Readings in the Theory of Knowledge:
A Primer for Young People

Douglas P. McManaman

Revised and Enlarged Edition

DPM Publishing
Aurora, Ontario

DPM also publishes its books in a variety of electronic formats.

Library and Archives Canada Cataloguing in Publication

McManaman, Douglas
Readings in the Theory of Knowledge: A Primer for Young People.
Aurora, Ontario: DPM Publishing. 2019

ISBN: 978-1-9991086-0-1

Cover by Jennifer Johnson, 2019.

Dedication

To the students of Father Michael McGivney, whose questions continue to inspire, shape and mold my writing.

Table of Contents

This book began as a series of short essays that I wrote for my students in the International Baccalaureate program of which the theory of knowledge course is a constituent part. My purpose was to make their lives a little easier and less anxious. The six prescribed titles from which they choose a title for the TOK essay they are required to write for the IB Organization are typically very lofty, even for graduate students in philosophy. Moreover, philosophy for high school students is difficult enough, but the theory of knowledge requires a basic introduction to philosophy as a pre-condition, at least if a student is expected to think carefully about knowledge issues and not "spout off" about things he knows absolutely nothing about. Without some background, theory of knowledge in high school can be a very frustrating experience for some students but, more importantly, a very dangerous course for everyone. With some background, however, the theory of knowledge can be very beneficial.

Another reason for writing this book was to bring some perspective to Catholic IB students who are serious about their faith. Philosophy has always had a very important place in the history of Catholic thought—it is still a required course of study in preparation for the priesthood. Catholics have a rich philosophical heritage that stretches all the way back to the beginning of the Middle Ages and one that is alive and still developing to this day. The Church has always taught that there is no conflict between faith and reason, and the works of some of the greatest Doctors of the Church, such as St. Augustine, St. Anselm, St. Thomas Aquinas, etc., were motivated by the desire to show that what Catholics choose to believe on faith is, although beyond the grasp of human reason, not contrary to reason. To achieve this end, they borrowed many ideas from wherever great ideas could be discovered and taken, which was and still is from all over the world (i.e., Averroes, Avicenna, Aristotle, Moses Ben Maimonides, etc.).

The very word 'Catholic' is from the Greek *katholikos (kata holos:* "about the whole"*)* which means 'all nations'. A thinker who is not internationally minded is not a genuine Catholic thinker. Moreover, anyone familiar with the development of Catholic thought, i.e., its progressive nature, should understand that "dogmatism"—in the sense of a stubborn unwillingness to develop and explore new avenues—ought to have no place in the mind of a Catholic. I began chapter 40 entitled "Models and Their Constituent Parts" by saying "I believe one of the most important objectives for a young student of the theory of knowledge is to come to some understanding of where necessity applies and where it does not apply. ...In other words, it is very important that we come to some appreciation of the scope of certainty and probability." I dare to say that most people, including most religious people, do not appreciate the scope of certainty and the vast scope of uncertainty in their intellectual lives; most people speak with an inordinately high level of confidence. The people in my life who have always exhibited a sense of self-doubt and who have cultivated a healthy skepticism regarding their current understanding of things are professional philosophers. And that was certainly the case with Socrates of Athens, who was informed by his friend, Chaerephon, that the Oracle at Delphi said he was the wisest man in all of Athens. Socrates knew he had no wisdom of which to boast, so he proceeded to interview all those most reputed for their wisdom. In the end, he realized the Oracle was right: "Well, I am certainly wiser than this man. It is only too likely that neither of us has any knowledge to boast of, but he thinks that he knows something which he does not know, whereas I am quite conscious of my ignorance…I am wiser than he is to this small extent, that I do not think that I know what I do not know" (*Apology, 21, d.* Trans. Hugh Tredennick*).

I remember the time I suddenly came down with a serious and painful illness. One doctor conjectured that it was polymyalgia rheumatica, but he wasn't sure. It turned out not to be, but in the end, no medical specialist was able to determine exactly what it was, and they all freely admitted as much. But there were plenty of people who "knew" what was wrong with me and what the origin of my illness was, and they were quick to point it out to me, i.e., "too much diet pop", or "that low carb diet", or "that protein powder you're drinking', etc. None of the latter, however, had spent as much as a day in medical school. Although the medical experts readily admitted their ignorance; those who had no background in medicine seemed to have the answers.

Most people are unaware of the scope of uncertainty that characterizes much of what they believe they know; which is why genuine dialogue is hard to come by today—it is hard to discuss ideas with those who know it all. And so theory of knowledge is a very important area of philosophical discourse and, if taught properly, is congruent with the fundamental principles of Catholic philosophical thought.

This work is a collection of readings; it is not a TOK course laid out on paper. There are many things that ought to be taught first in the context of the classroom that are not in this book, but the classroom should be the place where questions are pondered, claims are reflected upon, discussed and debated, etc. These readings are not meant to be definitive solutions, but spring boards from which to begin thinking about knowledge questions, to doubt or disagree, to challenge, etc.

Do not be intimidated by the mathematics found in the chapters on Bayes' Theorem and frequency type probability; the mathematics is simple compared to what is covered in the IB math curriculum. I encourage you to work through it with determination, especially chapters 10, 11, and 15 on deductive and inductive logic. The exercises and answers at the back of the book will help.

I have done my best to provide a foundation of principles that can be reflected upon in the light of other courses, i.e., history, chemistry, biology, economics, math, English, etc. Moreover, you should know that it is normal to have to read things two or three times; I have been studying philosophy for over 35 years now, and I still have to read specific works over a number of times. And that is only reasonable; for how can we expect to adequately grasp after just one reading what it took an author decades to discover and articulate. So the important thing to remember when reading philosophical material is to relax, especially if it seems as if you are not understanding a text as you think you should; and in that case simply put it down, and pick it up a few days later; for if you understand an idea 30%, you will understand it more the next time you read through it, and even more so after a third reading. Philosophical ideas slowly penetrate the mind as water gradually penetrates a sponge, and it is normal to suddenly understand a concept that you previously found incomprehensible and hadn't thought about in a while.

Preface to the Second Edition

As I said in the preface to the first edition of *Readings in the Theory of Knowledge*, this book began as a series of short essays specifically written for my Theory of Knowledge students in the International Baccalaureate program at Father Michael McGivney Catholic Academy. Since publishing the first edition, I have continued to write short essays for them, primarily to make matters somewhat easier for them—the prescribed titles from which they choose a title for their TOK essay are still very lofty, perhaps a bit too lofty for high school students. I have used these new articles in class over the years and knew that I would include them in a second edition if I ever got around to writing one. This work is a revised and expanded version of the previous work. The font has been increased to 12, thanks to the complaints of some of my students, and I have added some new chapters, specifically on necessary and sufficient conditions, independent and dependent variables, Jeffrey's Rule and what this rule might imply with respect to rumors, Burley's Rule and moral integration, a revised chapter on Inference to the best explanation, which, thanks to Nicholas Rescher, I now refer to as Inference to the Best Estimation; I also added a short introduction to plausible reasoning. These last two revisions were the result of discovering the writings of Nicholas Rescher; one day after school, shortly after publishing the first edition, I wanted to read something on ignorance, so I did a quick search on Kobo and found a book entitled *Ignorance: On the Wider Implications of Deficient Knowledge*, by Nicholas Rescher. Discovering Rescher gave me a new lease on teaching. I decided not to retire, but to study many of his writings and to find a way to make his thought accessible to my students. I've included only a tiny portion of the things I've put together for my students; the rest I reserve for a separate book to be entitled: *An Introduction to Plausible Reasoning.*

One of my principal goals in publishing the first edition was to have students come to a genuine appreciation of the scope of uncertainty in the pursuit of knowledge, especially with respect to their day to day inferences. That remains my goal, because things have not changed all that much in this regard. In fact, dogmatism has intensified. Knowledge is very difficult to acquire, and good thinking is about bringing maximal and consistent plausibility to our own epistemic framework (the set of data through which we interpret the world around us). As new data (or theses) are added to our existing set of data, the plausibility of much of that information changes and, if we are honest thinkers, we try to re-establish coherence and maximal consistency to that new data set. That will involve discarding theses or data that are inconsistent with new data that has greater plausibility.

This epistemic process is an ongoing one, which is why some of us—those who make the effort to think—change our minds very often throughout our lives. Science is a matter of plausible reasoning, which is why the history of science is evolutionary and revolutionary (the history of science is, among other things, a veritable graveyard of discarded hypotheses). So too is philosophy an evolutionary process— although the history of philosophy has had a very different kind of trajectory. All knowledge is subject to the same evolutionary law.

One important lesson to take away from this fact is the importance of avoiding the habit of "over-stating your case". We do not always know for certain whether our data is correct (most often, the plausibility index of the data on which we ground our conclusions is less than certain), nor do we ever know whether we have enough information and whether the plausibility of our current conclusions will change as a result of additional information in the future, etc. Hence, the importance of cultivating a certain degree of epistemic humility. But the spirit of dogmatism—that stubborn unwillingness to examine new data for fear of upsetting the applecart of one's own conceptual framework—is alive and well in the world, especially among those who see themselves as open-minded progressives. This is ironic, because we seem to pride ourselves on being an open society. We are very far, however, from being the open society we imagine ourselves to be. We are not critical thinkers until we begin to question the plausibility of our sources, reject outright the epistemic hubris that characterizes so many talking heads and political pundits in mainstream media, and learn to suspend our disbelief. This book aims to help further that end among young people.

Author's Biography

Douglas McManaman studied Philosophy at St. Jerome's College in Waterloo, and Theology at the University of Montreal. He was a regular columnist for the Canadian Messenger of the Sacred Heart and Catholic Insight Magazine, and continues to write for Lifeissues.net, and the Catholic Educator's Resource Center. He is the author of *Why Be Afraid?* (Justin Press), *Basic Catholicism, Introduction to Philosophy for Young People*, and *A Treatise on the Four Cardinal Virtues*. He has been interviewed twice on EWTN Radio, The Good Fight with Barbara McGuigan. He is a Permanent Deacon for the Archdiocese of Toronto and the current chaplain of the Catholic Teachers Guild. He has been teaching Religion and Philosophy to senior high school students for over 30 years; he is currently teaching at Father Michael McGivney Catholic Academy in Markham, Ontario, Canada. He is the past president of the Canadian Fellowship of Catholic Scholars.

There are more things in heaven and earth, Horatio, than are dreamt of in your philosophy.
Hamlet, Act 1. Scene V

The fundamental cause of the trouble is that in the modern world the stupid are cocksure while the intelligent are full of doubt. Bertrand Russell, The Triumph of Stupidity (1933).

The right attitude in philosophy is to accept aims that we can achieve only fractionally and imperfectly, and cannot be sure of achieving even to that extent. It means in particular not abandoning the pursuit of truth, even though if you want the truth rather than merely something to say, you will have a good deal less to say. Pursuit of the truth requires more than imagination: it requires the generation and decisive elimination of alternative possibilities until, ideally, only one remains, and it requires a habitual readiness to attack one's own convictions. That is the only way real belief can be arrived at. Thomas Nagel, The View from Nowhere, "Introduction".

As I have admitted that every problem arises out of some kind of knowledge, and therefore presupposes knowledge, you may ask whether my remark that science begins and ends with problems could not be replaced by the remark that science begins and ends with knowledge. My answer is, 'Yes-provided you mean (as I do) by knowledge something like problematic or hypothetical or tentative knowledge rather than unproblematic or settled knowledge.' Settled knowledge does not grow. I have often said myself that science begins and ends with theories. But I used the term 'theory' in a very wide sense, in a sense in which it includes myths and all kinds of expectations and guesses. I never use it in the sense of a settled or proved or established theory, for I do not think that such a theory exists. A theory always remains hypothetical, or conjectural. It always remains guesswork. And there is no theory that is not beset with problems. Karl Popper, The Myth of the Framework. 156-157.

1 Introductory Thoughts on the Nature of Opinion

A good place to begin a conversation on the nature of knowledge is to discuss the following claim: "Every opinion is just as "valid" as any other opinion". At the root of this rather widespread belief is the contention that "Everything is a matter of opinion after all, and so one would have to be arrogant to hold that one's own opinion is more "valid" than any other".

Leaving aside, for the moment, the question about what validity in this case means in the strict sense, an intelligent person can offer a series of compelling arguments in favor of the above. In fact, I recall having a discussion with a friend of mine in our staff lunchroom about some philosophical question or other, when a supply teacher who was eavesdropping decided to throw in her two cents. She began to defend the post-modern position that all knowledge is a construct and thus whatever is "true" is only so relative to the larger "system" that was constructed and of which "truth" is merely a part. Truth is relative, in other words. The more we tried to qualify her point, the better her arguments became—I cannot reproduce them here, because I cannot recall them in all their detail; they were, however, complex and rather impressive. She had very insightful things to say about the limitations of human knowing, the implications of cultural limitations and the limits of language, the degree to which human beings make wrong inferences every day, the little that we know at any one time, etc. We agreed with many of her insights; we agreed that she was, for the most part, right. However, she drew a conclusion that we thought undercut everything she argued up to that point. She claimed that we really don't know anything, that possessing truth is not possible at all, and that we can be certain of nothing. If that is true, then what do we make of her insights into the limitations of human knowing with which we had no issue? Do we take them seriously? Do we dismiss them?

In order to begin to resolve this problem, let us consider just what an opinion really is. If you reflect a moment, you'll notice that we do not regard every conclusion we draw as being a matter of opinion. We do not pretend that the conclusion of a mathematical problem, for example, is an opinion. But is it an opinion if I conclude, after only a few days at the start of a new semester, that one of my students would make a good nurse, because she is cheerful and kind? Indeed, it is an opinion. The difference between the conclusion of a mathematical problem worked out without any errors and my judgement that this young lady would make a good nurse, is that I cannot be entirely certain about the latter, that is, I might be wrong, especially if my judgment is made solely on the basis of evidence gathered all within a sample space of a few classes. It is true that all good nurses are joyful and kind, but it does not follow that all those who are joyful and kind will turn out to be good nurses. I may discover that the jovial student in front of me lacks the mental capacity to pass even a single required course at the university level.

In other words, an opinion may or may not be true; it could be mistaken. All I can say about an opinion of mine is that *it is possibly the case* that I am right. That, of course, implies that it is possibly the case that I am wrong.

I might claim that the desk on which I am writing is about 4 feet wide, but to discover whether or not my opinion is right, I need a standard by which to determine the correctness of my judgment. What is that standard? The answer, of course, is a ruler of some kind, a measuring tape or a yard stick. Without a standard, there is no way to measure my judgment. What, then, is the standard that is the measure of my opinion that this young lady would make a good nurse? The answer is certainly not her plans or goals. Indeed, she might want to be a nurse, but she might also be mistaken about her own abilities. Rather, she is the standard. In other words, it is not true that she will *probably* make a good nurse, or *probably* not make a good nurse. Rather, she will either make a good nurse or will not make a good nurse; she either has all the qualities and abilities that a person needs to become a good nurse, or she doesn't. Probability is in me, not in her. I am not certain at this point whether she does or does not possess the required qualities; all I see after a few days is her demeanor, and so it is my judgment that possesses a degree of probability. She, this human being in her total reality, is the measure of my judgment. If it turns out that she does not have the necessary qualities and abilities that will allow her to successfully complete a nursing program, then my opinion is wrong. In other words, reality or real being is the measure of our opinions.

We can look at this from another angle. An opinion is a judgment that may or may not be true (i.e., it is possibly the case that my judgment that she will make a good nurse is wrong). We all understand what it means for something to be "possibly the case that…" It means that "it is not necessarily the case that…" If something is necessarily the case, we see that "it cannot be otherwise". It is not my opinion that 5 X 20 equals 100, for example. I know it does; I see that it cannot be otherwise. In other words, I grasp the necessity of the conclusion. An opinion lacks precisely that condition; if I do not see the necessity of my conclusion, at best I have a very well founded opinion that may or may not be true to reality.

To hold that absolutely every claim or judgment is a matter of opinion is to hold that there is no existing standard by which to measure the truth of a particular opinion. In other words, we cannot know anything for certain, or what amounts to the same thing, we cannot grasp the relationship of necessity between the conclusion and the premises from which it is drawn. But if we cannot ever apprehend the necessity of a conclusion—because knowledge is impossible—, then we have never apprehended the necessity of a conclusion or claim (if we cannot make a square circle because the existence of a square circle is impossible, it follows that we have never seen one). How then did we ever acquire the idea of "necessity" in the first place?

The apprehension of "necessity" is the condition for the possibility of understanding what it means to lack necessity, that is, what it means for something "to be possibly the case…" In other words, if everything were a matter of opinion, we wouldn't know it, that is, we wouldn't know what an opinion is.

We know, however, that an opinion is a judgment that may or may not be true. We may not know much in this world, but at the very least we know with certainty that an opinion is *necessarily* a judgment that is *possibly* wrong. Moreover, our understanding of reality might very well be almost infinitesimally thin, virtually nothing compared to the infinity of all there is left to know, but at least we know that real being is the measure of what we know—which is why we continue to test our opinions, to measure them against the yardstick of reality. In other words, we attempt to verify them, confirm them, or if you are a good and honest scientist, to falsify them. If it were not so, that is, if real being were not the measure of our opinions, then knowledge and opinion would be conflated; thus, whatever I think is true would in the end be true, because I think it. And if we really believed that, we wouldn't dare to argue with anyone, or demand that a hypothesis be tested, because deep down we would believe that whatever anyone thinks is true, is in fact true. We would not regard anyone's judgements or claims as opinion, but as knowledge.

And even if someone were to disagree with everything I've written thus far, that disagreement would nevertheless imply that my opponent in debate grasps "necessity", for what he asserts, essentially, is that what I've argued is not necessarily true.

2 *A Thought on the Origin of Necessity*

An opinion is a judgment that may or may not be true. In other words, the one holding the opinion does not know whether or not his judgment is correct, because he does not see the necessity of his conclusion, only its possibility (perhaps a good possibility or not). Now, we only understand "what is possibly the case" against the background of "what is necessarily the case". What, then, is the origin of this idea of necessity?

I would argue that the clue that might resolve this problem lies in the standard that moves a judgement from the level of an opinion to the level of knowledge. That standard is real being, that is, the realm of the real. For example, the truth of my opinion that the man seen running from the crime scene was 6 feet tall and in his mid-20s is measured by what he really is (he was 5 ft., 8 and 34 years of age). It seems to me that the concept of necessity is, first and foremost, derived from our apprehension of being or existence (existential judgment). You stand before me, and before I know anything about what you are specifically, I apprehend "that you are". That apprehension is an existential judgment that "you are"; and you necessarily exist, as long as you exist. In other words, *nothing can both be and not be at the same time and in the same respect* (the principle of non-contradiction). I apprehend the necessity of this principle immediately upon apprehending "what is".

It is impossible to deny with any consistency the principle of non-contradiction; one would have to use it in order to deny it, that is, treat it as true for as long as one maintains that it is false. In other words, if the principle of non-contradiction is not true, then contradictories can be true at one and the same time. Thus, to deny the principle would be to affirm it, and vice versa.

Another formulation of the principle is that of identity: *each being is what it is.* We know that a carrot is a carrot, not a rabbit. A being is not "what it is not", thus it is what it is. A being is necessarily identical to itself. If it were not so, all discourse would be impossible.

My apprehension of "what" you are (essence), which is simultaneous to my apprehension "that" you are (existence), is gradual. We only know what a thing is through its activity, and observing a thing's activity takes time. My understanding of "what" you are (for example, my understanding of human nature) lacks the degree of necessity that my existential judgment possesses. I may mistakenly conclude that something I observe in you is universal, that is, common to every member of the species. Only gradually do we come to apprehend what belongs to a thing's nature, and this gradual coming to understand what a thing is involves a great deal of self-correction.

My apprehension of your very existence, however, is not subject to degrees. You either are or are not, there is no in between. This is traditionally referred to as the principle of the excluded middle (*a being either is or is not, there is no in between*).

Hence, the claim that we can never possess certainty of anything has to be false. If certainty is absolutely outside our ability to enjoy even for a moment, knowledge would be impossible, and we would have no apprehension of "what is necessarily the case"; how then could we have any idea what it means to be "possibly the case"? And how would anyone know what an opinion is? We could say nothing definitive about what an opinion really is, much less that everything is a matter of opinion and that every opinion is just as valid as any other opinion.

3 Is Everything Changing?

"You cannot step into the same river twice; for other and yet other waters are ever flowing on." Heraclitus

"Everything is changing, and nothing is permanent". To test whether or not this is true, let us consider the implications of the claim for knowledge. If we suppose that everything before us is changing in such a way that nothing at all endures throughout the change, that is, there is nothing permanent, does it not follow that knowledge of things is impossible? Does it not follow that ultimately there are no such things as "things"? What can anyone who claims to know anything be said to know? Whatever he knows has changed entirely.

It is true without a doubt that we live in a world that is constantly changing, but isn't my apprehension of a permanent "something" the condition for the possibility of knowing that this something has changed? My wife has changed over the years. I know that because I know that something about her has endured, namely, she has endured, and she is a "being", not a pure becoming. In other words, she is the subject of the many changes she has undergone. Without that enduring subject, change is unintelligible.

The alternative, it seems to me, is to maintain that all that has endured is a sound, a word, a name. In other words, it is language that gives rise to the illusion of permanency; it is language that gives rise to the illusion that we live in a world of "beings" or "things" that endure, or things that are the subject of the changes they undergo. If this is the case, then it would seem that all knowledge is indeed a construct, a product of language. Truth is no longer the adequation between what is in the mind and what is, because there is no "what is", there are no beings to know, there is just "becoming". Reality is unknowable, unintelligible, and absurd. Truth, rather, is something relative to a language system that has evolved over time. In itself, there is no such thing as truth, just as there is no such thing as "thing".

That is why Heraclitus is also able to claim that "To god all things are beautiful and good and just, but men have supposed some things to be unjust, other things just."[1] In other words, men have supposed that there is some sort of objective criterion by which they can measure the rightness or justice of a course of action, as if there is such a thing as an objective injustice. However, just as a yardstick that is continually changing cannot provide a stable and accurate measurement, so too there is nothing in the realm of the real that can provide a permanent and enduring measure of a just and unjust course of action.

Perhaps the God of Heraclitus is the measure of what is just and right, one might object. Perhaps all things are beautiful and good and just because in the end, God will bring it about that beauty, goodness, and justice will have the final word. But for someone like Heraclitus who is committed to the principle that all is change, this is not so: "God is day-night, winter-summer, war-peace, feast-famine. But he changes like (fire) which when it mingles with the smoke of incense, is named according to each man's pleasure."[2]

If everything is changing such that nothing is permanent, then it follows that the principle that "each being is what it is" (the principle of identity) is false. Each being is not what it is, for there is no "being" to speak of; rather, being is a product of speech. The principle of identity becomes a product of language, and it is a principle that has to be constructed in order to be able to carry on meaningful discourse. In other words, it is a construct necessary for the fiction that is called "science".

There is, however, a difficulty with this argument. How is it possible to assert that the principle of identity, or what amounts to the same thing, the principle of non-contradiction, is false? The principle of identity assures us that contradictories cannot be true at one and the same time (i.e., each being is what it is, not what it is not), and so if it is asserted to be false, one seems to be implying that those who hold it to be true are wrong, pure and simple. But, if identity or non-contradiction is false, then those who hold it to be true are right

---

[1] Fr. 102, Porphyrius *in Iliadem 4, 4*. Quoted in G.S. Kirk & J.E. Raven. *The Presocratic Philosophers: A Critical History with a Selection of Texts*. Cambridge: Cambridge University Press, 1957. 193

[2] Fr. 67, Hippolytus *Ref. IX, 10, 8*. Quoted in *Ibid.*, 191.

precisely because they are wrong; in other words, contradictories are true at one and the same time. In other words, it doesn't matter what anyone says, for whatever is said is true because one has said it.

That is why I would argue that the theory of knowledge is not first philosophy. Rather, being is first, and so the philosophy of being is prior to the theory of knowledge, and one's theory of knowledge depends on one's philosophy of being.

4 *Truth in Perspective*

Is there or is there not any such thing as "absolute" truth? It all depends on what we mean by absolute truth. If by "absolute truth" we mean that what I see and understand at this moment, from my particular vantage point, is such that nothing more can be said about it that will add to my understanding, then no, there is no such thing as absolute truth, at least when it comes to human beings, who are not omniscient.

If by "absolute truth" we mean that I see the world without any influences stemming from my own subjectivity, such as unknown biases or unconscious inferences, then no, there is no such thing as absolute truth. If by "absolute truth" we mean that my own intellectual frame of mind and specific interests do not focus and thereby limit my grasp of the real, so that my apprehension of the real is complete and unamenable to revision and further enrichment, then no, there is no such thing as absolute truth.

But if by "absolute truth" we mean that I am capable of coming to a genuine, objective, albeit limited understanding of a real or existential state of affairs, then yes, there is absolute truth; to deny it implies that one has something to say about human knowing, that is, one has come to a genuine grasp of a real or existential state of affairs of human knowing, i.e., its limits, its vulnerability to unknown influences, etc.

A group of masters paint the same scene; each one has his or her own style, and they all have the ability to capture and express on canvas what they see and how they see it. Each work is different, and each one is exhilarating. Certainly one might be more beautiful than another—although articulating just how this works is very difficult—, but let us assume that all of them are masterpieces, so beautifully done that it is beyond our ability to evaluate them in relation to one another. Can it be said that one of them alone is an objective and absolute representation of the truth of the scene in question? I don't think so. They are all beautiful and accurate expressions of the contemplative gaze of the artist, which is opened up onto the real world. Their grasp upon the real is indeed objective; for only a subject apprehends an object. In fact, a being only becomes an object through the existence of a knowing subject. Prior to that, it is indeed a being *per se*, but not an object. In other words, subjectivity is the condition for the possibility of objectivity. Just as it is through my own subjectivity that I come to an objective grasp of the real world, so too it is through their subjectivity (the artists) that my grasp of the real is enlarged and expanded. I will often learn to see things about the world through the subjectivity of another that I otherwise would have missed. Thus, there is no coming to grasp the real outside the limitations of a knowing subject. That is absolutely true and denying that is absolutely false.

But what if the artistic depiction of some aspect of the world is not true to the facts, but is a caricature of sorts, a misinterpretation rooted in unconscious biases, for example? It seems to me that the very fact that one is able to eventually uncover this is testimony of our ability to grasp the real, that is, to possess truth.

If, however, the denial of absolute truth is meant to imply that we cannot grasp the real, that man is the measure of all things (Protagoras), then it seems to me that the denial of absolute truth is absurd; for nothing can be both true and not true at the same time and in the same respect (i.e., it would have to be true and undeniable that man is the measure of all things and at the same time that there is no absolute truth that is undeniable and the measure of my mind).

The denial of truth is often grounded on the supposition that the very idea of "truth" is incompatible with the facts of subjectivity, in other words, with the fact that human beings see things from a limited, particular, and even biased perspective. Since each one of us sees the world from our own particular point of view, how can any one of us claim to be in possession of truth?

The basic idea behind the denial of "absolute" truth seems to be that objectivity can only be had on condition that subjectivity is eliminated, and since one cannot eliminate subjectivity (the mind) and all that it implies (limitations), one cannot possess truth (objectivity).

On the other hand, if it is only through a knowing subject that something becomes an "object" of knowledge, then perhaps subjectivity is the condition for the possibility of "objectivity". For example, consider a world without persons, that is, intelligent subjects capable of knowing things outside themselves. Instead, only inanimate things and, let's say, plant life exist. In such a world, there would be no "objects" as such, only existing things. An object is the correlative of a subject. An apple is not an object for another apple or a rose bush, and a rock is not an object for a tree, etc. These become objects of knowledge *in relation to* a knower, for a knower is the subject who knows beings outside of himself. What he knows become the *objects* of his knowledge.

What I am suggesting is that there is no incompatibility between having a limited perspective and possessing truth, even truth that is "absolute". More specifically, there is no truth (objectivity) *without* a subject who sees and knows the world from a limited perspective. And far from keeping me from an objective apprehension of the real, perhaps some of my biases are just what I need to open me up onto the realm of the objective.

In short, the objective world is so rich in meaning that only a knowing subject will grasp its existence and meaning partially, incompletely, but truly.

Intuition

It is not possible to deny the existence of truth without implying it. For if there is no truth, then it is objectively and absolutely true and we ought not to deny the claim; for we ought not to deny what is in fact true. But if there is no truth, there is no need to worry about denying what in fact ought not to be denied, because there is no truth to deny.

In other words, denying the existence of truth is circular and inevitably violates the first self-evident principle of non-contradiction, which runs: "Nothing can both be and not be at the same time and in the same respect". This principle is necessarily and absolutely true, for it cannot be definitively denied without using it. Our knowledge of this principle is immediate, intuitive, initially pre-conscious, and it is the starting point of all subsequent knowledge.

Our apprehension of the principle of non-contradiction follows upon our intuitive apprehension of being. When I know anything specifically, I *first* know that it "is". Whatever is, "is", and not "is not". It is because we have real contact with existing natures outside the mind that we know with certainty all the other first principles that are implied in the intuitive apprehension of being. For example, to know that whatever is, is, is to know that each being *is what it is*, not what it is not (the principle of identity). Thus, an Oak tree is an Oak tree, not a tomato. Unless each being is what it is, we cannot conclude anything about anything whatsoever.

Moreover, because we know that "is" and "is not" are not identical, we know immediately and with certainty that from nothing comes nothing (the principle of causality). It is on account of this that we know pre-consciously that whatever is, has that *whereby* it is. In other words, whatever is, to the extent to which it is, possesses a *sufficient reason* for its being, so that it is capable of explaining itself to intelligence.[3] With a little self-reflection, we become aware that we have always known this principle pre-consciously; for we have a tendency to ask questions; in so doing we seek the sufficient reason or causes of things (science). We naturally know that for every effect, there is a cause that explains it, and we know that the effect cannot be greater than the cause; for if the effect exceeds the cause, then a portion of the effect (something) has come from nothing and lacks sufficient reason for being. But this is not possible, since "nothing" is not something.

There are more principles that can be uncovered by intelligence and their implications can be unraveled through careful reasoning, resulting in genuine insights into the ultimate nature of things (philosophy). The laws of being that can be uncovered by intelligence all apply to whatever is. In that sense, human persons can possess knowledge that is absolute, universal in scope, and necessarily true— albeit incomplete.

---

[3] Jacques Maritain, *A Preface to Metaphysics*, London, Sheed and Ward, 1948. 97-105.

Now although everything that exists "is", there is nevertheless a greater complexity to real things than that which is contained in the simple idea of being. There are various kinds of beings in the world and their complex natures are known gradually, through experience, that is, by observing their various activities. Non-living things have certain properties that can only be known through observation and experiment, and living things too have specific properties that inanimate things do not possess; animals have certain faculties that plants do not have, etc. In other words, the world is complex and rich in variety.

Although we are capable of possessing a genuine knowledge of things, our knowledge is not exhaustive. As we move from the realm of concepts that are the more universal (i.e., being as such, or 2, 3, 4, 10 x 3, the properties of a triangle, etc.) to the realm of the particular (this person named John, that work of art, these circumstances, Poland, etc.), the more we become aware of the limitations of our own perspective. The realm of the particular is so rich in detail and contains so many layers of meaning that although what we apprehend might be objective and absolutely true, our knowledge of it is often only partial. But it is precisely the limited perspectives of other human persons that can enlarge my own limited perspective. It is because their limited perspectives open them up to what is true—and beyond my limited purview—that it is in my best interest to learn to see aspects of this world through their eyes. This does not mean there is no universal truth; much less does it imply that contradictories can be true at one and the same time. It simply means that genuine dialogue with others can enlarge my world and enrich my possession of the truth.

I recall the day I asked a friend of mine to accompany me on a short walk for some fresh air after a few hours of marking exams while both of us were visiting a friend in a small Ontario town. Had I gone by myself, I would have missed out on the brief education in Victorian style homes that I received in that half hour walk. He has always loved architecture, and he came alive as we were walking through that old neighborhood, noticing the great works of art underneath so many tasteless attempts at renovating them. As a result of my friend's excitement, I began to see the neighborhood through his eyes; in fact, I continue to see old neighborhoods through his eyes. In other words, I have been introduced to a better and more extensive apprehension of the real as a result of my friend's bias (slant) and limited perspective. And although our knowledge bears upon the same thing outside of us, for my friend there are far more layers of meaning contained in the judgment "This is a house" than there is for me.

The human person is so complex that he can be known through a variety of angles. He can be known psychologically and emotionally, philosophically, theologically, morally, politically, historically; he can be known empiriometrically, but even an empiriometric knowledge of the human person is had also from various angles, i.e., histologically, neurologically, biochemically, physiologically, etc.

It isn't a slant (bias) or perspective that keeps a person from a deeper apprehension of the truth, but prejudice, which is a prior or premature judgment. It is appetite that is usually at the root of prejudice, and it is disordered appetite that adversely affects a person's judgment (Appetite is twofold: the sensitive appetites from which arise the eleven basic emotions, and the will or rational appetite). Disordered passions (i.e., inordinate love of self) tend to cloud judgment, and the rational appetite will determine what a person allows himself to see or know—consider the expression: "There are none so blind as those who will not see".

That is why a person will not acquire the intellectual virtues without the moral virtues, for disordered passions rebel against reason. One virtue in particular that plays a central role in the acquisition of truth is humility, which is the moderate love of one's excellence. If a person lacks humility, he cannot tolerate the awareness of his own limitations and perfectibility, and so he is not moved to enter into dialogue with others in order that his own possession of the truth may be enlarged and enriched.

Concluding Thoughts

The notion that subjectivity renders objectivity impossible is an assumption that ought to be more carefully scrutinized. When a person writes a letter, his purpose is to communicate *what* is on his mind. Without an intelligent subject to receive the communication, the letter is perhaps nothing more than lines of ink and cellulose fibers. But of course, the letter is much more than that. Without an intelligent subject to receive the letter, the fullness of *what it is* objectively cannot be properly apprehended.

Similarly, consider the claim that color and sound are not real, since without the perceiving subject, there are only sound waves and reflected light. And since it is true that sound waves are not sound, and reflected light is not color, color and sound, so it is argued, are not objective qualities of things, that is, outside the mind and in the thing, but merely within the perceiver.

It seems to me that this reasoning involves the assumption that objectivity requires the elimination of subjectivity. Perhaps, however, subjectivity is required in order to possess the objective, and so only through a subject who has the power to perceive is it possible to objectively grasp certain aspects of real existing beings, such as their colors and their sounds, just as it is only through an intelligent subject that the complete reality of that hunk of cellulose fibers with ink markings can be known. The reason for this is that being exists ultimately for a knower, that is, for intelligence.

An objective knowledge of history, albeit incomplete, is also possible. Indeed, *each being is what it is* (the principle of identity), yet *what it is* can be misunderstood or understood more or less fully by one person than by another. So too an historical document can be misinterpreted or interpreted more or less perfectly by one person than by another. A line or two in Aristotle's *Physics*, for example, might be correctly interpreted by two people and mean the same thing to both of them, but what Aristotle says there can be more completely understood by the scholar who has been pondering Aristotle's principles for 30 years from various angles than they would be by the student who has spent only a year thinking about them.

Moreover, it is also possible that *what* a person says or writes can, either immediately or in time, be better understood by someone other than the author himself. But none of this is possible unless human persons are, by their sentient and intelligent nature, opened up onto the realm of real being.

The position articulated here is very different from post-modern relativism, which begins with the premise that the realm of the real is in itself unintelligible and absurd, because it is in a pure state of flux. Post-modernism looks to man as the measure of what is true and meaningful, for things have no meaning in themselves, for all that is meaningful is locked into the subjectivity of the written or spoken word. The paradox, however, is that if this is so, dialogue becomes pointless and ultimately groundless. Everything becomes a matter of opinion, and no opinion has any more validity than any other, for even the rules of logic are constructs. Moreover, the only law governing human choices is that which originates in the will of the majority, or the powerful. If human intelligence and reasoning cannot arrive at a genuine apprehension of the objective and absolute principles of a universal and natural moral law—because truth is not possible—, then power is all that is left to govern human beings.

5 *Some Thoughts on the Degrees of Abstraction*

All our knowledge begins in sensation; as Aristotle said: "Nothing is in the intellect that is not first in the senses". Sensation, however, is not the same as thinking. Sense perception is limited to material singulars (i.e., I see this cat and that tree, I feel the surface of this desk under my fingertips, etc.); but ideas, however, are abstract. The mind possesses ideas, which are not the same as images in the imagination. Ideas have a universal scope to them. For example, I perceive (sensation) this man, but my mind conceives "man" in general. In other words, I know that this particular thing that I sense is a particular instance of the kind (genos) of being we call "man". I touch this particular light bulb, but my mind knows what it means to be a light bulb in general (it possesses the idea of "light bulb").

Without going into detail on how the genesis of universal ideas might work, let us just say that the mind abstracts or "separates out" the intelligible content (idea, concept, nature) from the particular thing, and the result is a universal idea abstracted from individual matter (the particular material thing). Because that intelligible content or idea (i.e., "human", "canine", "feline" etc.) has been separated from the singular material thing (John, Fido, this cat, etc.), it does not refer solely to any individual (particular) thing, for example John, but covers all men; the concept "quantity" does not refer to any particular quantity, such as this quantity of milk in this particular carton in front of me, but covers all that is essentially a quantity (number, pounds, yards, centimeters, etc.), and the concept "science" does not refer to any particular science, but covers all science.

Natural Science

An important point that has a number of important implications for the theory of knowledge is that there are degrees of abstraction, that is, the mind is capable of abstracting to a greater or lesser degree. The physical or empirical sciences take place on the first level of abstraction. What this means is that the mind of the biologist, for example, abstracts from the single sensible material thing (ie., this bone, these organs, this tissue, etc.), but not from common sensible matter (i.e., bone, organ, tissue in general). The scientist studies this cadaver not in order to understand this cadaver, but to understand the anatomy of all bodies. So he does not abstract from bone, muscle, tissue, etc., only this bone, this muscle, this tissue, etc.

Ideas like "cell", or "branch", or "oak tree", or "photosynthesis" are all ideas at the first level or degree of abstraction. These concepts do not refer to any particular cell, branch, or tree, but only "cell", "branch", or "tree" in general. They are universal concepts. Cells have quantity, and so too do branches and oak trees; but the ideas "oak tree", "cell", "tree", etc., do not include any particular size.

Mathematics

The mind is able to abstract even further when it considers quantity separated out from its sensible matter. For example, a cell is generally round, so too is the sun, but the mind can abstract circular from sensible matter and consider the properties of the circle abstracted from it. To do so, one does not need to know anything about the properties of the cell, or what exactly the sun is, or various metals that might possess a circular shape. The mind also abstracts number from the multiplicity of individual material things to consider number alone. In the real world, we find a multiplicity of things (real beings), but the mind is able to separate out number alone from the particular thing (whatever it might be), such as 2, 10, 50, ½, ¼, etc. Instead of 5 apples and 1 basket, the mind considers 5 and 1 by themselves, leaving things behind. This, the second degree of abstraction, is the level on which the mathematician operates.

The Philosophy of Being (Metaphysics)

The mind is capable of abstracting even further; it can abstract from quantity and any other particular "mode of being" (such as "when", "where", "quantity", "quality", "substance", "activity", etc.) or object of study (i.e., living being, human being, mobile being, inanimate being, logical being, etc.) in order to consider "being" simply insofar as it is being. In this way, the mind focuses on the properties of being. In other words, just as the mind can focus on the properties of water (chemistry - first degree of abstraction) or the properties of living things (biology - first degree of abstraction) as well as the properties of quantities such as triangles, circles, numbers, etc., (mathematics – second degree of abstraction), the mind can also focus on the properties of being in so far as it is being—not insofar as it is circular, and not insofar as it is living, or chemical, etc.,.

This is metaphysics or the philosophy of being (third degree of abstraction). The philosophy of being is the highest level of abstraction; for it is not possible to abstract any further, for there is nothing wider than being (beyond being is non-being, or nothing).

What is interesting to note and perhaps explore further later on is that the more abstract the level on which a person reasons, the greater the certainty of its conclusions. When the intellect abstracts, it separates its object from matter, and the greater that separation or abstraction, the more able we are to discern the necessity of our conclusions, thus the greater the certainty. It is as if matter renders things more opaque to the mind.

As an example, consider something we know that belongs to the third degree of abstraction, such as "whatever is, is one". In other words, one is a property of being. We know this with certainty, for if a being is not one insofar as it exists, but two, then it is not a being, but beings (plural). We also know with absolute certainty that nothing can both be and not be at the same time and in the same respect (the principle of non-contradiction). One cannot deny it without acknowledging it as true. For example, to assert that the principle of non-contradiction is false would imply that it is true at the same time and in the same respect, and so it would be pointless to deny it; so if a person denies it, he does not see that it is pointless to do so. Thus, he rejects the contradictory claim. But if the principle of non-contradiction is false, all contradictory claims are just as true as the contradicted claims.

Furthermore, we know with certainty that a2 + b2 = c2, but that has to be worked out or discovered. Not every human being knows that this is true; it is not immediate and intuitive, as is our knowledge of the principle of non-contradiction. Pythagoras was the first to discover this, but everyone knows immediately (perhaps not explicitly) that nothing can both be and not be at the same time and in the same respect. Thus, mathematics is certain, but mathematical knowing is less extensive than the knowledge of the first principles of speculative reason.

Finally, we know that the boiling point of water is 212 °F and that the freezing point is 32 °F, but we are not able to reason to this conclusion, nor can we determine the temperatures mathematically. That universal truth has to be arrived at through empirical investigation (experiment).

On the level of the material singulars (particulars), we have very little certainty. For example, although we may be able to determine that a certain number of radon atoms will disintegrate within a particular time, exactly which ones will disintegrate out of this collection is not certain (all we have are probabilities). Although we may be able to arrive at a percentage of students who will be away from school tomorrow, it is not possible to determine with certainty who will be away tomorrow as a result of a cold or flu.

Ethics

The science of ethics corresponds to the same pattern. The virtue of prudence (the mother of the virtues) is the application of universal moral principles to particular situations. As a result, there are aspects of ethics that are clear and certain, but as we approach the level of the particular, moral matters can become rather murky, that is, things become less certain. For example, it is obvious to everyone that "good is to be done and evil is to be avoided" (the first principle of morality).

A more intermediate moral precept would be the following: "Treat human persons as ends, not as means to ends". As a principle, people generally agree with this. In other words, its truth is clear. It is not always clear, however, whether a particular behaviour in a specific context is an instance of treating another as a means to an end. We all agree that loving another simply for the sake of what he or she does for you is a violation of that principle, but it is less certain whether Artificial Insemination or *In Vitro* Fertilization is such an instance.

This is not to imply that moral truth is impossible to achieve on the level of the concrete particular. Rather, it means that on this level there are more things to consider, which is why the virtue of prudence contains a number of virtues that are its "parts", such as reasoning, memory, docility, circumspection, caution, foresight, and shrewdness. These are needed to deal adequately with particular situations. In order to make prudent decisions that will achieve one's end without choosing to harm another or oneself and without making matters worse, we need an ability to learn from experience, which is memory; circumspection enables us to consider the relevant details within a situation, and docility enables us to seek advice from others with experience. With experience comes foresight and caution.

And so it is not enough to have a theoretical knowledge of ethics; nor is it enough to have lived. One needs both in order to apply the one (universal moral principles) to the other (particular situations).

History

History deals entirely in the realm of the particular; for it is the study of the past, and so the historian does not operate on a level of abstraction, as does the scientist or the mathematician. That is why history is not a science. It is, however, a way of knowing.

Certainty is very difficult to come by at this concrete level. The historian will formulate hypotheses and will proceed to test them in a way that is proper to his discipline. The reason for the uncertainty involved in the study of history is that it is the evidence or the facts that come first, and the historian must inference his way to the best explanation of those facts, and as we will see when we study inferencing more thoroughly, there are often a number of possible explanations that can account for the facts. Like the work of a homicide investigator, history requires a great deal of labor, i.e., a great deal of research, reading through archives and documented evidence, and careful interpretation of the facts in evidence.

Faith (natural faith)

Faith means trusting in what somebody tells you because you have evidence that the speaker is well informed about the subject and is honest. We have faith in our family doctor that the prescription he writes for us is not going to kill us; we put our faith in the pharmacist that he or she did not make a mistake on the dosage and that what we are given to take is going to help us—unless we studied pharmacology. We trust our mechanic when he tells us he fixed the brakes—we simply get in the car, drive, wait for a red light, and only then do we discover whether or not our faith was well placed. The world of science relies heavily upon faith—no scientist can repeat every experiment and study done in the past, nor even the most recent studies. We trust that data has not been falsified. Now that trust has been betrayed very often in the past; in 1998, a British surgeon and medical researcher published a study claiming a link between the measles, mumps and rubella vaccine, and autism. It took years to discover that the claim was fraudulent. But in that time, some children died as a result of the faith placed in that claim.

6 Can Two People Be Right?

The mission statement of the IB Organization includes a line to the effect that others with their differences can be right. And so, we can ask the question: "Can two people or two different cultures also be right?" The simple answer to this question is that it depends on whether the two perspectives are contradictory, or merely different.

Firstly, contradictories cannot be true at one and the same time. This follows from the intuition of being and the principles that follow from that intuitive grasp. Before I know anything specifically about something, I first know that it "is". Unless I know that it "is", I cannot know "what it is". And so, the first principle of all speculative reasoning is that "nothing can both be and not be at the same time and in the same respect". To deny this is to suggest that being and non-being are identical, and if that were so, then it would follow that "each being is what it is not" (i.e., an elephant is a rose bush), which of course is absurd.

And so if it is true that you are reading this page, it cannot be the case that at the same time and in the same respect you are not reading this page. You could, however, be reading this page and not reading it at the same time but in a *different respect*; for example, you could be reading it with your eyes, but not really concentrating on it, and thus failing to grasp what is being said. In this sense, we can say that you are reading it and not reading it at the same time. Both statements are right.

Now, the higher the level of abstraction on which we are thinking, the more certainty we will enjoy. That is why mathematics enjoys tremendous certainty; for it takes place on the second level of abstraction (one has abstracted quantity from sensible matter in order to consider it alone). It is on the lower levels of abstraction, however, that things become more complex. The reason is that as we approach the sensible realm (the realm of the particular), our knowing participates more completely in the limitations of sense perception. For example, from one vantage point, the city looks quite peaceful (the person is looking at the city from the 40th floor balcony of a building), but from another person's vantage point, the city appears rather chaotic (she is looking at the city from the 1st floor balcony of her apartment). Both are right, but they are correct from two completely different angles; they are not contradicting one another—two different perspectives often complement one another. In other words, "difference" is not the same as "contrary".

That is why within those areas of knowledge that are the least abstract, we often find different points of view to be more or less right. In the area of history, for example, there might be "more to the story". An historian might be right about a particular fact, but another historian might also be right in insisting that the fact should be seen against the background of a much larger picture before one can conclude this or that. But contradictories cannot be true at one and the same time, neither in history nor within any other area of knowledge.

If anyone is going to deny this point about contradictory positions, he or she usually does so within the context of a discussion bearing upon a moral issue. But the point made here certitude and degrees of abstraction applies to this particular area of knowledge as well (ethics). Recall that prudence is the application of universal principles to particular situations. The more universal the principle, the more we will agree with one another. For example, everyone agrees that "good is to be done, evil is to be avoided" (the first principle of morality). As well, virtually everyone agrees that "one ought not to do to another, what one does not want done to oneself" (the golden rule). Disputes begin to arise on a much more concrete level of discussion, for example, whether this or that particular course of action constitutes such an injustice.

If, however, the deliberate and intentional destruction of human life in the womb, for example, cannot be justified under any circumstances, then it follows that the position that it is permissible to intentionally destroy a developing human life is incorrect, and vice versa.

But this example is still relatively abstract, so let us consider an issue or dispute that takes place on a more concrete level. Some teachers argue that there are too many assemblies and classroom interruptions; they make it very difficult to do an adequate job on the curriculum, especially the IB curriculum.

Now there were a number of points of view on this issue. Can all of them be right? In a manner of speaking, yes. How many assemblies are too many? That is difficult to determine; for there are so many factors to take into consideration, not just the IB curriculum. Liturgies are part and parcel of a Catholic environment, OSAID has an end to achieve, the social science department wants to instill certain values in students with regard to Remembrance Day, etc. Administrators have to deal with every objection and try to create the conditions that will meet the needs of everyone involved, including teachers, students, parents and senior administration at the board level, etc. There are so many angles from which to consider this issue, which is why it is no easy task to resolve.

It should be increasingly clear how intelligence participates more fully in the limitations of sense experience as we approach the level of the concrete particular. There are teachers who want fewer assemblies, some are indifferent, and others, including students, do not want their own particular initiative scrapped, while other students would like to see less interruptions, etc.

Administration sees the tremendous good that is accomplished by many of these assemblies, and so they are torn. Who is right? Can they all be right? Indeed, they can, but from a particular angle (i.e., from the angle of a classroom teacher, from the angle of a high achieving student trying to prepare for university, from the angle of a grade nine student who is having a tough year, from the angle of a teacher with an initiative, from the angle of an administrator, etc.).

There is a larger picture, however, and the right decision—and there is indeed a right decision—can only be made by those who are willing to do the hard work involved in taking in the larger picture. The right decision will not necessarily be a solution, but a trade-off. What makes matters very difficult, however, is the person who is resolved to look at the issue from his particular angle alone, thus refusing to see the matter from another angle. As a result, he fails to appreciate the limitations of his own perspective. It is only much later, when he takes on an administrative position, for example, that he finally comes to realize that things are not as simple as he once thought they were.

7 The Shortest Proof of the Mind's Immateriality

The shortest and simplest proof for the immateriality of the mind is the following:

> *The simplest of all ideas is "being", or "is". As such, being cannot be divided, for being has no parts. The instrument or tool that delivered the idea of being to the knower must be simple and without parts. Hence, the mind is an immaterial power, and it is indestructible; for one cannot destroy or divide or tear apart what is simple and immaterial.*[4]

Explanation

The simplest of all ideas is "being", or "is". For example, I know that I am, that you are, that the clock is, that my cat is, the tree in my front yard is, etc. The idea of being is not only the simplest, it is also the absolutely first idea: before I know anything more specifically or precisely, I at least know that it "is", that it exists.

Now, "is" cannot be divided. Consider a single line. A line is divisible, and when it is divided, it becomes two. A circle can also be divided. When we divide it, it becomes two (two halves). Whatever has parts is divisible.

Now, to be something with many parts is to exercise a kind of multiplicity (a single whole having many parts). For example, relative to me, a rectangle has a front part, a middle part, and an end part, however imprecisely marked, and each part is outside the other part. There is a middle part, and two end parts.

Consider too that a human being has a hand, a foot, a forearm, a torso, etc. Although the parts are continuous, each part is outside the other part. So, my hand is not my foot, my foot is not my torso, etc. Divide a line in two and we know that this part of the line on the left side of the division is not that part of the line on the right side of the division.

---

[4] Vincent E. Smith, *Idea Men of Today*. Milwaukee: Bruce Publishing Company, 1950. 392

Now, being (is) cannot be divided. *Being has no parts.* What would it mean for this part of being to be outside of that part of being? To be outside of being is to not exist, because outside of being is non-being, and non-being is nothing. So, the idea of being cannot be a line, or a circle, or any other quantity. The idea of being is absolutely simple, without parts, and thus indivisible.

The instrument or tool that delivered the idea of being to the knower must be simple and without parts. Hence, the mind is an immaterial power, and it is indestructible; for one cannot destroy or divide or tear apart what is simple and immaterial.

8 Is Everything Relative?

Consider the claim: "Everything is relative. Nothing is absolute". Is this true? Let's begin by asking ourselves what it means to be relative. Something relative can only be understood "in relation to" something else. The left side of a stone **depends upon**, or can be understood only **in relation to**, the observer or some other reference point. So, left and right are indeed relative. I can't tell someone to meet me on the left side of the school, for that depends on a point of reference (i.e., the left side when looking at the school from the corner of McCowan and Fourteenth Ave).

"Tall" is also a relative term, not absolute. A person is tall in relation to the observer, or in relation to the average height of those around him. If the observer is shorter than the person observed, or if those around the observed are shorter, the observed will appear tall. If the observer is 7 feet tall, the person may not be tall at all, but short. Hence, to understand something that is relative (R) depends on understanding X, but if X is relative, then understanding it (X) depends on understanding Y. If Y is relative, then understanding Y depends on an understanding of something outside of it (W), etc. Consider the diagram below:

R   X   Y   Z   Z1   Z2   Z3   Z4   Z5   etc. ad infinitum   ∞

If everything is relative, then there is no ending (i.e., no Z_{end}) and the series continues *ad infinitum*. In other words, the series of dependant factors is indefinite or infinite.

But not everything can be relative in that series of dependents. There must be a first (principle, source) that is **not relative,** but absolute (independent). The reason is that if there is no absolute, that is, no first principle, then our understanding of **R** depended upon understanding an infinite series, and that would mean we could never achieve an understanding of **R** (such as the simple assertion that "Bilaal is tall"). Our understanding of **R** would **depend upon** understanding an **indefinite** or infinite (without end) number of factors or causes. In other words, our understanding would remain **indefinite;** we would never "reach" understanding, just as one could never reach a destination that is an infinite number of inches away. If we know anything that is relative, it means that something in our knowledge is not relative, but absolute.

9 Thoughts on the Principle of Causality

A cause is a principle (source) from which something proceeds with dependence. All causes are principals, but not all principles are causes. The principle of causality is the principle that from nothing comes nothing. Another way of expressing this same principle is to say that *nothing moves itself from potentiality to actuality except by something already in actuality*. A more popular way of formulating this same principle has been to say that *a thing cannot give what it does not have*.

Now, how can we be certain that the principle of causality is absolutely and necessarily true? How can I be certain that "from nothing comes nothing" or that "a thing cannot give what it does not have"? The certainty is derived from the principle of non-contradiction, which in turn is derived from existential judgment, or the apprehension of being. If something comes from nothing, then nothing **is** something (i.e., it is "something" from which something can proceed). But if nothing is something while it is still nothing, then contradictories are true at one and the same time; thus, if "something" is the contradictory of nothing and nothing is something as much as something is nothing, then to fail is to pass and to pass is to fail, to lie is to tell the truth and to tell the truth is to lie, to eat is to starve, and vice versa, etc.

If something could move itself from potency to act, for example, if a stone which is at rest (but potentially in motion), could move itself from potential motion to actual motion on its own, then it would be giving to itself what it does not have; it does not have motion, yet it gives itself motion--i.e., something comes from nothing. But this once again violates non-contradiction. To deny the principle of causality is to assert that a thing can simultaneously 'have' and 'not have' a specific perfection in the very same respect. If a pool ball could move itself from rest to motion, then it could impart to itself what it lacks; it would both have and not have the very same motion. But the truth of the matter is that the pool ball receives a perfection that it lacks, namely motion, from an actually moving ball, which in turn receives its motion from another actually moving ball, etc.

The principle of causality is often formulated thus: *The effect cannot be greater than the cause.* This is necessarily true because a being can only give what it has, not what it does not have. If the effect can be greater than the cause, then the cause can give what it does not have; for this would mean that from nothing comes something. If I have only 10 dollars, I cannot give you 100 dollars. If you end up with 100 dollars, $90 of that money is unaccounted for. I can account for the 10 dollars, but not for the remaining $90.

The reason why we naturally seek to know the causes of things is because we immediately know, consciously or unconsciously, that for every effect there is a cause that accounts for the effect. Or, to put it another way, we immediately know that there is a sufficient reason that something is so, such that it is capable of explaining itself sufficiently to the intellect, thus satisfying the intellect, at which point we stop searching for the reason or cause.

This principle is naturally known (pre-consciously or consciously), it is grasped through intuition (an immediate apprehension by the intellect), and it is self-evident. It cannot be demonstrated through reason because reason needs the principle of causality to demonstrate anything. If I give you reasons that prove something or other, I say something like "this is true on account of such and such", or, "this is true because such and such". For example, Robert asks questions *because* Robert is rational. But Robert is rational *because* 1) all men are rational, and 2) Robert is a man. Twice we use "because" in order to account for the fact that Robert asks questions. In other words, to deduce a conclusion from two given premises is to employ the principle of causality; the conclusion depends upon the term 'man'. The principle of causality is required to prove anything at all, and one cannot prove a principle by using it—that is the fallacy of "begging the question" (assuming the point we are trying to prove). If the principle of causality were not true, we could not prove anything at all, and science would be impossible. Most importantly, if one denies the principle of causality and provides "reasons for" denying it, then it seems that one uses it in order to deny it.

Some Possible Implications

In the previous chapter, we argued that an infinite series (or regress) of causes is impossible (i.e., an infinite or indefinite series of relatives fails to account for a definite understanding of something relative). Imagine now a chandelier held up by a single series of links. When looking up, we cannot see the top, and let us assume that there is no empirical way to see the top. It is possible to know, however, that if the chandelier is actually suspended, that is, if it is off the ground, it follows necessarily that there is a finite number of chain links, no matter how many links there may be. The suggestion that there might be an infinite number of chain links is repugnant to the intellect. That, of course, is no proof that there is not an infinite number of links. But an infinite number of links, as an explanation of the suspension, is insufficient to the intellect; for each link in the chain is dependent upon the link above it; in other words, the sufficient reason for the first link holding up the chandelier is the link directly above it, and the sufficient reason or cause of that link holding up the first link is found in the third link above it, etc.

Each link on its own is insufficient to account for the suspension of the chandelier; the sufficient reason for each link actually doing what it does is outside it (each other link). The entire series of links is nothing other than the sum of its parts, which is each individual link. If the series of links stretched on to infinity (indefinitely), there would be no sufficient reason for the suspension of the chandelier—in other words we'd have an infinite number of insufficient reasons for the suspension of the chandelier. The chandelier would not be actually or definitively suspended, but would be forever "potentially" suspended, or what amounts to the same thing, indefinitely unsuspended. It is, however, actually suspended, which implies that there is not an infinite number of links holding up the chandelier, but a finite number. Thus, there is a relatively independent something that is first, such as a beam of sorts.

The principle of causality, which is derived from non-contradiction, implies that since nothing can impart to itself what it does not possess, every change from potentiality to actuality depends on something already possessing that actuality—whatever that actuality is (i.e., actual motion, an actual quality, a quantity, a perfection of some kind, etc.). For any series of causes—whatever the motion might be—, there is a first cause that is uncaused, or a first mover that is unmoved. Or, we can refer back to the chandelier: each link in the chain is a dependent cause (dependent upon the link above it); the first cause is an absolutely independent cause.

It is important not to imagine or picture this, but to "think it", that is, to keep our reasoning on an abstract level, just as in doing math, we abstract number from the concrete (1, 2, 3, from three apples) in order to free ourselves to discover more than would otherwise be possible. That there is a first uncaused cause behind every motion or change is true with regard to any change or motion whatsoever, i.e., locomotion, change in quality (i.e., color, habit, shape, etc.), quantity (growth), etc.

Moreover, it is possible to make the case that if the effect cannot be greater than the cause, then the first uncaused cause cannot be less than the effect or the sum of the total combination of effects, for that would imply that something can give what it does not have (or comes from nothing). Consider the motions found in the world; they are intelligible, such as the development of a flower, the birth of a calf, a shooting star, the fall of a leaf, the budding of a leaf, etc. The motions are also experienced as beautiful and good. In other words, we experience the world as intelligible (knowable), good (desirable), and beautiful (harmonious and radiant). Thus, the first uncaused cause must possess intelligence, goodness, and beauty to an eminent degree, otherwise the effect would acquire perfections that are lacking in the first cause. This first uncaused cause is what some people mean by "God".

Now this argument is rather sketchy, especially the above paragraph. It is not as compelling as it could be if more and smaller steps were taken—it may not be compelling at all. It needs to become much thicker and richer. Nevertheless, it is still a sound argument when it is properly understood, and, we would argue, it might account for the fact that man has always possessed a natural sense or knowledge of God, however confused and general it might be.

10 *A Review of Some Basic Deductive Logic*

Logic is the study of how to reason validly. A number of very interesting knowledge questions arise within the context of logic, especially inductive logic, which we will begin to treat shortly. But to better appreciate what is involved in the logic of induction, it is best to go over some of the basic principles of deductive logic.

There is a distinction between a valid argument and a sound argument. A valid argument is one that follows the basic rules of logic. The premises of the argument might very well be false, and the conclusion might very well be false, and yet the logic might be flawless. For example:

All women are sports fans (major premise)
Hitler was a woman (minor premise)
Therefore, Hitler was a sports fan (conclusion)

The above syllogism is an example of an unsound argument that is logically valid. In other words, the argument does not violate any of the rules of logic. To better understand this, let us review some of the fundamentals.

Firstly, a categorical syllogism (i.e., the one above) is made up of categorical propositions, which are complete sentences with a subject and a predicate (i.e., all women are sports fans). The subject of a proposition is "that about which something is said" (i.e., women); the predicate is "that which is said about something" (i.e., sports fan). The copula joins or separates the subject and the predicate (i.e., is/is not; are/are not).

You'll notice that there are three terms in a categorical syllogism. In the syllogism above, the terms are "sports fan", "Hitler", and "woman". These are called the major term, the minor term, and the middle term respectively. The major term is always the predicate of the conclusion (i.e., sports fan), the minor term is always the subject of the conclusion (i.e., Hitler). The middle term, which is the most important term in a syllogism, is never in the conclusion but appears twice in the premises (woman). Moreover, the major premise is the one that contains the major term, the minor premise is the one that contains the minor term.

Now, there are only four ways to formulate a categorical proposition; two affirmative ways, and two negative ways. We can affirm that: "All women are sports fans"; and we can affirm that: "Some women are sports fans". Or, we can deny that all women are sports fans, universally or particularly. For example, we can deny it universally by asserting: "No woman is a sports fan"; or we can qualify our denial: "Some women are not sports fans".

All S is P (universal affirmative)
Some S is P (particular affirmative)
Some S is not P (particular negative)
No S is P (universal negative)

The universal affirmative (All S is P) is called an A statement; the particular affirmative is called an I statement. The particular negative is called an O statement, and the universal negative is called an E statement.

A = All S is P (universal affirmative)
I = Some S is P (particular affirmative)
O = Some S is not P (particular negative)
E = No S is P (universal negative)

We need to become familiar with one more term before we can proceed to the rules, namely, **distribution**. We speak of terms that are either distributed or undistributed. Imagine that I am given a box of pens and have been asked to distribute them to the students. Halfway through giving them out, the fire alarm sounds and we evacuate. The box of pens is undistributed. In other words, less than 100% of the pens in the box were distributed. If, however, I was able to give each student a pen before the fire alarm sounded, the box of pens would be distributed. In other words, 100% of the pens in the box have been given out.

A distributed term covers 100% of the things referred to by it; an undistributed term covers less than 100% of the things referred to by it. Consider the proposition: All woman are sports fans. "Women" is distributed, because the term "women" as it is employed in the A statement "All women are sports fans" covers 100% of the things referred to by it, namely female human persons. Note that affirmative statements involving single individuals are treated as A statements, i.e., Debbie is a human person (i.e., All of Debbie is a human person).

In the context of an I statement, such as "Some women are sports fans", the term "women" is undistributed, because it covers less than 100% of the things referred to by it, namely female human persons.

For the same reason, "women" is undistributed in the context of the O statement (Some women are not sports fans).

In the context of the E statement, "No women are sports fans", the term "women" is distributed. In other words, 100% of women are not sports fans (not one among women is a sports fan).

The predicate is also either distributed or undistributed. In the statement "All women are sports fans", the predicate (sports fans) is undistributed; the reason is that only some sports fans are women, not all—some are men. Similarly, all dogs are animals, but not all animals are dogs (some are human, some are birds, reptiles, etc.). For the same reason, the predicate of an I statement is undistributed.

The predicate of an E statement, however, is distributed. Consider that "No cats are doctors". This means that 100% of doctors are not feline (not one of them is a cat).

The predicate of an O statement is also distributed, but some people find the explanation difficult. Perhaps the following might help. Assume for a moment that 95% of the student body is East Indian, and there are only 50 students who are not East Indian. Hence, "Some students are not East Indian". The principal makes an announcement: "Would all those students who are not East Indian report to my office immediately". Five minutes later, the 50 non-East Indian students are

in the principal's office. The predicate "East Indian" is distributed in
the context of an O statement because 100% of East Indian students
are not in the principal's office.

Consider the following statement/distribution chart in which the
distributed terms are underlined:

A = All <u>S</u> is P
I = Some S is P
O = Some S is not <u>P</u>
E = No <u>S</u> is <u>P</u>

Immediate (deductive) inference

Consider the following implications. Note that ⊢ means "implies"
or "entails" (i.e., we can immediately infer with necessity that…) and ~
is the negation sign, which reads "it is not the case that…"

A ⊢ I This means an A statement immediately implies (presupposing
of course the same subject and predicate) the I statement. For example,
all snakes are poisonous implies some snakes are poisonous (assuming
the subject satisfies the condition of existential import—i.e., at least
one instance of the subject exists).

A ⊢ ~(O) An A statement implies the negation of the O statement.
For example, all snakes are poisonous implies immediately that "it is
not the case that some snakes are not poisonous".

A ⊢ ~(E)

E ⊢ O

I ⊢ ~(E)

~(A) ⊢ O

~(E) ⊢ I

~(I) ⊢ E

~(I) ⊢ O

~(O) ⊢ A

~(O) ⊢ I

E ⊢ ~(A)

E ⊢ ~(I)

~(I) ⊢ ~(A)

O ⊢ ~(A)

~(O) ⊢ ~(E)

Consider too the following unwarranted implications, which will help underscore the limits of knowledge. To indicate that they are unwarranted, we will employ the following symbol: ⊣ , which means "does not imply or entail, or cannot be deduced from". For example, given that "it is not the case that All S is P", one cannot deduce that No S is P—to do so would be unwarranted. The fact that "it is not the case that All men are Italian" does not permit us to conclude that No men are Italian.

~ (A) ⊣ E (E is not deducible from ~ (A), but remains unknown).

~ (A)⊣ I (i.e., If we know "it is not the case that all men are geniuses", we do not thereby know that some men are geniuses)

~ (E) ⊣ A (If we know that "it is not the case that no men are geniuses", we do not thereby know that all men are geniuses)

~ (E) ⊣ O (…and we do not thereby know that some men are not geniuses; they could all be geniuses for all we know).

I ⊣ A (knowing that some men are geniuses does not tell us whether or not all men are geniuses)

I ⊣ O (knowing that some men are geniuses does not tell us whether some men are not geniuses)

O ⊣ E (knowing that some men are not geniuses does not tell us whether no man is a genius)

O ⊣ I (knowing that some men are not geniuses does not tell us that some men are geniuses)

Now we are ready to discuss the rules. Before reading further, however, it might be a good idea to work on some of the exercises in Appendix D at the back of the book.

Rules

An invalid categorical syllogism violates at least one of the following rules. The conclusion of a syllogism that violates one of the rules is called a *non-sequitur*, which means "the conclusion does not follow necessarily from the given premises". In a valid categorical syllogism, the conclusion follows necessarily from the given premises. This does not mean, however, that the conclusion is true. If the premises are false (or only one of the premises is false), the argument is unsound, even though the logic is valid. Consider the following:

All men are giraffes
My pet cat is a man
Therefore, my pet cat is a giraffe.

The following are the rules for the categorical syllogism:

1. In a valid categorical syllogism, the middle term must be distributed at least once. The following is an example of a syllogism with an undistributed middle term:

All iron is <u>malleable</u>
All gold is <u>malleable</u>
Therefore, all gold is iron

The middle term is "malleable" (which I have underlined), and in this syllogism it is the predicate of both the major and minor premise. The major and minor premises are both A statements, and if you look at the statement/distribution chart above, you will notice that the predicate of an A statement is undistributed.

2. In a valid categorical syllogism, any term that is distributed in the conclusion must be distributed in the premises. The following is an example of a syllogism that violates this rule.

All teenagers are familiar with the difficulties of high school
No grandparent is a teenager
Therefore, no grandparent is <u>familiar with the difficulties of high</u>
<u>school</u>

The conclusion is an E statement, and the predicate of an E statement is distributed. The major term, however, is undistributed in the major premise (the major premise is an A statement).

3. No conclusion can be drawn from two negative premises. The following is an example that violates this rule:

No student of this school likes liver
No one who likes liver lives on Rideau crescent.
Therefore, no one living on Rideau crescent is a student of this school

This is obviously a *non-sequitur*; there might be 50 students living on Rideau crescent who are students of this school.

4. A valid categorical syllogism can have no more than three terms (no conclusion can be drawn from a syllogism with more than three terms):

All clowns like cotton candy
All cotton candy is sweet
Therefore, ……………..

There are four terms in the above syllogism: "clowns" "cotton candy" "people who like cotton candy", and "sweet". To see this clearly, all one has to do is rewrite the propositions by bringing out the copula. Hence,

All clowns are people who like cotton candy
All cotton candy is sweet
Therefore, ……………..

5. In a valid categorical syllogism, if a premise is negative, the conclusion must be negative.

No dogs are doctors
Some doctors are meat eaters
Therefore, some meat eaters are dogs

The premises in the syllogism above are true and the conclusion is true, but the conclusion cannot be deduced with certainty from the given premises (the conclusion simply does not follow).

11 The Conditional Syllogism

The most important kind of argument for the theory of knowledge, it seems to me, is the conditional argument. It looks like the following:

If John eats a rich dessert, then his blood sugar level will rise.
John ate a rich dessert.
Therefore, John's blood sugar level rose.

The major premise of a conditional syllogism takes the form "If p, then q" (If John eats a rich dessert (p), then his blood sugar level will rise (q)). The symbol for this relation, which is called material implication, is an arrow: →

p → q
p
q

The "if" clause of the major premise (p) is called the antecedent, the "then" clause (q) is called the consequent. The antecedent in the above syllogism is "If John eats a rich dessert", the consequent is "then his blood sugar level will rise".

The minor premise of the conditional syllogism is either an affirmation of the antecedent, or an affirmation of the consequent; or it is a denial of the antecedent, or a denial of the consequent. The symbol for negation is ~, for example,

p → q
~p
~q

In real terms, this argument would read as follows:

If John eats a rich dessert, then his blood sugar level will rise.
John did not eat a rich dessert.

Therefore, John's blood sugar level did not rise.

Consider the following:

If John eats a rich dessert, then his blood sugar level will rise.
John ate a rich dessert.
Therefore, John's blood sugar level rose.
(Affirming the Antecedent/Modus ponens)

If John eats a rich dessert, then his blood sugar level will rise.
John did not eat a rich dessert.
Therefore, John's blood sugar level did not rise.
(Denying the Antecedent)

If John eats a rich dessert, then his blood sugar level will rise.
John's blood sugar level rose.
Therefore, John ate a rich dessert.
(Affirming the Consequent)

If John eats a rich dessert, then his blood sugar level will rise.
John's blood sugar level did not rise.
Therefore, John did not eat a rich dessert.
(Denying the Consequent/Modus tollens)

Now, two of the forms are valid, and two are invalid. A conditional syllogism of the form "affirming the antecedent" (called Modus ponens) is valid, as well as the form "denying the consequent" (called Modus tollens). Consider the following:

If John eats a rich dessert, then his blood sugar level will rise.
John ate a rich dessert.
Therefore, John's blood sugar level rose.
(Valid – affirming the antecedent)

If John eats a rich dessert, then his blood sugar level will rise.
John's blood sugar level did not rise.
Therefore, John did not eat a rich dessert.

(Valid – denying the consequent)

And so, if the premises are true and if the reasoning is valid, then we can be certain of the conclusion (it is necessarily true). Hence, if the premises of the above two arguments are true, then the conclusions are necessarily true.

However, we ought to become very familiar with the invalid forms. Consider the following:

If John eats a rich dessert, then his blood sugar level will rise.
John did not eat a rich dessert.
Therefore, John's blood sugar level did not rise.

This is an instance of "denying the antecedent", and it is invalid, which means the conclusion does not follow necessarily (with certitude) from the given premises.

"Affirming the consequent" is also invalid:

If John eats a rich dessert, then his blood sugar level will rise.
John's blood sugar level rose.
Therefore, John ate a rich dessert.

The conclusion cannot be deduced with certainty from the given premises; for although John's blood sugar level rose, the reason may not be that he ate a rich dessert; he may have had a cup of coffee, or a sugar free treat that is high in carbohydrates, etc. These possibilities apply to both arguments, rendering both of them invalid.

Before reading further, try to complete the exercises in Appendix E at the back of the book.

12 Necessary and Sufficient Conditions

Science in general is a knowledge of things through their proper causes. But instead of speaking of the causes of things, it is much more convenient to speak about the conditions of something, either the conditions of an occurrence, or the conditions of a thing's existence, or the conditions of something being true. For example, we can ask the question: "What is the cause of a functioning automobile?" This is a very ambiguous question; in fact, it is really not a good question. A better question is: "What are the conditions for a functioning automobile". For there is no single cause of a functioning automobile, but there are a number of conditions.

Conditions are divided into 1) necessary and 2) sufficient. For example, a high school diploma is a necessary condition for going to university, but it is not a sufficient condition for university. In other words, without a high school diploma, a young man will not be going to university. But a young man with a high school diploma is not necessarily going to university either. He may have a diploma, but if his marks are not good enough, then he will not be accepted to the program. In other words, the diploma by itself is not sufficient.

Necessary Conditions

Let's define the two more precisely. In doing so, I will use the variables we are already familiar with from our treatment of the conditional syllogism, specifically the major premise of a conditional syllogism:

$$p \rightarrow q$$

A condition q is necessary if its non-existence or non-occurrence or falsity guarantees the non-existence or non-occurrence or falsity of p. For example, spark plugs are a necessary condition for the functioning of the car. In other words, without spark plugs, the car will not start. Or, graduating with a 90% average is a necessary condition for being accepted into such and such a program (i.e., medicine). What this means is that without a 90% average, one is not going to medical school. Or, being human is a necessary condition for being married. If you are not human, you are not going to be married.

Looking at this from the perspective of the conditional syllogism reveals its cogency:

If this car starts, then it has spark plugs.
It does not have spark plugs.
Therefore, it will not start.

If you get accepted into medical school, then you have a 90% average.
You do not have a 90% average.
Therefore, you will not get accepted into medical school.

If you got married, then you are human.
You are not human
Therefore, you are not married.

All these are valid arguments, for they all take the form of denying the consequent.

$p \rightarrow q$
$\sim q$
$\sim p$

q is a necessary condition for p (without q, there is no p)

Sufficient Conditions

A condition p is sufficient **if and only if** the existence or occurrence or truth of p guarantees the existence or occurrence or truth of q. For example, achieving 30 credits is a sufficient condition for graduating from high school. Having the flu is a sufficient condition for having a fever, that is, if you have the flu, then you have a fever. And, although functional spark plugs are a necessary condition for a functioning car, they are not a sufficient condition, for one also needs a functional transmission, gasoline, battery, starter motor, etc.

Looking at this from the perspective of the conditional syllogism also reveals its cogency.

If you have 30 credits, then you will graduate.
You have 30 credits.
Therefore, you qualify for graduation.

If you have the flu, then you have a fever.
You have the flu
Therefore, you have a fever.

If you drive 20 km over the speed limit on this road between 1 and 1:30 in the afternoon, then you will get a ticket (ceteris paribus).
You drove 20 km over the speed limit on this road between 1 and 1:30.
Therefore, you are getting a ticket.

All these are valid conditional syllogisms, for they all take the form of affirming the antecedent:

$p \rightarrow q$
p
q

Note the following converse relations:

If q is a necessary condition for p, then p is a sufficient condition for q.

And, equivalently,

If p is a sufficient condition for q, then q is a necessary condition for p.

For example: if being a female is a necessary condition for being a mother, then being a mother is a sufficient condition for being a female.

And, if being a mother is a sufficient condition for being a female, then being a female is a necessary condition for being a mother.

These are important distinctions, because the scientific method is about testing claims regarding certain causes or conditions. Later on, we will also be referring to epistemic conditions (both necessary and sufficient).

Before reading further, try to complete the exercises in Appendix F at the back of the book.

13 Independent and Dependent Variables

The terms that we will be familiar with by the end of this chapter are the following: *independent variable; predictor variable; experimental variable; irrelevant variable; dependent variable; outcome variable; confounding variable; third variable; control variables.*

If we are going to pursue one or more of the experimental sciences—even the social sciences (psychology, sociology, etc.)—, we will soon enough come across the terms independent and dependent variables. These are used in the context of research. The terms sound very technical and rather abstract, but they are really quite straightforward, especially when looked upon within the context of the conditional syllogism.

Let's say you have an outbreak (i.e., acne). You will likely ask yourself: "What is the cause of this?" You realize there are a number of possible factors that can account for the outbreak. It might be something you ate, or it might be the change in weather, or it might be stress, that is, any number of things, etc. We can't assume the cause; rather, we must in some way test the antecedent we posit as the cause.

The **dependent variable** is the outcome, the result (the effect), that is, the outbreak (i.e., acne). The "cause of" or "reason for" the outbreak is the **independent variable**. The independent variable is sometimes called the **predictor variable** or **experimental variable**. This is what it looks like in the context of the conditional syllogism:

If I eat chocolate (independent variable), then I breakout (dependent variable)
I had a breakout today (dependent variable/outcome variable)
Therefore, I ate some chocolate (conclusion)

As you can see, this is **affirming the consequent**, and affirming the consequent is invalid. So, the conclusion does not follow necessarily from the given premises. It might be the case that chocolate is the reason I had an outbreak, but it is not necessarily the case. It has to be tested. In other words, the independent variable has to be subject to experiment. That is why it is called the **experimental variable**. It is also called the **predictor variable** because we "predict" that it is chocolate that causes the outbreak. So, we have to subject the predictor variable (the independent variable) to experiment; for it might not be the chocolate at all.

How do we test it? We manipulate the independent variable. So, you are told not to eat chocolate for two weeks and we'll see if you have a breakout.

The result: you had a breakout. Conclusion? It is not the chocolate that is the reason for your breakouts. So, chocolate is an **irrelevant variable**.

So now you predict another variable: greasy French fries. The reason you suggest this is that every time you have a breakout, it always happens after you eat French fries. So perhaps French fries are the reason for the breakouts.

The French fries are your independent variable (predictor variable, or experimental variable). However, there might be a **third variable**, which is called a **confounding variable**. You see, it is also true that whenever you have a breakout, you are also under a lot of stress (i.e., exams, tests, the start of a new school year, going on a date, etc.). Furthermore, every time you are stressed, you get a craving for French fries. You think the French fries are causing the breakout because the breakout always occurs after you eat the fries. But it may not be the fries at all; the cause may be the stress.

And so we have to test each variable. So ,we have an independent variable: French fries; a dependent variable: breakouts, and finally a third variable (called the confounding variable): stress.

The doctor tells you to stop eating fries for a month, but you still breakout, and it's June. The fries are an irrelevant variable, but the stress is a possible factor (a possible predictor variable, or independent variable). It's June, and exams are coming, so you are stressed, and you breakout. It is highly likely that the stress is causing you to breakout. Let's remove the stress and see if you breakout. No exams or tests for one year. The result is that you did not breakout at all.

**If you have stress, then you will breakout
I had no stress this year.
I did not breakout.**

Notice, however, that this syllogism takes the form of denying the antecedent, which is invalid. So, although it is true that you did not breakout, it is not necessarily the case that the reason is that you did not have a stressful year. It is probable, even highly likely, but it is still not entirely certain.

That is why science is fundamentally uncertain. It is very difficult to achieve perfect certainty in the sciences. All we have in the end are our best estimates.

There is one more variable to speak of, namely, **control variables.** These are factors that must be kept the same throughout an experiment. In order to properly discern the relationship between the independent and dependent variable, certain factors must be held constant. For example, I have been asked to test two different types of badminton birdies made by two different companies. I decide to test them on two different days. Basically, I want to compare them to see which one is better in terms of flight. However, if the results of the experiment are going to be reliable, I will have to hold constant certain control variables. For example, if I were to test one birdie on a bright and sunny day, without the slightest breeze in the air, and the other birdie on a cloudy and windy day, my conclusion about their quality would be unreliable; for the differences in their flight might be due to factors other than the quality of the birdie, such as the weather, or even the person testing the birdie, the kind of racquet he is using, etc. So, the weather is a control variable that must be held constant in this case. Another control variable is the athlete testing the birdie. We cannot have one athlete testing the birdie on one day, and a different athlete on another. So too, we cannot use one badminton racquet on one day, and different quality racquet on another. We must test the birdies while holding constant the control variables: same weather conditions, same athlete, same racquet, etc. If the flights of the two birdies are significantly different within the same conditions (with the control variables held constant), we know the flight difference was not due to the differences in weather, or the quality of the racquet, or the player, etc., for these were held constant.

A test will be declared unreliable if it turns out that control variables were not held constant. What makes matters difficult is that we often do not know whether there are control variables that we missed. Testing badminton birdies is much easier than comparing and explaining the gender pay gap., for example. There are far more variables that have to be taken into consideration before we draw any definitive conclusions about the causes of such a gap.

Why they are called "independent" and "dependent" variable should be clear at this point. The outcome, such as a fever, depends on the flu; it is not the flu that depends on the fever. The flu is independent of the fever. The flu is a sufficient condition for a fever, but a fever is not a sufficient condition of the flu—the fever could be the result of some other variable, such as food poisoning, or another virus.

The Residual Fallacy

Now, the claim that income disparity between men and women is the result of unjust discrimination must undergo the same kind of testing. Hence,

If there is income discrimination against women in the workforce, there will be income disparity between men and women
There is income disparity between men and women.
Hence, women are victims of income discrimination in the workforce

Once again, we know this is a deductively invalid argument, so it must be tested. Other variables might account for the outcome or dependent variable (income disparity), such as quantity of education, quality of education, type of degree one has, years of experience (often interrupted by maternity leave), skill level, number of hours worked on a weekly basis, etc. All these must be held constant. If income disparity disappears when we control for certain confounding variables, then discrimination becomes an irrelevant variable.

The two groups under consideration are "men with university degrees" and "women with university degrees". There are, however, other variable predictors that come to the fore as a result of a more precise analysis of the general category of university or college degree. To hold years of education (quantity) constant is not enough, for there are qualitative differences as well that have to be take into consideration. Qualitative differences are a variable predictor, and quality can be measured by academic performance, the ranking of the university, or the difficulty and remuneration factor in the particular field of study, etc. In terms of remuneration capacity, it is unreasonable of me to expect a master's degree in philosophy to equal a master's degree in biochemistry or electrical engineering degree; most industries have no use for a person with a graduate degree in philosophy but do have a place for a person with a master's in biochemistry or engineering—philosophy majors are more likely to be waiting on tables after they earn their degree; engineers are usually working as engineers.

The category of "university educated" women and men is problematic from another angle. University graduates include people who go on to postgraduate study, and this too influences income. The ratio of women and men with postgraduate degrees differs from the ratios of those with university degrees. At the bachelor's degree level, women outnumber men, but men outnumber women by more than a two to one ratio at the master's level and by 59% at the PhD level. So when we compare university educated men and women, which includes those who have gone on to pursue postgraduate work, we are really comparing apples and oranges.[5]

If we wish to compare men and women at the PhD level, we discover once again disparities between men and women, and changing

---

[5] Thomas Sowell *The Vision of the Anointed* New York: Basic Books, 1995 37-42

ratios. Women receive 37% of all PhDs; moreover, the areas of study differ significantly from those of the 63% of males who receive a PhD. The PhDs which men receive tend to be more heavily concentrated in math and science and other fields of greater remunerative capacity. Women received almost half of the PhDs in the social sciences, and more than half in the area of education. Men received more than 80% of the PhDs in the sciences and more than 90% in engineering. Not even the social sciences are equally remunerative; two people with a social science degree may show a difference in income if the one degree is in sociology while the other is in econometrics; a degree in econometrics has greater remunerative capacity—and more men enter econometrics than do women.[6]

It is simply not the case that the disparity of income between men and women is due to discrimination any more than the disparity of income between me and Oprah Winfrey is due to a pervasive discrimination against philosophy teachers.

The fallacy at the heart of the claim that women make less than men for doing the same work is the fallacy of assuming that all variables left unexamined must be equal so that all residual differences in outcome (in this case, income) can be attributed to discrimination. Such a conclusion is always underdetermined, and it is very often unwarranted.

White Privilege

The concept of "white privilege" can also be looked upon the light of this fallacy; for the contention that "white privilege" is the reason that a majority are successful and white, while a minority are less successful and "not white", I would argue, is also rooted in the residual fallacy. To illustrate, I will simplify by dividing society into two groups: East Indian minority that makes up 30% of the population, leaving the white majority at 70%. Let it also be that 20% of the Indian population are very successful (2 out of 10). Since the Indian population

---

[6] *Ibid.*

constitutes 30% of the society that is a white majority, it follows that 6% of the entire population is East Indian and very successful. We will also assume 50% of the Indian population are middle class (5 out of 10). That means 15% of the entire population is East Indian and middle class. Finally, we will say that 30% of the East Indian population are poor (3 out of 10); that is 9% of the entire society are poor East Indians.

In the white population, which is the remaining 70%, 10% are white and very poor (1 out of 10), or 7% of the entire population, while 60% of the white population are middle class, or 6 out of 10, which means 42% of the entire population are white middle class (since 70% of the population is white). And finally, we will say that 30% of the white population are very rich, or 3 out of 10. That means 21% of the entire population is white and very rich.

Looking at the entire population:

Indian minority (30% of population)	White majority (70% of population)
6% = very successful	21% = very successful
15% = middle class	42% = middle class
9% = poor	7% = poor

Out of their own respective population:

Indian minority (30% of population)	White majority (70% of population)
20% = rich	30% = rich
50% = middle class	60% = middle class
30% = poor	10% = poor

As we can see when considering their respective populations, a greater percentage of East Indians are poor (⅔ more), and a greater percentage of whites are rich (⅓ more) and middle class (16.7% more).

The residual fallacy consists in assuming that all unexamined factors that might contribute to an explanation of this particular phenomenon are equal, such that all remaining differences in outcome can be attributed to discrimination, or white privilege.

But such an assumption needs to be tested. Other possible variables include: educational backgrounds, educational standards (i.e., medical schools in India are not the same as medical schools here, different degree requirements, which call for extra schooling in Canada, etc.), different educational opportunities in India, so those who emigrate here have a different distribution of low skilled versus skilled labor; initial language barriers, lack of connections (family or business connections), the time it takes to acquire credit, or differing initial economic conditions (i.e., my parents arrived from India with nothing, so they did not inherit anything from anyone, while your parents inherited money when their parents died, which permitted you to open your own business, because your parents put that money in savings, etc.).

Consider this last condition: parents arrived from India with nothing, did not inherit anything from anyone, while some white students inherited money when their parents died, which permitted them to open their own business, etc. This is privilege, without question, but it is not essentially white. Whiteness is incidental. It is simply the result of circumstances belonging to one country (Canada) that are different from those of another country (India).

We can compare your parents with the parents of that white student, but we can also compare your parents with the parents of another white student whose parents did not inherit anything. Both are white, but both do not enjoy the same level of privilege. Thus, privilege, like income, is circumstantial, while "white privilege" is categorical. The residual fallacy in this case involves assuming that the distribution of "privilege" is due to the color of one's skin, or the "category" to which one belongs by virtue of one's color. However, there are a multitude of factors that keep a large percentage of white people and their children from "privilege", namely, a poor work ethic, poor choices, a sense of entitlement, lack of talent, drug use that has had adverse effects on brain development, etc. Such factors also keep some members of a minority group from achieving a level of "privilege" available to them in this country. But it has been factors opposite the aforementioned, namely, a good work ethic, hard work, character, talent, persistence and good decisions, etc., that account for the level of privilege that many people, white or brown, currently enjoy. Indeed, some who enjoy privilege may not fit that description, but may have inherited all they have. However, such privilege cannot be sustained without those factors (i.e., determination, imagination, a good work ethic, industriousness, etc.).

Once a generation has passed and the language barrier is no longer a factor—because the children of East Indian parents went to public school and now speak fluently and they have the same educational opportunities as white children, and are achieving comparably with white children and in many cases better than many of the white students, since the Indian work ethic is significantly better—, we should see a change in the difference in percentages in the latter table above; they should eventually equal out at the very least. If white privilege is nothing more than a fallacy rooted in prejudice, then not only will they equal out, they might even tip in favor of some minorities. And this is just what has happened among the Asian population. In 2001, 31% of Chinese in Canada—both those born in Canada and foreign born—had a university education, while the national average was 18%. Furthermore, Chinese who immigrated to Canada in the 90s and who were of prime working age had an employment rate of 61%, 19% lower than the national average only eleven years later in 2001. The fundamental issue here, however, was the recognition of foreign qualifications. But, the employment rate for Canadian-born Chinese men who were of prime working age was slightly above the national average (86%), and the employment rate for

Canadian born Chinese women of prime working age was 83%, which was higher than the national average, which was 76%.[7]

---

14 *Do I Exist?*

A poster put out by the IB Organization entitled 'Do I Exist?' represents British philosopher A. J. Ayer making the claim—against the "naïve realism" of the Greeks—that you cannot prove that you exist. Many students notice it, laugh, and then wonder not so much whether or not it is true, but whether or not anyone would in all seriousness make such a claim. The answer is, not many, but yes, there are some who would.

Indeed, I cannot prove that I exist. The fact of the matter is that I do not need to. A proof is a demonstration, a deduction that carries the force of necessity. Thus, a proof takes the form of a demonstrative syllogism:

All A is B
J is A
Therefore, J is B

The conclusion follows necessarily from the given premises. The reason is that the conclusion is contained in the premises and simply needs to be "deduced" or drawn out (if all A is B and J is A, then it necessarily follows that J is B). But all deductive syllogisms depend upon simpler acts of the intellect, such as judgment. For example, All A is B (All triangles have angles the sum of which equals 180 degrees, or, All men have a rational nature, or Some students are not Italian, etc.). Judgments, however, presuppose simpler acts of the intellect, namely, simple apprehension: "Man", "rational", "sum", "angle", "Italian", etc.,. It is these simpler apprehensions that judgments combine or separate (i.e., No dog is a doctor). The idea that your existence cannot be proven is rooted in a failure to distinguish between acts of the intellect. More specifically, it involves limiting knowledge to the conclusion of a syllogism. But knowledge begins before we get to that point.

Now, before I apprehend anything specific about a thing, at the very least I apprehend that it 'is'. "Is" or being is absolutely first. There is nothing prior to 'is'. We know this because what is prior to 'is' either a) exists or b) does not exist. If it exists, then it 'is'. But what does it mean to say that 'is' is prior to 'is'? They are identical. Hence, the second option, namely, what is prior to 'is' does not exist, which means that nothing is prior to 'is' or being. The idea of being is therefore the absolutely first idea.

From whence did this idea arise? It came from my contact with real being or existence. I make existential judgments. What this means is that not only do I know "what a thing is" (simple apprehension), I also apprehend, simultaneously, "that it is" (existential judgment). I know what you are (a human being), but before I know that with any precision and depth, I at least know 'that you are'. My understanding of 'what' (essence) you are might be well off the mark, but my apprehension 'that you are' cannot be off the mark. If one denies this by insisting that my judgment that what I apprehend to exist might be mistaken, that it might turn out to not really exist, presupposes that we already know what it means to 'really exist' as opposed to 'not really exist'. Nevertheless, whatever you turn out to be—i.e., a mirage, a dream, or a real being outside my mind, I at least know 'that you are'.

Thus, the apprehension of 'existence' is the condition for the possibility of all further reasoning. So of course you cannot prove through a demonstrative syllogism that you exist; you don't need to, because your existence is self-evident to you, and my existence is immediately evident to you.

To claim that you cannot prove that you exist is like making the argument that "although you can prove to me that the sum of the angles of a triangle are 180 degrees, you cannot prove that there is any such idea as triangle". Why would anyone feel the need to prove that? If you are proving that the sum of the angles equals 180 degrees, you can only do so on condition that you know what you are talking about, which are "triangles". When we prove anything, we are proving *something about something*. For example, we are proving that 'if a man cannot move at a rate of 400 miles an hour on foot or in a car, then he could not possibly have made his way to that town, 400 miles away, to commit the murder'. But proving something about something presupposes that we are talking about something (is), whether that turns out to be 'time', a human being, the nature of speed, the nature of movement, the guilt of a criminal, etc. Being or 'is' is the starting point of all proof, not the finishing point. To say that you cannot prove that you exist—as if that's a meaningful claim—, is like saying that you cannot make the starting line the finish line. Of course, every child knows that the finish line is not the starting line. To suggest that we cannot know the starting line because it is not the finish line is just sophisticatedly disguised nonsense.

15 *A Note on Uncertain Inference*

A valid **deduction** carries the force of necessity. This means that if the premises are true and the reasoning is valid, then we can be certain of the conclusion, because the conclusion follows necessarily from the given premises. The reason is that the conclusion is contained in the premises and only needs to be "educed" therefrom.

Consider the conditional arguments below; the reasoning is valid, and as long as the premises are true, we can be **certain** that the conclusion is true.

If a doctor does not wash his hands after performing an autopsy, then he will increase the spread bacterial infection.
This doctor never washes his hands after performing autopsies.
Therefore, he increases the spread of bacterial infection.
(Valid: Affirming the Antecedent)

If atoms are ultimate particles, they are indivisible.
Atoms are not indivisible.
Therefore, they are not ultimate.
(Valid: Denying the Consequent)

If one eats lots of vegetables and fruit, then one reduces the risk of cancer.
One eats lots of vegetables and fruit.
Therefore, one has reduced the risk of cancer.
(Valid: Affirming the Antecedent)

Consider now the following **uncertain** conditional arguments:

If Henry has moral scruples against drinking, then Henry never drinks.
Henry never drinks.
Therefore, Henry has moral scruples against drinking.
(Affirming the Consequent: Invalid deduction)

If the defendant is willing to testify, then he is innocent.
The defendant is not willing to testify.
Therefore, the defendant is not innocent.
(Denying the Antecedent: Invalid deduction)

If life exists on Mars, then Mars has an atmosphere.
Mars has an atmosphere.
Therefore, life exists on Mars.
(Affirming the Consequent: Invalid deduction)

To inference is to *draw a conclusion without the available evidence.* In other words, the conclusion is "information transcending"—the conclusion is not contained in the premises. Now because evidence is missing, the conclusion is risky (inconclusive), that is, it may be false; thus, it is not necessarily true, but possibly true. It is for this reason that we shall limit the use of the term "inference" to induction; for **inductive conclusions** (i.e., conclusions of an inductive argument) are **underdetermined**; as such they lack the compelling force of necessity. Essentially, we jump to a conclusion without the evidence needed for a necessary conclusion, and thus our conclusion is only probable—to some degree or another (i.e., under, over, or around 50%).

The word "hypothesis" comes from the Greek words *hypo* (under) and *thesis* (proposition); the hypothesis is the proposition or supposition that lies under (hidden behind) the evidence, as a **possible** explanation of the evidence—it has only an underdetermined status, so to speak. Consider the invalid conditional syllogisms above. Notice the minor premise in the first example: Henry never drinks. This is an example of *affirming the consequent*, which is an invalid form. But notice that the consequent (Henry never drinks) is the only piece of evidence that is given to us. What can we infer as *the reason for* the fact that Henry never drinks? We can infer nothing with any certainty. There are, however, a number of possibilities (hypotheses), i.e., he can't stand the taste of alcohol; he is an alcoholic and belongs to AA; he has moral scruples against drinking (i.e., he is a Mormon), etc. We don't know for certain. The antecedent, namely that **Henry has moral scruples**

against drinking, is one hypothesis, or one possible explanation of the evidence, and so the conclusion that **Henry has moral scruples against drinking** might be true, but it is not necessarily true. There is a **probability** that the conclusion is true, but at this point the degree of probability is unclear (i.e., is it over 50% or under 50%? In other words, is there a 0.3 probability that the conclusion is true, or a 0.8 probability that the conclusion is true?).

Consider the second uncertain conditional argument above. What can we infer as *the reason for* the fact that '**The defendant is not willing to testify**'? We can infer nothing with any certainty, but there are a number of possibilities (possible antecedents or hypotheses). He might be guilty and is afraid that he will be found out if cross-examined; he might be innocent and is afraid that the cross-examination will trick the jurors into believing that he is not innocent; he might be innocent and feel no need to testify, since the interview he had with police after the incident was played for the jurors, and he feels there is nothing more to add, etc. The conclusion of the argument, namely **the defendant is not innocent** is invalid, that is, it lacks the force of necessity. It is a *non-sequitur*. As an inference made solely on the basis of the fact that he is not willing to testify, the conclusion has a possibility of being true, but at this point we cannot assign a number that indicates the degree of probability (i.e., a low probability of 0.3; or a high probability of 0.8, that is, between 0 and 1).

As further evidence is gathered, however, the degree of probability begins to change. For example, if Henry goes to Church every Sunday, the probability that our conclusion is true (i.e., that Henry has moral scruples against drinking) increases. But he could be Catholic, and Catholics do not have moral scruples against drinking. If evidence comes forth that he is not a Catholic, but attends a Church in an area where there is a Mormon Church on the NW corner of the street, and a Catholic Church on the SE corner, then the probability that our inference is correct is even higher (there is perhaps a 0.5 chance that the hypothesis that he has moral scruples is correct, thus increasing the probability that our inference corresponds to the truth). If Henry is

Catholic, then he will park at the Catholic Church on Sunday (highly plausible), but if he is a Mormon, he will park at the Mormon Church (highly plausible). If we see that his car is regularly parked at the Mormon Church on Sundays, then it is highly plausible that he is a Mormon and that he has moral scruples against drinking, and the hypothesis that would include that he is Catholic and has no moral scruples against drinking becomes implausible.

The investigative method always seeks the best and most consistent estimation within the context of the entire set of data at our disposal; however, even the best estimate is always tentative, for there is always the possibility that new information will change the plausibility of our current position. A theory, even when it is tested, can be no more than an inadequate explanation that puts forth causes that show consistency with the effects in question, but are not known with certainty to have a necessary connection with those effects. Philosopher Vincent E. Smith writes:

> The lesson in astronomy should never be forgotten. For almost two thousand years, the geocentric theory seemed to most men of learning to be an adequate explanation of heavenly appearances. Then came Copernicus. Today, according to Einstein, either a heliocentric or geocentric hypothesis may be used in order to map out the motions of the world.[8]

---

[8] Vincent Edward Smith, *The Elements of Logic*. Milwaukee: Bruce Publishing Company. 1957. 228

16 *Conditional Statements and the Dangers of Inferencing*

Consider the following major premises of a possible conditional argument

Example #1

If his engine seizes up, then his car will end up on the shoulder of the road.
If his transmission fails, then his car will end up on the shoulder of the road.
If he gets a flat tire, then his car will end up on the shoulder of the road.
If he can't wait to get to a bathroom, then his car will end up on the shoulder of the road.
If he wants to stop for a jog out in the country, then his car will end up on the shoulder of the road.
If his car gets stolen by kids who just want a quick joy ride, then his car will end up on the shoulder of the road.

Example #2

If the principal is a mean and vindictive man, then he will carry around a very serious demeanor.
If the principal just received news that his wife is in the hospital, then he will carry around a very serious demeanor.
If the principal has been fasting for 24 hours and is very hungry, then he will carry around a very serious demeanor.
If the principal just had to suspend someone that he did not want to suspend, then he will carry around a very serious demeanor.
If the principal hates young people, then he will carry around a very serious demeanor.

Example #3

If a student is lazy and does not care about school, then he will arrive late to school.
If a student is feeling very sick and missed the bus as a result, then he will arrive late to school.

If a student's bus was late, then he will arrive late to school.
If a student's parents are always fighting and he's feeling rather depressed and can't get himself motivated, then he will arrive late to school.
If there was an accident on the road and roads were closed, then he will arrive late to school.

Example #4

If my husband is ungrateful and inconsiderate, then he will leave his coat on the couch and forget to greet me (his wife).
If my husband has had a stressful day and is rushed to do something the minute he gets home, then he will leave his coat on the couch and forget to greet me (his wife).
If my husband is going through a mid-life crisis, then he will leave his coat on the couch and forget to greet me (his wife).
If my husband is very preoccupied with certain issues, then he will leave his coat on the couch and forget to greet me (his wife).

As you can see from the above, there are a number of possible antecedents (to the left) that can account for the consequent (on the right). Each antecedent can be regarded as a hypothesis (H_1, H_2, H_3, H_4, H_5, etc.), and the consequent can be regarded as the available evidence.

That is why making inferences on the basis of the consequent (available evidence) yields only a possibility (probability), not a necessity.

Induction begins with the consequent (the evidence), we then inference in order to explain the evidence. The inference, however, has only a degree of probability (between 0 and 1); for there are other possible explanations (hypotheses). As evidence is gathered, the possibilities are gradually narrowed down by more precise degrees of probability. For example, consider the first example above; if I learn that he never jogs, then the probability that he wanted to stop for a jog out in the country is rather low. If I eventually learn that he never takes his car in for oil changes, but simply adds oil when it is low, then the probability that it is either one of the first two alternative antecedents (hypotheses) increases. Similarly, if I learn the principal has 8 kids (in

#2), then the likelihood that the last alternative (i.e., hates young people) explains the serious demeanor decreases.

The human emotions, if disordered, can blind the intellect to the possibilities that can account for the evidence; disordered emotions can incline us to *settle on one alternative* and treat that alternative as the only one, when in fact it is only a possibility. For example, if a teacher has a mood disorder, he may rush to judgment when a student walks in late, settling for the possibility that the student does not care about school. As he settles on that alternative and treats it as a necessity rather than a possibility, other emotions begin to arise, such as anger, and so he reacts with anger. The student feels slighted because in his mind, he didn't do anything wrong (and anger is a response to a perceived injustice), he's late because traffic was stopped due to an accident, etc.

When, towards the end of the school year, I am exhausted and under pressure, I begin to make inferences that are quick and often wrong. It is my emotional state that inclines me to settle upon the alternative that will bring me some sort of relief. When I am tired, I have little patience for certain people, and I tend to misjudge the reasons for what it is they are doing. That is why I try not to place a great deal of trust in the way I see and interpret things at the end of a school year.

17 Inductive Arguments (Inferences)

Most of our day to day reasoning, not to mention the scientific method, is inductive. Deduction, as we have seen, is a mode of reasoning in which the conclusion is contained within the premises and need only be educed: i.e., **all men are rational; some living things are men; therefore, some living things are rational.** The conclusion of an inductive argument, on the other hand, is not contained in the premises, and so inductive conclusions are risky (inconclusive). It is only inductive arguments that provide grounds for accepting, on the basis of reason, **new information**. In other words, if we were limited to accepting only that which could be established by deductive means, we would never go beyond that which we already have available in the premises of an argument, because all the information in the conclusion is contained in the premises. For example, **some living things are rational** is included in the premises 1) **all men are rational** and 2) **some living things are men**.

To repeat, a large amount of work in the natural and social sciences is inductive in character. This means that conclusions are often made on the basis of observations **in a number of cases,** and then they are generalized to cover as yet unobserved cases. Let us examine four kinds of inductive arguments: 1) **induction by enumeration**, 2) **the statistical arguments**, 3) **modified induction by enumeration**, and 4) **analogical arguments**.

Induction by Enumeration

Consider the following argument, which is an instance of induction by enumeration:

Since 90% of the eggs sampled from Bill's chicken farm have been grade A, 90% of all the eggs on that farm are grade A.

90% of sampled E are A
Therefore, 90% of all E are A

The evidence before us is a sample of eggs, and from there we infer that the reason that 90% of that sample are grade A is that 90% of all the eggs on Bill's farm are grade A. Consider too the following example of induction by enumeration:

81% of all Canadians favor the Prime Minister's position on an increase in the federal tax on gasoline. We know this because a recent poll showed that 81% of Canadians polled favored his position.

81% of polled A are F
Therefore, 81% of all A are F

Both arguments are a generalization based on a sample.

The fundamental difference between induction and deduction is that if the premises are true in an inductive argument, the conclusion is **probably** true, though it might be false. The reason for this possibility is that **the conclusion contains information that is not contained in the premise**. In our first example, the conclusion is about all the eggs on Bill's farm, while the premise only gives us information about those eggs that were sampled. Because of this, it follows that the degree to which our conclusion is probably true depends on two important factors: 1) the **size** of the sample, and 2) whether or not the sample is **representative**.

In order for a sample to be properly representative, the parts of the sample must be widely distributed. Consider an urn full of marbles; I deposit 80 red marbles in it, and 60 yellow marbles on top of the red, and 30 black marbles on top of the yellow without mixing them all up. The marbles are not properly distributed, and so anyone who reaches in and takes one marble, then another, and another, etc., will end up with an unrepresentative sample. He may conclude that 90% of the marbles in the urn are black. If the pollster sampled from one city only, or one section of a city (i.e., Little Italy), the degree to which the conclusion is probably true would be low; for his sample is

91

unrepresentative. In other words, the conclusion is inductively invalid. Or think of a deck of 52 cards; if you choose 7 cards, you may end up with 4 clubs, 2 hearts, 1 diamond, and no spades. In your sample, 57% are clubs, 29% are hearts, 14% are diamonds, and 0% are spades. You could not infer that 57% of the entire pack are clubs, 29% are hearts, 14% are diamonds, and none are spades. The sample is too small, and unusual occurrences are to be expected when the sample size is small.

Consider two more examples of induction by enumeration:

Breanne received an 'A' in every course she has so far taken; therefore, she will get an 'A' in all her remaining courses.

100% of past M have been A
Therefore, 100 percent of future M will be A

In this example, all the courses that Breanne has taken so far are a **subset of** all the courses she will take. This particular argument predicts future occurrences on the basis of past occurrences. Once again, the conclusion is probably true, but it may be false.

Consider the following:

None of the IB students interviewed thought that final exams were very well scheduled. Hence, no IB student thinks that final exams are very well scheduled.

0% of interviewed S are I (impressed)
Therefore, 0% of all S are I

Like the previous example, this argument draws a conclusion that is a generalization about all the members of a particular class based on a sample of the class. In fact, this is the general feature of all examples of induction by enumeration.

We can generalize the above argument forms as follows:

Y% of observed A are B
Therefore, Y% of all A are B

(where Y is equal to or greater than 0 and equal to or less than 100)

The Statistical Argument

An inductive argument can also be **statistical**. In this case, we begin with information about all members of a class, and we draw a conclusion about a particular member of that class. Once again, the conclusion is only probable, not necessary. Consider the following:

80% of the pigs on this farm are healthy. Since Fred is a pig on this farm, Fred is healthy.

80% of all P are H
F is P
Therefore, F is H

Consider too the following:

Most of the remarks made by Brenda are insulting. The next remark made will be insulting because Brenda will make the remark.

More than half of all R is I
N is R
Therefore, N is I

The following example appears to be different, but on closer inspection, it has basically the same form:

60,000 of the tickets in the drum were purchased by people from Markham, 15,000 of the tickets were purchased by people from Newmarket, and 5000 of the tickets were purchased by people from Aurora. The winning ticket will be drawn from the drum. Hence, the winning ticket was purchased by someone from Markham.
(T = tickets in the drum; M = tickets by people from Markham; D = drawn or winning ticket)

75% of all T are M
D is T
Therefore, D is M

In a good inductive argument in the form of a statistical syllogism, **more than 50% of the class in question must have the property in question**. The generalized form of this argument is as follows:

Y% of all A are B (where Y is greater than 50 and less than 100)
X is A
Therefore, X is B

Modified Induction by Enumeration

In the two argument forms above, we made inferences about all the members of a class based on the results of **sampling some** of the members of the class (induction by enumeration), and we made inferences about a particular member of a class given information about **all the members** of a class (statistical syllogism). Now we shall examine an argument form which enables us to make inferences **about a particular member** of a class given the results of **sampling some of the members of the class**. These arguments are instances of modified induction by enumeration. For example:

87% of IB students polled were dissatisfied with the scheduling of final exams. Since Shikha is an IB student, she is dissatisfied with the scheduling of final exams.

87% of polled IBS are D
S is IBS
Therefore, S is D

To understand why this is a good inductive argument, consider the following induction by enumeration:

87% of polled IBS are D
Therefore 87% of all IBS are D

Assuming that the sample was large enough and representative, the above is an example of a valid (reasonably warranted) induction by enumeration. Now, consider the following statistical argument:

87% of all IBS are D (the conclusion of the above argument)
S is IBS
Therefore, S is D

This is a standard statistical syllogism, and it is valid because over 50% of the members of a class are dissatisfied. We know this because that is our conclusion taken from a valid induction by enumeration.

Consider the following invalid modified induction by enumeration:

10% of the students polled favored the principal's proposal. Banushan is a student, and therefore Banushan favors the principal's proposal.

The form of this argument is:

10% of observed S are F
B is S
Therefore, B is F

The relevant parts of this argument are the following:

10% of observed S are F
Therefore 10% of all S are F

10% of all S are F
B is S
Therefore, B is F.

Although the first argument satisfies all the conditions required for a good induction by enumeration, the second argument is not an acceptable instance of a statistical syllogism; for the percentage of students that are in favor is not greater than 50%. Hence, the above example of modified induction by enumeration is unacceptable.

The general argument form of modified induction by enumeration is the following:

Y% of observed A are B (where Y is greater than 50% and less than or equal to 100)
X is A
Therefore, X is B

Analogical Arguments

The final type of inductive inference we deal with in this chapter is very important in the sciences, especially paleontology: the analogical argument. The general form of this particular kind of inference is the following:

$$X = (p_1, p_2, p_3...., \text{we "estimate" } p_n+1) \text{ on the basis of:}$$
$$Y = (p_1, p_2, p_3...., p_n+1)$$

What this means is that x, which is a particular thing or a class of things, possesses certain properties $\{p_1, p_2, p_3,.....p_n\}$ in common with some y (another particular thing or class of things), and it is this fact that is the basis for the inference that x possesses some other property (p_n+1) that y also possesses.

An example of an analogical induction is the following:

y = Rodents are mammals, and they possess a nervous system that includes a developed brain.

x = Human beings are mammals, they possess a nervous system that includes a developed brain.

95% of rodents died when they ingested solanine ($p_n +1$)
Therefore, 95% of humans will die if they ingest solanine.

There are three conditions that determine reasonable warrant for this type of inductive argument:

1) The more properties that x and y have in common, the greater the warrant for the estimation.

2) The more relevant the shared properties are $\{p_1, p_2, p_3,...p_n\}$ to property p_n+1, the greater the warrant. For example, the property of a nervous system is relevant to the property of being affected by a toxin like solanine.

3) Relevant dissimilarities must also be taken into consideration; the more dissimilarities there are and the greater their relevance, the weaker is the warrant. For example, mice and humans have many dissimilarities, but most of those dissimilarities are not relevant to the effects of certain toxins, but the size difference might very well be relevant, when it comes to testing for carcinogens, for example. The dosage a rodent will need to receive in order to develop a specific pathology might very well amount to, proportionately, half a ton for a human being.

The following is an example of an unwarranted analogical induction:

x = Keefe is Chinese, he wears glasses, likes to shop at the Pacific Mall, and is good at Math.
y = Ethan is Chinese, he wears glasses, likes to shop at the Pacific Mall, ...therefore Ethan is good at Math

The Halo effect is also an example of an unwarranted analogical induction. Consider the following:

$$J = \{p_1, p_2, p_3....p_n\}$$
$$G = \{p_1, p_2, p_3....p_n+1\}$$

George is kind, personable, attractive, goes to Georgetown U, and is generous (p_n+1).

John, whom I just met, is kind, personable, attractive, goes to Harvard, ...I infer that he will be willing to give to our cause.

The inference is unwarranted because the evidence available (kind in social settings, attractive, university educated) are not entirely relevant to the property of generosity.

Before reading further, see if you understand the basics of induction by completing the exercises in Appendix G and checking your answers at the back of the book.

18 Induction by Enumeration and Thin Slicing

Consider the following major premise of a conditional syllogism:

If 65% of the marbles in this urn are blue and 35% are red, then 65% of my sample will be blue and 35% will be *read.*

This is true **as long as** my sample comes from a well-mixed urn (a well **distributed** urn of marbles); if it is well distributed and if my sample is large enough, my sample will be **representative** of the whole. That is why pollsters have to take careful measures to make sure their samples are representative if the results are to be accurate—people are not distributed like marbles in an urn.

When we do a poll, we begin with the existing state of affairs (the consequent, or the effect), and we draw a conclusion about the **antecedent,** which is the **whole. The cause or reason for the effect is the whole (antecedent), while the effect is the sample (consequent)**. So, the sample has to be representative of the whole, but society is not organized like a well-mixed urn. We have communities, i.e., Jewish, Italian, Asian (Markham), etc. Hence, we cannot select from Markham only, or from China town only, or the Italian area of Toronto only, etc.

The sample has to be large enough and representative, thus we have to select randomly from Markham, randomly from the Italian area, randomly from the Jewish area, etc. Nor can we select only from Facebook, because only a certain kind of person (within a certain range) uses Facebook; nor can we select only from LinkedIn, because only a certain type (within a range) of person uses LinkedIn. We must make sure to sample from a widely representative population.

Now, to meet someone for the first time and receive a certain "vibe", and then proceed to make an inference on the basis of that "vibe" is to **thin slice**. If in your experiences your "vibes" often turn out to be correct, it is safe to say that you are good at **thin slicing**. Think of a slice of bread. By cutting off a thin slice, you get a sense of what the whole loaf is really made of. If your thin slice tastes good, and it tastes like banana bread, then it is probably true that the whole loaf is a good tasting loaf of banana bread.

If you are intuitive, that is, if you are a good thin-slicer, then you know intuitively what to look for when you meet someone for the first time. The way he or she looks at you, what they choose not to say, how they speak of others, their eyes, clothes, etc., all relay a host of information, some of it relevant, some irrelevant. One gets a sense of the whole person, if one possesses good intuition.

Recall that induction by enumeration involves drawing a probable conclusion about an entire population on the basis of a sample. Thin slicing is a form of induction by enumeration. You are sampling, and then you are drawing a conclusion about the whole person based on that sample. Some people know what to look for, others do not. Some people are often misled by irrelevant clues, like niceness, clothes, smile, charismatic quality, smooth talker, etc. But some people look for the relevant clues; they have an eye for the significance of what is **not said**, what a person does not say in response to what someone else says, for example. They pay attention to how patient a person is in times of difficulty, how he treats those who are not of any benefit to him, the tone of his voice, the look in his eyes, the level of sincerity, whether he's too good to be true, etc.

What is happening here is that a person is sampling the right things, just as a pollster asks the right questions. Thin slicing is done quickly, rapidly, but it is a case of inferencing. Not everyone can thin slice well, especially when it comes to people. One needs a great deal of experience, and I would argue that one has to know oneself well from within.

19 *Abstractive Induction, Existential Judgment, and Reasoning*

A student once remarked: If all knowledge begins in sensation (begins with the particular), then all knowledge begins with induction, and if all knowledge begins with induction, and induction is only probable knowledge, then nothing is certain.

This is a very thoughtful remark. For it is true that "nothing is in the intellect that is not first in the senses"; thus, all knowledge begins in the realm of the concrete particular. The first act of the intellect is simple apprehension, or what some thinkers have referred to as "abstractive induction". The second act of the intellect is existential judgment, and finally, the third act of the intellect is reasoning, which is both deductive and inductive.

Now, abstractive induction (the first act of the intellect) is different from inductive reasoning. Inductive reasoning presupposes or depends on abstractive induction. One cannot reason inductively unless one knows "what" one is talking about. We cannot begin to determine the probability of schizophrenia given the evidence, or the probability of specific symptoms given that a person has schizophrenia, unless one knows what "schizophrenia" is in the first place, or what an "illness" is, or what "evidence" is, or what "probability" is, etc. And that's just what "abstractive induction" is; it is the first act of the intellect which apprehends the "whatness" or essence of things.

The mind is an immaterial power, and what it does first is it abstracts the "intelligible content" (i.e., the essence of the thing or action or relationship, etc.) from the particular phantasm, that is, from all its individuating conditions. The mind conceives that intelligible content (the concept, the idea) abstracted from the particular, which is why it is universal in the mind, while outside the mind it is a particular instance of a tree, or a man, or an act of justice, etc.

Existential judgment, the second act of the intellect, is the apprehension of the very act of existence of the being before me. I know "what" you are through the first act of the intellect, but at the same time I apprehend "that you are" (that you exist) through existential judgment. The first act of the intellect, abstractive induction

101

(or simple apprehension) is incomplete, considered in itself. It is perfected in the act of existential judgment. The first act of the intellect grasps "a potentiality for existence", while through existential judgment I immediately apprehend that this being before me is more than "what it is" essentially; in other words, the act of existing of this being does not add anything to the nature of this being, that is, it does not change it specifically in any way; rather, it is this being's existential actualization. I know what it is, but I also know something more, namely, "that it is", and the intelligible content of this apprehension is not a concept (it is not an essence), but it is an intelligibility other than the intelligibility of the "essence"; it is an intelligibility that is the perfection of the "whatness" that I apprehend in the first act of the intellect, namely the intelligibility of its existence.

The reason that the apprehension of a being's act of existing is not included in the first act of the intellect is that apprehending "what" a thing is does not tell me whether or not it exists. After years of study, I may know something about the nature or essence of dinosaurs, but knowing "what" they are is not to know "that they are" (their existence). If existence were included in a thing's nature, then knowing "what" it is would be enough to know "that it is". Whatever belongs to the essence of a thing belongs to it necessarily (triangles are necessarily three sided, animals are necessarily living, a man is necessarily risible, etc.). In knowing "what" a man is, for example, I know that a man is necessarily "rational" (has the ability to reason) and "sentient" (has the ability to sense). But the act of existence of a particular man is not part of that conception; rather, I apprehend that existence through a different act of the intellect, namely existential judgment. I know "what" you are, and I know "that you are". I can now reason (the third act of the intellect) deductively, for example, I know that "All men are rational", and I judge that you (a real being) are a man; therefore, I conclude that "You are rational". I can also reason inductively; for I know that 87% of students in this school are East Indian, and so I conclude that you, a student of this school, are East Indian. This latter conclusion is a valid inductive argument, it is only probable, but it depends on two more fundamental acts of the intellect in order to be achieved.

Moreover, the first act of the intellect admits of degrees; as I observe a thing's activity (how it behaves, how it reacts, etc.), I gradually come to know "what it is" more fully. At first, I may only know it to be a substance of some kind, but as I continue to observe its activity, I begin to see that it is a living thing, and then an animal of some kind, etc. As I begin to study it using a method that is investigative (scientific), that is, a deliberate method that aims to gather data beyond our ordinary experience, my knowledge of "what it is" becomes richer with precision and detail (i.e., I know it has a heart that pumps blood, nerves, muscles, etc.). It is that method, the scientific method, that is highly inductive, and the conclusion of an inductive mode of reasoning is probable. Before I can employ the scientific method, however, I must know "what" I am investigating. In other words, inductive reasoning should not be confused with abstractive induction (simple apprehension).

And so, as a medical student, I am certain that I am learning more and more about "human" physiology, anatomy, and histology, etc. I may not be entirely certain of the cause of a specific type of cancer, but I know, generally speaking, what cancer is, and I know what "human" is, just as I know what "reasoning" is, what induction and deduction are, etc.

20 The Round-Trip Fallacy

The following is a valid statistical argument:

87% of oranges in this box are grade A.
This orange is from this box.
Therefore, this orange is grade A.

The truth of the conclusion has high probability. A subtly defective statistical argument, however, is the following:

87% of oranges in this box are grade A.
This orange is grade A.
Therefore, this orange came from this box.

This has been called the Round-trip fallacy.[9] The terms in the major premise have been flipped, as it were. The major premise is "87% of the oranges in this box are grade A", but the lazy mind reads it as "87% of Grade A oranges are in this box". The results of this subtle fallacy are invalid conclusions that can have serious repercussions. For example, let's assume statistics show that 99% of terrorists are Muslim. Consider the following statistical argument:

99% of all terrorists are Muslim.
John is a Muslim.
Therefore, John is a terrorist. (i.e., a good probability that this is true)

Or,

Most of the criminals on First 48 are black.
Celon is black.

---

[9] Nassim Nicholas Taleb, *The Black Swan: The Impact of the Highly Improbable.* New York: Random House Trade Paperbacks, 2010. Chapter 5, "Confirmation Shmonfirmation" [Kobo version]. Retrieved from http://www.kobo.com.

Therefore, Celon is a criminal. (i.e., a good probability that this is true).

As Nassim Taleb points out, the confusion is very trivial, but it is a crucial mistake. "Unless we concentrate very hard, we are likely to unwittingly simplify the problem because our minds routinely do so without our knowing it"[10]

Consider the terrorist example above; the major premise is: "99% of all terrorists are Muslims". A lazy mind reads it as "99% of all Muslims are terrorists". A proper statistical argument using the correct major and minor premise is the following:

99% of all terrorists are Muslim.
John is a terrorist.
Therefore, John is a Muslim.

The truth of the conclusion has a high degree of probability, but it is still underdetermined, so there is a possibility that John is a non-Muslim terrorist (i.e., Jewish, Latino, Chechnian, etc.). The erroneous version, however, is seriously mistaken; for there are about 2 billion Muslims in a world of about 7 billion. Thus, about 30% of the world's population is Muslim. If there are about 10,000 terrorists in the world, 99% of whom—we assume—are Muslims, then 9,900 terrorists are Muslim, out of the 2 billion Muslims in the world. That gives us .00000495; or 0.000495 %. Thus, it is very unlikely (very low probability) that a Muslim in your neighborhood is a terrorist. Consider, however, the practical implications of such a trivial logical error.

Let us return to our original example:

87% of oranges in this box are grade A.
This orange is grade A.
Therefore, this orange came from this box.

---

[10] *Ibid.*

There is an even lower probability that this grade A orange is from this box, considering how many grade A oranges there are in the world compared to how many oranges are in this box.

Another variation on this fallacy is to equate absence of evidence with evidence of absence. In other words, **absence of evidence is not evidence of absence**. For example, little or no evidence of violence is not evidence that this person is not violent. In chapter 22, we will introduce the concept of the null hypothesis; at this point, however, let it be said that the null hypothesis simply means that between samples of the population of whatever it is we are testing for (samples of behaviour, samples of popcorn, samples of people on medication, or samples of a new drug, etc.), there is no significant difference, and thus any observed difference is due simply to, chance, sampling or experimental error. For example, we want to know something about the relationship between our hypothesis that this criminal is no longer violent and evidence of violence; for he's behaved quite well these past three years, thus we start with a null hypothesis that he is not violent (status quo); we assume, therefore, that there is no significant difference between samples of his behaviour, that is, nothing that raises red flags. The symbol for the null hypothesis is H_0.

This statistical method is called significance testing, which we will look at more closely later on. In the meantime, consider the following:

$$H_0 \rightarrow \sim E$$
$$\sim E$$
$$H_0$$

If he's not a violent man (H_0), then we will not see significant evidence (to be specified).
We have not seen specified evidence.
Therefore, there he is not a violent man (i.e., there nothing wrong, nothing to worry about, all is well).

This is an instance of **affirming the consequent**, which is logically invalid. Hence, the conclusion is unwarranted. On the basis of a lack of evidence, we concluded that the null hypothesis is true. But all we know is that we have not seen evidence that puts our null hypothesis in doubt, at least not to a degree that we decided beforehand would be significant, and so that lack of evidence simply confirms our null hypothesis. However, a lack of evidence does not prove a null hypothesis, nor does confirmation prove a hypothesis; rather, it is falsification alone that proves a hypothesis wrong. Hence, we do not know whether or not the null hypothesis is true; that has to be tested directly.

The following are examples of popular confusions of absence of evidence with evidence of absence. Each one is, of course, a *non-sequitur*.

1) Little or no evidence of narcissism is evidence that a person is not a narcissist.

This is false; for this person is careful, he is devious and underhanded, so he leaves no evidence of his narcissism.

2) No evidence of a disease is evidence that a person does not have a disease (i.e., no evidence of cancer is evidence that a person does not have cancer).

This is false; a person may very well have cancer that no test has yet been able to detect.

3) No evidence of a terrorist threat is evidence that there is no terrorist threat.

Again, this is false; little or no evidence of a terrorist threat is not the same as evidence that there is no terrorist threat (or no significant terrorist threat). The terrorists might be careful, blending nicely into the daily life of the society they wish to eventually terrorize.

4) No evidence that this person is innocent is evidence that he/she is not innocent (guilty).

False. This person might have been at the wrong place at the wrong time; he/she was alone when the murder took place and just happened to be seen near the place where the body was recovered on the very day that the pathologist determined that it was dumped there. Thus, there is no evidence of his/her innocence; but that does not mean there is evidence that the person is not innocent.

5) No evidence that this person is the killer is evidence that he is not the killer.

False. He is a cunning and careful criminal, so there is no evidence that he killed his victim.

6) No evidence of understanding is evidence of a lack of understanding.

Again, this is not necessarily true; for some students with a serious learning disability (output disability) show little or no traditional evidence of grasping concepts, but they may very well understand a great deal of what is taught. Of course, there would have to be some evidence, some way of knowing that he has learned something, but the evidence is typically unconventional, such as the teacher has their attention the entire time, or their questions reveal a profound grasp of the concepts.

7) No evidence of interest (yawning, head down, etc.) is evidence of a lack of interest.

Some students who appear to be bored and uninterested in class talk of little else when they are outside of class, i.e., at home. Or, they might desperately want to be there but are suffering from a sudden onset of an illness, or sleep deprivation, etc.

21 Thoughts on Being Wrong

One day I walked into a used bookstore and cafe that I used to frequent regularly, and I was tempted by the sight of the various slices of pie on display. However, they appeared to be the very same slices I saw a week earlier when I was there last, so I said to the young man working the counter: "These pies are not fresh, but are just on display, right?" He was rather put off by my comment/question and responded with a tinge of anger: "No, these pies are fresh and are baked daily."

"Oh, okay," I said, suddenly aware that I was mistaken; for the pies that I was spying looked exactly the same, in every way, as the slices I saw the previous week. Of course, I did not argue with the young man who was clearly upset at my inference, but ordered a slice and a cup of coffee, after which time he became more pleasant.

After eating the slice and drinking the coffee, I went to look for the philosophy section of the bookstore. In previous years, it used to be in the middle shelf towards the front, but those shelves now contained biography and travel, etc. I knew where the religion section was, and I had gone through all their books the previous week, but I wanted to see what they had in philosophy. So, I asked him where I could find philosophy, and he immediately turned towards the religion section and pointed, but I immediately said: "That's the religion section". He made his way towards it and said: "That's Religion and Philosophy", and he was right, the philosophy section was next to it under the tag "Philosophy", which I'd missed. Once again, I was mistaken; for I had assumed I had enough data to oppose his judgment, that he did not know where his philosophy section was and that he was confusing it with religion.

I went to study the books on the shelf and soon realized that I'd seen them before, a week earlier, but had forgotten that this was the new section of philosophy books. My memory failed.

In this short span of about 15 or 20 minutes, I had made a wrong inference about the slices of pie, and I'd assumed that I knew his store better than he did, and I realized that my memory failed. His emotional reaction at my first mistake is understandable, for it had the potential to do harm: had anyone overheard, my inference might have planted a seed of doubt in their minds, which in turn could negatively impact sales.

The only reason I am aware of my errors within this short span of time is because I am disposed to think of real-life situations that illustrate knowledge problems. Had I not, like most people, been so disposed, I would have quickly forgotten these mistakes. In fact, I would probably not have become explicitly aware of them at all; I would have suppressed the knowledge; for it is not a pleasant experience to be proven wrong, to discover that you have been mistaken. We feel stupid or ashamed, so we are not inclined to focus on our errors, much less experience any kind of fascination with them. We do, however, remember moments when we were right, for we relate them to others and sometimes even ridicule those who, in the circumstances, were wrong. Although such incidents are far less frequent than the incidents in which we are wrong, we tend to forget the latter.

I was mistaken three times at the very least. If I were to focus, however, on the inferences I made to myself within the course of those 20 minutes, the number would be much higher. How many great books did I pass over, because I inferred they contained nothing that would be of any importance for me? I made quick inferences about the people who had entered the store, all on the basis of their manner of dress and comportment. How likely is it that were I to suddenly possess information about their past, I would discover that my initial inferences were too thin to be taken seriously even for a moment? Based on past experience, I would have to say highly likely.

What we gradually realize when we pay close attention to those times when we've discovered we were wrong is that human intelligence is profoundly limited; it is limited by virtue of the fact that what we know naturally are existing material natures, limited and varied by matter. Human knowing is initially inductive; thus, we draw risky conclusions all the time. Those conclusions lack necessity and so are only probable.

Within those 20 minutes, I did not feel stupid for being wrong—although I have no doubt that I looked rather stupid to this young fellow. Being wrong is a normal epistemic state of affairs. That is why I have come to believe the logic of induction is far more important than the finer details of deductive logic; for our day to day reasoning is a matter of induction and thus full of risk.

One of the most pervasive errors people commit today has to do with distribution: "All that is true makes sense", just as "All giraffes are animals" (the subject is distributed, the predicate is undistributed); but to flip this is a common error: "All that makes sense is true". This is no truer than "All animals are giraffes". Our risky conclusions, that is, our inferences, often **make sense**; however, they are often mistaken.

Progress is slow in this world, and it will not pick up speed when we stop being so wrong; that's not possible. Progress will begin to happen when we become aware of our radical limitations, that most of our conclusions are the result of an inference to the most plausible estimation, often drawn without sufficient evidence, the result of impatience and affected by a very weak memory. It is our level of confidence that is one of our biggest problems; people tend to draw conclusions with a level of confidence that has no rational basis whatsoever.

A Thought on Multiple Inferences

How is it possible for someone to be so wrong about a particular person, a group of persons, a culture or a nation? One way to look at this is from the point of view of the basic rules of probability, specifically the multiplication rule. A major problem with our inferences (going from evidence to conjecture) is that they are rarely singular. A single inference has a degree of probability; let's assign an 80% probability as a thought experiment (i.e., the probability that John, who said he was going to place A, probably went instead to place B after a quick visit to place A—because I know that John likes comfortable living quarters, not the rough quality that is typical of place A). Our inferencing, however, rarely stops there. On the basis of that first inference (which actually is not really first at all, but an inference made on the basis of a prior inference or series of inferences), we make another inference, perhaps one that has an 80% probability, and on the basis of that inference, we infer something else in order to make sense out of the previous inference—again, let's assign a 70% probability to that one. In the end—if we were to stop here, which is unlikely—, we are left with a conclusion that has a rather low probability of being entirely true; in this case a 45% probability or 0.45 (.8 X .8 X .7 = .45). Perhaps that is why very often we discover that we are well off the mark about a particular person, culture, nation, or issue.

22 *An Introduction to Bayesian Inferencing (Abduction)*

There are two types of probabilities: 1) belief type and 2) frequency type. In this chapter we focus on belief type probability (Bayes' Theorem). Belief is a matter of degree, and we can represent that belief in terms of probability. For example, I see a woman and just by her appearance, I believe she is married, that is, I infer she is married. Of course, I am not certain, but the probability of my hypothesis P(H) can be represented by a number between 0 and 1 (0 = I am certain it is false; 1 = I am certain it is true). Let's say I believe there is a 30% chance that she is married P(0.3). Shortly thereafter, she is pushing a stroller, and because of that additional piece of evidence, my belief that she is a married woman P(H/E) has increased significantly P(0.7). Bayesian inference seeks to determine the posterior probability of the hypothesis given the evidence P(H/E). The following is the formula for Bayes' Theorem (/ = division):

$$P(H/E) = P(H)P(E/H) \ / \ P(H)P(E/H) + P(\sim H)P(E/\sim H)$$

This may look difficult, but it is not. The symbol ~H simply refers to the complement of the hypothesis. Thus, if P(H) is .3, then P(~H) is .7; If there is a 30% probability that she is married, there is a 70% probability that she is not.

Imagine that you have been called to Jury duty;[11] a robbery took place in Markham, and let's assume that given the evidence, there are two alternative hypotheses (two possible gangs): 1) a member of the Markham Terrors committed the crime, or 2) a member of the Renegades committed the crime. The Renegades always wear blue bandanas, and the Markham Terrors always wear dark yellow ones. Now, 85% of the street robberies in the past have been committed by members of the Markham Terrors, who always wear yellow bandanas; the rest have been committed by the Renegades. On a dark and misty

---

[11] The fundamental structure of this example is based on a scenario I found in Ian Hacking's *Introduction to Probability and Inductive Logic*. Cambridge: Cambridge University Press, 2001. 72-73.

night, a kid robbed an old man, assaulted him and ran off. Anushka witnessed the whole thing and she insists that it was a kid wearing a blue bandana. The officer had her tested under conditions similar to those on the night of the accident, and 80% of the time she correctly reported color. Which hypothesis has the greater probability?

A) a Markham Terror gang member did it (yellow bandana).
B) a Renegade gang member committed the crime (blue bandana).

After witnessing her testimony in court, you all went off to deliberate.

Juror #1 (Alisha) said: "The probability that the criminal was wearing blue is 80% or 0.8." I say we convict the Renegade gang member.
Juror #2, (Austin) said: "It is more likely that the criminal was a Renegade, but the probability is less than 0.8.
Juror #3, (Kathlyn) said: "It is just as probable that the criminal was wearing dark yellow as that it was light blue. There is equally probability here."
Juror #4, (A.J.) said: "It is more likely than not that the criminal was wearing dark yellow. I say there is reasonable doubt and we should not convict this Renegade gang member on the basis of the evidence we have. We need more."

On the basis of the information, which juror is correct?

Let's work on the solution:

Let Y = A criminal selected at random wears a yellow bandana. $P(Y) = .85$, or 85% (since 85% of the street robberies in the past have been committed by the Terrors).
Let B = A criminal selected at random wears blue. $P(B) = .15$ or 15%.

It is important to note that Y and B are the **base rates** or prior probabilities; this is important because we have a tendency to ignore base rates, focusing instead, almost exclusively, on the evidence at hand; the result is that our statistical intuition is often mistaken.

Let W_b = Anushka (the witness) states that the criminal is wearing blue. $P(W_b/B) = 0.8$. This means the probability that the witness says he's wearing blue, given that he is actually wearing blue; I.e., the probability that she is correct. Now, keep in mind that $P(W_b/B)$ is $P(E/H)$, that is, the probability of the evidence given the hypothesis. Thus, what is the probability of the evidence, which is that Anushka states that the criminal is wearing blue, given that he is wearing blue? It is 0.8 or 80%.

Thus, $P(W_b/Y) = 0.2$. This means the probability that the witness says he's wearing blue given that he's wearing yellow is 0.2 or 20%; i.e., the probability that the witness is mistaken. In other words, what is the probability of the evidence given the alternative hypothesis $P(E/\sim H)$?

Now, we want to know the probability of the hypotheses given the evidence $P(B/W_b)$ and $P(Y/W_b)$. In other words, what is the probability that the criminal is a Renegade gang member given that the witness says it was? And what is the probability that the criminal was a Markham Terror gang member given that the witness says it was a Renegade gang member?

B (blue bandana) in this case is the *hypothesis* that we are testing, and W_b is the *evidence*. Using Bayes' Theorem, we determine the following:

$P(B/W_b) = P(B)P(W_b/B) / P(B)P(W_b/B) + P(Y)P(W_b/Y)$

$P(B/W_b) = (.15 \times .8) / [(.15 \times .8) + (.85 \times .2)] = .12/.29 = 41\%$

$P(Y/W_b) = P(Y)P(W_b/Y) / P(Y)P(W_b/Y) + P(B)P(W_b/B)$

$P(Y/W_b) = (.85 \times .2) / [(.85 \times .2) + (.15 \times .8)] = .17/.29 = 59\%.$

And so it turns out that A. J. is right, "It is more likely than not that the criminal was wearing dark yellow."

Although we may never know with *certainty* whether it was in fact a kid wearing a blue bandana who actually robbed the man (unless more evidence is forthcoming, like DNA testing), we are **certain** that it is *more likely* (more probable) than not that it was a yellow bandana (Markham Terror Gang). Given the little evidence at our disposal, we should find reasonable doubt. We need more evidence that will shift the probability over towards the blue bandana (that is, toward the witness's testimony).

If we focus only on the witness's accuracy (80%), we will vote to convict the accused, who wears a blue bandana. In other words, if we simply focus on the evidence (as most people do) and ignore the prior probabilities of the hypotheses (ignore base rates), we risk a wrongful conviction and we will vote in a way that is contrary to the logic of probability.

If we were to consider the base rates alone (85% and 15%)—and I am not suggesting that we do—we would vote more in accordance with the logic of probability, even though our judgment of the probability will turn out to be greater than what it actually is (i.e., 85% vs. 59%). If we take everything into consideration and calculate the probabilities, that is, if we do **not** ignore the base rates and include the witness's accuracy, there is still a greater probability (59% vs. 41%) that the criminal was wearing yellow (less than the actual base rate of 80%, but nevertheless a greater probability than that the criminal was wearing blue).

Thus, we should not be too quick to favor the witness. Yes, she is right in color identification 80% of the time, but the base rates tell another story and are a very important factor here.

Now, because the opposing hypothesis has a greater probability, this does not mean that the crime was committed by a member of Markham Terrors, who wear yellow. The crime still could have been committed by a Renegade. Given only the witness's testimony and its accuracy as well as the base rates, we cannot convict the Renegade because there is reasonable doubt. If the base rates were different, if 75% of the crimes were committed by the Markham Terrors and the witness is wrong 25% of the time in color identification at night, then the probabilities change. There is now a 50% probability that the criminal was wearing yellow—thus a 50% probability that he was wearing blue (the two hypotheses have equal probability). The case has to get thrown out, unless more evidence is forthcoming. And if 90% of the crimes are committed by the Markham Terrors (yellow) and our witness is right 75% of the time in color identification at night, in other words, her accuracy decreases from 80% to 75%, but the base rate increases, then there is now a 75% greater likelihood that the criminal was wearing yellow and that our witness is wrong. The increase in the base rate was significant here.

However, if 75% of the crimes are committed by the Terrors in yellow (our base rate decreases) and our witness is right 95% of the time (her accuracy increases), then it is 86% more likely that the crime was committed by one of the Renegades (blue).

23 Jeffrey's Rule and the Power of Rumors

Our day to day existence is full of opportunities to hypothesize; in fact, most of our decisions involve comparing evidence for various and competing hypotheses (i.e., can I trust this person? Is this person upset with me? Is this a good company to work for? etc.). When we think about the probabilities for certain hypotheses, we do so relative to our current set of background knowledge, as well as our prejudices, beliefs, etc. However, we learn new things all the time; in other words, new evidence surfaces, and in light of that new evidence, we might think to adjust the probabilities of our hypotheses. For example, consider our taxi scenario in which a witness, with an 80% accuracy rating, testified that it was a blue taxi that sideswiped another vehicle. What would happen if a new witness were to come forward to testify that she believed it was a green taxi that did so? Would we be moved to revise our judgment of probability? Unless we had some sort of incentive to continue to believe it was blue (i.e., we were threatened, or bribed, etc.), we would probably, on an intuitive level, revise our belief about our original hypothesis. If the new witness were to say it was blue, according to a Bayesian calculus, the probability that it was a blue taxi would increase significantly.

Recall there was a 41% probability that it was a blue taxi, a 59% probability that it was a green taxi (the base rates are: 15% of taxis in town are blue, and 85% are green).

$$P(H/E) \text{ or } P(B/W_b) = .15 \times .8 \ / \ .15 \times .8 + .85 \times .2 = .41$$

Thus, 41% is our posterior probability. But should a new witness come forward—who also tested 80% for accuracy—to testify that the car was blue, consider what happens to our new calculation. Let us refer to the new evidence as F.

$$P(H/E \ \& \ F) = P(H/E)P(F/H\&E) \ / \ P(H/E)P(F/H\&E) + P(\sim H/E)P(F/\sim H\&E)$$

$$P(B/W_b \& 2^{nd}W_b) = P(B/1^{st}W_b)P(2^{nd}W_b/B \& 1^{st}W_b) /$$
$$P(B/1^{st}W_b)P(2^{nd}W_b/B \& 1^{st}W_b) + P(G/1^{st}W_b)P(2^{nd}W_b/G\&1^{st}W_b)$$

$= .7354$, or a 74% probability that it was blue.

Note that if the new witness had said that it was a green taxi that she saw, then the probability that it was a blue taxi would have decreased to 15%.

Thus, new information (experience) changes the probability of our inferences. That is what experience does, generally speaking; it alters the degree of probability of our beliefs, either by strengthening them, or weakening them, and it does so continually.

However, the problem with the above is that learning does not always proceed in such neat and tidy steps, such as:

1. We come into new evidence (E)
2. We employ Bayes' theorem.
3. We then come into another new piece of evidence (F)
4. We re-apply Bayes' theorem.
5. Etc., continually updating our posterior probabilities.

Some learning does proceed that way (i.e., laboratory, surveys, etc.), but in real life, we often change our viewpoint on the basis of information that is far less precise. Sometimes the new evidence is merely a rumor, something we overheard, an inference that another person might have made on the basis of very little evidence. We might choose to ignore the inference or the rumor, but I will argue that doing so is far more difficult than we might want to admit. If we know that there is a good probability that the rumor is true, we can revise our opinions, but we cannot do so with Bayes' theorem, because rumors offer us no certain information (E) to use in the theorem (i.e., P(E/H), or the probability of the evidence given the hypothesis.

Logician and probability theorist Richard Jeffrey revised Bayes' theorem to manage such new and uncertain information.

Consider the following (note the asterisk *)

P(H) = the probability of the hypothesis.
P(H/E) = the probability of the hypothesis given the evidence before the rumor.
P*(H) = the probability of the hypothesis in light of the rumor.
P*(E) = the probability of rumored evidence.

Jeffrey's Rule: P*(H) = P(H/E)P*(E) + P(H/~E)P*(~E).

What is a rumor? It is a piece of information that could be true or false. Many rumors are the result of an inference, and so they have only a degree of probability. Consider the following scenario:

G = You will receive a good education if you go to City District High School.
R = If you go to this school, you might get stabbed, robbed, bullied.

One cannot use Bayes' Rule, because we do not have the likelihoods: P(E/H).

Jeffrey's rule: P*(G) = P(G/R) P*(R) + P(G/~R) P*(~R)

P(G/~R) = the probability that you will receive a good education if you go to CDHS, given that there is no rumor. 80%.
P(G/R) = the probability that you will receive a good education at CDHS, given that there is bullying, stabbings, etc. 10%
P*(R) = the probability that the rumor is true. 75%
P*(~R) = the probability that the rumor is not true. 25%

1. P*G) = the probability that you will receive a good education at CDHS in light of the rumor.

P*(G) = .1 x .75 + .8 x .25

.0750 + .20 = 28% chance that you will receive a good education in light of the rumor.

A 50/50 Rumor

What about a person who simply has no idea whether or not the rumor is true. In other words, what if there is no real foundation for the rumor, nothing that inclines us to believe it or disbelieve it.

Citizen who has no clue:
$P^*(R) = .5$
$P^*(\sim R) = .5$

.1 x .50 + .8 x .50
.0500 + .40 = .45, or 45% chance that you will receive a good education in light of the rumor.

An Improbable Rumor

Now, let's say I don't trust the rumor, because although I've been retired from that school now for 10 years, I haven't heard anything bad. Moreover, I believe the rumor is based on prejudice: i.e., lots of Indian, Sri Lankan, and black students, and some people jump to conclusions without any substantial evidence.

Consider the mathematical evidence that rumors have influence nevertheless.

Me:
$P^*(R) = .25$ (a 25% chance that a bullying problem developed since my absence)
$P^*(\sim R) = .75$ (a 75% chance that the rumor is unfounded and rooted in prejudice)

$P^*(G) = .1$ x .25 + .8 x .75

.0250 + .60 = 62% chance that you will receive a good education in light of a rumor that we might not even trust. Our probability calculation has gone from 80% to 62% on the basis of a rumor that we find lacks credibility. Hence, rumors still influence.

The question at this point is whether this can be regarded as a mathematical look at what takes place on an intuitive level. If the two levels are parallel, then a rumor that began as a rapid and unfounded inference inevitably affects our probability calculus. It alters our inferences, reducing or increasing their probability, and it does so all on the basis of an inference that is itself only probable. How much credibility do we give the rumor? We may choose not to give it credibility at all, but it is there, at the back of our minds, and it does influence us nonetheless (a rumor with a 25% credibility dropped the probability of the hypothesis that one can receive a good education at CDHS). Rumors influence us especially when we receive additional evidence that confirms the new hypothesis that results from the rumor (P*(H), because confirmatory evidence is more vibrant than disconfirmatory evidence.

The things people choose to us say about others inevitably influence the way we perceive them. The problem is people often believe things that are downright false or highly unlikely, and yet they assert these beliefs with tremendous passion and a sense of certainty, and if we admire the source, we are often moved to believe what they say. If they are not careful and if we are not careful, we will find ourselves passionately hanging on to beliefs that we mistakenly think are truths, and if we act on those beliefs, we may end up doing a great deal of harm to ourselves and others.

24 *Frequency Type Probability (Part I)*

Bayesian inferencing is about inferencing to the best hypothesis. In other words, we look for the probability of the hypothesis given the evidence P(H/E). Frequency type probability is about calculating the probability of the evidence, given the hypothesis P(E/H). We refer to this as bell curve probability. A number of knowledge issues arise out of this particular type of inferencing, but before treating any of these, we should become familiar with some of the basics. To that end, I have come up with a fictional scenario having to do with popcorn.

Recall the last time you made popcorn. Remember how it sounded? One kernel, then two or three begin popping, then a few more, then many more begin to pop, and soon the popping breaks out into an all-out machine gun series of pops, which soon begins to die down gradually, and then three, then two, then one pop at the very end. That's what a normal probability distribution sounds like; a normal probability distribution looks like a bell curve.

We call this a frequency type probability, for we do not know which popcorn kernel is going to pop at any one time, but we do know that there is a 68% chance that it will pop within a certain time span, and a 95% chance of popping within a slightly larger time span, etc. Or, we can put it like this: 68% of the kernels will pop within this specified time frame, 95% of the kernels will pop within this wider time frame, etc.

In order to provide a sense of how frequency distribution works, allow me share the results of an experiment that I carried out, the results of which are a rough approximation. We start with 173 kernels of popcorn; we pour the kernels into an unusually large pot that has been heating up with oil on the bottom. Thirty seconds later, the first two kernels pop; about five seconds later, the next two kernels pop; about five seconds after that, two more pop, etc. At the one minute mark, four kernels pop, and another four pop one second later; and there is a steady increase. The sounds reach a crescendo at the 70 second mark, and it begins to die at about the 75 second mark. After

80 seconds, the popping sound has noticeably died down. Four kernels pop at 83 seconds, and 3 kernels pop at 88 seconds, etc. At 118 seconds, two kernels pop, and the final kernels pops at the 2 minute mark.

The mean (average) of the distribution is 72.93 seconds (or 73 seconds). The standard deviation (σ) is a measure of the dispersion of the data from the mean. In this case, the standard deviation is 13.90 seconds (14 seconds) seconds $\pm$. What this means is that 68% of the popcorn kernels will have popped between 59 seconds and 87 seconds, which is 1 standard deviation (1σ) from the mean (73 seconds). But 95% of the kernels will have popped within 2 standard deviations, that is, between 45 seconds and 101 seconds; and 99.7% of the kernels will have popped within 3 standard deviations, that is, between 31 seconds and 115 seconds. This means that 2.5% of the kernels will pop before 45 seconds and 2.5% of the kernels will pop after 101 seconds. Which ones exactly? We simply don't know.

The standard deviation is calculated using the following formula: $\sqrt{}$ $[\sum (X_1 - X)^2 + (X_2 - X)^2 + (X_3 - X)^2 + \ldots /n]$, where X stands for the mean (73 seconds), while X_1, X_2, X_3, etc., stand for each observed result; for example, X_1 is the first popcorn kernel that popped, and this took place at the 30 second mark. So, $(X_1 - X)^2$ is $(30 - 73)^2 + (30 - 73)^2 + (35 - 73)^2 + \text{etc.,}. /173$. The standard deviation is the square root of the sum of each observed result minus the mean squared, divided by the total number.

If we were to plot the data on a chart, this is what our frequency distribution would look like:

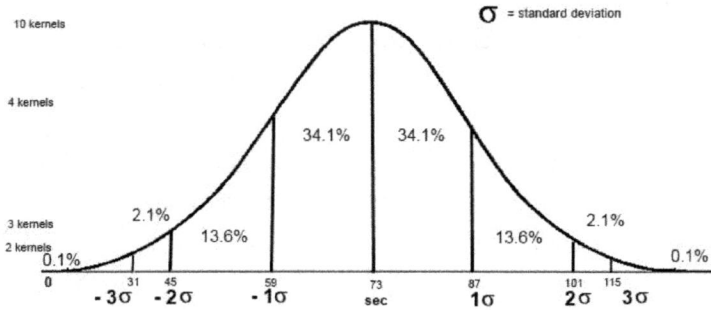

Our mean is 73 seconds; the jar of popcorn, which contains 173 kernels, takes about 120 seconds to pop completely.

Now, we have genetically modified our popcorn in the hopes that we could achieve a faster popping time. Let's test for whether or not we have achieved our goal. Our null hypothesis (H_0) is that this genetic modification does *not* affect the time of popping. Our alternative hypothesis (H_1) is that this genetic modification is responsible for popped corn in less time.

At this point, we introduce the concept of the **standard error**. The standard error measures the dispersion of *the sample means* (which is a smaller sample); for we are not going to use 173 kernels of popcorn to test this again, because in this fictional scenario, popcorn is expensive; rather, we are going to use a smaller sample. So we ask: "How closely do we expect the sample means, i.e., the means of the smaller packages of popcorn, to cluster around the population mean (the larger population of kernels in our study, which is 73)?

The standard deviation measures dispersion in the larger population; in our case, it measures the dispersion of time measured in seconds of all the popcorn in our study. The standard error measures the dispersion of *the sample means* (we have five smaller samples of popcorn, each containing 40 kernels, for example). If we draw repeated samples of 40 kernels from the larger population of popcorn kernels, what will the dispersion of the sample means look like? The standard error is *the standard deviation of the sample means.*

A large standard error will mean that the sample means are spread out widely around the population mean; a small standard error means that they are clustered relatively tightly. Our sample means will cluster more tightly around the larger population mean as the size of each of our samples gets larger. As our sample size gets larger (i.e., from 30 to 80), the standard error gets smaller, since large samples are less vulnerable to distortion by extreme outliers. As the sample size gets smaller, the standard error will get larger. The formula for the standard error is: $s/\sqrt{n}$

Returning to the popcorn example, the standard deviation is 14 seconds. If the small sample contains only 40 kernels, the standard error is $14/\sqrt{40} = 2.21\pm$ seconds from the mean; two standard errors (2σ) is $4.42\pm$ seconds, and three standard errors (3σ) is $6.63\pm$ seconds

We expect that 68% of all sample means will lie within one standard error of the population mean, and 95% of all sample means will lie within two standard errors of the mean. If our sample mean is within two standard errors of the population mean, that gives us a 95% confidence level that the null hypothesis is true.

In other words, if we have 100 small samples, we expect (if the null hypothesis is true) that 68 of these sample means will be within 70.79 and 75.21 seconds. 95 of these 100 samples of 40 kernels will lie within two standard errors of the population mean, that is, 95 of these sample means will be between 68.58 and 77.42 seconds. We can expect only 5 samples to lie outside (outliers) two standard errors of the population mean. So, if a small randomly chosen sample of new popcorn has a mean of 67 seconds, it is unlikely that the null hypothesis is true (although it is possible). If a small sample of new popcorn has a mean of 64 seconds, the probability is very high that the alternative hypothesis is true, for 64 seconds is more than 3 standard errors from the mean.

The **p-value** is the probability of obtaining a test statistic at least as extreme as the one that was actually observed, assuming that the null hypothesis is true, or $P(D/H_0)$. In other words, we are going to assume that the genetically modified popcorn is no different than any other. If the sample mean is more than two standard deviations above or below the mean, we have a p-value of less than .05 (p-value < 0.05). This means that the probability of obtaining a sample like that, given our null hypothesis is true, is less than 5%. The mean time of popping popcorn is 73 seconds, with a standard deviation of 14 seconds, so if our new sample has a mean that is two standard errors below the mean of 73 seconds, as was said above, it is improbable that our null hypothesis is true, and thus more likely that our alternative hypothesis is true. In other words, our results are significant at the 5% level. Our conclusion is that either the null hypothesis is true, in which case something very unusual and improbable occurred by chance, or the null hypothesis is false.

In the context of frequency type probability and hypothesis testing, we often speak of a type I and type II error. A type I error is the incorrect rejection of a true null hypothesis. In other words, it is a false positive. A type I error leads one to conclude that a supposed effect or relationship exists when in fact it does not (i.e., our genetically modified popcorn caused this sample to pop faster, when in fact it did not). A type II error involves the failure to reject a false null hypothesis (it is a false negative). Here, our test fails to detect the change. Thus, we conclude that the difference between the sample mean and the population mean is insignificant, when in fact it is significant. A blood test designed to detect a disease, but fails to detect the disease in a patient who has it, is a real example of a type II error. Another example is a clinical trial of a medical treatment that fails to show that the treatment works when in fact it does work.

If we are subject to a type I error, people will buy our genetically modified popcorn, but there will be no difference in cooking time between that and regular popcorn. If we are subject to a type II error, we give up the development of this new popcorn, believing that it does not work, when in fact it does. People could begin eating their popcorn much more quickly, but they have been deprived of that thanks to a type II error.

25 Frequency Type Probability (Part II)

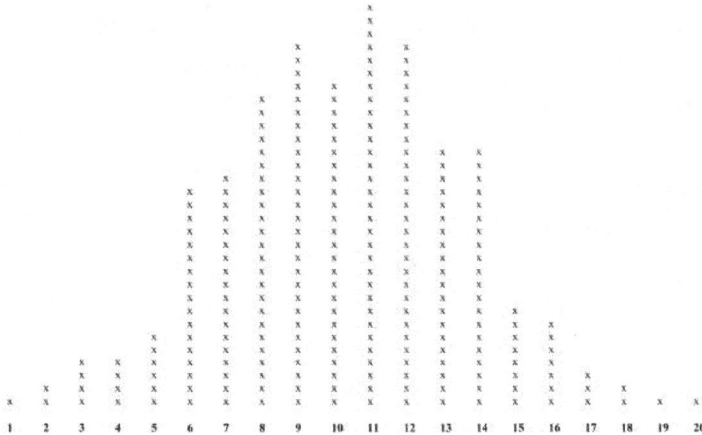

```
                          x
                          x
                          x
              x           x     x
              x           x     x
          x   x   x   x   x     x
          x   x   x   x   x     x
          x   x   x   x   x     x
          x   x   x   x   x   x   x   x
      x   x   x   x   x   x   x   x   x
      x   x   x   x   x   x   x   x   x
      x   x   x   x   x   x   x   x   x
      x   x   x   x   x   x   x   x   x
      x   x   x   x   x   x   x   x   x
      x   x   x   x   x   x   x   x   x
      x   x   x   x   x   x   x   x   x
      x   x   x   x   x   x   x   x   x   x
    x   x   x   x   x   x   x   x   x   x   x
  x   x   x   x   x   x   x   x   x   x   x   x
  x   x   x   x   x   x   x   x   x   x   x   x   x
x   x   x   x   x   x   x   x   x   x   x   x   x   x   x   x
 1  2  3  4  5  6  7  8  9 10 11 12 13 14 15 16 17 18 19 20
```

Let us have 250 people flip a fair coin 20 times and record how many heads each one of them flipped. We chart the results (above); then we calculate the standard deviation, which in the above scenario turns out to be 2.9 (or 3; 10-3/10+3), or between 7 and 13. Thus, 68% of the students tossed 7-13 heads out of 20. Two standard deviations will be 10-6/10+6, that is, between 4 and 16. In other words, 95% of the students will have tossed between 4 to16 heads out of 20 tosses. What is the probability of flipping 2 or even 3 heads out of a possible 20? Or, what is the probability of flipping 17, 18, 19, or 20 heads? The p-value is defined as the probability of obtaining a more extreme result, further into the tails of the null hypothesis distribution, given that the null hypothesis is in fact true. In other words, what is the probability of obtaining a result greater than 2 standard deviations? The answer is a less than 5% probability. The p-value $= < 0.05$.

Now, consider the following. If we give all these students (250) fair coins, only about 2.5% will flip 2, 3, or 4 heads, and about 2.5% will flip 17, 18, 19 heads. The distribution above will inevitably be smoother (look more like a Bell) if the population flipping the coins is larger (i.e., 2000 or so).

Now, we want to carry out an experiment. We wish to know if a coin is fair or biased. So, we want to know the probability that this coin is biased. Our null hypothesis is that the coin is fair. We give someone a coin and tell him to toss the coin 20 times. He does so. He flips heads twice, and tails 18 times. Can we infer that he has an unfair coin? That the coin is biased? In other words, does this evidence show that the null hypothesis is probably false?

A large majority of researchers in the past thought so, and some still believe so today. But this is false. The probability that the null hypothesis is false is a matter of Bayesian inference: $P(H/E)$. Frequency type probability is about $P(E/H)$, that is, what is the probability that someone will flip 2 heads out of 18, given that the coin is fair? All we can infer from the evidence is that either the null hypothesis is false (the coin is biased) or something unusual has happened. That's it. In the experiment above, something unusual did happen, namely two people tossed heads twice, three people tossed heads 3 times, 2 people tossed heads 18 times, etc. Given that the coin is fair, most people will not achieve such results, only a few. It has nothing to do with what they are wearing or whether they are good looking or what their horoscope says, it is a purely statistical phenomenon.

So, if someone flips heads twice, that does not prove that the null hypothesis is false (that the coin is biased), nor does it strongly suggest that the null hypothesis is false. It is a subtle point, but the confusion has led to painful repercussions in the fields of medicine and economics, to name only two. Let's compare this to Bayesian inference. You flip the coin 20 times and you get 2 heads out of 20.

$$P(H/E) = P(H)P(E/H) / P(H)P(E/H) + (\sim H)P(E/\sim H)$$

You were given that coin out of a box of coins, 95% of which are fair, 5% are biased. The biased coins have been tested, they show extreme bias 95% of the time, 5% of the time we get a false positive, that is, they tested positive for "unbiased" (alternative hypothesis) when the coin was biased (null hypothesis).

.95 x .05 = 0.0475
.0475 + .0475 = .095

50% probability that the coin is fair or unbiased. A 50% probability that the null hypothesis is true. That is significantly different than 2.5% probability that the null hypothesis is true (that the coin is fair).

In other words, there is a significant difference between telling someone "There is a 50% chance that you will experience serious side effects from this drug" and "There is a less than 3% chance that you will experience serious side effects from this drug". I might take the risk at 3%, but not the 50%, nor 40%, nor even 30%. And yet, it is the 50% that is accurate, because that was the result of calculating $P(H/E)$. The 3% was the result of measuring the probability of the evidence given the null hypothesis, not the probability of the null hypothesis.

A Point on Opinion Polls

We saw that induction by enumeration involves making an inference about all members of a class on the basis of a sample of some of the members of that class. A valid induction by enumeration requires a large enough sample and most importantly a representative sample.

People are leaving the polling station. The result (evidence) is 53% voted Conservative, 47% voted Liberal, etc. You, a journalist, want to report on who is the likely winner of this election. Can we infer with a rather high degree of probability that the conservatives are going to win the election? The mathematics of probability will not entirely dispel the uncertainty, but it will help narrow down the degree of probability.

You conduct a simple exit poll of 500 representative voters on Election Day. You discover the following:

Conservative: 53%
Liberal: 45%
NDP: 2%

Let's use the Conservative candidate as our proportion of interest. We need to find the standard error for this exit poll.

$$\sqrt{p(1-p)/n}$$

$\sqrt{.53 \, (.47)/500}$
$\sqrt{.00049} = .02$
2% margin of error.

We know that roughly 68% of the time, we can expect the sample proportion to be within one standard error of the final result; 95% of the time, we can expect the sample proportion to be within two standard errors of the final result; 99.7% of the time, we can expect the sample proportion to be within three standard errors of the final result. What does this mean? It means we have 68% confidence that the Conservative party is going to win this election. Why?

Conservative: 53% ±2
Liberal: 45% ±2
(When we calculate the standard error of the Liberal proportion, it also comes to .02).

This means that 68 times out of 100, our exit poll results will be within one standard error of the final election outcome. So, the final election outcome could be 51% Conservative, and 47% Liberal. In other words, in the worst-case scenario for the Conservatives, the Conservatives would still win the election.

But what about the other 32%? Indeed, 68% is not a high confidence level. Why are we not 95% confident that the Conservatives will win? A 95% confidence level requires 2 standard errors, which is ±4. In this case, we have the following:

Conservative: 53% ±4
Liberal: 45% ±4
NDP: 2%

Thus, it is very possible that the Conservatives will finish with 49% of the vote, and the Liberals will finish with 49% of the vote. Thus, we cannot say with certainty who will win this election. But, let's try a larger exit poll. Instead of 500 people, we poll 2000 people. The larger the sample, the more tightly will the bell curve cluster around the proportion. In this case, our standard error is 1%, and so if in our new sample, 53% of voters leaving voted Conservative and 45% voted Liberal, we would have a 95% confidence level that the Conservatives are going to win this election.

26 *A Thought on Type I and Type II Errors and Intuition*

As we pointed out in the previous chapter, we speak of a type I and type II error in the context of frequency type probability and hypothesis testing. A type I error is the incorrect rejection of a true null hypothesis (a false positive), leading us to conclude that a supposed effect (i.e., a disease or condition) or relationship exists when in fact it does not exist. We conclude that the reason for the observed result is that the alternative hypothesis is true, for example, he is not normal, but has schizophrenia; in truth, however, he does not. A type II error involves the failure to reject a false null hypothesis; it is a false negative. We conclude that a supposed effect (i.e., disease or condition) or relationship does not exist (i.e., all is normal) when in fact it does (i.e., all is not normal). In the context of a controlled experiment, it means our test fails to detect the change or the disorder. Thus, we conclude that the difference between the sample mean and the population mean is insignificant, when in fact it is significant. For example, a blood test designed to detect a disease, but fails to detect the disease in a patient who has it, is an example of a type II error, as is a clinical trial of a medical treatment that fails to *show* that the treatment works when it really does work.

Because we are very poor intuitive statisticians, we tend to make type I and type II errors frequently without realizing it. Our tendency to think fast is part of the problem, not to mention our tendency to fall into a normalcy bias (our tendency to underestimate the possibility of a disaster—"don't be ridiculous, it can't happen here").

Most people, I would submit, are easily deceived about evil and character disorder. We readily allow ourselves to be hoodwinked, to be fooled by the dynamic personality, the "nice guy" who, when talking to us, makes us feel as though we are the most important person in the world, says all the right things, that is, things we want to hear, etc. We trust so readily in our intuition that we disregard base rates or prior probabilities, past performance, or the smaller clues that—if we were to pay close attention to them—suggest we ought to slow down think things through more carefully, that this person I work with may not be who he appears to be. In this regard, people tend to fall into a type II error. They believe all is well (or very well) with a person or situation when in fact it is anything but. In a statistical context, it is similar to settling upon a significance level (p-value) that is too small (.01, or .005, etc.). As I said above, the normalcy bias contributes to this as well; we have a tendency to conclude that since a disaster of this or that magnitude has never happened to me before, it simply won't happen to me ever (induction by enumeration). Thus, clues that a disaster is immanent are interpreted optimistically, and gaps in the evidence and ambiguities are used to infer a situation of much lesser gravity.

There is an ever present danger, however, of a false positive, the result of intuitively settling upon a significance level that is perhaps too wide (10 or 20%?). It is easy for some people (usually people who have been hurt in the past) to rush to judgment that something is far more seriously wrong than it actually is. For example, a person who is simply immature, who has not outgrown the mild narcissism of a normal but earlier stage of development, who is imprudent, etc., gives limited but similar evidence, that is, clues that might suggest a pathological narcissist, but he might turn out to be nothing of the sort. Those clues are quickly interpreted as evidence that the alternative hypothesis is true.

27 Fallacy of the Transposed Conditional

In the context of frequency type probability, that is, in the context of significance testing (testing for p-values), there is a fallacy that we need to be on the watch for; it is a fallacy that can have serious repercussions in the areas of economics, medicine, and psychology, to name a few. It is a misinterpretation of what a p-value means; the misconception has its roots in the fallacy of the transposed conditional (or the inverse probability fallacy).

The correct definition of a **p-value** is: "…the probability of obtaining a given result (or a more extreme result, further into the tails of the null hypothesis distribution), given that the null hypothesis is in fact true."[12] In other words, the p-value is equivalent to $P(E/H)$, or more specifically, the probability that data has occurred, given the null hypothesis, or $P(D/H_0)$. The p-value is **not** the probability of the null hypothesis given the observed data $P(H_0/D)$. The fallacy of the transposed conditional equates the two: $P(D/H_0) = P(H_0/D)$.

It seems that the root of this fallacy is a misapplication of the argument form **denying the consequent**, to which we were introduced in chapter 11 (The Conditional Syllogism). The formal name for **denying the consequent** is Modus tollens. Consider the following:

If a person comes down with the flu, then he will have a fever.
I do not have a fever.
Therefore, I do not have the flu.

This is deductively valid. Consider then the following form:

$A \rightarrow \sim B$
B
$\sim A$

[12] Pawel Kalinowski, Fiona Fidler, and Geoff Cumming (2008). "Overcoming the Inverse Probability Fallacy: A Comparison of Two Teaching Interventions". *Experimental Psychology* Vol 4(4): 152-158. DOI: 10.1027/1614-2241.4.4.152.

This is deductively valid, for it is simply an instance of Modus tollens (denying the consequent):

If I am healthy, then I will not have a fever.
I have a fever.
Therefore, I am sick.

The reason the above arguments pose no problems is that they are made up of **categorical premises**. What if we were to use **probabilistic statements**, which is what statistical reasoning is about? Would the logic work? Consider the following variation on of an example originally presented by Pollard and Richardson (1987):[13]

$C \rightarrow \sim MP$
MP
$\sim C$

If you are Canadian, then you are probably not an MP.
Stephen Harper is an MP.
Therefore, Stephen Harper is probably not a Canadian.

This is valid according to the principles of deductive logic (Modus tollens), but the logic is clearly absurd; for Stephen Harper is a Canadian.

When researchers engage in Null Hypothesis Significance Testing (NHST), they are replacing categorical propositions with probabilistic premises, and when that happens, the logic breaks down. Consider the following:

If an orange is from this store, then it is probably not rotten (because 97% of the oranges in this store are grade A).
The orange from this crate from this store is rotten.
Therefore, the orange is probably not from this store.

---

[13] *Ibid.*, 153.

If H, then ~E
E
~H

The important point to keep in mind is that this is **the basic structure of NHST**:

If the null hypothesis is true, then it is probably the case that you will not see this evidence (i.e., rotten orange, MP, etc.)
I see this evidence.
Therefore, the null hypothesis is not true.

Returning to our genetically modified popcorn scenario:

If the null hypothesis is true, then it is probably the case that you will not see the evidence (a faster popping time that is significant, i.e., greater than 2 standard deviations).
This sample has a faster popping time (greater than 2 standard deviations).
Therefore, the null hypothesis is not true.

This is a statistically invalid conclusion; for the conclusion, notice, **is about the null hypothesis**, but frequency type probability seeks to know $P(E/H)$, not $P(H/E)$; it is Bayesian probability that seeks $P(H/E)$. Where frequency type probability ends, Bayesian probability should begin. In other words, a significance test is the beginning, not the end of research.

Let's consider a scenario using imaginary data. The probability that you are going to be sick (vomit) given that you have food poisoning $P(E/H)$, is not the same as the probability that you have food poisoning given that you are sick $P(H/E)$. It is almost certain that if you get food poisoning, you will be sick, but it is far from certain that you got food poisoning given that you are vomiting (you might have the flu that is going around). Let's fabricate some data:

$P(H_0)$ = The null hypothesis; one does not have food poisoning: .98 (Most people do not get food poisoning when they dine out). $P(H_1)$ = The alternative hypothesis, one has food poisoning. 0.02 (very rare).

Using frequency type probability, we determine that:

$P(E_v/H_1)$ = .97 (The probability that you will vomit given that you have food poisoning) $P(E_v/H_0)$ = .03 (The probability that you will vomit given that you do not have food poisoning).

Can we conclude that $P(E_v/H_0)$ = $P(H_0/E_v)$? No, we cannot. Consider the following using Bayes' Theorem.

$$P(H_0/E_v) = P(H_0)P(E_v/H_0) / P(H_0)P(E_v/H_0) + P(H_1)P(E_v/H_1)$$

.98 x .03/.98 x .03 + .02 x .97 = 60%

There is a significant difference between 3% and 60%. A researcher using the Fisherian mode of probability calculation might reject the null hypothesis and conclude that you have food poisoning on the basis of a 0.03 significance level. Using Bayes' Theorem, the probability that you do not have food poisoning given that you are vomiting is 60%.

Deirdre McCloskey and Stephen Ziliak have written on the importance of understanding this fallacy. In their article entitled "The Unreasonable Ineffectiveness of Fisherian"Tests" in Biology, and Especially in Medicine", they reiterate an argument made by statistician Jacob Cohen, who applied this fallacy to the topic of the misdiagnosis of schizophrenia. The incidence of schizophrenia in adults in the United States is about 2%.

Let H_0 (our null hypothesis) = the person is normal (.98).
Let H_1 (our alternative hypothesis) = the person is schizophrenic (.02).
Let E_s = our test result on the person in question is positive for schizophrenia.

Now, a proposed screening test is estimated to have at least 95% (> 0.95) accuracy in discovering schizophrenia (E_s/H_1) and about 97% (.97) accuracy in declaring a truly normal case "normal" (E_n/H_0).

$P(E_s/H_1) = > 0.95$
$P(E_n/H_0) = .97$

So, the probability of a diagnosis of schizophrenia given the person is normal is less than 5%, which is statistically significant.

$P(E_s/H_0) = < .05$ [statistically significant: $p = 0.05$]

Now, McCloskey and Ziliak make the point that a researcher in the Fisherian mode (frequency type probability, which seeks $P(E/H)$) would, in the face of such evidence, reject the hypothesis of normal (H_0) and conclude that the person is schizophrenic. We can only imagine what might come after that (i.e., being committed, medication, the patient begins to see himself in a particular way, etc.). But—and this is the important point—the probability of the hypothesis given the evidence **is not what has been tested** $P(H_0/E_s)$. The probability that this person does not have schizophrenia given a positive test for schizophrenia $P(H_0/E_s)$ is rather strong (about 60%), and not less than 3% (as the Fisherians or frequentists believe). Let's calculate this using Bayes' Theorem:

$P(H_0/E_s) = P(H_0)P(E_s/H_0) / P(H_0)P(E_s/H_0) + P(H_1)P(E_s/H_1)$

.98 x .03/.98 x .03 + .02 x .97 = .6025 = 60%

As you can see, this is significantly different from $p = .03$. This is an example of how the fallacy of the transposed conditional (which occurs when we rely exclusively on frequency type probability in the context of medicine) can have serious repercussions on the lives of individual persons. So, out of 50 cases testing as schizophrenic out of a population of 1000 people tested, 30 of these are false positives (misdiagnosed as schizophrenics). Ziliak writes: "The example shows how confused—and humanly and socially damaging—a conclusion from a Fisherian 5% science can be. One of us has a good friend who as a child in the psychiatry–spooked 1950s was diagnosed as schizophrenic. The friend has shown since then no symptom of the disease. But the erroneous diagnosis—an automatic result of the fallacy of the transposed conditional—has kept him in a state of dull terror ever since. Imagine in other arenas, with similarly realistically low priors, the damage done by the transposed conditional—in scientific work or diet pills or social welfare policy or commercial advertising or the market in foreign exchange. Once one considers the concrete implications of such a large diagnostic error, such as believing that 3% of adults tested for schizophrenia are not-schizophrenic when the truth is that 60% of them are not-schizophrenic, and realizes that, after all, this magnitude of diagnostic error is governing NASA and the departments of cardiovascular disease and breast cancer and HIV health policy, one should perhaps worry."[14]

The important point is that a significance test is only the beginning, not the end of the research. A type I error (the incorrect rejection of a true null hypothesis, that is, a false positive) is, in some contexts, far more harmful to a person than it would be in other contexts.

Concluding thoughts

To test your understanding of the fallacy of the transposed conditional, answer the following true/false survey (Oakes, 1986; Haller and Krauss, 2002). Imagine there is a treatment that we suspect

---

[14] Deirdre N. McCloskey and Stephen T. Ziliak (2009). "The Unreasonable Ineffectiveness of Fisherian "Tests" in Biology, and Especially in Medicine". *Biological Theory* 4(1) 2009, 44–53. Konrad Lorenz Institute for Evolution and Cognition Research. 45-46.

may alter performance on a certain task. You compare the sample means of both the control and the experimental groups. Now, imagine that we use a simple independent means t-test and your result is significant ($t = 2.7$, d. f. $= 18$, $p = 0.01$). In other words, the p-value is 0.01—i.e., the probability of this evidence or data, given that the H_0 is true, is 1%. Check off each of the statements below as "true" or "false." Note that "false" means that the statement does not follow logically from the premises. Also, several or none of the statements may be correct.[15]

1. You have absolutely disproved the null hypothesis (you have absolutely disproved that there is no difference between the population means).
[ ] true/false [ ]

2. You have found the probability of the null hypothesis being true.
[ ] true/false [ ]

3. You have absolutely proved your experimental hypothesis (that there is a difference between the population means).
[ ] true/false [ ]

4. You can deduce the probability of the experimental hypothesis being true.
[ ] true/false [ ]

5. You know, if you decide to reject the null hypothesis, the probability that you are making the wrong decision.
[ ] true/false [ ]

---

[15] Gerd Gigerenzer (2004). "Mindless statistics". *The Journal of Socio-Economics* 33. 587-606. DOI: 10.1016/j.socec.2004.09.033. 594-595.

6. You have a reliable experimental finding in the sense that if, hypothetically, the experiment were repeated a great number of times, you would obtain a significant result on 99% of occasions.
[ ] true/false [ ]

Haller and Krauss (2002) posed these questions (originally devised by Oakes, 1986) to teachers and students from psychology departments at six German universities; 30 statistics teachers, which included psychology professors and teaching assistants, 39 professors and lecturers of psychology who do not teach statistics, and 44 psychology students. Every statistics teacher taught null hypothesis significance testing (NHST), and each student had successfully passed one or more statistics courses. Not one student, however, noticed that **all of the statements were false**; each student marked as true one or more of the illusions about the meaning of a p-value.[16]

We can ask why this is the case? The answer is that the students inherited the "p-value illusions" from their teachers. 99% of the professors and lecturers marked true to one or more of the above statements. 80% of the statistics teachers shared these misconceptions with their students.

The most frequent illusion was #5: "You know, if you decide to reject the null hypothesis, the probability that you are making the wrong decision." For example, if the p-value is p = 0.03, there is a 3% probability that you are making the wrong decision. In other words, there is a low probability that your decision to label this man schizophrenic is wrong. As we saw above through Bayesian probability calculation, there is a high probability that a diagnosis of schizophrenia is wrong, that is, a 60% probability that he is not schizophrenic. Allow me to comment briefly on each statement:

Statement #1 is false: "You have absolutely disproved the null hypothesis (you have absolutely disproved that there is no difference between the population means)." The reason is that inductive conclusions are undetermined, not absolute. What it means is that the

---

probability of the data is 0.01 given that the null hypothesis is true. At this point, we need to test the hypothesis directly (Bayesian inference).

Statement #2: "You have found the probability of the null hypothesis being true." It does not mean that there is a 1% probability that the H_0 is true. We do not know the probability of the hypothesis, because we simply did not test for it.

Statement #3: "You have absolutely proved your experimental hypothesis (that there is a difference between the population means)." Not at all. Again, inductive conclusions are undetermined; so the rhetoric of certainty ought to be restrained. What is needed at this point is to test the null hypothesis.

Statement #4: "You can deduce the probability of the experimental hypothesis being true." Again, this statement is about the hypothesis, whereas p-value is about the data.

Statement #6: "You have a reliable experimental finding in the sense that if, hypothetically, the experiment were repeated a great number of times, you would obtain a significant result on 99% of occasions." This is called the replication fallacy, which equates the probability of the data with the probability of similar results if the research were repeated. The problem is that this could only happen if the H_0 were true; but a p-value does not tell us whether or not the H_0 is true.

Earlier studies by Oakes (1986) in Britain showed results slightly worse. Now, if students inherited these misconceptions from their teachers, where did the teachers acquire them? The answer is: their textbooks. Guilford's *Fundamental Statistics in Psychology and Education* (first edition, 1942) was the most widely read in the 40s and 50s. Guilford actually said that hypothesis testing reveals the probability that the null hypothesis is true: "If the result comes out one way, the hypothesis is probably correct, if it comes out another way, the hypothesis is probably wrong" (p. 156).[17] However, p-value is the probability of the data (or more extreme data), given that the H_0 is true.

---

[17] Quoted in *Ibid.*, 596

What is being tested is the data, assuming the hypothesis is true; it is not the hypothesis that is being tested.

There are other authors who also taught the erroneous notion that level of significance specified the probability of hypothesis, such as Anastasi (1958), Ferguson (1959), Lindquist (1940), Miller and Buckhout (1973), Pollard and Richardson (1987), Mulaik et al. (1997), and Nickerson (2000).[18]

---

[18] *Ibid.*

28 *False Positives and the Importance of Base Rates*

Base rates are far more important than most people realize. We often fall victim to a representation heuristic[19], which involves a tendency to give undue weight to our impression of a person, without adequate consideration of that person's background. In other words, we tend to ignore prior probabilities. How often do we see young teachers hired on the basis of a good interview, while a more competent person with a proven record but who does not interview as well, is rejected. A disciplined investor, however, pays close attention to base rates and demands to know something about past sales, total revenues, profits, etc., before investing money in a project or business that looks good on the outside; for he pays the price for being careless, while it is students who pay the price for the careless decisions of an administration or school board. The general public are not so careful. This is especially evident during election time, when most people concern themselves with impressions, rather than prior probabilities, background information, past experience, etc.

Base rates are especially important with regard to medical diagnoses. Imagine that you are about to be tested for a disease. You are informed that the test has a 99% accuracy rate, that is, it is right 99% of the time. Moreover, if you do not have the disease, the result will come back negative with a 99% probability. You decide to go ahead and are tested for the disease; the result comes back positive. Should you panic? You probably will. That is why you need to consider the base rate of the disease.

This particular disease, you eventually discover, is very rare; only 1 in 10,000 has the disease (0.0001). That means among one million people, only 100 have the disease (in a country of 30 million, 3000 have the disease).

So let's test one million people at random. Because the test is accurate 99% of the time, it will give a false positive 1% of the time.

[19] Daniel Kahneman, *Thinking Fast and Slow*. Anchor Canada, 2011. *Chapter 14 "Tom W's Specialty"* [Kobo version]. Retrieved from http://www.kobo.com.

Thus, the test will say that 1% have the disease. Now, 1% of 1 million is 10,000. At this point you begin to relax, because you realize that there is a high probability that you are not among the 100 people who have the disease, but a member of the 9,900 false positives (a false positive is a result that indicates you have the disease, when in fact you do not).

You were afraid with this:

$P(E/H)$ or $P(E_p/D)$ = the probability that you are tested positive given that you have the disease.

But you are relieved to discover:

$P(H/E)$ or $P(D/E_p)$ = the probability that you have the disease given that you are tested positive for it.

The fear you experienced was the result of intuitively committing the fallacy of the transposed conditional, as if $P(E/H) = P(H/E)$.

And so we need to keep in mind that if the base rate of the disease is very low, even a very reliable test can be misleading, which in turn can cause unnecessary stress—9,900 are a lot of false positives, and that's a lot of unnecessary stress on close to 10,000 people for every million tested. That is why a reliable test can be trusted only when applied to a population "at risk", that is, where the base rate for the disease is rather high.

Let's do the math involved in this scenario:

$P(D)$ = the hypothesis that an individual has the disease. This is our base rate, which is $1/10,000$ or $.0001$

$P(E_p/D)$ = the probability that one is tested positive given that one has the disease is 99% or $.99$

$P(E_p/\sim D)$ = the probability that one is tested positive for the disease, given that one does **not** have the disease, which is 1% or .01.

$P(\sim D)$ = the probability that you do **not** have the disease is 9,999/10,000 or .9999.

We want to know what is the probability that you do not have the disease, given that you are tested positive for it, or

$P(\sim D/E_p)$? Once again, we use Bayes' Theorem.

$$P(H/E) = P(H)P(E/H) \ / \ P(H)P(E/H) + P(\sim H)P(E/\sim H)$$

$$P(\sim D/E_p) = P(\sim D)P(E_p/\sim D) \ / \ P(\sim D)P(E_p/\sim D) + P(D)P(E_p/D)$$

$$.9999 \text{ x } .01 / .9999 \text{ x } .01 + .0001 \text{ x } .99 = .99$$

Hence, there is a 99% probability that you do not have the disease, given that you have tested positive for it.

It should be obvious at this point that widespread testing for a relatively rare disease becomes a moral issue. Although such widespread testing will certainly make some company a great deal of money, it will also cause many others to experience a great deal of unnecessary stress.

We are not certain who these "victims" are going to be but understanding something about uncertainty enables us to see what is not readily obvious on the surface. In other words, we are certain that a significant number of people are going to be adversely affected by what will initially be experienced as "bad news". This will lead to further testing, which is costly, both emotionally and financially. One could put forth a persuasive argument that such a test should not be administered *en masse*, but only to a section of the population that is deemed at risk.

A failure to understand something about uncertainty (probability), that is, a failure to appreciate what uncertainty is and how significant a small space of uncertainty may turn out to be can have profound negative repercussions. Again, most people are woefully unaware of the uncertainties in their judgments and speak with great confidence. In other words, most people speak with a rhetoric of certainty that is completely unwarranted.

29 *Thoughts on Probability, Order, and Memory*

What is interesting about inductive logic using the mathematics of probability is that we can discern an objective order that makes inductive reasoning possible. We can come to an understanding of this order on some level. In other words, we are able to arrive at certainty on one level, about something we cannot be certain of on another level. We are not certain which color bandana it was, but we are certain that there is a greater probability that it was not the blue one, but a yellow one.

Consider what we can do with a standard pack of 52 cards. A dealer deals the top card, and he tells you that it is either red, or clubs, but not which. What is the probability that it is an ace? In other words, what is $\Pr(A/RvC)$? A & (RvC) is equivalent to an ace of clubs, or a red ace (diamonds or hearts), for a total of 3 aces. Hence, 3 cards out of the 39 RvC cards are aces. Thus, the conditional probability is:

$$P[A/(RvC)] = P[A \& (RvC)] / P(RvC)$$

$$P(RvC) = 39/52$$
$$P[A \& (RvC)] = 3/52$$
$$= 3/39 = 1/13$$

Thus, the probability of drawing an ace given that the dealer dealt a red card or a club is $1/13$, or 7.7%.

We don't know whether the dealer dealt an ace or not, but we do know that the probability that he has done so is about 8%, which is a rather low probability. In other words, there is about a 92% probability that he did not.

Now, a deck of cards is a well ordered artifact. We could not calculate the probability without that order. A standard deck contains 52 cards, and 13 of these are hearts, 13 are clubs, 13 are spades, and 13 are diamonds. We also have 12 face cards.

It is also necessary to thoroughly shuffle those cards (around 7 times), and shuffling is a determinate activity, carried out with a purpose (final cause), namely, to achieve a random distribution (uniform distribution). Without this underlying order as well as a knowledge of it, calculating probability would be impossible. In other words, all knowledge depends upon order (intelligibility).

Sometimes the order exceeds our ability to understand in all its details, but inductive reasoning using the mathematics of probability enables us to make some sense out of this order, to 'tame it', to some degree at least. In short, probability depends upon order. Without an ordered universe and an intellect to grasp the intelligible structures of things (their motions) through simple apprehension (or abstractive induction), we could not set out to determine probabilities.

As intuitive statisticians, we are very poor. Statistics helps us tremendously, and it is in light of statistics that we come to recognize how deficient our intuitive statistical inferences really are (this is especially true of frequency type inferences). Part of the problem is our memory. We suffer from "duration neglect"[20]; that is, we tend to remember peak experiences, especially those that occur at the end of an experience. This is true, it seems to me, when it comes to positive peak experiences (the sight of the baby after a painful delivery causes the new mother to forget everything that just happened) as well as negative peak experiences (a bad ending to a performance causes us to forget all the good that led up to it). We learn from experience, but how much we learn from experience depends upon our memory.

However, what we remember depends, in large part, upon what interests us, that is, what it is we find significant. I remember some of what I notice, but not everything; there is a great deal that I notice every day that I forget, because it does not bear in any significant way on what it is that interests me (I will remember seeing a new book by my favorite author at a Chapters, or a book that will have some relevance for the courses that I teach, but the vast majority of the titles that I read will quickly fade from memory). But consider how much there is that we do not notice. Others notice things that I simply miss, and they remember some of it because it has significance for them.

---

[20] See *Ibid.*, Chapter 35 "Two Selves".

Much of what we remember depends on character, on the kind of person we have made ourselves to be by the choices that we have made. Two people of entirely different character, possibly even opposing character, **interpret reality very differently**. They do not have the same interests, and so they do not notice the same things, nor do they remember the same things. They learn from experience at a different rate, and what they learn from experience is very different from one another.

Most of our everyday knowledge is a matter of inferencing. We begin with the evidence, with something we see, and we make inferences that bear upon a possible antecedent. Our conclusions have probability only, but they very often **feel right**, they appear to us as correct, and yet we tend not to be aware of their precarious nature. Moreover, the feeling we get when we apprehend something that is true is the very **same feeling** we get when we apprehend something that is false (because we are not aware that it is false). As we get older, we learn from our mistaken inferences—some of us, at least—, if we are open to learning. Stubbornness, pride, an oversized ego, etc., keep us from learning from experience, from revising our conclusions, at least in certain significant areas. A bad memory also keeps us from self-correction and the growth that results from that—i.e., we have forgotten how wrong we were. So if we have a need to feel right, we will avoid self-correction.

It is a truism to say that we are unaware of what we don't know, but it is not a truism to say that we are, for the most part, *unaware that we are not aware of what we don't know*—we should become aware that there is much within our immediate vicinity that we are almost completely ignorant of. It makes a difference to know that there is so much that we don't know, that our inferences are only probable, that we are poor intuitive statisticians, that our emotions incline us to particular judgments or conclusions, and that our conclusions are thus risky. We often speak with a very high confidence level, much higher than is warranted. The reason has a lot to do with how we feel, that is, with the emotions—being wrong feels the same as being right. In other words, there are no negative emotions that automatically arise out of an erroneous inference.

30 The Investigative Process: An Introduction to Mill's Methods (Canons of Induction)

In searching for the cause, we are searching for the condition or circumstance in whose presence the event is present as well, and in whose absence the event is
absent as well. Mill's methods of induction are best regarded as an illustration of the investigative process, that is, the stages that an investigator goes through in searching for the cause of an event or phenomenon.

Now, you are the investigator, and your job is to solve the case of this mysterious illness by a series of inferences. You begin by interviewing all those who became ill. You discover that they all happened to eat at the same restaurant the previous evening. The restaurant is a buffet. You determine what each of them had. After you gather your evidence, you begin making inferences to the best possible explanation at this point. You employ the **Method of Agreement**:

"If two or more instances of the phenomenon under investigation have only one circumstance in common, the circumstance in which alone all the instances agree, is the cause (or the effect) of the given phenomenon".[21]

	Fried rice	Curry goat	Jerk chicken	King fish	Food poisoning
Anushka	Yes	Yes	Yes	Yes	Yes
Malavan	Yes	No	No	Yes	Yes
Nick	Yes	Yes	No	No	Yes
Vanessa	Yes	No	Yes	No	Yes

If the Curry goat was the cause of the food poisoning, Malavan would not have become ill. If the Jerk chicken was the cause of the food poisoning, both Malavan and Nick would not have become ill. If the King fish was the cause of the food poisoning, then Nick and Vanessa would not have become ill. So, our best inference at this point

---

[21] John Stuart Mill, *A System of Logic*, Book III, Chapter VIII, §1. London: John Parker, West Strand. [Kobo version]. Retrieved from http://www.kobo.com.

is that the fried rice is the cause of the illnesses. Our conclusion, however, is tentative; it possesses only a degree of probability.

But there is more to this buffet than goat, chicken and fish. You pay a visit to the restaurant and see that they offer spring rolls, roast beef, and shrimp as well. So you return to Anushka and Malavan and proceed to inquire of them.

Direct Method of Agreement

	Spring rolls	Roast beef	Shrimp	Fried rice	Food poisoning
Anushka	No	Yes	Yes	Yes	Yes
Malavan	Yes	No	No	Yes	Yes

You eliminate the spring rolls as the cause, because Anushka does not eat them, yet she became ill. So, the roast beef and the shrimp are possible causes. But after interviewing Malavan, you rule out the roast beef, because he did not have any, and yet he too became ill. That leaves the shrimp and the fried rice as possibilities. Anushka had shrimp, but Malavan did not. If it were the shrimp, Malavan would not have become ill. Thus, the probability of the hypothesis (that it is the fried rice that explains the illness) has increased somewhat. But our conclusion is still rather **underdetermined**.

Meanwhile, your partner is interviewing other students who were there that night. She gathers evidence, but unlike your evidence, which is **positive**, her evidence is **negative**. She's found two young students who did not get sick, so she begins to make inferences on the basis of that evidence, using the Inverse Method of Agreement.

Inverse Method of Agreement

	Spring rolls	Roast beef	Shrimp	Fried Rice	Food Poisoning
Alexis	Yes	Yes	No	No	No
Sajee	No	Yes	Yes	No	No

It appears to her that fried rice might account for the illnesses, but she concludes that more evidence is needed. She calls you on her cell phone and asks to get together over lunch to pool the evidence, but she would rather go somewhere other than the buffet restaurant. You agree, and you begin sharing your findings. You employ the Double Method of Agreement in order to see whether the probability of your hypothesis increases.

The Double Method of Agreement

	Spring rolls	Roast beef	Shrimp	Fried rice	Food poisoning
Anushka	No	Yes	Yes	Yes	Yes
Malavan	Yes	No	No	Yes	Yes
Alexis	Yes	Yes	No	No	No
Sajee	No	Yes	Yes	No	No

The Double Method of Agreement is a **combination** of the Direct Method of Agreement and the Inverse Method of Agreement. The Direct Method of Agreement by itself establishes reasons to believe that a certain condition or circumstance was the cause of the illness; so too the Inverse Method of Agreement. By combining the two methods, the Double Method simply gives us **more reason** to infer that it was this condition or circumstance that was the cause. Thus, it increases the probability that it was this condition that explains the consequent (event, or phenomenon). You are thrilled with the results, and you are about to conclude that you are certain that the fried rice is the cause. But your partner tells you that he has gathered further evidence that he has yet to organize and study. He's interviewed Amy, Rita, Michelle, and Brandon, and so you study the results.

	Spring rolls	Curry goat	Jerk chicken	Fried rice	Food poisoning
Amy	No	Yes	Yes	Yes	Yes
Rita	Yes	Yes	No	Yes	Yes
Michelle	Yes	No	No	No	No
Brandon	No	Yes	No	No	No

You are elated. You believe that your case is very strong. Your inference that the fried rice is the cause of the food poisoning now has a rather high degree of probability [$P(H/E) = >. 5$]

Still, your partner is not fully satisfied. We need, she points out, some further evidence that will increase significantly the probability of our original hypothesis—and thus increase our level of confidence. She decides to interview two people who have the same taste in foods and the same eating habits. This allows her to employ the Method of Difference.

The Method of Difference

Mill writes: *If an instance in which the phenomenon under investigation occurs and an instance in which it does not occur,* **have every circumstance in common save one***, that one occurring only in the former, the circumstance in which alone the two instances differ, is the effect, or the cause,* **or an indispensable part of the cause***, of the phenomenon.*[22]

Ben and Claudia have very similar eating habits and they like the same things. Ben got sick, however, while Claudia did not.

	Spring rolls	Curry goat	Jerk chicken	Fried rice	Food poisoning
Ben	No	Yes	Yes	Yes	Yes
Claudia	No	Yes	Yes	No	No

Thus, your best explanation is that the fried rice is the cause of the illness; for this hypothesis has the greatest probability. Thus, the rice is likely **the cause** of the illness, or an indispensable part of the cause of the illness.

As you can see, a controlled experiment is really the employment of the Method of Difference. The researcher controls for various factors so that every circumstance is had in common. If we are going to test for whether or not diet soda is better for weight loss than regular soda, we need to control for other factors. For example, many people

---

[22] See *Ibid.*, Book III, Chapter VIII, §2.

who drink diet pop also eat foods high in carbs, or they drink beer, etc. So, for accurate results, we need to control for these factors. We need candidates who are similar in all respects except one. That is the Method of Difference.[23]

Mill writes:

> *It thus appears to be by the Method of Difference alone that we can ever ...arrive with certainty at causes....The Method of Agreement is chiefly to be resorted to as a means of suggesting applications of the Method of Difference, ...or as an inferior resource in case the Method of Difference is impracticable. ...The indirect method, therefore, can only be regarded as a great extension and improvement of the Method of Agreement, but not as participating in the more cogent nature of the Method of Difference.[24]*

As a final note, allow me to quote philosopher of science Peter Lipton (emphasis mine): "Mill's methods have a number of attractive features. Many of our inferences are causal inferences, and Mill's methods give a natural account of these. In science, for example, the controlled experiment is a particularly common and self-conscious application of the Method of Difference. The Millian structure of causal inference is also particularly clear in cases of inferential dispute. When you dispute my claim that C is the cause of E, you will often make your case by pointing out that the conditions for Mill's methods are not met; that is, by pointing out C is not the only antecedent common to all cases of E, or that the presence of C is not the only salient difference between a case where E occurs and a similar case where it does not" He continues: "Of course, Mill's methods have their share of liabilities, of which I will mention just two. First, they do not themselves apply to **unobservable causes** or to any causal inferences where the **cause's existence**, and not just its causal status, is inferred.

---

[23] Bram Van Heuveln. A Preferred Treatment of Mill's Methods: Some Misinterpretations by Modern Textbooks. *Informal Logic: Reasoning and Argumentation in Theory and Practice.* Vol 20, No 1 (2000). Retrieved from http://ojs.uwindsor.ca/ojs/leddy/index.php/informal_logic/article/viewFile/2252/1696

[24] Mill, *op.cit.*, Book III, Chapter VIII, §3.

Secondly, if the methods are to apply at all, the requirement that there be **only a single agreement or difference** in antecedents must be seen as **an idealization**, since this condition is never met in real life. **We need principles for selecting from among multiple agreements or similarities those that are likely to be causes, but these are principles Mill does not himself supply.**"[25]

---

[25] Peter Lipton. *Inference to the Best Explanation*, London: Routledge, 2004. Chapter 1, "Induction", [Kobo version]. Retrieved from http://www.kobo.com.

31 A Brief Introduction to Plausible Reasoning

Plausible reasoning works with the data of our conceptual framework, some of which is established fact, and some of which is the result of both deductive and inductive inference. What distinguishes deductive from inductive reasoning is that in the case of deductive reasoning, the conclusion is contained in the given premises, while in the case of the latter (inductive reasoning), the conclusion is not; rather, the conclusion is the result of a jump or leap—we speak of jumping to conclusions. As an example of a simple deductive argument, consider the following:

All the marbles from urn A are red
The marble in my hand is from urn A
Therefore, the marble in my hand is red

Assuming that the data is correct, the conclusion follows necessarily from the information contained in the first two premises. Consider, too, the following:

If you come down with the flu, then you will have a fever
After taking your temperature, the doctor declares that you do not have a fever
Therefore, it follows that you do not have the flu

Again, all the information that allows us to assert rather conclusively that you do not have the flu is contained in the data provided. Let us enlarge the set of data and attempt a more elaborate puzzle. Consider the following set of data:

Roha, Ariba, and Saad are very devout Muslims who faithfully observe Salat (daily prayer) every day, regardless of where they are. Roha generally does not use the subha (prayer beads) on Thursdays, and without the struggles with writing that affect some of her friends, writes some of the finest poetry in the school. Saad,

who suffers from migraines, will always recite subha on Mondays, and is not known for his eloquent speeches. The person with a gift for eloquent speaking always recites subha on Thursdays.

There is enough information or data contained in the set above to work out which student has which gift, and which day of the week they can be found reciting subha, and what difficulties they struggle with.

	R o h a	A r i b a	S a a d	M o n d a y s	W e d u	T h u r s	P o e t r y	A r t i s t	S p e a k e r
Struggles with writing									
Suffers from migraines									
Struggles with math									
Poetry									
Artistic									
Eloquent speaker									
Recites subha on Monday									
Recites subha on Wednesday									
Recites subha on Thursday									

The above is a relatively simple puzzle and working it out is a matter of simple deduction. We know that Roha does not use her prayer beads on Thursdays nor does she struggle with writing; rather, she writes the finest poetry. So, under her column we can place an X beside "Struggles with writing" and an X beside "Recites subha on Thursday." We can also place an X, under her column, beside "Artistic" and "Eloquent speaker", and place an O beside Poetry - which allows us to place an X beside "Poetry" under Ariba and Saad's name. Saad suffers from migraines, so in his column we can place an X beside "Struggles with writing" and "Struggles with math", and an O beside "Suffers from migraines". This allows us to place an X beside "Suffers from migraines" under Ariba and Roha's name. This in turn allows us to see that Roha struggles with math and Ariba struggles with writing.

We can also place an X, in Saad's column, beside "subha on Wednesday" and "subha on Thursday", and an O beside Monday. That permits us to place an X under Roha and Ariba's name in the Monday row. Doing so allows us to see that Roha recites subha on Wednesday, which leaves Ariba as the one who recites on Thursday. Since the one with the gift of eloquent speaking recites subha on Thursdays, we know that Ariba is the fine speaker, which leaves Saad as the artistic student.

Puzzles such as these can become much more challenging, but even with more challenging puzzles, the information required to solve them is contained in the data either explicitly or implicitly. What is particularly interesting about deduction is that much of the information is implicit, and it takes some serious effort to make it explicit; doing so opens up avenues that permit us to make other pieces of implicit information explicit as well.

Most people tend to find such difficult puzzles far too taxing and will not make the effort, but completing such puzzles is, although relatively difficult for some people, still rather insignificant. Consider that in this world there are matters far more serious, such as moral, economic, or political matters. Moreover, the data regarding such moral, economic, or political matters is, in many cases, available (such as general principles and patterns), which means it is possible to make important points explicit through a process of deduction, points that are implicit in the explicitly known data. Many of us, however, are unaware of such basic and important moral, economic, or political implications of the available data because we are very often unwilling to make the effort required to draw out the logical implications of the data that we possess explicitly. This is especially true with regard to moral matters, because there are certain conclusions bearing on certain issues that many of us would like to be false, or beyond resolution.

Plausibility and Systematicity

What is interesting about such logical puzzles, especially the more difficult ones, is that each piece of data fits into a larger whole, very much like the pieces of a jigsaw puzzle. In the correct and completed product, there are no gaps or incongruities; all the needed parts are integrated into a unity. The correctly completed puzzle is also cohesive, that is, each piece of data is connected to other pieces of data; for if some piece of data is out of place, that is, assigned to the wrong place, then other pieces of available data will be affected and the whole puzzle will lack consistency and coherence; thus, the completed puzzle would not fit the entire set of given data (clues provided); a number of inconsistencies result, and so the puzzle in the end lacks harmony, elegance, and congruity. To see this, all we have to do is pay attention to what happens when we complete the puzzle and discover there are errors. What we discover are conflicts.

These properties, namely, **completeness, inclusivity, unity** and **integrity, cohesiveness** and **coherence, functional simplicity** and **economy, elegance, symmetry, consistency** and **coordination of parts**, etc., are the properties of the correctly completed puzzle, that is, logically consistent data ordered according to the information provided. These properties are **the parameters of cognitive systematicity**. A puzzle is like a system with many parts unified into a functional and coherent whole.

The most important point I wish to make, however, is that in the real world, we rarely, if ever, have complete and reliable information. In that light, consider how much more difficult such a logical puzzle would be to complete if the information available was not entirely reliable, that is, to some degree uncertain, only plausible (minimally, moderately, or highly). Like a chain, our conclusion would only be as strong as our weakest piece of data (i.e., our weakest link).

Consider too how much more difficult the puzzle would have been to solve had the information been overabundant; for example, if we were informed that Saad, who suffers from migraines and has failed math twice, sometimes recites subha on Mondays and Thursdays and won a public speaking contest a few years ago, and the person with a gift for eloquent speaking recites subha on Wednesdays and Thursdays, etc., we would have a much more difficult time determining who's who. In other words, an overabundance of information makes matters more difficult because, ultimately, we find ourselves in the position of needing further information to resolve conflicts that inevitably arise.

This is the reason why deductive puzzles like the one above can take less than a half hour to complete, but knowledge from the predominantly inductive sciences (i.e., chemistry, physics, biology, astronomy, etc.) takes centuries to develop and are never complete. Deductive reasoning is relatively simple because all the information needed to derive an absolutely certain conclusion is contained in the premises. Hence, the conclusion is determined, certain, that is, it necessarily follows from the given premises.

Inductive reasoning is not so simple, because the conclusion of an inductive argument is "information transcending". This means that the conclusion is not contained in the data provided by the premises; it "transcends" the data, or goes beyond the available information, that is, makes assertions that are inconclusive and possibly false. Inductive reasoning involves "jumping" to a conclusion, and the goal of inductive reasoning is to estimate the most reasonable jump, that is, to discover the most fitting estimate.

Consider the following puzzle: A carrot, a pile of pebbles, and a pipe made from a cob of corn are lying together in the middle of a field. Our task is to estimate why that is the case. Here we begin with facts in evidence and proceeding to infer the reasons for the facts (the antecedent, prior conditions or causes that account for the facts in evidence). Instead of the luxury of a conditional thesis, such as "if he has the flu, then he will have a fever", all we know are the facts in evidence and it is up to us to determine why—and of course there are a number of candidates (possible hypotheses). There are very often a number of possibilities that can explain any piece of evidence, but not all are equally fitting. One rather striking explanation for the carrot,

pebbles and pipe lying together in a field is that during the winter, on
that very spot, someone had built a snowman using a carrot for a nose,
a pipe, and pebbles for the eyes and mouth. Although such an estimate
is fitting, it lacks the force of deductive necessity, that is, it is
inconclusive; it has only a degree of plausibility. If the field were in
Florida, this estimation would lack plausibility, but if the field is not a
carrot field but perhaps a park located in a state or province that
typically has lots of snow during the winter months, and plenty of
children around, the inference that a snowman once stood here
becomes much more plausible.

Our day to day reasoning is a matter of plausible reasoning, which
is a combination of both deductive and inductive argumentation. A
large part of the set of data available to us, possibly the most part, is
made up of theses or propositions that are not established facts, but
which have only a degree of plausibility - either minimal plausibility
(.2), moderate plausibility (.5), or a rather high degree of plausibility (.8
or .9). Moreover, our data base is always incomplete. And that is the
fundamental reason why it is very difficult to know whether many of
the conclusions we draw are absolutely or only putatively true, for an
argument is only as strong as its weakest link. What is putatively true
will be that set of data out of a number of other sets of data that has
maximal plausibility. Whereas some subsets of data had to discard
highly plausible data in order to maintain logical consistency, the
maximally plausible and consistent set of data is our best estimate
(putatively true).

In order to demonstrate in very simple terms how this works, let
us limit ourselves to three pieces of data. Using the two variables p and
q to stand for the following two separate propositions:

Saad struggles with math (p).
Roha struggles with math (q)

Consider the following set of data: $\{\sim p, \sim q, p \vee q\}$

This is translated as:

~p = Saad does not struggle with math (which, on the basis of our background knowledge, we will say is highly plausible, or .9)

~q = Roha does not struggle with math; (which we will say is minimally plausible, or .2)

p v q = Either Saad struggles with math or Roha struggles with math; (which is a highly plausible thesis, or .9)

   The cardinal principle in plausible reasoning is: **save the most plausible data.** Each piece of data above, however, is plausible on its own, but as a set of data, it is logically inconsistent, which means we are forced to discard a piece of data in order to bring consistency to the set. It cannot be true that "Either Saad struggles with math or Roha struggles with math" if it is also true that "Saad does not struggle with math" and "Roha does not struggle with math". And so, this state of affairs demands that we restore consistency, and we can only do so by discarding a piece of data. This gives us three possible alternatives:

1. We can abandon p v q: "Either Saad struggles with math or Roha struggles with math", which is a highly plausible thesis (.9). In doing so, we are left with the following subset:

S_1 = Saad does not struggle with math and Roha does not struggle with math}.

2. We can abandon ~p: "Saad does not struggle with math", which is also a piece of data with high plausibility (.9), and this leaves us with the following subset:

S_2 = Roha does not struggle with math, and either Saad struggles with math or Roha struggles with math}.

3. Finally, we can abandon ~q: "Roha does not struggle with math", which is minimally plausible (.2), and this leaves us with the following subset of data:

S_3 = Saad does not struggle with math, and either Saad struggles with math or Roha struggles with math}.

The first alternative discards a highly plausible piece of data; the second alternative discards a highly plausible piece of data as well, but in the third alternative, the discarded data is minimally plausible (.2).

The first alternative, S_1, contains one piece of highly plausible data (.9) and one piece of minimally plausible data (.2), but the price for this subset is the loss of a highly plausible thesis (.9). The second alternative, S_2, also contains one piece of highly plausible data (.9) and one piece of minimally plausible data (.2), but it too incurs a heavy loss, the dismissal of a highly plausible thesis (.9). The third alternative, S_3, manages to discard minimally plausible data and keep two pieces of highly plausible data.

All three subsets (S_1, S_2, and S_3) are consistent, but S_3 is maximally plausible. From this set of data, we can conclude that since either Saad struggles with math or Roha struggles with math, and it is almost certain that Saad does not struggle with math, it follows that it is highly plausible that Roha struggles with math. And of course, this is consistent with our background knowledge of Roha and Saad; for example, Saad loves physics, but Roha loves literature, and it is unlikely that Saad would love physics if he struggled with math; moreover, Roha avoided courses that require math prerequisites, which might suggest that math is not her strong point. Of course, it is entirely possible that new data could upset the plausibility index of this conclusion—we might learn that Saad would like to study physics but is unrealistic about his intellectual abilities and that Roha is so mathematically adept that she finds the subject unchallenging and boring, etc.

A correctly resolved logical problem has the properties of completeness, inclusivity, unity and integrity, cohesiveness and coherence, functional simplicity and economy, elegance, symmetry, consistency and coordination of parts, etc., but it is these very properties that are the criteria for resolving a problem that is a matter of plausible reasoning, that is, when our goal is a matter of determining the best or maximally plausible estimate. Hence, the most plausible set of data (out of which our current estimate is constituted) will be that which is most complete, inclusive, integral, cohesive and coherent, the most functionally simple and elegant, etc. And since a system is a group of interrelated and interacting elements that constitute a unified whole, properties like completeness, inclusivity, cohesiveness, coherence, simplicity and elegance are the **parameters of cognitive systematicity.**[26]

Logical puzzles of a deductive nature, such as the one above, are contrived; data is carefully selected and other data left out precisely in order to make possible a definitive conclusion. The real world, however, is just not like that; reality is far more complex. Data that is at our disposal is typically overabundant and inconsistent, and the data needed to resolve an impasse is often missing. Moreover, the data we have at our disposal is rarely "established fact" but is for the most part only minimally or moderately plausible. Hence, the best we can hope for is a best estimate that is putatively true, not definitively so.

Concluding Thoughts

When a conclusion of an argument makes sense to us, that is, when it is coherent, we have a tendency to assume that we have, as it were, a completed puzzle on our hands, a conclusion that enjoys the force of deductive necessity and that what we see is all there is to see. But what we see is not all there is. Although all that is true "makes sense", it is not the case that "all that makes sense is true" (i.e., all humans are animals, but not all animals are humans). With the introduction or discovery of new data, it often happens that what was earlier our best estimate is now relegated to a much lesser degree of plausibility and what was earlier estimated to be far less plausible

---

[26] Nicholas Rescher. *Induction*. Pittsburgh: University of Pittsburgh Press, 1980, 31-32.

becomes maximally so. What "makes sense" in a very limited context is often discovered to be inconsistent and incoherent in a larger context. In other words, in time we often discover that what we thought was "true" and complete is far from it. New information reveals that this or that piece of data has been improperly placed, that "this" or "that" is not the case, and that the world outside the mind is far more complex than we initially realized.

The problem with some writers, i.e., political pundits on the left and right, very conservative theologians, religious or political fundamentalists, etc., is not so much the conclusions that are logically drawn from their pool of rational data; rather, it is that the circle of data from which conclusions are educed is profoundly limited. Very often what is deduced from the principles they work with is indisputable, but the circle of data is too limited to guarantee anything more than a truth candidate, and it is precisely this "sense of incomplete information" that seems to be lacking today. Without an empirical orientation, we tend not to suspect that our storehouse of data might very well be significantly incomplete. Hence, the epistemic overconfidence with which most people make assertions. All our ideas are derived from the world of experience, for nothing is in the intellect that was not first in the senses (peripatetic axiom). Indeed, our ideas are universal, but they are nonetheless limited by the effects of matter, that is, sense perception and our dependence upon observation of a thing's activity in order to grasp the natures of things—and things always act in time. It is only gradually, in time, that our information base is enlarged, and so we always seem to be in a position to revise the plausibility index of some of our data and rethink the beliefs we previously held. If this rarely happens today, it is only because thinking takes effort and patience, and most people lack the patience required to "suspend disbelief" and the willingness to expend one's energy thinking, listening, reasoning, and revising.

32 *Plausibility and Probability*

It is important not to confuse plausibility with probability; the two are not the same. As Nicholas Rescher points out, plausibility is about the reliability of the sources which issues or authorize claims.[27] In this case, "sources" includes a wide variety. For example, various persons who make claims, such as experts or eye witnesses. Sources also include non-personalized historical sources, such as oral tradition, newspaper accounts, common knowledge, rumors, etc. It also includes our own observational information sources, such as our senses, and our memory. Also included are intellectual sources, such as reasonable inference, conjecture, hypothesizing, assumptions, etc. Finally, certain authorizing principles count as a source having a degree of plausibility, such as simplicity, or the principle of uniformity, consistency, coherence, etc.[28]

To provide a better sense of how plausibility differs from probability, consider that the probability factor decreases with each additional piece of data. For example, let it be that each of the following pieces of data has a probability factor of 80% (0.8). Hence,

The car was blue: 0.8
The car was going 20km over the speed limit: 0.8
The car was driven by a Sri Lankan woman: 0.8
The Sri Lankan woman had a child in the car: 0.8

What is the probability that all these factors will be found together (i.e., a Sri Lankan woman, driving a blue car, with a child in the back, driving 20 km over the speed limit)? Following the multiplication rule, we arrive at the following:

$p(f1) \times p(f2) = .64$
$p(f1) \times p(f2) \times p(f3) = .5$

---

[27] Nicholas Rescher. *Plausible Reasoning*. Amsterdam: Van Gorcum, 1976. 6
[28] *Ibid.*, 6

p(f1) x p(f2) x p(f3) x p(f4) = .4

The probability that these factors were all together is 0.4, which is improbable (less than 50%).

Plausibility, however, does not work like that. For example, Mike witnessed the hit and run. He says the car was a blue mustang, it was driving very fast in a 50 km zone, he said it was a Sri Lankan or East Indian woman at the wheel and she had a child in a car seat in the back. Mike is a reliable witness; he is not a liar, he has very good eyesight, he has no reason to lie. It is moderately to very plausible that Mike is correct with respect to the entire report. In other words, the conjunction of each point does not diminish the plausibility factor as it does the probability factor. Moreover, 0.2 in the context of probability indicates a 20% probability, which is highly improbable, but .2 in the context of plausibility means minimally plausible. Also, 0.4 in the context of probability also indicates an improbability (less than 50%), but .4 in the context of plausibility indicates moderate plausibility.

33 Inference to the Best Estimation

The method employed by an investigator trying to solve a crime as well as the work of an historian is fundamentally inductive; the method is a matter of inferencing to the best explanation or estimation.[29] The experimental sciences (empiriometric) employ an investigative method, and so the scientific method as well is fundamentally a matter of inference to the best explanation. The general form of inference to the best explanation is the following:

F is the case
S affords the best-available systemization of all the determinable F-relevant facts
S entails X
Therefore, X is the case (or at least can presumably be accepted as such[30]

Consider the following scenario:

We are in a suburban neighborhood, it is Saturday morning. Mr. Smith, who lives at #6 Forest Hill Cres, wakes up, grabs the paper, and notices that his tires have been slashed. His car, a Corolla, is parked on the street in front of Jeff Sinclair's house, who lives at #7 (parking is allowed on the opposite side of the street only, the side with odd number houses). The police are called.

They ask Mr. Smith: "Who do you think could have done this?" He has no clue; for he has no enemies. The police begin to look for clues. They notice broken glass on the road. On closer inspection, they noticed that it is glass from a beer bottle. It looks as if one or possibly two bottles were smashed. Nothing else seems out of place.

---

[29] I am convinced that the logic of the scientific method is more a matter of inference to the best systematization (Nicholas Rescher) and not inference to the best explanation. But to do justice to this will require a separate book, which is forthcoming.

[30] Nicholas Rescher. *Epistemic Principles: A Primer for the Theory of Knowledge*. New York: Peter Lang, 2017. 147.

The officer infers that there was probably a party late last night (Friday). They ask Mr. Smith to verify the hypothesis, and he says he's a deep sleeper, and he went to bed at 8 o'clock and heard nothing.

They proceed next door and ask Mrs. Robinson at #8, and she says there was a party at #11 across the street, and it was loud, and continued till about midnight. She was observing everything from her window until about 5 minutes before midnight, but she didn't see anything out of the ordinary. She tells them that the people living in #9 have been on vacation overseas for over a week now. But Mr. Sinclair at #7, who often parks on the road and drives a Toyota Camry, was home yesterday, so perhaps he knows something.

They visit Mr. Sinclair's home, but he's away. An hour later, he pulls into his driveway. He slept at his mother's house in the next town just south of where this is all taking place.

After some inquiry, the officer discovers that Mr. Sinclair, living at #9, is a rather impatient man. He has a low tolerance for nonsense. Living at #11 is a family, the parents of whom are often away on business trips. They have two boys, twins, 19 years of age. The one, Carlos, is unemployed, a high school dropout, and he's not looking for a job. Furthermore, he hangs out with friends who have had some involvement with the police; the other, Juan, is hard working and lined up a job with Microsoft. He's often sent overseas on business as well.

The one officer asks himself: "Why would Mr. Sinclair sleep at his mother's house, when he can sleep at home?"

Mr. Smith comes out and tells the officer that there is one person who is perhaps angry at him. Last year, he yelled at a grade 7 boy from a nearby elementary school who was bullying a smaller and much younger boy. Smith was so angry that he demanded the kid follow him back to the school, where he reported everything to the principal. The kid was suspended for 3 days. His name is Johnny McPherson, but Mr. Smith hasn't seen him since that day.

The police officer asks Mr. Smith about Carlos, living at #11. He has a good relationship with Carlos and has hired him for the third summer in a row to mow his lawn, whenever it needs mowing. Carlos is happy for the opportunity to make some money.

The officer finds out where little Johnny McPherson lives. He's home, and he is very skinny, appearing to weigh about 90 pounds. When asked if he knew Mr. Smith, he did not know who the officer was referring to. Then, when the officer mentioned the person who had him suspended last year, he remembered. After a few questions, Johnny said to the officer: "I deserved to be suspended. I was going through a difficult period back then. My parents were going through a divorce. The suspension did me some good."

He decides to ask Mr. Sinclair why he went to his mother's. Sinclair said: "I couldn't get to sleep from all the noise and loud music coming from #11, so I drove to my mother's not far from here. At about 11:00 p.m., I did ask them to stop the party, but they would not". The officer asked him: "Why didn't you call the police?" He answered: "I told them I would, but I decided not to. I just left. In any case, I hadn't seen my mother in a few weeks, so I was due for a visit."

Out of the following alternatives, which is the most fitting estimate as to how the tires got slashed?

1) Johnny McPherson was lying. He used this as an opportunity to get back at Mr. Smith, thought the party would be a good decoy.

2) Mr. Sinclair was angry for being compelled to drive to his mother's house to sleep, so he slashed the tires of the car, mistakenly believing that the car belonged to Carlos or one of his friends.

3) There is a group of teenagers who like roaming the streets at night. They typically walk around the neighborhood at about 11:00 p.m., but rarely ever past 11:30 p.m. (they have a curfew). They heard the commotion at #11, wanted to get in on the action, but were refused, so they left, and on the way saw the car and slashed the tires in anger, mistakenly believing that the car belonged to Carlos or one of the partiers.

4) The police arrived at midnight because someone further down the road called them. They told Carlos and his friends to call it a night. One of the friends, thinking that Mr. Smith's car was Mr. Sinclair's, slashed the tires in revenge. Carlos told the friend that Sinclair drives a Toyota, which is true, but he did not specify (Camry or Corolla), so the friend, thinking Mr. Smith's Corolla was Mr. Sinclair's car because it was parked in front of his house, slashed the tires, not realizing that he was slashing Mr. Smith's tires.

As you can see, each alternative is **plausible**, but they are not equally so. We cannot be certain of any one, but the alternative containing a set of data that is maximally plausible is the best estimate. Johnny could be lying, but it is unlikely that a grade 8 kid with such immoral character—given that he slashed the tires—could deliver such a line as "I deserved to be suspended. I was going through a difficult period back then. The suspension did me some good." Those, however, with a criminal personality are often smooth talkers and devious. Thus, there is a possibility that he is the culprit.

Mr. Sinclair could have slashed the tires, believing the car belonged to a partier, but it is highly plausible that he would know that Mr. Smith parks his car on the road and that he drives a Corolla. So, it is rather unlikely that he would mistakenly slash the tires. This alternative requires that we discard highly plausible data, namely that if Sinclair is familiar with Smith's car, then he will not slash his tires by mistake.

One of the kids from the group of teenagers that typically wanders the streets is a possibility, but Mrs. Robinson said nothing was out of the ordinary; she was watching the street through her window until 11:55 p.m. It is highly probable that she would have seen and heard these teenagers make their way to the door, only to be rejected. She mentioned nothing. Carlos said nothing about them either.

The most coherent and maximally plausible estimation is that someone at the party slashed the tires, in retaliation for Mr. Sinclair supposedly calling the police. Carlos would have known Mr. Smith's car, but not one of his friends, many of whom have had some involvement with the police in their lives. So, the police begin looking closely at each of Carlos' friends.

The last alternative seems to be the most fitting. The premises on which it is based are **secure**, the reasoning on the basis of the set of data that entails the conclusion is **tight**, the explanatory account is **natural** and quite **simple**, it is in **harmony** with our broader understanding of how things work, and the set of data is **consistent**.[31]

---

[31] Nicholas Rescher. *Epistemic Principles: A Primer for the Theory of Knowledge.* New York: Peter Lang, 2017. 144-147.

34 *Amtrak Sunset Limited Crash: An Illustration of Inference to the Best Systematization*

This train wreck was the derailing of the Sunset Limited, an Amtrak train that was crossing the Bayou Canot bridge in Mobile, Alabama. 47 people were killed in this wreck, and 103 were injured. It happened on September 22, 1993. This was one of the deadliest train wrecks in the history of the United States, and the deadliest in Amtrak's history.

The facts of the case

The tugboat Mauvilla was the first to report the accident. The FBI arrived at the site to investigate the possibility of terrorism. Thus, terrorism was the **first hypothesis**. Divers recovered the **event recorder** from the Bayou, which indicated that the train was traveling over 70 miles an hour. The recorder indicated that there was no break application, which means that whatever caused this crash, the engineer simply did not see it.

Investigators also discovered that the signals on the track just before the bridge were green. If the rail were to break—i.e., as a result of an explosion—, the break in the electric current would have caused the light to turn red, indicating that the train should stop and proceed no further. Clearly the rail was not destroyed beforehand. So it appears that this would rule out a bomb—at the very least, it decreases the probability that a bomb destroyed the bridge.

The bridge was built in three sections: the southern section, which was a 165 foot steel truss bridge, and the center section, which was a 140 foot steel girder originally designed to pivot so that river traffic could pass through—it was this center section that was completely destroyed. The third part of the bridge was held up by wood pilings.

Despite the fact that the pivot section was never used, investigators discovered that it wasn't connected properly; there were not enough tie downs to hold it securely in place. Investigators, however, had a **second hypothesis**: perhaps the wood pilings underneath the water deteriorated as a result of damage by wood destroying organisms. So they checked the wood piles underneath the water. There was no deterioration of the piles that contributed to the collapse. So, investigators eliminated one more hypothesis.

At this point, investigators began to study the three concrete piers. When they looked closely they discovered that the steel plates used to connect the bridge to the concrete had been displaced 48 inches out of alignment. Also, one of the metal girders had been sheared off as if struck on the end by a powerful force. They measured the spacing of the girder's rivets and compared them to scratches along the sides of the train's engine. It was discovered that the rivets made the scratches along the side of the engine. But how, they wondered, did the train hit the outside of the bridge?

Coast Guard investigators then began interviewing eyewitnesses; perhaps they have information that will in turn provide a lead towards **a plausible hypothesis**—at this point, there is none.

They begin by interviewing the crew of the tugboat Mauvilla. The tugboat was pushing six barges (each barge is about 195 feet, and it was pushing 3 wide and 2 long; that turns out to be 400 feet of steel out ahead of the actual vessel). The Mauvilla was making a routine run up the Mobile River. The tugboat pilot called in three hours before the accident reporting that the fog was heavy. He said that half an hour before the train wreck (2:20 a.m.), he steered the barges around a bend in the Mobile River and noticed on his radar what appeared to be another tugboat. He said he steered towards it hoping to tie onto it until visibility improves. But before that could happen, the pilot said his tugboat ran aground. At about 2:50 a.m. the Mauvilla's crew heard a crash and then saw a fire through the fog.

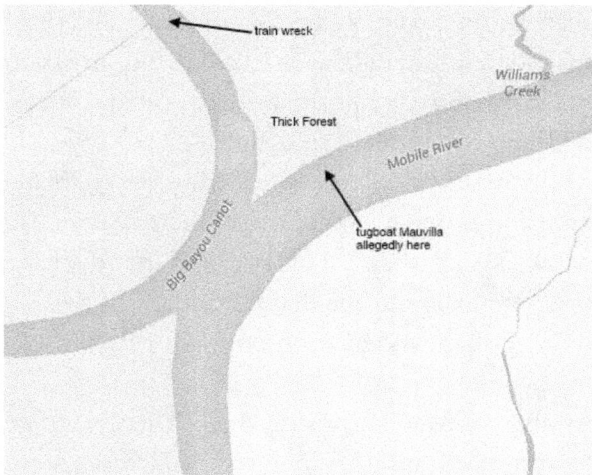

Investigators ask the question: if the Mauvilla was on the Mobile River, how could they see an accident on the Bayou Canot, 6 miles away? The Bayou Canot is the river that runs north, the Mobile River continues east. Between the Mobile River and the Bayou Canot bridge is thick forest, so if the tugboat is positioned east up the river, how is it that anyone was able to see the flames from the train?

This is the **question** that allows for the discovery of a more plausible hypothesis. Perhaps the Mauvilla was not on the Mobile River, but on the Bayou Canot. Perhaps the captain thought he was going around a bend on the Mobile River, when in fact, he was going around the bend on the Bayou Canot, at that point where it begins to go north, and did not realize it due to the thick fog. The Mauvilla did not have any maps on board, not even a compass; it had radar, but the pilot was not trained to use it.

After investigators heard the pilot's story, they went back to investigate the bridge in light of this new evidence, which provided a hypothesis. They returned to the concrete pier that was holding up the bridge structure and studied it. They noticed fresh damage to the concrete on the pier; it seemed something had hit the point of the pier. Now they began to wonder whether the damage was caused by the barges. Certain data are beginning to acquire greater plausibility; for example, it is plausible that the tugboat did not run aground on the

Mobile River and that it was actually on the Bayou Canot and hit the bridge. It is very plausible that the tugboat that Willie Odom saw on the radar was not a tugboat after all, but the bridge. Perhaps it was the Mauvilla that caused the Sunset Limited to derail.

After studying the concrete pier, they returned to the tugboat and examined the left barge and found a similar mark; there was an indentation in the metal, like a T shape. This suggests that the barge hit the top part of the concrete pier, and the diamond point of the concrete pier caused the T shape indentation on the metal of the left barge.

The other barges also revealed surprising clues. There were vertical scrapes on the others and indentations. When they pulled the steel girder out of the water, they did a visual inspection and noticed that the vertical steel members called "stiffeners" around the side of the girder had been bent flat against the girder, and so investigators measured the distance between the stiffeners and the vertical marks on the barges; they were a perfect match.

Investigators discovered concrete chips on the Mauvilla's front left barge. The concrete chips along with samples from the concrete pier were sent to the FBI lab for analysis. They were identical in composition. Each mix of concrete is unique, having a very specific composition, i.e., a specific amount of rocks, sand, cement, and water, etc. Investigators slice the concrete pieces into very thin samples or slices and compare them under a microscope. The concrete found on the barge was the same as that found on the pier. The barge ended up striking the bridge 48 inches out of alignment. The collision bent the track into an S shape; it did not break the track, and that is why the light on the track did not turn red—had the current been broken, the light would have turned red and the engineer would have stopped the train.

The conclusion is that the operator of the tugboat mistakenly turned down the Bayou Canot, which was closed to commercial traffic. He mistakenly thought it was a bend in the Mobile River, and this mistake was due to the thick fog. The tugboat he thought he saw on the radar was really the Bayou Canot Bridge; he thought he had run aground, but he had really hit the bridge.

35 *Searching for Hypotheses: A Note on Asking the Right Question*

Finding and asking the right "contrastive" question is often the door that opens the way to the hypothesis from which we can infer the best explanation; for it allows us to eliminate those hypotheses that fail to explain the contrast, and the best explanation is the inference that best explains the contrast.

Recently I saw a documentary about a brutal murder of a wealthy woman who was going through a bitter divorce. The prime suspect in the murder was her husband, but at the time of the murder, which took place in a parking garage, he was in the courtyard of the office building from which they had come—he was in full view of the surveillance camera (before, during, and after the murder). That answers the question: "Where was he at the time of his wife's murder?" He was right there on his cell phone, while his wife was being brutally stabbed in the parking garage of that very building. One could even see people, who were in the courtyard with him, walking quickly in the direction of the woman's screams, in an attempt to see what was happening.

But it was only when the investigator began to wonder why he did not so much as look up, let alone make his way over to where everyone else was heading, but stood right there in his place, that the case began to unravel. The hypothesis that might explain the fact of his not moving is that he knew who was screaming; it was his wife, who was being killed by someone he had hired. In other words, he did not move because he was not curious; it was expected.

It was the right question (a contrastive question) that opened up the avenue that led to the hypothesis that best explains the mystery, after those hypotheses that failed to explain the contrast were eliminated.

What can we infer from the following blood drop on the floor next to a body?

The simple inference is that this came from the man on the floor who died of a stab wound to the chest; it is just one of many drops of blood going from the living room to the kitchen. The following is a sample of the other drops in the room.

Why is there blood rather than no blood? The answer is that the man was stabbed, and that left an open wound that bled.

But what if someone were to ask a different question as a result of a different interest? For instance, "Why is the first blood drop round, while the others are elongated, having the shape of a Q-tip?" This is a different question, and it opens up a whole new avenue to explore. The questioner takes note of the contrast in the shape of the drops. The elongated drops are explained as the result of falling from a moving body. The bleeding man was moving towards the kitchen, which is the direction towards which the sharp end of the drop points. This can be verified through a simple experiment.

So why is the first drop rounded? Shouldn't it also be elongated? The first blood drop is a low velocity drop from someone who was stationary, contrary to the elongated drop that came from someone moving in a particular direction. This requires some sort of explanation. This gives rise to the hypothesis that perhaps these blood drops are from two different people. DNA testing would reveal that indeed, the elongated blood drops came from the dead man; while the single round drop came, more than likely, from the perpetrator of the crime who was standing over his victim, and who must have cut himself while stabbing the victim.

It was that new question rooted in a new interest that enabled us to understand better the antecedent, thus enabling us to explain the evidence.

Different questions rooted in different interests highlight what would otherwise remain hidden. This is evident in the interpretation of texts. When we approach a text from a particular vantage point, that is, within a particular frame of mind, with particular interests that are very different from what interested us in previous years, certain aspects of the text stand out for us, that is, certain lines and ideas are highlighted that were in the penumbra when we read this same text previously. That is why we acquire a much better grasp of a text or book when we read it later, for the second or third time.

36 Thoughts on Inferencing

It is very important that we come to an awareness of the degrees of certainty available to us on each level of abstraction. As you know, the lower the level of abstraction on which a science is conducted, the less certainty we enjoy. So much of what we conclude on the level of concrete particulars is really the result of induction. That means that much of what we think we "know" is tentative, perhaps not really knowledge at all, but belief. We believe that such and such a person is arrogant, or a nice guy, or honest, or we believe that this celebrity thinks she's better than others, and we believe flax seed oil is good for us—unless of course we've done the science—, and we believe he is guilty of the crime for which he is charged, or that he is not guilty of the crime for which he is charged, etc. In my experience, most people are not aware of the underdetermined nature of such conjectures and habitually confuse them with genuine knowledge, which is why they attribute far more certainty to what they think they know than is warranted. How do we know they do so? We know because they are so passionate about their convictions and are often so closed to dialogue.

Consider how few people there are who are genuinely open to serious discussion that subjects their deepest convictions to critical scrutiny. Most people are simply not interested in discussing the issues, the evidence, the questions, the gaps in their arguments, the possibilities, etc., whatever the issues. What is the reason for this? I suspect it has a great deal to do with the emotions; in other words, it has a great deal to do with ethics. Being right feels wonderful; certainty feels good; and very few are willing to endure the feeling of being wrong. It takes a great deal of humility to admit to having been mistaken.

Now humility is a virtue, and the virtues dispose the emotions to readily submit to the demands of reason with ease. For a humble man or woman, it is easy to give way to the truth, and it is difficult to hold on to something he or she knows to be false. A humble person is not passionate about his views; if he is passionate about anything, it is the truth, not his views. Now the virtues are connected to one another; one cannot have humility, but not temperance, or temperance but not fortitude, etc., and so a virtuous person is temperate. He is not attached to the emotional complacency of being right, or the emotionally satisfying feeling of certainty. But that cannot be said for the majority of people.

The way to greater peace in this world is through a greater openness to dialogue; but of course, that's easier said than done. Dialogue is emotionally difficult for those who are inordinately attached to the emotional satisfaction of being certain. And so once again, it boils down to virtue. The way to peace in this world is not through some ideologically based construction of a system of government, but personal virtue.

Moreover, it is this same attachment to feelings of complacency that inclines others to neglect the labor involved in drawing out all the logical implications of the first principles of speculative and practical reason, *of which we can be certain*. Here, the discomfort associated with the prospect of having to reform one's life (in the case of moral discoveries) or acknowledge what one was comfortable refusing to acknowledge (i.e., the existence of absolute moral precepts, or God, etc.) outweighs the satisfaction of enjoying a level of certitude in these areas (morality, metaphysics, etc.). One has to love truth more than the pleasures of sense before this will ever be reversed.

37 *Further Thoughts on Inferencing and the Limitations of Knowing*

The predominant problem today is not that people don't know enough—that is the norm, and it is to be expected in light of the limitations of human intelligence, imposed by matter, time, and sense perception. Rather, the problem is that most people *don't know that they don't know*. Moreover, many are simply not willing to know that they do not know much of what they think they know.

In fact, it isn't "knowing" *per se*, but "believing" that makes up most of what we consider "knowledge"; most people fail to appreciate the extent to which this is true and its implications. For the most part, we live by "belief", in the sense that so much of our "knowledge" base is made up of inferences having varying degrees of probability (or plausibility). For example, it is true that I know that this woman is my teacher, that she is a human being, that she knows the English language, etc., but I believe she is a genuinely good person—which is why she is nice to me—, and I believe that what she's teaching me is not simply made up purely out of her imagination, but properly researched; and I believe she has my best interest at heart—but I don't know that—, and I believe the school principal is a mean spirited and vindictive man (I infer that from his demeanor), and I believe that the person I call my "best friend" is truly a good friend; and I believe that the pills handed to me by the pharmacist are going to help heal my strep throat and not kill me, etc. These inferences do not all have the same degree of probability, and it is reasonable for me to believe much of what it is I infer, i.e., that the approaching car is not going to swerve and run me over, for the odds are in my favor that it will not.

But as we get older, and if we are honest, we begin to realize that many of the inferences we made while we were young and which became a constituent part of our knowledge base in light of which we interpreted much of our later experiences, were in fact wrong. For example, many people who have held on to resentment towards their parents will later on, after having children of their own, begin to acquire a better understanding of the decisions and perhaps even the mistakes their parents made; for they now understand some of the anxieties that go along with parenting, the stresses of adult life, etc. They didn't see that before, for it was not part of their experience, and they simply assumed that whatever they were not aware of simply did not exist or was irrelevant. They begin to realize that they made inferences on the basis of very limited information, the limits of which they failed to appreciate when they were young. Such examples can be multiplied many times over. Wisdom is partly the result of having a great deal of experience in being wrong.

The fact of the matter is that we speak too quickly—especially when we are young; for we tend not to be aware of the degrees of probability—often low probability—of what it is we think we know to be true, and so we speak out boldly and confidently, we write letters of complaint, we raise objections or threaten, etc., because in our minds the feeling of certainty is proof positive that what we think is so is simply the truth. We conflate possibility and necessity; it is experience and age that gradually separate the two in our minds—if we allow ourselves to learn from experience.

Indeed, there is so much that we as individuals do not need to know personally, because *the impossible is not and cannot be a need*, and it is not possible to know enough. After all, what is enough? We have one another; and not knowing what this implies is a problem (i.e., we have one another to depend on); for there is only a small sphere in which each of us can perhaps be somewhat justified in "thinking fast". In other words, there is only a very small area in which any of us can rightfully pronounce on matters with a degree of certainty, and it is usually a much smaller sphere than we tend to believe it is. Outside of that tiny sphere, we are practically lost, and so we need to keep quiet and listen to others speak.

When a person is quick to take it upon himself to educate those in his immediate vicinity about almost anything and everything, he has already come to the conclusion—for whatever reason—that others don't know what he is about to offer them—or do not know about it to the same degree he does. If he continues to speak and offer his "knowledge" unsolicited, he has concluded that their minds are, as it were, smaller spheres within the larger and all-embracing sphere of his own intellect. This is epistemic arrogance, and the world of an arrogant man is a very small world to be living in. Others can enlarge my mind if I acknowledge the possibility, but to do so requires that I become less in my own eyes. As Ralph Waldo Emerson writes: "Shall I tell you the secret of the true scholar? It is this: Every man I meet is my master in some point, and in that I learn of him."[32]

This is not to suggest that we cannot possess certainty. Indeed, we can and do, for the very idea of certitude did not arise from nothing—from nothing comes from nothing. Being or existence is given in knowledge (existential judgment), and the higher the level of abstraction on which we think, the greater the certainty we enjoy. But the light of clarity, certainty and necessity can and often does blind us to the opaque, to the possible and the contingent, and so much of the reasoning we carry on from day to day is a matter of inferencing, which is characterized by uncertainty, opacity, and contingency.

---

[32] Oliver Wendell Holmes, *Ralph Waldo Emerson*. Boston: Houghton, Miffin, 1884. 289.

38 *The Fallacy of Composition*

The fallacy of composition involves attributing to the whole what belongs to a part of the whole, or, attributing to the part what belongs only to the whole. One of the most interesting points about probabilities is that we are very poor intuitive statisticians, and that includes professional statisticians. What I mean is that professional statisticians carefully input data and of course they employ the mathematics of probability, and in doing so, they are acting as professional statisticians; but when outside the office, they, like everyone else, tend to make statistical inferences intuitively, and when they do so, they are often just as wrong as the rest of us.

Induction by enumeration is a kind of inference that begins with a sample, and draws a conclusion about the whole, i.e., k% of this sample is good quality, therefore k% of the whole is good quality. A statistical argument, conversely, begins with facts about the whole and proceeds to make an inference about a part of the whole, i.e., k% of Canadians like hockey; John is Canadian, therefore John likes hockey. The validity of an argument of induction by enumeration depends on the size of the sample and whether it is properly representative (i.e., opinion polls must sample from all minorities and all socio-economic sectors).

The fallacy of composition attributes to the whole what belongs only to a part, or vice versa. In other words, it attributes necessity where there is only probability. For example, despite what appears to be reckless driving in Rome, I didn't see one accident while I was there for two weeks. Thus, I conclude that driving is much safer in Italy (i.e., I conjecture that fast driving makes drivers more alert). Or, I saw many cars in Italy that are worth over 150 thousand dollars; therefore, I conclude that Italy is a prosperous nation.

In the former instance, my experience was only partial (a part), and I made the mistake of treating my limited experience as a sample from which to make an inference about the whole of Italy. I need a far greater sample and a more representative one (i.e., I need to sample not merely from the month of August, when most Romans are on vacation, and I need to sample from outside of Rome as well) in order to validly infer anything about road safety in Italy. In our minds, however, we tend to think our sample size is large enough and entirely representative. Again, this is primarily because we are lazy; we would rather draw conclusions quickly and without too much effort. In other words, we want closure. For example, we think a 15-20 minute interview is enough to determine whether this person will, on the whole, be a great teacher, a reliable employee, etc. We think a few dates are enough for us to determine whether we can spend the rest of our lives with this person, that is, whether "on the whole" he is a good and trustworthy individual; for he was charming while dating and while I was seeing him for only part of the time, but does that mean I can infer that on the whole, he is what he appears to be in those limited and partial moments?

Other examples of the fallacy are the following: Such and such is a good school. Therefore, this student must be a good student, because she graduated from that school. Or, that teacher must be good, because he teaches at that school. Consider the following: My experience in that city on this vacation was wonderful. Thus, I make an inference that I would be happy living there for the rest of my life because I was happy there for a small portion of a lifetime. Or, on the whole, this person is very intelligent. Therefore, every opinion he holds is a very intelligent and well thought out opinion.

We can see how this fallacy in this context begins to blend into the fallacy of misplaced authority: "Einstein is very intelligent and is a preeminent scientist. Therefore, what he said about education is worthy of respect". If we were to formulate this as a valid argument of induction by enumeration, perhaps it would look something like this: "80% (?) of the things Einstein says about physics is highly enlightened. Therefore, the next thing he says about physics will be highly enlightened". As far as this argument goes, it has high probability and is thus inductively valid. But the fallacy of composition would confuse what belongs to a part with what belongs to the whole. Thus, "80% (?) of the things Einstein says about physics is highly enlightened.

Therefore, the next thing Einstein says (without qualification) will be highly enlightened". In other words, 80% of the things he says about a small sphere of knowledge (physics) might be highly enlightened, but that does not mean that 80% of the things he says belonging to the general sphere of knowledge (on the whole) will be enlightened. It is often the case that when experts "spout off" about issues outside their narrow field of expertise, their insights are not significantly sharper than that of the average person in society.

When growing up, I never encountered anyone who had later on committed suicide. In fact, I never encountered anyone who was clinically depressed. What inference can I make on the basis of that experience? Not much, at least nothing with any real validity. The sample size is too small and unrepresentative. To draw a conclusion on such a basis, which is very common, is to fall into a bias that Daniel Kahneman refers to as WYSIATI (What You See Is All There Is).[33] Circumstances have changed a great deal since I was a child, and we talk about things now that we never used to talk about, such as mental illness, clinical depression, domestic abuse, out of wedlock pregnancy, homosexuality, etc. Our own individual experience is a sample, and very often it is an insufficient sample. Nevertheless, that does not seem to keep us from making inferences about the whole (the whole subject matter, or whatever it is we are commenting on) on the basis of that limited part.

Other examples of the fallacy in the context of science include the following reductionisms: Atoms have no color. This table is made up of atoms. Therefore, this table has no color." Or, "Atoms are mostly empty space. This table is made up of atoms; therefore this table is mostly empty space. Hence, solidity is an illusion".

---

[33] Kahneman, *op. cit.*, Chapter 7, "A Machine for Jumping to Conclusions".

39 Some Basic Induction Biases

Induction begins with evidence and aims for the most plausible hypothesis (antecedent) as an explanation of the evidence. Just as there are deductive fallacies, such as the fallacy of the undistributed middle term, or the informal fallacy of begging the question (assuming the point that needs to be proven in order to prove the point), so too there are inductive fallacies called biases and heuristics (an aid to problem solving that is not necessarily optimal) that are in large measure responsible for the inductive errors to which we typically fall prey— and of which we are, for the most part, unaware.

Confirmation Bias

One of the most pervasive biases is the **confirmation bias**. This is the tendency to look for confirmatory instances of a hypothesis and to ignore evidence that disconfirms the hypothesis. Confirmation does not prove a hypothesis correct; rather, disconfirmation proves it is erroneous. For example:

If violence is a propensity specifically characteristic of the male psyche, then we will see many and far more instances of male violence against women than vice versa.
This year alone there were *k* instances of domestic violence against women (evidence).
Therefore, the propensity to violence is a characteristically male phenomenon.

This is an instance of affirming the consequent, and it is deductively invalid. The minor premise (i.e., "This year alone there were k instances...") is the evidence before us. The conclusion is only a possibility and thus requires further investigation. We may look at this particular form of the conditional syllogism, affirming the consequent, as an inductive argument. Because we are lazy minded, we have a tendency to settle upon the antecedent, which is the hypothesis (i.e.,

...violence is a propensity specifically characteristic of the male psyche), and so every news item of a woman who is the victim of male aggression becomes a verification or confirmation of the hypothesis, for it is felt to be a significant piece of evidence because it stands out and is easy to remember, and it stands out only because it confirms the ruling hypothesis, giving rise to a very real emotional complacency.

Consider that **if John killed his mother, then there will be evidence of a motive** (i.e., life insurance policy). That John was in debt and needed money to pay those debts and that his mother recently took out an accidental death insurance policy and named John as the beneficiary confirm the hypothesis that he killed his mother. But this does not prove he did so. Investigators know this, but the average person who places a great deal of confidence in his intuitive inferences is rarely aware of this.

What is needed at this point is more attention to possible evidence that disconfirms the original hypothesis. It often happens, however, that such evidence is overlooked, because it lacks a certain kind of significance, that is, it lacks the emotional resonance that confirmatory instances possess; for example, the disconfirming evidence that most violence against children is perpetrated by females, or that the rate of murder and violence in women's prisons equals or surpasses that of men's prison facilities, etc., are easy to overlook, because such disconfirming evidence suggests we're back to the drawing board, a prospect that can be exhausting.

The Narrative Fallacy

The **narrative fallacy** is a close cousin of the confirmation bias. Reality is vast and very complex; it exceeds our ability to fully understand. The past is especially difficult if not impossible to master, and we seem to have an aversion to uncertainty and opacity—with the exception of moral matters; here we love ambiguity, for we believe it allows us to do what we please. It takes a great deal of effort to refrain from constructing a coherent narrative that offers an explanation of complex phenomena.

In the words of Nassim Taleb, "the narrative fallacy addresses our limited ability to look at sequences of facts without weaving an explanation into them, or, equivalently, forcing a logical link, an arrow of relationship upon them. Explanations bind facts together. They make them all the more easily remembered; they help them make more sense. Where this propensity can go wrong is when it increases our impression of understanding".[34]

Ideologies are coherent narratives that weave an explanation into complex realities, such as the feminist ideology that interprets all history as a struggle between man's desire to subjugate women, or the anti-American and anti-corporate narrative that is suspicious about everything America does and reads negative motives into everything produced by large corporations. This fallacy is a relative of the confirmation bias; for whatever confirms the narrative has significance for us, and whatever disconfirms it hardly ever noticed.

But more to the point, narratives "make sense" out of very complex phenomena, and we begin to mistake "making sense" with "truth". Consider the following categorical proposition (A statement): "All that is true makes sense". It does not follow, however, that "all that makes sense is true". The subject of the statement "All that is true makes sense" is distributed, the predicate, however, is undistributed. Just as it is true that "All giraffes are animals", it does not follow that "All animals are giraffes".

A further difficulty is that human beings have a tendency to stubbornly persist in the narratives they've held on to for years, for they provide emotional security in many ways, and after many years, so much has been invested emotionally that it is almost inconceivable that one would be open to revision, that is, to letting go of the narrative and moving on to something more true to the facts.

It is always tempting to weave a narrative into the complexities of history; I've done it myself. It makes history so much more manageable

---

[34] Taleb, *op. cit.*, Chapter 6, "The Narrative Fallacy".

and easier to remember. Furthermore, what makes narrative construction so attractive is that confirmatory evidence abounds, lending the illusion that history is much less complex than it really is. It is very far from clear, however, whether or not my cause and effect narratives are true, or whether they are nothing more than a sophisticated version of the *post hoc, ergo propter hoc* fallacy, by which we erroneously conclude that because B happened after A, B happened because of A.

We also notice the narrative fallacy at work in our tendency to attribute causal relevance where there is nothing more than statistical relevance. Again, this is a matter of imparting cause/effect imagery that helps to "make sense" out of complex and random phenomena. Consider, for example, regression to the mean, which refers to a random variable that departs unusually from the mean, but then returns to normal. This has been referred to as the Sports Illustrated Jinx; for how often has it happened that an athlete featured on the cover of Sports Illustrated one year has a rather disappointing season the next. There is no cause/effect relationship between his performance and the fact that he is celebrated on the cover of the magazine. He is featured in the magazine as a result of an outstanding year; but as the variable increases in number (i.e., number of games played), there is always a regression to the average. I recall the day Stuart Manley shot a hole in one at the ISPS HANDA World Cup of Golf in Melbourne (Nov, 2013); he scored an 11 on the following hole. There's no use looking for a cause; it is a statistical phenomenon.

We see the narrative fallacy at work in our tendency to answer erroneously basic statistical questions bearing upon concrete information. Consider the following:[35] Jill, a 28-year-old, single, passionate and outspoken woman who majored in philosophy, is a strong social justice advocate who has picketed against injustices a number of times. In light of this information, which has greater probability? a) Jill is a bank teller; b) Jill is a bank teller and an active

---

[35] Ian Hacking. *Introduction to Probability and Inductive Logic*. Cambridge: Cambridge University Press, 2001. 65.

feminist; c) Jill is a bank teller and an active feminist who takes yoga classes.

Most of us choose the alternative with richer narrative content, i.e., c) or b), rarely a), mistakenly believing that c), for example, has greater probability. In other words, b) and c) are more concrete and tend to correspond to an already existing narrative. But, $P(A\&B) \leq P(A)$, and $P(A\&B\&C) \leq P(A\&B) \leq P(A)$. In other words, b) and c) imply a), and so there is a far greater probability that Jill is a bank teller than that she is a bank teller and an active feminist. Thus, the $P(a) \geq P(b) \geq P(c)$.

We seem to have a natural aversion to the abstract, but the irony is that we often use general statistical categories to bolster our narratives, such as "the wealthy 1%", or "the bottom 5%", or "household income", etc., to bolster an anti-corporate or anti-capitalist narrative. However, those flesh and blood human beings who occupied the category of top 1% for a given year are rarely the same ones in that category five years hence; the same is true for the bottom 5%; human beings move through these categories, which are themselves static. Furthermore, that household income for one ethnic group is double or triple that of another is not necessarily evidence of discrimination, especially when the average number of working household occupants for the one ethnic group is much higher than it is for the other (*per capita* income is a more accurate criterion).[36]

The **just world fallacy** is a species of the narrative fallacy: "What goes around comes around"; "Everyone gets what he deserves". If a person is bullied, or is a victim of some terrible injustice, there is a tendency to look for evidence that bolsters an existing narrative that he or she must have done something to deserve it, for the prospect of genuine evil is frightening. The flip side of this fallacy is to automatically regard the perpetrator as a victim, i.e., of environmental conditions, such as poverty or an abusive parent, etc.

It is important to make sure not to invest a great deal of ourselves into our hypotheses, that is, we need to keep a very open mind, one

---

[36] Thomas Sowell. *Economic Facts and Fallacies*. New York: Basic Books, 2011. Chapter 5, "Income Facts and Fallacies" [Kobo version]. Retrieved from http://www.kobo.com.

that is ever open to revision, and to develop not so much a passion for the viewpoint we hold as much as a passion for the truth, wherever it may lead us. We have to learn to become very comfortable with the prospect that we've been wrong all these years.

The Availability Heuristic Bias

The most pervasive bias, it seems to me, is the **availability heuristic bias**, again due in part to our lazy mindedness. A heuristic is a mental shortcut; instead of taking the long way, which involves thought and perhaps some investigation, we rely on a shortcut to get to where we wish to go. These shortcuts that we are inclined to take open us to a greater likelihood of error. This particular heuristic describes our tendency to judge the probability of certain events on the basis of our ability to readily think of examples of them. We make decisions and/or judgments on the basis of information that is readily available, believing that what we see is all there is to see (WHAT YOU SEE IS ALL THERE IS (WYSIATI).[37] In other words, if we do not see it, it does not exist. This bias is rooted in a lack of awareness of the limitations that sense perception imposes on human intelligence.

The problem is not that we do not know enough—we will always not know enough—, rather, the problem is that we don't know that there is so much that we don't know—or if we do, that knowledge is purely theoretical, not yet having any serious impact on the speed at which we make inferences and decisions. If we kept at the forefront of our minds an awareness that there is a veritable universe of knowledge within so many different areas of knowledge of which we are completely ignorant, we would think and judge much less quickly than we typically do. But keeping such awareness at the forefront of the mind is much more difficult than we tend to imagine. As a classroom teacher, there is so much that goes on in the school that is outside my purview, and thus outside my awareness. I recall as a young teacher how often I would make inferences bearing upon the administration,

---

[37] Kahneman, *op. cit.*, Chapter 7, "A Machine for Jumping to Conclusions".

on how inadequately they are doing their job or how "imprudent" their decisions were, all on the basis of the knowledge that was within my limited range—I was a young teacher with only a few years of experience. It was only when I became good friends with a vice principal and had spent more time in the office as a result of a unique schedule that my eyes were slowly opened to how little I knew in the way of the overall happenings of a typical school day.

A fine article on the topic was written by 19th century economist Frederic Bastiat, entitled: *That Which is Seen, and That Which is Not Seen*. He writes: "In the department of economy, an act, a habit, an institution, a law, gives birth not only to an effect, but to a series of effects. Of these effects, the first only is immediate; it manifests itself simultaneously with its cause - it is seen. The others unfold in succession - they are not seen: it is well for us, if they are foreseen. Between a good and a bad economist this constitutes the whole difference - the one takes account of the visible effect; the other takes account both of the effects which are seen, and also of those which it is necessary to foresee. Now this difference is enormous, for it almost always happens that when the immediate consequence is favourable, the ultimate consequences are fatal, and the converse. Hence it follows that the bad economist pursues a small present good, which will be followed by a great evil to come, while the true economist pursues a great good to come, - at the risk of a small present evil".[38]

---

[38] Frederick Bastiat. *That Which is Seen, and That Which is Not Seen,* 1850. Retrieved from http://bastiat.org/en/twisatwins.html. Economist Thomas Sowell writes: "When I was an undergraduate studying economics under Professor Arthur Smithies of Harvard, he asked me in class one day what policy I favored on a particular issue of the times. Since I had strong feelings on that issue, I proceeded to answer him with enthusiasm, explaining what beneficial consequences I expected from the policy I advocated.

"And then what will happen?" he asked.

The question caught me off guard. However, as I thought about it, it became clear that the situation I described would lead to other economic consequences, which I then began to consider and to spell out.

"And what will happen after that?" Professor Smithies asked.

As I analyzed how the further economic reactions to the policy would unfold, I began to realize that these reactions would lead to consequences much less desirable than those at the first stage, and I began to waver somewhat.

"And then what will happen?" Smithies persisted.

Bias in the media contributes to availability heuristic. There is so much that is not covered in the media, for one reason or another, that is far more important than what is typically covered. Part of the reason that certain news items are selected has to do with the narrative fallacy or confirmation bias: certain news items confirm a narrative, whether that is a left wing narrative or a right wing narrative. It is precisely the availability heuristic bias that is the reason most people are overly-credulous and have inordinate trust in the mainstream media. They naturally believe that whatever is not covered by mainstream media is not newsworthy.

Anchoring

It was anchoring that lost me close to 4 thousand dollars when trading in my old car for a new one. I was offered only $4000 for my 2008, which I declined. I was then asked to offer a fair price. I didn't come prepared, so I said $6000. After about 15 or 20 minutes of apparent negotiations in the back, the slick salesman returned to say that the battle was hard fought, but we won: $6000 it is. I discovered later that I should have received $9,500 for it, which then would have been sold for a good profit. I was anchored low, and it affected my judgment of the value of my own car.

I can walk into a classroom with a jar full of about 200 marbles and ask students to estimate the total number. If I privately instruct a student to offer the first estimate at 400, the overall average of the class estimates will be much higher than if I gave no instruction to anyone.

By now I was beginning to see that the economic reverberations of the policy I advocated were likely to be pretty disastrous— and, in fact, much worse than the initial situation that it was designed to improve.

Simple as this little exercise might seem, it went further than most economic discussions about policies on a wide range of issues. Most thinking stops at stage one. In recent years, former economic advisers to Presidents of the United States— from both political parties— have commented publicly on how little thinking ahead about economic consequences went into decisions made at the highest level…Short-run thinking is not confined to politicians but is often also found among the population at large. Nor is this peculiar to the United States or even to Western societies." *Applied Economics*. New York: Basic Books, 2004. Chapter 1, "Politics versus Economics: One-Stage Thinking" [Kobo version]. Retrieved from http://www.kobo.com.

Students are unconsciously influenced by the first estimate. I have found that in marking papers, I have for years been unconsciously subject to anchoring. If a student makes a good impression on me early by asking a brilliant question, I have it in my mind that she is brilliant, and that affects my expectations and the way I see and evaluate her work henceforth. I tend to mark high, even when her work is not where it should be. I also find that when a student does well on the objective section of a test, my evaluation of her essay, which I mark later, is biased in her favor. Since I have become aware of that and now mark their essays without knowing who wrote them (the names are on the first page only), the averages have decreased somewhat.

A first impression is an anchor; and it is remarkable how many people continue to allow themselves to be blinded by their first impressions. Some people have very dynamic personalities, and that acts as an anchor. That is why it is very difficult for some people to believe that such a "nice guy" could be so cold and indifferent, or stingy, envious, cunning and devious.

Representation Bias (Ignoring Base Rates)

We also have a tendency to identify representation with probability. Allow me to use an example borrowed from Daniel Kahneman's *Thinking Fast and Slow*. A man named Steve is selected at random from a representative sample. A neighbor describes him as follows: "Steve is very shy and withdrawn, invariably helpful but with little interest in people or in the world of reality. A meek and tidy soul, he has a need for order and structure, and a passion for detail." Kahneman asks: **"Is Steve more likely to be a librarian or a farmer?"** [39]

Since Steve more closely resembles a librarian, most people rely on that fact alone and infer that there is a greater probability that he is a 'librarian' than a farmer. But in this case, intuition is contrary to the logic of probability. There are twenty farmers to every one librarian

---

[39] Kahneman, *op. cit.*, "Introduction".

(20:1); that is an important base rate. What most people do when they answer this question is that they ignore the base rate and substitute a question that is much easier to answer, which is: "What is the probability that a librarian would have such personality traits?" That's not the same question as "Is Steve (a random pick) more likely to be a librarian or a farmer?" The former is $P(E/H)$, that is, the probability that a person gives evidence of these traits, given that he is a librarian; the latter is $P(H/E)$, and to determine this requires $P(H)$.

Let us say the answer to the question about the probability that a person will give evidence of specific personality traits, given that he is a librarian is rather high. The question, however, is: "Is Steve, a person selected at random from a representative sample, more likely to be a librarian or a farmer?" That is a question that takes a bit more effort to answer, because it requires a bit of research (a knowledge of the ratio of farmer to librarian), so we tend to substitute that question for an easier one. The answer to the former question can be answered intuitively, but the answer to the latter question cannot.

The point is we are lazy thinkers; we are subject to a representative bias. We are inclined to make an intuitive inference based on representation, not on prior probabilities; our quick intuitive inferences are often wrong precisely because we ignore base rates and trust too readily in our limited experience—this bias is a close relative of WYSIATI. The prospect of slowing down and thinking about the correct answer is less appealing; perhaps thinking slowly makes us feel slow, and we assume "slow" means "stupid". But slow is prudent, and prudence is not stupidity; on the contrary, imprudence is practical stupidity. It is better to think than to "spout off", and too many people today "spout off" about things they know virtually nothing about, on the basis of their limited experience and the intuitions that arise from it.

Ignoring base rates is easy because we often don't know them. For example, how many of us knew that nine Canadians die of Asthma every week? More often than not, **we arrive at our own base rates**, and the base rates we determine on our own are often incorrect. This is so because our personal base rates are often based on experience, and for the most part we are not aware of the **limitations of our experience**. For example, according to the experience of a typical Canadian, a pastry is not breakfast (unlike the Italian), and sweets such as chocolate bars are popular snacks; but we take it for granted that this is universal.

Often people ask me about the state of Catholic Education in Ontario, but I have only had experience in three different high schools in my teaching career. How can I make an accurate inference on the basis of such limited experience? I know only three Toronto area high schools. I have no experience in the elementary schools; I have no experience of schools in the rest of southern Ontario, northern Ontario, or in the Ottawa area, etc. Moreover, there is so much that I am not aware of in the school that I am currently in. I don't know how many of the students practice their faith, and I don't know how many teachers practice. In fact, I am often surprised to discover that so and so is a fervent Catholic; but the very fact that I have experienced surprise would suggest that I have made prior inferences which were later discovered to be incorrect. But if I were to tell this person what I think is the state of Catholic Education in Ontario based on my limited experience, it is very likely that he would accept what I say as an accurate assessment based on my 30 years of teaching experience. In other words, it is likely that he would treat it as an expert opinion, which is anything but an expert opinion.

Hindsight Bias

The failure to appreciate the limitations that sense perception imposes on human intelligence seriously affects our ability to **predict** with any kind of accuracy. All I have to do to be reminded of my own lack of skill in this area is to think back to when I was in high school. I "knew" what I was going to be, and if today I were to enter a time machine and visit myself in the past, to inform me of what I was going to end up doing in the future, I would have declared my older self "insane". I also recall being told that by the time I am an adult, the internal combustion engine would be obsolete and that all cars would be electric.

Our predicting abilities are very much like google maps: if you have ever driven a long distance using instructions provided by google maps, you understand what I mean. On my way to New York, I found myself driving through beautiful countryside and small towns. The shortest distance took me about 12 hours, while a longer distance would have taken me to New York in 9 hours. The computer program is "abstract", so to speak; it does not factor in mountains, speed zones, stop signs, small towns, etc. How many of us start the day with a set of plans that includes running all sorts of important errands, yard work, reading, etc., only to end the day with not even half of it done? Even something so simple as going from the lunch room to my office to get a book to read during lunch had not worked out in the concrete as I'd predicted it would, that is, as it worked out so neatly in my mind; I made my way to the stairs, unclipped my keys, which then fell out of my hand and through an opening in the stairs, falling to the floor below, which led me there, which is the reason I then encountered a former student on that floor, which led to conversation, after which time the thought of walking all the way up three flights of stairs to get a book had become too exhausting, etc. None of this was factored into my original plan, nor could it be.

We continue to predict with confidence because we have not learned to become skeptical of our abilities; in other words, we have not learned from the past. Our mistakes drift from memory—after all, who wants to be reminded of their limitations? Perhaps what happens is that we construct a narrative to explain the past, so that in our minds we fool ourselves into believing we have figured out where we went wrong and on that basis persuade ourselves that we are now able to predict with accuracy (hindsight bias).

I would argue there are two kinds of intuition: 1) **intuition of the first principles** (intuition proper), and 2) a **secondary intuition**, which is a rapid reasoning process that is both inductive and deductive.

The latter, it seems to me, corresponds roughly to Daniel Kahneman's System 1. Nassim Taleb summarizes it well:

> System 1, the experiential one, is effortless, automatic, fast, opaque (we do not know that we are using it), parallel-processed, and can lend itself to errors. It is what we call "intuition," and performs these quick acts of prowess that became popular under the name blink, after the title of Malcolm Gladwell's bestselling book. System 1 is highly emotional, precisely because it is quick. It produces shortcuts, called "heuristics," that allow us to function rapidly and effectively. Dan Goldstein calls these heuristics "fast and frugal." Others prefer to call them "quick and dirty." Now, these shortcuts are certainly virtuous, since they are rapid, but, at times, they can lead us into some severe mistakes. This main idea generated an entire school of research called the heuristics and biases approach (heuristics corresponds to the study of shortcuts, biases stand for mistakes).[40]

Intuition of the first principles is intuition in the proper sense; for it alone is an immediate apprehension of a fundamental law of being that is self-evident (i.e., each being is what it is; nothing can both be and not be at the same time and in the same respect, etc.). Intuition in the proper sense is the immediate apprehension of the first principles of speculative reason.

Intuition in the secondary sense (System 1) only appears to be immediate, but it is in fact a rapid reasoning process that is based on premises that are either known to be true or assumed to be true. Consider the intuition we often have about someone, for example, i.e., an intuition that "this man cannot be trusted", or that "he's a nice guy", etc. This is the result of a rapid reasoning process, a string of rapid inferences based on our experiences. This is the reason that our intuitions are often wrong when we are young; we simply do not have

---

[40] Taleb, *op. cit.*, Chapter 6.

enough experience, and we place too much confidence in the accuracy of our rapid inferencing.

Secondary intuition, it seems to me, often works like this: You meet someone for the first time; you have an intuition, which is the product of pre-conscious and rapid inferencing. For example, he reacts to something you said, he has a look on his face, and makes a remark, etc., and you quickly make a series of inferences as to the possible cause of or reason for (i.e., hypothesis, or antecedent) this behavior: 1) he is a bit arrogant, or 2) he's superior in some way, or 3) he knows something I don't, or 4) he's an envious person, etc. Now these inferences are not explicit, but implicit, that is, you are not explicitly aware of these four possible alternatives, as if you had articulated them to yourself.

Years later you reflect upon the evidence that has accumulated over time, and you conclude that he is this or that kind of person, which was one of the alternatives in your pre-conscious and rapid inferencing years earlier. For example, you finally discover that he really is an envious person, and there's almost no doubting it. You say to yourself: "I knew it! I knew it all along".

But you did not know it all along. This is **hindsight bias**; what we forgot is that there were other possibilities or alternatives that we implicitly knew as well, but the evidence that has accumulated now makes this one alternative stand out in our memory, as if it were the only one, and so we think that we should have listened more carefully to our intuition years earlier. What really happened at the beginning, however, is that we simply treated that alternative as one among other possible alternatives, probably refrained somewhat from making a definitive judgment, and years later it appears that we had before us only one alternative, and so we mistakenly think to ourselves: "I should have listened to my intuition."

That counsel, namely "that I should have listened more carefully to my intuition", is the reason we do not learn from experience as much as we could. That's simply bad counsel. The question is: "Were there clues that were significant back then, whose significance I overlooked?" The fact of the matter is that there will always be clues or pieces of evidence that we will overlook, because their significance is unknown to us, for they can only be understood in light of what lies ahead, which of course is unknown to us. We need to be aware that at every present moment, our ability to predict is severely limited, because the possible significance of each piece of evidence in the complex network of evidence before us is opaque and thus uncertain. That opacity disappears as we look back (hindsight is 20/20, as they say).

I might have learned from one experience or two in the past, but the future could have unfolded differently, and I would have learned something else entirely; moreover, there is so much more to learn, so many factors that I am not aware of, some of which I will eventually become aware, and some of which I might never become aware. Thus, it seems to me that the idea that learning from experience is some kind of asymptotic phenomenon in which we gradually get closer to perfecting our ability to learn from the past so that we are more able to accurately predict what will happen in the future is ultimately an illusion. If it were not an illusion, we should grow more confident in our intuitions and predictions as we age; I would argue that it is wiser that we become less confident.

The Murder of Dorothy May Donovan

I often use the story of the murder of Dorothy Donovan to illustrate a case in which it appears highly unlikely that the accused is innocent, but who in the end turns out to be so. She was 70 years old when she was found stabbed to death in her home. Nothing at all was missing from the home, and she had not been sexually assaulted. She had one son, Charles Holden, for whom she took out an insurance policy; he was the sole beneficiary.

The police took Charles in for questioning. He claimed that at around midnight on June 22, 1991, while leaving a Hardee's restaurant, a black man approached and asked if he could get a ride to the hospital, for his sister was having a baby. Initially, Charles said no, because he wasn't going very far—he only lived a few blocks away. After some pressure, however, he changed his mind and gave the man a lift. Shortly thereafter, Charles stopped at an intersection (in Delaware, just outside of Harrington) and told him this is as far as he can drive him. The hitchhiker got angry and started attacking him. Charles said he opened the door, got out and ran. The hitchhiker grabbed a screwdriver from the floor of the truck and ran after Charles, and the fight continued at the intersection. Charles stopped and agreed to take the man to where he wanted to go, but as the hitchhiker made his way around to the passenger side, Charles jumped in, locked the door, and drove off. The hitchhiker tried to run after him, but he soon gave up.

Charles did not want to turn and proceed home, which was half a mile from where he'd left the hitchhiker, in case he would recognize the truck in the driveway and possibly take revenge, so he continued to drive around. Finally, he returned to his trailer, which was beside his mother's house, but he noticed someone lurking about who looked like the hitchhiker. So, he decided not to pull into the driveway; instead, he called the police from a local pay phone. An officer came and went with him to his trailer and then next door to his mother's house (Dorothy Donovan). They saw that the back door window had been broken and there was blood inside the house. They proceeded up the stairs to Dorothy's bedroom and found her lying dead; she'd been stabbed to death.

The facts at this point are that nothing was stolen from the house, so we can infer with relative certainty that this was not a robbery. She was not sexually assaulted, and Charles refused to take a polygraph. What motive could anyone other than Charles have for killing this woman? And what is the likelihood that a hitchhiker would eventually turn down the right street and, out of all the houses to choose from, find Charles' mother's house, break in and kill her in retaliation for not being given a lift to the hospital? How would he know who she is and where she lives? And why would he do so? In revenge for not being given a lift further up the road? The probabilities are extremely low. Moreover, Dorothy Donavan recently took out an accidental death insurance policy and Charles was the sole beneficiary, and he needed money to pay back his debts.

The forensic team found a bloody palm print on the stair railing, which did not match Charlie's palm print. Moreover, witnesses at the Hardee's confirmed that there was indeed a hitchhiker. Finally, the DNA evidence did not match Charles.

Although the evidence confirming parts of Charles' story began to favor him, the narrative was still rather difficult to believe (improbable). And so authorities began to speculate that perhaps Charles hired someone to kill his mother. Perhaps the hitchhiker was the hired killer.

15 years later, a DNA match finally surfaced. The killer was Gilbert Cannon of Delmar, MD. He was high on cocaine at the time when he got a lift from Charles Holden, and he said to police that he selected that particular house owned by Dorothy Donovan because it was the first house he could find that appeared to be vacant. He had no idea that the woman who surprised him was Charles' mother.

The police, understandably, thought the story was ludicrous. So too do students, upon hearing it for the first time. But was it really? When we don't know the outcome and all we're given are the facts in evidence and the prior probabilities, it seems highly unlikely. But after knowing the outcome, that is, in hindsight, it begins to appear more likely. The account is a clear and coherent narrative, and it appears to have greater probability when seen in the rear view mirror, so to speak. Before knowing what actually took place, the story seems too outlandish to be true, after knowing what actually took place, it appears too outlandish to be false. It is tempting to conclude: "We should have known better". We can well imagine Charles regretting not taking the man further up the road, to exactly where he wanted to go. He was thoughtful enough to infer the possibility that the hitchhiker could turn down his street, recognize the truck, and commit further violence. His decision not to pull in the driveway right away was prudent; but there are limits to what we are able to predict.

We tend to forget the opacity that characterizes the initial state of affairs; and so we regard our judgment or decision as a mistake, more serious and blameworthy than it is in reality. We have an unrealistic perception of the gravity of the error. That forgetfulness of the initial opacity allows us to perpetuate the illusion that we are more able to accurately predict than we really are, and so we continue to make predictions with confidence.

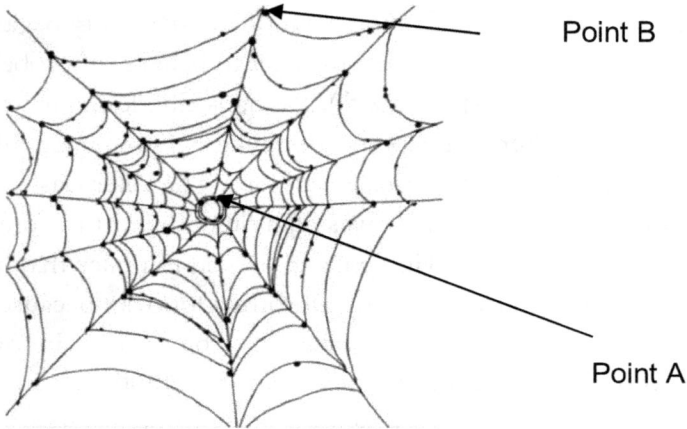

Point B

Point A

    The opacity that characterizes the beginning of an investigation, or an ordinary inferential judgment, is much like the web of a spider. Consider Point A the initial point of an investigation, or the starting point of an ordinary inference. You witness a particular behavior, and you want to make an inference towards a hypothesis that will best explain the behavior or piece of evidence (the consequent), which is represented by Point B. Note all the possible avenues that one can take to get to Point B starting from Point A.

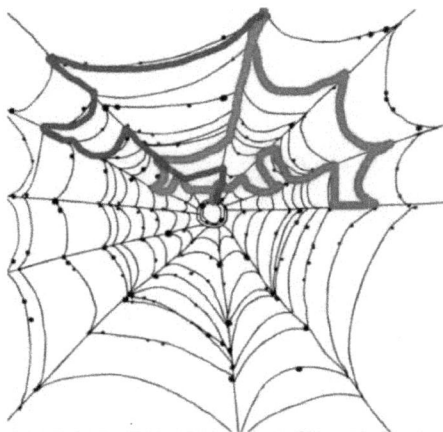

A person might be devious, or he might simply be immature, or he might have simply had a bad day, etc. Note that the web has 12 possible lines or avenues that converge in the center; but there are more than 12 possible avenues to get to a particular point, such as point B (more than 12 possible antecedents of the consequent). For there are small pathways connecting the lines or avenues, lanes which become wider as we climb up the web. I can take Point A as my initial avenue, and the simplest route that can "explain" point B is linear (straight north). But there are a number of possible turns that could have been made, in other words, there are a number of possible routes that can account for the evidence at Point B. My previous experience (blue) taught me a number of things about a certain kind of behaviour (B); but that in no way entails that behind this same behaviour is the same series of antecedents that led up to it in the previous case. I am tempted to make an inference that this time around, the route traced out in blue will explain Point B. But that is a mistake. It is possible, but it is not necessarily the case. This time around I may discover that another set of antecedents has led to the same place (purple or red).

After I finally discover the truth that explains the evidence, the opacity that characterized our initial state of affairs vanishes somewhat, and if we were correct in our inference, we tend to attribute far greater probability to the possibility after the fact than it had at the beginning.

This is hindsight bias.

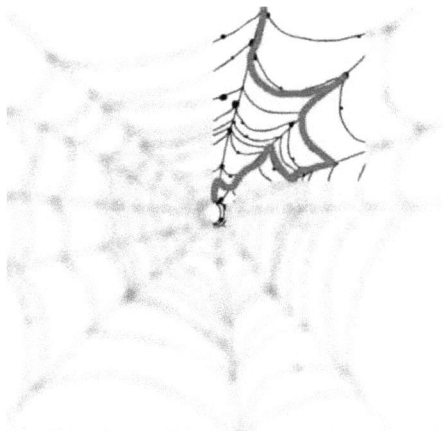

When I get to the end and look back, I see the route I took; it has more density, it is more vivid, and all the previous alternatives fade from memory. If I were required to provide a number that represents the probability that this particular route accounts for the evidence, my estimate would be much higher than what I would have estimated it to be at the beginning. Why? I've forgotten about the other possible alternatives. In light of new information, I offer a new probability, i.e., 90%. In actual fact, however, there was great opacity at the beginning. If we were wrong in our prediction, our error fades from memory; if we were right, we tend to take credit for it, as if we were able to determine the probability at the start. Our inference is often a matter of luck, unless of course we have a tremendous reservoir of experience behind us.

Sherlock Holmes stories might very well contribute this defect. Contrary to Holmes, his reasoning is not at all a matter of deduction, but induction. Moreover, his inductions are quite unrealistic; for there are far more possible alternatives that can explain a given piece of evidence, such as mud on a shoe, than the one Holmes quickly settles upon. In reality, inference is never obvious, and crime often takes years to solve. The hindsight bias is operative because Doyle is writing fiction; he possesses the ending, he knows the outcome; the reader does not. And so the reader is hoodwinked. Doyle puts himself in the reader's shoes, knowing that there are many possible alternatives or hypotheses that explain a piece of evidence, but he has Holmes declare one alternative with great confidence, lending the illusion that his inference had far greater probability than it would in reality; thus, the reader feels intellectually deficient next to the brilliant Sherlock Holmes. We live the hindsight bias, but it is the hindsight bias that makes Sherlock Holmes much more fascinating to read.

In the end, hindsight bias keeps us from learning from our mistakes, for it tends to keep us from re-evaluating our capacity to make accurate predictions. It keeps us from coming to a deeper appreciation of the limitations that sense perception imposes upon human intelligence.

Survivorship Bias

To illustrate what is meant by survivorship bias, consider the probability of flipping a coin five heads in a row: P(HHHHH). There is a 1 in 32 probability of doing so, which is rather low. But as a thought experiment, let's take a classroom of 32 students and get them to flip a coin. All those who flip heads are allowed to live; those who flip tails will be shot. Once we've eliminated those who flipped tails, around half, we flip once again. 8 more students are shot. We do this a third time, and a fourth, and finally a fifth time. One student is left standing.

He alone can write about the experience, and he can come up with any narrative he wants, theological or otherwise, to "explain" the amazing achievement of flipping five heads in a row. But the narrative explains nothing. It is a statistical phenomenon, and those who are able to challenge his narrative are dead.

If he is foolish enough to believe his narrative, we can visit another classroom, load the gun, and do it all again. This time around, however, I'm willing to bet against our survivor.

Examples in real life include stories, for example, of a school whose test scores continue to improve every year. Should the principal receive an award? Not necessarily. More information is needed. It could be that the dropout rate is high, and for a number of reasons. The standards might be so high—unreasonably high—that average or below average students cannot keep up; they begin to "fall through the cracks". Thus, we can have a school of very poor and uncommitted teachers who can only teach those students who essentially can and do teach themselves. The inference is made, namely, that this is a great school: "Just look at those test scores" or "look at the quality of those students". A narrative is often constructed to explain the phenomenon. But this is the narrative fallacy; for it may be nothing more than survivorship bias. The school down the road may have lower test scores, but it might also be a better school, that is, a school that provides a better education and has a more dedicated staff of teachers. It just has more low achieving students, who bring down the average. Bringing down the average, however, is not the same as bringing down the quality of education.

40 *Is Everything We Say Biased?*

The word "bias" is from the French word *biais*, "slant", or "slope". An incline is slanted. A person who is biased leans in a particular direction. Take politics as an example, a journalist who "leans" left is biased to the left, a journalist who "leans" right is biased to the right.

So what exactly does it mean to say that everything we say is biased? Let's assume for a moment that this is true; everything, regardless of the truth claim, is said within the framework of a bias, an inclination, a slant or angle. What exactly is being claimed here? Does it mean that we simply cannot trust what anyone says, because it lacks objectivity? Does the claim "everything we say is biased" include the claim itself?

If it is true that absolutely everything we say is biased and there's no escaping it, then the statement is a truism. Sure, everything we say is biased; now let's get on with the real task of determining whether what I am about to argue regarding this historical point or that moral claim is true or not.

If it means that we simply cannot trust what anyone says, because it lacks objectivity, then we have to ask how it is possible to achieve objectivity. How can I escape from my own subjectivity in order to acquire an unbiased grasp of what it is I am trying to understand? The problem, however, is that I cannot escape from my subjectivity. An object of knowledge is only such in relation to a knowing subject. Subject and object are correlative terms. Moreover, there is a two-fold mode of knowing in the human person: sensation (which we share in common with brute animals), and intellection. "Nothing is in the intellect that is not first in the senses"; thus all knowledge begins in sensation, but ends in intellection, that is, in the apprehension of simple universal concepts, which when combined become judgments that are either true or false (i.e., all men are rational), and which in turn become premises to syllogisms which end in a conclusion (i.e., therefore, John is rational).

What this means ultimately is that human knowledge participates in the limitations of sense perception. We gradually come to understand the natures of things through their activity (we observe how a chemical reacts, or how an animal behaves, etc.). Our knowledge of the nature of a thing is not instantaneous, but gradual. Moreover, we only see the world through a particular vantage point. If you look out the window of the classroom every day, you become familiar with the neighborhood from a particular angle; you don't see it from the south of where you are, looking north; someone else does, namely the one who lives in that house over yonder. As a result, you see things that she might not, while she sees things that you might not.

Similarly, someone growing up under an oppressive regime will experience freedom here in Canada much differently than the spoiled child who was raised in freedom and privilege. Both are biased, that is, both see the world from an angle (a slant). And so, it is simply not possible to see the world from an unbiased perspective. To do so, one would have to be an angel, an immaterial substance of a rational nature - or God.

Does that mean, however, that it is no longer possible to say anything that is simply true? Of course not. In fact, it is often the case that a bias is exactly what one needs in order to be able to finally see the truth. How many people thought a certain way when they were young, but changed years later after more life experience? How many of us were highly critical of certain people, like our own parents, when we were young adolescents, but upon experiencing the difficulties of parenting our own children, came to the realization that "I had no idea what I was talking about back then"? What happened? We began to see parenting from a different angle, from a different vantage point, that is, with a different slant, namely, from the angle of a parent with a host of responsibilities, fears and uncertainties, that were simply absent in childhood. That "angle" or slant (bias) opened up a whole new world that initially we had no idea existed. Only within that framework was it possible to finally understand our parents' behaviour.

St. Thomas Aquinas speaks of two kinds of moral knowledge: scientific and connatural. A morally good man who never read a book or took a course on ethics can, however, possess moral knowledge by a kind of connaturality (or knowledge through inclination). This means that he or she knows the right course of action in a given circumstance through an interior "leaning". She knows from within, for she is inclined to choose the morally noble course of action because she possesses the virtues. This is what Aquinas is referring to in the following: "Now rectitude of judgment is twofold: first, on account of perfect use of reason, secondly, on account of a kind of connaturality with the matter about which one has to judge. Thus, about matters of chastity, a man who has learnt the science of morals judges rightly through inquiry by reason, while he who has the habit of chastity judges rightly of such matters by a kind of connaturality."

Consider an Olympic figure skating or gymnastics competition. To the rest of us who are not skaters, the competitors all look equally skilled, but if the judge was a former skater or gymnast, he or she will see obvious grades of perfection among the competitors. The judge correctly judges of the quality of each athlete by a kind of connaturality; he or she knows "from within", for he or she is athletic, thus has acquired the skill or quality of being a skater or gymnast, and possessing that quality from within enables him or her to judge rightly concerning matters pertaining to that specific sport. So too, a person who has become musical will be able to judge the performance of a piece much better than one who is not at all musical, and a person who is a skilled artist will be able to judge a work of art much better than one who is not at all artistic.

Thus, in some cases at least, it turns out that bias is really the only way to objectivity (truth). An unbiased observer would make a lousy judge of music, or art, or gymnastics, and a person lacking the virtues (which are inclinations or biases), such as a criminal, would make a lousy judge of moral character.

It is not bias that blinds the intellect, but the wrong bias that impedes right judgment. We wouldn't have the mother of one of the competitors judge the competition, because often we see what we want to see; a mother, for example, might not see the flaws in her daughter's performance. She has the wrong bias for judging a gymnastics competition. Love for her daughter does not equip her to judge a sport, but it does enable her to judge a host of other things regarding the child (i.e., how best to speak to him/her in this or that situation, what the most fitting Christmas present would be, etc.).

So too, who best to teach a subject like Church history? Someone whose ruling passion is anti-Catholicism? Or someone who loves the Church? The answer to this question is not all that simple. The one who has no love for Catholics might be more willing to look at the sins of the Church throughout the centuries; and so his presentation of Church history might be more complete than, say, the one who simply cannot look objectively at the difficult facts. But it is also true that the one who despises Catholicism might not be willing to look more deeply into the causes and conditions of those difficult facts for fear of discovering what he would rather not discover, and that the one who loves the Church is more willing to dig more deeply into the mire to better grasp the facts of history. Both have a bias, and that is inevitable, but it is not always clear which bias is acting as an impediment and which one is acting as a channel of a more complete knowledge.

An honest scholar is one who loves truth more than he loves himself and is one who has become aware of his biases—as far as that is humanly possible. He is one who will allow the right biases to take him more deeply into the complexities of the discussion in order to find the treasure he's looking for, and he will not allow the wrong biases, his own bigotries perhaps, to keep him from listening to those who can open him up to a world that he otherwise would not have known.

What all this suggests, it seems to me, is that Aristotle was right when he said that it is not possible to acquire the intellectual virtues without first possessing the moral virtues, such as honesty, which is a part of justice. He must have been advanced in years to have had such an insight.

41 Is the Falsification Principle Falsifiable?

A theory is genuinely scientific if and only if the theory is falsifiable. Observational predictions that confirm a hypothesis do not prove the hypothesis, because in principle, other hypotheses might also account for the same evidence. It is disconfirmatory evidence, that is, evidence that is incompatible with a theory that definitively proves a theory false; thus, in this light, there is a fundamental uncertainty that accompanies the scientific method. Karl Popper, who first proposed the falsification principle, writes: "…every scientist who claims that his theory is supported by experiment or observation should be prepared to ask himself the following question: Can I describe any possible results of observation or experiment which, if actually reached, would refute my theory? If not, then my theory is clearly not an empirical theory. For if all conceivable observations agree with my theory, then I cannot be entitled to claim of any particular observation that it gives empirical support to my theory. Or in short, only if I can say how my theory might be refuted, or falsified, can I claim that my theory has the character of an empirical theory."[41]

The question whether the falsification principle is itself falsifiable is, I would argue, rooted in a confusion between two distinct areas of knowledge, namely science and philosophy. The falsification principle is a principle that follows upon the very logic of the scientific method. In other words, it is the result of a certain kind of inquiry, that is, a certain kind of reasoning. The kind of reasoning that allows us to determine that the falsification principle is a sound principle is different

---

[41] Karl Popper, *The Myth of the Framework*, New York: Routledge, 1994. 88. He also writes: "Agreement between theory and observation should count for nothing unless the theory is testable, and unless the agreement is found as the result of serious attempts to test it. But testing a theory means trying to find its weak spots. It means trying to refute it. And a theory is testable only if it is (in principle) *refutable*….the decisive function of observation and experiment in science is criticism. Observation and experiment cannot establish anything conclusively, for there is always the possibility of a systematic error through systematic misinterpretation of some fact or other. But observation and experiment certainly play an important part in the critical discussion of scientific theories. Essentially, they help us to eliminate the weaker theories. In this way they lend support, though only for the time being, to the surviving theory – that is, to the theory which has been severely tested but not refuted." *Ibid.*, 89-90

from scientific reasoning. The former is deductive and philosophical; the latter is inductive and investigative. The former is the fruit of an inquiry about science; science, however, does not concern itself with science, it concerns itself with the causes of cancer, or the reason one is hearing voices, or why wood burns, etc. In other words, the falsification principle is not a scientific hypothesis. The reasoning that leads us to this principle occurs on a higher level of abstraction. Inquiry that takes place on the first level of abstraction, on the contrary, is inductive, and inductive conclusions are underdetermined, that is, they lack the force of necessity and are thus only probable. That is why hypotheses need to be tested. But the philosophy of science, or the logic of science, is not the result of reasoning on the first level of abstraction. Logic is not empirical science.

If you come down with the flu, you will have a fever. The doctor took your temperature and found that you do not have a fever. Thus, the antecedent has been falsified, that is, you do not have the flu. But this is a conditional syllogism of the form of **denying the consequent**, and that yields a certainty, not a probability. **Affirming the consequent**, however, yields only a probability. Thus, if you come down with the flu, you will have a fever. The doctor took your temperature and found that you indeed have a fever. He will **not** conclude that you have the flu; he knows better. Those not trained in medicine often do not and are wont to conclude that you have the flu. Such a conclusion, however, is invalid; it is not necessarily true, only possibly true. Therefore, the hypothesis that you have the flu needs to be tested further. When investigating a hypothesis, we look for evidence that falsifies it, because evidence that confirms the hypothesis does not prove the hypothesis, because another hypothesis might very well account for the same evidence, or in this case, another disease might have one of the same symptoms (i.e., fever). Thus, affirming the consequent is simply a matter of corroborating a hypothesis, which strengthens it, but does not prove it. To falsify a hypothesis is to discover a consequent that can be denied, and thus the antecedent or hypothesis can be validly denied. In this case, we are certain that the antecedent or hypothesis is false.

The falsification principle is rooted in the very laws of logic (the rules of inference), and so the falsification principle is not falsifiable, any more than first principles are falsifiable. But that does not mean they are assumptions. To demand that they be falsifiable in order to count as knowledge is to demand that the pre-scientific knowledge that is the condition for the possibility of science be reduced to or treated as scientific knowledge.

42 Thoughts on Randomness and Predictability

Matter is not only the principle of corruption or mutability, it is the principle of variety or multiplicity. It is matter that allows a form to be multiplied into a variety of individual instances. For example, there is only one "humanness" and one "triangularity", but matter allows that form to be multiplied into a multiplicity of humans or triangles, all having the same form, but each one a unique instance of that form.

Moreover, matter is that which renders things opaque to scientific scrutiny; for there is nothing opaque about a geometric triangle, but when matter takes the form of a triangle, there is now an almost infinite number of possible instantiations that bring with them a host of unpredictable factors, at least initially unpredictable. For example, a triangular metal sign will rust, unlike the triangle that exists as an idea in the mind of the mathematician. After a time, we expect it to rust under certain conditions, for we have learned something about the nature of metal from experience, but I did not predict that it would cut my hand when I picked it up; now I know to be more careful next time. A wooden box rots; a cement pyramid does not last as long as one made of steel, etc. Understanding material natures is a matter of induction, unlike mathematics, which is a matter of deduction. In the real world, we need more than an understanding of a thing's nature or essence, because a real material thing is far more complex than its form would suggest.

Now, **chance** is the intersection of two lines of action ordered to an end. In a world of material substances that act for ends (for every agent acts for an end), there is an infinite variety of possible intersections, and none in particular are foreseeable. I mow my lawn one day and an apple falls from the tree onto my head. That is a chance happening, an intersection of two lines of action ordered to an end (my act is ordered towards cutting the lawn, the fall of the apple is ordered toward the ground). My neighbor decides to mow his lawn around the same time; we did not plan that; it is a chance occurrence. I did not know it was going to rain; that was not part of my plan to walk to the mailbox; nor was it part of my plan of action to slip on the mud on the way to the mailbox. It was part of my friend's plan to marry a man, but a man is a rational animal, and so there is so much about the person she married that she had not predicted—much that is good, and much that is not that pleasant to have to deal with. It is his material nature that gives rise to the unforeseeable. Human beings, because they are living sentient creatures, have sensitive appetites, and the eleven basic emotions arise from those appetites, and appetite follows upon knowledge, or what we might believe initially to be knowledge. Very often our inferences are wrong, but they give rise nevertheless to certain emotions, like fear, sorrow, and a mix of despair, or possibly anger, etc. Those emotions can incline us to a sudden course of action that makes life very difficult for us and for others, something we had not anticipated. So too, wrong inferences can give rise to joy, but a false joy, and the elation can incline us to a course of action that is destructive in the long term—and normally none of us deliberately plan our own destruction.

There is a complexity of factors that render others, including ourselves, impossible to fully understand and their behaviour almost impossible to predict. And so, although I hired this person to work for me, his mood disorder was not part of my plan. It was unforeseeable; it was a matter of chance. In fact, it was not included in his plan either, which included working for me for the summer. He had no idea that he was genetically disposed to a mental illness and that an accidental fire at home would give rise to a degree of stress that would act as a trigger to the illness. He did not see it coming; no one did. But his trip to the hospital resulted in a host of chance occurrences, intersections that were also unforeseeable.

Matter brings so much variety and complexity to the universe, and in doing so it makes it so unamenable to prediction. I know what walking to the corner store involves, but I cannot factor in that which I simply cannot see, and there are a myriad of possible outcomes that always escape me. I may pull a muscle on the way; I may get hit by an SUV crossing the light; I might witness a hit and run or a robbery and a shooting; I might be temporarily but adversely affected to the clerk's mood and conduct towards me, etc.

Form or essence, the intelligible content of things and actions, allows a certain degree of predictability. We all have the same nature, a rational nature, and so I predict that you will ask a host of questions, purchase things at the lowest price possible, etc. An apple tree is a certain kind of thing that can be studied, and in doing so, we come to grasp the nature of the thing and how it acts; thus, we can predict that it will begin to grow apples in the spring and that they will begin to fall off the tree in the Fall. In fact, it is through the activity of things that we gradually come to grasp their natures with increasing precision; i.e., I know more about the nature of man than I did as a toddler. Initially, I know something is a being (thing), then a living thing, and on closer inspection I see it is an animal, but it is a different kind of animal than the ones I am used to. It behaves differently; what it does is similar to what other animals do, but in other ways it is unique. I find no evidence of rational activity, however, so I cannot yet infer intelligence or the ability to reason. In other words, I observe no activity that cannot be explained by an appeal to external and internal sensation and sense appetite, etc. Nevertheless, there is much about the things I understand that evades my ability to predict; for I am told that these animals usually live to a certain age, but this one might die tomorrow, as a result of an unforeseeable intersection of two or more lines of action (the activity of a virus and its own act of breathing, etc.).

Chance writ large is randomness, and this randomness is very different in texture than the ludic randomness[42] that is employed to illustrate basic statistical concepts (i.e., games, such as dice, or coin flipping, or the roulette wheel, etc.). A pair of dice has to be crafted carefully so as to be free of bias; so too a coin and a roulette wheel. Still, the possibilities of a coin flip are so numerous that we are left with a space of uncertainty and thus a probability (i.e., P(.5)), and a number of flips provides an intelligible pattern, a bell curve. But reality is much larger than the Gaussian bell curve, that is, reality is much larger than a

---

[42] Taleb, *op. cit.*, Chapter 9, "The Ludic Fallacy, or the Uncertainty of the Nerd".

mathematical model. A controlled experience like a game of roulette is Gaussian, but reality is not cut and crafted so carefully. Probability is much larger than the small 'r' randomness (probability) associated with gambling. The ludic fallacy identifies the two, confusing small 'r' randomness with chance writ large, or large 'R' randomness. Nature, as far as I can tell, does not produce unbiased objects.[43]

History is a vast network of intersections, that is, random occurrences. That is why we need to be careful with historical narratives; they lend the impression that history is much simpler and neater than it really is.

Consider the expression: "You are on the wrong side of history". I've been accused of that, and so I have begun to wonder what it means. Does it mean that history will judge the position I take on an issue—or action (whatever it is)—to have been wrong? And does it not presuppose that we are able to say where history is going? Where it is headed? Are we able to predict to that extent? How is it that a person who cannot even foresee what his own predicament will be in a week's time can somehow predict where history is headed? And what is the criterion by which we claim that someone is on the wrong side? Is it a matter of numbers? If there is a majority on "this side", does this mean necessarily that it is the right side? Does history always move in the right direction? Does it always move in the direction of progress? Are our judgments in hindsight always right? Was Joe Kennedy on the wrong side of history? He was not in favor of opposing Hitler. One could say he was on the wrong side of history, but he, as well as many others, did not foresee that. And what if history turned out differently? What if Hitler succeeded? What, then, would constitute the right side of history? And what role does hindsight bias play in this expression?

---

[43] Taleb, *op. cit.*, Chapter 15, "The Bell Curve, That Great Intellectual Fraud". See also Shankar Vedantam. "Put Away The Bell Curve: Most Of Us Aren't 'Average'". *NPR* (May 3, 2012). Retrieved from http://www.npr.org/2012/05/03/151860154/put-away-the-bell-curve-most-of-us-arent-average. See also Josh Bersin. "The Myth Of The Bell Curve: Look For The Hyper-Performers". *Forbes* (February 19, 2014). Retrieved from http://www.forbes.com/sites/joshbersin/2014/02/19/the-myth-of-the-bell-curve-look-for-the-hyper-performers/

43 Thoughts on Inferencing, Narratives, and the Need to Explain

Daniel Kahneman asks readers what to make of the following: "A study of new diagnoses of kidney cancer in the 3,141 counties of the United States reveals a remarkable pattern. The counties in which the incidence of kidney cancer is lowest are mostly rural, sparsely populated, and located in traditionally Republican states in the Midwest, the South, and the West."[44]

Almost immediately, we begin to speculate on the possible causes, and our inferences bear upon everything from cleaner air or water, a better diet, to a simpler lifestyle. But then he asks us to consider that counties in which the incidence of kidney cancer is highest are mostly rural, sparsely populated, and located in traditionally Republican states in the Midwest, the South, and the West.[45] Immediately, we speculate on the probable causes, everything from alcohol, excessive tobacco, lack of good medical care, etc.

Other similar scenarios illustrate the same tendency within us; for example, about as many boys as girls are born in hospitals every year. Many babies are born every week at City General Hospital, but in Rural County Hospital, only a few babies are born every week. A normal week is one where between 45% and 55% of the babies are female. An unusual week is one where more than 55% are girls, or more than 55% are boys. This year, unusual weeks (64% boys one week; 37% boys another week, etc.) were more common at Rural County Hospital than at City General. Why would that be?[46]

Typically, we begin to speculate on the possible causes and we soon begin formulating hypotheses, in an attempt to "make sense" out of these unusual phenomena. But there are no causes that explain these results; these are statistical phenomena. The more frequent the instances or the larger the sample, the more we expect to see a *regression*

---

[44] Kahneman, *op. cit.*, Chapter 10 "The Law of Small Numbers".
[45] *Ibid.*
[46] Hacking, *op. cit.*, 192.

to the mean. In other words, these are instances of the law of small numbers. A higher instance of kidney cancer in rural counties is to be expected, because of lower numbers (sparse population); so too a lower instance of kidney cancer is to be expected in more sparsely populated areas—in light of the law of small numbers, that is.

In order to understand this better, imagine that I deposit 30 blue marbles in an urn, along with 25 green marbles, 20 white marbles, 15 yellow, and 10 red. We mix them up thoroughly to achieve a uniform distribution. If I were to reach in and grab a sample, I expect to have in my hand a majority of blue marbles, followed by a smaller number of green marbles, a still smaller number of white marbles, etc. But that is not what always occurs. Sometimes I have more green marbles than blue, or more yellow marbles than white, or more red than yellow. I certainly do not always end up with a sample containing 30 % blue marbles, 25% green, 20% white, etc. There is no cause that explains these unusual distributions; it is simply the law of small numbers. As I continue to draw marbles, record their numbers, and replace them in order to draw and record again, the more we see a regression to the mean, for example, the more the blue marbles will average out to 30%, the green to 25%, etc.

These statistical experiments are important because they highlight our natural tendency to think in terms of causes, or more specifically, to attribute causes where there are none. Causes do explain, for science is a knowledge of things through their proper causes. Moreover, understanding, which is achieved when we grasp the cause, is emotionally satisfying, and many of us, in particular the young, are uncomfortable with uncertainty and "not-knowing"; it is more comfortable, for example, to drive on a clear and sunny day than it is to drive in the fog or in the dark. But the above problems are not causally relevant, only statistically relevant.

This desire for explanation has to be carefully monitored. In other words, we have to become aware of it, because the desire for explanation is often so immoderate that we very quickly settle for explanations that are emotionally satisfying, that "feel right", that "make sense", but are not necessarily true. As was said above, all that is true makes sense, but not all that makes sense is true. That is why simple ideologies are very attractive. They appear to explain, to make sense out of reality that is too complex to fully comprehend, and following upon an ideology that we have embraced are plenty of confirming instances (confirmation bias). However, there is good reason to be suspicious of ideological narratives that are clear, simple, and coherent, and that satisfy us emotionally because they help "make sense" of a complex world.

The more abstract the principle, the simpler it is, and the more certainty we possess. For example, the most abstract principle is non-contradiction (nothing can both be and not be at the same time and in the same respect), or the principle of identity (each being is what it is), as well as the principle of causality (from nothing comes nothing), etc. But as we move to the level of the concrete particular, things become much more complicated and varied, not to mention much more uncertain. This is what bothered Rene Descartes, who was a mathematical physicist and who was impatient with philosophy's many schools of thought; he desired a philosophy that was as certain as mathematics, neatly deduced from absolutely certain principles and which would result in universal agreement. He never achieved what he set out to achieve.

The more we approach the realm of the concrete particular, the more we move towards the realm of the probable. What we claim is "knowledge" on this level is very often and for the most part, on closer inspection, not really knowledge at all, but belief, conjectures, a series of inferences that have crystalized into an intellectual framework in which aspects of the world appear a certain way, and in which other aspects remain hidden from view, inferences that are rooted in basic induction biases of which, for the most part, we are unaware, inferences constructed on the basis of first impressions and under the influence of the latter (the halo effect)[47] and inferences constructed on

---

[47] See Kahneman, op. cit., "Exaggerated Emotional Coherence (Halo Effect)" in Chapter 7.

the basis of specific memory associations that enable us to "make sense" out of our world. The anti-corporate narrative, for example, might make a certain amount of sense out of things, but it is not necessarily a narrative true to the facts.

That is why we need to be very careful of narratives that propose clear and simple dichotomies, such as "corporations bad/union good"; or "Israel bad/Palestinians good", or "the rich are bullies/the poor are victims"; "establishment bad/rebels good"; "conservatives bad/liberals good"; "liberals bad/conservatives good", etc.

On a very abstract level, truth is clear, precise, and certain; it is also simple. It is simple because it is divested of matter and its contingencies. The realm of the particular is fraught with contingencies, and this makes clarity much more difficult, and it usually renders simple dichotomies impossible. Yet simple dichotomies are emotionally satisfying, because they "make sense" out of complex realities. That is why those who embrace an ideological narrative, such as the anti-Israel narrative, will refuse to adjust their view when evidence is made available that the reality of the situation is far more complex than their narrative would suggest. They defend the construct for psychological reasons, but the truth of the matter is far more complex, messy, and replete with ambiguity and uncertainty. Truth cannot be nicely slotted into an ideological construct, without shaving off so many details and facts in the process; it is easier to make facts fit the theory, but that involves ignoring those facts and details that will not readily fit into the ideological narrative (ideological narratives always involve selection bias).

Moreover, confirming instances of a hypothesis and an observational prediction do not establish conclusively the hypothesis. Disconfirming instances do, however, conclusively disconfirm it, but we tend to ignore disconfirming instances, we don't see them, for we are so focused on confirming instances that the disconfirming instances lack significance or impact, sort of like missing the gorilla in the selective attention test.[48] I can become so prejudiced against the rich that I cannot see that their decisions to take risks and invest in up and coming entrepreneurs is actually a service to the common good of the civil community; all I see are actions motivated by greed. So too, the rockets launched into Israel are interpreted as acts of despair and powerlessness as opposed to murder and hate: "Please remember the children growing up in Sderot. And their anxious parents and grandparents. And of course their neighbours on the other side of the Gaza border, whose despair and powerlessness directs those rockets. They all cry out for our prayerful understanding."[49]

Simple narratives can do a great deal of harm. I remember counselling one person who'd lost everything and who was on the verge of a nervous breakdown, and who was told by his Baptist pastor that his wife was in hell and that his illness was due to diabolical possession. The reason is simple: it was either allow new evidence to disconfirm a "religious" ideological narrative (that in order to get to heaven, one must explicitly acknowledge Jesus as Savior and Lord), thus introducing into one's life uncertainty and less emotional complacency, or remain emotionally complacent and simply tell them the answer that makes life so much simpler, regardless of how that might affect him. Or, I tell others that corporations are greedy and indifferent to justice, and that they should never work for Walmart, because Walmart is a big corporation, and big corporations are bullies, and bullies are bad and have all the power. The disconfirming evidence that the fall of Blackberry provides is never allowed to enter into the picture. In short, we need to learn to deal with uncertainty and to think on the basis of principles, not ideological systems and coherent narratives that are prepackaged.

Uncertainty, however, can become a comfortable position too, in particular for those committed to an immoral lifestyle. Their love of uncertainty is nothing other than a fear of moral clarity and a conflict

---

[48] Christopher Chabris and Daniel Simons. *The Selective Attention Test* (1999). [Video file] Retrieved from http://www.theinvisiblegorilla.com/videos.html

[49] ZioNation – Progressive Zionism and Israel Web Log (August, 26 2007). Retrieved from http://www.zionism-israel.com/log/archives/00000408.html

of conscience. Again, what is genuinely uncertain, most people treat with the confidence of absolute certainty, but that which we can know with relative certainty, such as universal moral precepts, most people relegate to the realm of the perpetually ambiguous.

44 *A Note on Narrative Construction*

The narrative fallacy describes our tendency to weave a meaningful narrative between facts, a narrative that "makes sense" out of those facts, a narrative that is not necessarily "true to the facts", if you will; for there are too many facts missing. Thus, narrative construction is a kind of inferencing, and it is by virtue of its meaning, that is, its coherence and the causal relationships inserted between the facts, that we tend to infer that the narrative is far more probable than not.

At the end of a school year, I noticed that a student of mine has the same surname (an unusual name) as a student I taught the previous year, and because both were in the same program (IB), separated by only a year, I inferred relatively quickly that the two were siblings; for it has happened before that a brother and sister were in the same program, separated by only a year or two. Within this particular program, which is only a few years old, the frequency of two students with the same surname turning out to be siblings was higher than both turning out to be completely unrelated; hence, my inference that the two were siblings.

And so I imagined the older sibling coaching the younger one, informing her on what to expect for the following year, how to prepare for exams, what pitfalls to avoid, how to choose a good presentation topic, etc., and I imagined this discussion taking place around their kitchen table, etc. At the graduation, I actually went looking for the younger sibling, expecting her to be there watching her brother graduate, but she was nowhere to be seen. Later on, at the beginning of her final year, I asked her why she did not show up to her brother's graduation. She told me he's not her brother and that she's never spoken to him before.

From a statistical point of view, the unusual occurrence of two people with the same surname turning out to be siblings is to be expected in light of the fact that the program is relatively young. Over a period of ten years or so, however, the number of unrelated students having an identical surname will certainly outnumber related students, as it has done in the school at large (outside of this relatively new program). This is simply a case of the law of small numbers (i.e., unusual occurrences are more probable when numbers are low).

But notice the narrative I readily constructed, all on the basis of very scanty evidence. It was easy for me to believe that the two were siblings without any evidence because it was easy to imagine that the one student is in the program "because" the other was in the program. It is this "because" (the cause being) that lends credibility to the narrative. It is much more comfortable to have a meaningful narrative that "explains" a few facts in evidence than it was to have an enduring question mark in my mind; explanations give closure, unanswered questions leave doors open.

We engage in narrative construction all the time, but for the most part we are unaware of the fictional nature or low degree of probability of many of those narratives. Narrative construction has more to do with a need for closure, or meaning, than it does with the truth; narratives are part of our personal epistemic model through which we see and interpret the world; it is only later on that we eventually discover that aspects of that model are wrong, and if we are honest, we make revisions.

45 Models and their Constituent Parts

I believe one of the most important objectives for a young student of the theory of knowledge is to come to some understanding of where necessity applies and where it does not apply. Certitude is the result of seeing the necessity of a conclusion (it cannot not be true); if necessity is outside our grasp, we experience uncertainty, a degree of probability or perhaps plausibility (either high, low, or moderate). In other words, it is very important that we come to some appreciation of the scope of certainty and probability.

It is indefensible to categorically deny certitude; one would have to be certain that one cannot enjoy certainty, which is contradictory. However, it is safe to say *that most of what is in the mind* is characterized by a degree of uncertainty. Consider once again the following inference:

If p, then q
q
p

This is a standard inference people typically make, and it is invalid from a deductive point of view. The conclusion is not necessarily true, thus the conclusion is uncertain.

If a person has diabetes, then he will experience extreme fatigue.
The facts in evidence before us are that this person experiences extreme fatigue.
Therefore, he has diabetes.

The conclusion "makes sense", but this does not mean it is true (all that is true makes sense, but not all that makes sense is true). Because it makes sense, however, most people are inclined to treat the conclusion as true, as having necessity and thus as certain, and if the hypothesis (the antecedent) is an injustice, they will react with indignation (i.e., If the teacher is partial, he will give me a low mark; I received a low mark; therefore, he's partial).

What you will notice, if you carefully listen to people, is that they treat most of their inferences as certain, and they believe their anger is warranted (or their sadness, or fear, etc.). The conclusion, however, is only probable and needs to be tested, and tested again, and tested further. Science is a matter of formulating hypotheses in order to account for the evidence—it is inductive, a matter of inferencing to the best explanation—, which is why testing is a constituent part of the scientific method. Roger Bacon, one of the pioneers of the scientific method, wrote: "We scientists of the human spirit shall experiment, experiment, ever experiment." The inferences people make every day also need to be tested empirically in some way, but outside the lab, most people treat their impressions and inferences are true and certain if they "make sense".

A model is *that through which we interpret*, at any one time, the data of our experience. All of us are subject to a model; for we are "subjects" who know, who interpret the real. The objects of our knowledge never appear in the fullness of their objectivity. Becoming aware of this is very important, especially for the sake of social harmony, dialogue, and progress. The models through which we interpret the world and all that is in it are made up of a number of things, namely, first principles, reasoned conclusions, inferences, language, experience, and biases and specific interests. That may not be all, but let's consider these.

1. **First principles, both speculative and practical**. The starting points (principles) of all knowledge are self-evident and intuitively grasped. This means they are apprehended immediately. If I know anything at all, I first know, albeit pre-consciously, that **each being is what it is** (the principle of identity); thus, I know that **nothing can both be and not be at the same time and in the same respect**. As a result of knowing this, I know that **from nothing comes nothing**, thus **the effect cannot be greater than the cause** (a thing cannot give what it does not have). I also **know that "what a thing is" (essence) is really distinct from "whether or not it is" (existence)**; for I can

know "what a thing is" without thereby knowing whether or not it really exists. Again, I may not grasp this explicitly, but it is implicitly known (knowing "what" a woolly mammoth is does not tell me whether or not it is).

There are also a host of practical principles (goods) intuitively known, such as human life, knowledge of truth, contemplation of beauty, friendship, justice, marriage, integrity, etc. These are intelligible human goods that are the motivating principles of human action, sought for their own sake; for I know through self-knowledge that I am naturally inclined to them and that I seek them as ends in themselves.

2. **Reasoned conclusions**: The model through which I interpret the world I experience is also made up of reasoned conclusions, some of which are true, but many of which are incomplete, such as my own moral reasoning. Most people know, as a result of reasoning on the basis of intelligible human goods and the first principle of morality (good is to be done, evil is to be avoided) that one ought not to do to another that which one would not want another to do to oneself, or that one ought not to harm others, or one ought to act reasonably, etc. But most people do not think about the further implications of these principles, that is, how they apply specifically in medical or economic matters, for example. The result is that most people apply them inconsistently. We also reason incompletely on the basis of the first principles of speculative reason. We know that contradictories cannot be true at one and the same time, but we do not bother to draw out the further implications of this principle, in order to evaluate some of the contradictory or inconsistent viewpoints we might hold. A physicist might conclude that solidity is an illusion, because an atom is mostly empty space, and yet he takes cover when he hears gunshots coming from the ghetto.

3. **Inductive inferences and beliefs**: A large part of the model through which we interpret the real is made up of inductive inferences that begin with the evidence (the facts, the consequent, etc.) and proceed towards a hypothesis (the cause, the antecedent, the sufficient

reason for, etc.). Inferences have probability only, thus they are uncertain and need to be investigated further. However, over time, many of these inferences have gone unchallenged and so they have crystalized, like honey in a jar, into what appear to us as solid truths. It is out of that crystallization that arises the illusion of necessity, which in turn causes us to "feel" that our inferences are certain. They are, however, nothing more than inferences and beliefs possessing the same degree of probability as they had originally, unless of course our knowledge base has changed, in which case we immediately recognize their status as probable, and thus uncertain. Because no one has challenged those inferences—since we tend to associate with those who think just like us—, we become increasingly convinced that they must be true, otherwise they would have been refuted. It is very difficult to convince someone of a mistaken inference when he has believed it for so long; often there is too much that has been invested emotionally for some people to allow their model to undergo revision.

4. **Language**: The model through which we interpret the real is limited and shaped in large part by the language we speak. Language both frees us to think, but it also limits, for a language embodies a cultural *weltanschauung*. When we learn another language, we begin to see how differently a nation sees the world. Some languages make distinctions that are not made in English, and those distinctions open our eyes to the richness and many-sided character of a particular phenomenon, like love, or happiness, etc.

5. **Our own limited experiences**. Knowledge begins in sensation, and what is in the senses depends on where we are and "when" we are and how long we've been there. Our personal experiences have contributed to an emotional frame of mind, and those emotions influence how we see and interpret things. Feelings can be very misleading, but we rarely suspect they are misleading us. We tend to regard them as evidence that we've interpreted things correctly—which of course is far from being necessarily true. For example, I feel angry; therefore, I have been a victim of an injustice (i.e., my interpretation of what has happened cannot be mistaken, for it feels as if I am right). But

the emotions incline us to settle upon a particular alternative, that is, to make a particular inference, and that is the inference that is likely to make us feel better (i.e., many people want something to be angry at). This is where prejudices arise. Moreover, there are often feelings of loyalty behind the inferences we've made over the years, or feelings of fear, or the desire for pleasure, etc.

Our experiences occur in a particular place and time in the world, and that concrete situation gives rise to many problems, and science arises out of those problems. In other words, specific interests arise within a concrete historical situation, and those specific interests give rise to specific questions, which open up very limited avenues to explore. Usually, we ask questions within an already existing tradition, which involves a typical way of asking questions. Sometimes a person has a radically different interest and begins to ask very different questions, which give rise to a new avenue to explore and possibly a whole new way of looking at things.

6. **Biases**. A bias is a slant. We are often unaware of them, but they influence the way we reason. The result is our conclusions are not as objective as we might think. All of us are subject to an availability heuristic bias, and we are inclined to believe that "What You See Is All There Is" (WYSIATI). Yet there is so much you and I have not seen and experienced and more that we never will. There is hindsight bias, anchoring, selection bias, statistical illusions, regression to the mean, etc. There are, as well, slants or biases of a different sort: I have particular interests, as was said above, and I ask particular questions that interest me, and the types of questions I ask arise out of a tradition, that is, out of my experiences within a community (i.e., the scientific community, my religious community, the educational community, etc.). My questions are often limited to those scientific questions congruent with the tradition and specific pattern in which I have been trained to think for many years. The same is true for the philosophical questions I pose, the moral, theological, or economic questions, etc. The moment I ask questions rooted in a different tradition, questions that do not conform to the pattern with which I am

familiar, I begin to experiment with a new paradigm, a new model. I.e., what if the criminals I am interviewing are feeding me the answers they know I'm looking for? Could I be the victim of their cunning and manipulation? What if it turns out that I've held onto an assumption that needs to be re-examined, namely, the assumption that they've been the victim of a bad environment, as the psychological community has inferred and which I was taught throughout my training in psychology? Such questions led to a paradigm shift for one renowned forensic psychologist.[50]

Concluding Thoughts

If a person has been preoccupied with an area of knowledge involving a high level of abstraction, such as mathematics or metaphysics, etc., he may tend to overlook the degree of uncertainty that belongs to the kind of knowledge that arises out of the ordinary level of our day to day inductions. He may be habitually inclined to attribute the light of certainty and necessity to an area of knowledge involving a lower level of abstraction, such as economics or history, a certainty these areas of knowledge do not enjoy. The converse can also take place (i.e., the historian or scientist concludes that nothing is certain). There is always a blend of certainty and uncertainty in our knowledge, that is, there are many clouds in the sky of our intellect, and there is much light that permeates those clouds (the light of necessity); however, the clouds still cloud, even for a pilot who flies during the day.

The model through which we see and interpret the world around us needs to be subject to critical scrutiny on an ongoing basis. To stop doing this is to get old, and there are young people who have gotten old too soon, and there are old people who still have the heart of a child. The young adult tends to lack an awareness of his limits, for he has had less experience in being wrong than those older than he, and so

---

[50] Stanton Samenow. *Before It's Too Late: Why Some Kids Get Into Trouble—and What Parents Can Do About It.* New York: Three Rivers Press, 2001. See also Stanton Samenow, *Inside the Criminal Mind.* New York: Crown Publishers, 2004.

he tends to exude overconfidence, is high energy, and is often reckless. If he refuses to allow the vast complexity of reality to change him, he inevitably becomes an old dog that refuses to learn new tricks.

The extremes we need to avoid are relativism on the one hand, and absolutism on the other. The western world in particular has embraced relativism because it wants to do what it pleases, and every culture, including western culture, inclines towards absolutism because we have an aversion to opposition and find uncertainty uncomfortable.

46 Continued Thoughts on Inferencing

Years ago someone made a remark about a colleague of mine; it was an inference on the basis of what in the final analysis turns out to be very scanty evidence. The remark was that this particular colleague is probably gay. The evidence is that he is single and close to 40 years of age. In light of the fact that less than 2% of the population have a homosexual identity (1.7%) and that the only evidence upon which this inference was based is that the man is single and close to 40, the probability that he is gay is certainly under 10% –which means there is a 90% probability that the inference is wrong. Still, it was made with what appeared to be a 95% confidence level.

I am not surprised anymore at the epistemic arrogance and over-confidence that is at the root of such rapid and unfounded inferences as they bear upon a wide variety of areas; it is rather typical of most people today. What I wish to call attention to in this short reflection is the power such risky inferences possess. Despite the very low probability that it is true, the remark has affected the way I see this man. I have no problem with the prospect that a colleague of mine is gay, but despite the fact that I have no idea whether or not he is—and that I do have a very good idea that the probability is very low that he is—, every time I look at him, I do so in light of someone's inference; in other words, when I see him, I see a gay man. I have to make the effort to remind myself, every time I see him, that I really don't know that.

What is disconcerting is that I never made the inference, someone else did, and it was passed on to me by an intermediary who likely gave it more credence than I did; my point has nothing to do with homosexuality; it has to do with the power of those inferences that in part make up the model through which we see and interpret the world around us. Note the power of this single inference having very low probability; without my knowing—at least at first—, it has affected the way I see and interpret a particular human being. If the inference is wrong—which it probably is—, the casual remark was profoundly unfair; for it has contributed to and helped perpetuate a misunderstanding of another person.

The epistemic model through which we interpret the world is made up of more than a single inference; it is made up of a collection having various degrees of probability, many of which have crystallized into what appear to us as self-evident truths. They are anything but.

If the model through which we interpret the world around us was constituted solely of inductive inferences, we'd be in worse shape than we are in. Our models are also made up of deductions that have the force of necessity, an apprehension of first self-evident principles both speculative and practical, rich experiences, correctly reasoned conclusions, and the languages we speak. It is the light emanating from these sources that tends to *fool us into believing* that the world is less complex than it really is and that our inferences possess greater probability than they in fact possess. The totality of our experiences, however rich, is limited, as is the language in which we think and as are the implications of those first principles that we have drawn out through reason. Our models need to be revised and reformed till the day we die. Most people, I dare say, settle for the undisturbed complacency that accompanies the feeling of certainty, which is why the model through which their reality is filtered is fixed and unyielding.

47 *A Thought on Epistemic Conditions*

Every parent sees it in his son or daughter: an almost complete lack of gratitude. But a good parent understands it, because she remembers when she was an adolescent and recalls her own ingratitude. It took years for her to see what her parents knew at the time, namely how lucky she was. The expression is "reality set in"; she came to see how difficult life really is and how hard she must work to give her children what they need, but her children do not see that—for the most part, at least—, and they are not able to see it. Everything comes easy to them; life is easy. They don't have the epistemic conditions needed to understand what it took their parents to get to the place where they are now. They, the parents, have those epistemic conditions; they have a wide enough experience to understand what their children simply cannot understand at this point.

Although every good parent understands this, the epistemological implications seem to be lost on them because they are not philosophers and, understandably, do not care to think about the implications. But, if reality set in, what was the child "knowing" prior to the moment reality set in?

The child sees the world through a model, one constructed on the basis of what he knows already, but also and probably for the most part on his imagination and what he would like reality to be. There is no doubt he is subject to an availability heuristic, as he and all of us always will be. But his complete lack of awareness of that heuristic was what allowed him to believe that his imagined world was the real world. In his case, how is it possible to talk about "objective truth"? Indeed, he sees the tree or the cat outside his mind, he makes existential judgments, comes to apprehend the natures of things gradually, but the contents of his consciousness of these things are rudimentary. A novel is far more than a dictionary; the world as he sees it has a narrative quality to it, and what he sees is, for the most part, what he has constructed.

As adults, it shouldn't be too difficult to acknowledge that the world as it appears to us now is simply that, the world as it currently appears to us. There is so much more to learn, and so much that we cannot learn at this time because the necessary epistemic conditions are absent and may remain so as a result of the limited circumstances in which we find ourselves.

What is an epistemic condition? Prior knowledge in all its diversity acquired through experience, which makes possible a specific intellectual posture, along with specific interests, questions, and problems to solve. Some of that knowledge will be certain, some will be a knowledge of uncertainties, a knowledge of probabilities that we once thought were certainties, a knowledge of limits, errors, failures, etc. I cannot make sense out of specific ideas or insights unless I come into the knowledge of other things first and am disposed in a particular way. There are experiences we will never have, and thus there are epistemic conditions that will never be, and that means there will be so much that will always be outside the purview of our understanding.

Communities also grow in understanding, and this is true of the Church as well. That growth is also the result of certain epistemic conditions that have been realized, certain experiences the community has undergone in its members. As an example of this in the context of the Church, consider the distinction between a proposition and an assertion. What the bible teaches (asserts) is very different than what is in the bible (propositions). Distinguishing the one from the other, however, is no easy task; the discernment takes place over time, that is, in history. Only gradually does the Church understand what is asserted in Scripture, that is, what the "word of God" is in the midst of what is written.

The fundamentalist, however, simply places total confidence in the way he interprets what he reads, without the slightest awareness of the precarious nature of induction as well as the role of epistemic conditions that go into establishing the epistemic model through which he currently sees the world and in light of which he interprets the Scriptures. The Catholic submits to the teaching authority of the

Church, but the Church as a whole develops her understanding of herself as she moves through history. This self-understanding is the *sensus fidelium* (sense of the faithful); the Church understands herself in her members, and the formulated teachings of the Church are the explicit formulation and expression of the sense of the faithful.

48 Some Thoughts on Epistemic Models

The whole problem with the world is that fools and fanatics are always so certain of themselves, and wiser people so full of doubts. Bertrand Russell

A model has a likeness to the original of which it is a model. Consider one you might have put together when you were young, i.e., an airplane, or a model of a famous structure (the Eiffel Tower, the Empire State Building, etc.). The model is easily recognizable; for there is a likeness to that which it represents (i.e., a good model of a 747 airplane has a likeness to a real one). It re-presents the original, that is, it "makes it present again" in your mind.

There is, however, a great deal about the model that falls short of the original. Some models are more detailed than others, have more content, and thus are richer representations of the original. What does this have to do with knowledge? In knowing anything, what is known exists in the knower *in an intentional* way. The idea that exists in the mind is the same "essence" that exists outside the mind—the former exists intentionally, the latter exists "really" as a particular existent; for a being is a composite of essence and existence, and essences are existentially neutral (i.e., they can simultaneously exist both inside and outside the mind). This does not necessarily mean one knows the essence of the thing completely or with great precision; rather, one simply apprehends "what" that thing is, albeit incompletely. Knowledge is a union between the knower and the known.

We have a host of concepts in our minds, which are incomplete apprehensions of what things are, and we have a myriad of judgments, reasoned conclusions (some of which are true), inferences, beliefs, and narratives that possess only a degree of probability. The totality of what is in the mind is a model, as it were. It is that through which we interpret the real. The world that we know, however, *is much larger and richer than what exists in us.* Our knowledge is imperfect; it is profoundly incomplete. What is in us is a kind of representation, an epistemic model; it is that through which the real is made present (re-presented) to us. I don't mean to suggest that what we know first and foremost is our ideas of things. On the contrary, we know beings first and foremost. But there is more to our knowledge than a collection of isolated concepts and abstract judgments. We express what we know about the world in a narrative, a sequence of cause and effect explanations that give meaning (sense, direction) to the real, which is of course already meaningful, but the real is intelligible in ways that are often beyond us at the moment. In other words, we begin to explain phenomena we encounter every day, such as wars we read about, homeless people, high taxes, etc., and our explanations are very often *made up of good guesses*—although we tend to think they are more than guesses.

Recently I listened to an attempt to explain modern art, that is, the reasons for certain developments within the history of art. Regardless of the quality of the explanation, it was a hypothesis in need of some sort of testing and corroboration. The problem with the argument, I thought, was that it was a hypothesis that could not be falsified; there was no way to disprove it. I don't mean to suggest that the argument was right and irrefutable; rather, it was very general and loosely connected. Although a hypothesis might make sense, it might very well be wrong nonetheless, or partly right and partly wrong; in other words, they are tentative, and so we ought to speak with a corresponding level of confidence, which often means a very low level of confidence.

We have religious views, political views, views about human nature and human behavior, metaphysical views, etc. The totality of our views is a kind of model. We interpret the world, the realm of the real, on the basis of everything we know and think we know so far. We make "sense" (meaning) out of our day to day perceptions on the basis of the "knowledge", or the data, beliefs and inferences that are available to us at the moment. We theorize, we speculate, we conjecture, and we react emotionally on the basis of what we have interpreted, which all takes place within an epistemic model, our own limited representation of what the world is, that is, our model of reality.

Like any model, however, it has a likeness to the real, because knowledge is a union between the knower and the known; but not everything within our minds is knowledge *per se*. In fact, one could argue that very little of it is. It only appears to be genuine knowledge because *our narratives* give "meaning" or sense to what we experience. However, *even false narratives and false hypotheses have meaning*. Truth is something else entirely. Much of what is in our minds is conjecture that we mistake for knowledge; much of it is faith and/or opinions that are in some ways more the result of loyalty than a genuine apprehension of the real. We imitate others, and we've been doing so since we were children; we think like the people whom we admire, and some of these might be our siblings, or parents, or our professors to whom we feel we owe loyalty. Of course, our only loyalty is to the truth, not to our siblings, parents, and former professors, etc. And although we owe loyalty to God above all, for He is Truth Itself, I might add that a great deal of our religious opinions is a matter of projection: much of what we see as the will of God is merely our own will, or our own conclusions that make sense to us at the moment. How much of our understanding of what constitutes the "will of God" has changed over the centuries? If our understanding of what constitutes God's will has changed significantly (i.e., we no longer burn heretics, nor label Jews as perfidious, nor cut off the hands of thieves or stone adulterers, or wipe out entire enemy populations, etc.), then there is room now for a dose of healthy skepticism regarding what we currently perceive to be God's will. This does not mean that it is okay to be moral or religious relativists—relativism is just another form of dogmatism or absolutism (i.e., "there are absolutely no moral absolutes and I am certain of it"). Rather, it means that we should avoid speaking with a rhetoric of certainty; we need to listen, ponder, question, raise possible objections, and learn to be at ease with "not knowing".

49 *When We Say: "I Just Can't See It"*

If you are around teenagers, you will often hear them use an expression like "I just don't see what's wrong with...", whether it is an economic issue you are discussing, such as the raising of the minimum wage, or a very subtle moral issue, etc. The tone of the expression "I don't see what's wrong with..." more often than not reveals it as a kind of argument, as if to suggest that "there can't be anything wrong with..., because if there were, I would see it."

The problem with the expression so employed is that it is a slight variation on WYSIATI (What You See Is All There Is), a bias at the root of the availability heuristic. We tend to make inferences on the basis of very scanty but readily available evidence, and we tend not to give serious consideration of the possibility that what we see is not all there is, that reality is much larger than what has hitherto been made available to us.

Of course, we "don't see what's wrong with..." That is a normal state of affairs; we don't see what's wrong with it (and many other things) until we actually do see what's wrong with it—and there are a number of ways to come to see something we simply did not see before. All throughout our lives we continue to discover things about issues, principles, people and places that we never dreamed we would. Life is full of surprises.

There's a vast space of reality that we don't see, and there are layers of reality that will remain forever beyond the purview of our minds and our ability to express in language. But most importantly, there are layers of reality that will only be uncovered under very specific conditions, and it may take years to acquire them. Many of these conditions depend on asking the right questions as a result of having to solve certain problems, and being positioned in a way that permits one to see what would otherwise be very difficult to see, and knowing the right people, finding oneself in the right circumstances, acquiring different interests, etc.

No conclusion about the truth of moral or other matters can be drawn from "I can't see what's wrong with..." For I cannot understand what it is like to be a bat or a snake, but I cannot for that reason conclude that there is nothing that it is like to be a bat or a snake. I don't know what it is like to be sexually abused, clinically depressed and suicidal; but it would be arrogance, for example, to infer that there is nothing that it is like to be "clinically depressed" and to then proceed to argue that such people only experience a low grade sadness that most of us experience periodically, and that all they need are some simple tools to help them cope.

"I don't see what's wrong with..." is an expression we often hear among the young because they simply do not have enough experience in being wrong to have become more acutely aware of their own limitations. But the expression and the rather dogmatic attitude behind it are found all too frequently in adults--who should know better. Those who are wont to declare "I just don't see..." stop investigating, or limit their investigation to a comfortable mode of thinking and a familiar angle, which permits them to go on within the complacency of being certain and right.

Take a contemporary issue. I might assert that I don't see what's wrong with the status quo in the Church regarding LGTBQ issues. However, I also don't know what it is like to be gay, or what it is like to have a male body and feel that I am a woman, or have a female body and feel that I am a man; I don't know what it is like to be a teenager who hears his friends talk about desires that he simply does not have, such as desire for the opposite sex. I can imagine partially, by comparing it to a similar experience, i.e., the isolation I experience when I learn that my friends are all going off to this or that place for the summer while I have to stay home, because we cannot afford to travel overseas; but something tells me that this does not quite carry the same weight as the former.

I can imagine what it is like to be terrified of the prospect of spending the rest of my life alone, and to have finally met someone who alleviates that fear, who is wonderful to be around. But when I do so, I imagine that this person is of the opposite sex. Imagine what it would be like to find no reprieve from loneliness in a person of the opposite sex, but only in a person of the same sex. Imagine further that you are a member of a Church that, for the most part, does not quite understand these desires and fears as those who have them might understand them, that avoids looking at the issues from the perspective of a person who has them or that limits the discussion to a level that is rather abstract, detached, and moral. Let's try to imagine what it would be like to be told that you must resign yourself to living alone for the rest of your life, *but you have to imagine that as someone who lacks the theological and moral understanding, the spirituality, and emotional stability that you possess.*

On the other hand, I might also be a person who does not see what all the moral fuss is about (i.e., "Do whatever you want, just don't hurt anyone"). I would say most people are in this category, and rarely do such people not overstate their case when discussing the issues— that is, "I don't see what's wrong with …" delivered with aggression. We ought to keep in mind, however, that there might be valuable insights just around the corner, moral principles and their implications that I cannot at this time see, but which others can; after all, there are people who have spent their lives thinking about these things, just as there are people who have spent a good part of their lives learning how to fly a commercial aircraft or master a musical instrument. I can't see what's so difficult about flying a 747 or playing the piano, until I actually try to do so, which I have not done as of yet; all I have to go on is what I have seen, and pilots and pianists make it look so easy.

This is a fundamental problem with the world we are living in, and it is an epistemic problem. From a theological standpoint, I would say it is an effect of that wound of Original sin that is traditionally referred to as concupiscence (of the flesh, of the eyes, and the pride of life), which includes the lazy tendency to make our own purview the measure of what is true, rather than to look to something larger (i.e., reality) as the measure. And so there is little dialogue, little discussion, a great deal of fear, anger, smirking and ridicule, not to mention a large pool of ignorance.

50 *When "I'm Right" is Your Default Position*

It is difficult if not impossible to argue with those whose default position is "I'm right". Those who operate within this default mode are not necessarily aware of the fact; it is a preconscious intellectual posture, and it results from confusing the light that comes from conclusions worked out within a particular intellectual model or paradigm, with the epistemic model itself. The model is limited, and so too the scope of its light, like the scope of a flashlight; in fact, it is often dark in comparison with an angle not yet discovered.

Many people lack an awareness of the role that epistemic conditions play in the development of knowledge, and as long as they do, they cannot escape from their default position, for they are not aware of the limitations of the intellectual universe in which they think. Inevitably, the result is that in his mind, those who argue against him are evidently wrong, and he simply has to find a way to get them to see what is clear to him; for they have to be wrong if being right is the default position. What results is an immediate telescope U-turn effect: when looking through the wrong end of a telescope, everything appears smaller than it actually is, especially people. Hence, their opponents in debate are summarily dismissed.

I believe that is why reading Socrates (the early dialogues of Plato) is so important. The dialogue typically ends without a resolution; at first it can be frustrating. The purpose of the dialogue, however, was to establish the conditions for a genuine discovery of the truth, or a closer approximation to it; for the dialogue typically ends in convincing us that we really don't know what we thought we knew. Only then are we able to learn; prior to that, there is no possibility of making any progress because there is just too much we think we know.

All science, including philosophy, begins with a problem. Karl Popper writes: "The work of the scientist does not start with the collection of data, but with the sensitive selection of a promising problem – a problem that is significant within the current problem situation, which in its turn is entirely dominated by our theories...the progress of science lies, essentially, in the evolution of its problems. And it can be gauged by the increasing refinement, wealth, fertility, and depth of its problems".[51]

In the light of the tentative nature of our hypotheses, theories, and overall intellectual frame of mind, our default position ought to be the awareness that the model through which we interpret the real might be insufficient; in fact, it is always incomplete, which is why knowledge never stops developing—at least it hasn't yet. I might lack a host of epistemic conditions that alone will enable me to see an issue in a whole new light. All we need to do to appreciate this more fully is reflect for a moment on the experience of having held onto a viewpoint for many years, only to discover that we were wrong; a significant point was overlooked because of the angle from which we were positioned.

St. Thomas Aquinas knew something about this, at least within the context of jurisprudence. Equity (epikeia), as Aquinas uses the term, is a virtue bearing on discrepancies between law framed from a very general position and the realm of the contingent. He writes: "…when we were treating of laws, since human actions, with which laws are concerned, are composed of contingent singulars and are innumerable in their diversity, it was not possible to lay down rules of law that would apply to every single case. Legislators in framing laws attend to what commonly happens: although if the law be applied to certain cases it will frustrate the equality of justice and be injurious to the common good…"[52]

Matter, which is a principle of individuation, renders things opaque to scientific scrutiny; for there is nothing opaque about logical entities like numbers or the most universal ideas, but when form exists in matter (i.e., this man as opposed to 'human'), at that point there are an almost infinite number of possible instantiations that bring with them a host of unpredictable factors; i.e., ill-disposed matter in utero can lead to brain damage, which in turn brings a myriad of difficulties

---

[51] Popper, *op. cit.,* 155-156.
[52] Thomas Aquinas, *Summa Theologiae* II-II, q. 120, a1.

to the life of a child; or the month in which one is born can produce real advantages or disadvantages for a child, etc.

Although philosophy is abstract and resolves its conclusions through reasoning (as opposed to empirical investigation), there is nevertheless a great deal of inferencing involved. We begin with the evidence of ordinary experience, and then we proceed to explain, to search out the first causes or reasons for this or that, but we always do so with a view to specific problems to solve, within a particular way of asking questions, with a mind disposed in a particular way, reasoning in a language that embodies modes of thinking of which we are often unaware, etc. In doing so, we often overlook distinctions, fail to grasp other important principles, or we will try to resolve newer problems within a paradigm brought about as a result of a very different set of problems and thus find ourselves somewhat hampered, etc. It can happen, as well, that newer problems can be dealt with satisfactorily using an older paradigm. In other words, philosophical knowledge is still always tentative. The default position that "I'm right"—even "I'm probably right"—is rooted in a mentality that fails to recognize even the tentative nature of philosophical resolutions.

51 Bayes' Theorem and Learning by Experience

All knowledge begins in sensation and ends in intellection. Being is given in knowledge; and being is first in our knowledge of anything. This means that before I know anything with any precision about what it is that is before me, I first know (judge) that *it is*. Indeed, I know immediately that it is a "what" (of a determinate nature), but initially that apprehension is imprecise, which is why I seek to penetrate its "whatness" (nature, intelligible structure, essence, etc.) more fully. Now, although existence is given in knowledge, there is nothing more on the side of existence to give, for there is nothing outside of 'is' but 'non-is' or nothing—a thing either is or is not, there is no in between (the principle of the excluded middle). However, on the side of a thing's "whatness", which is *really distinct* from its existence, there is so much to understand ever more fully. And so initially I know that it is a being of some kind, a substance of some kind, perhaps a living substance, and then given further evidence I apprehend that it is a living sentient substance (an animal), and given more evidence I grasp that it is a living sentient rational substance, etc. This deeper penetration into *what it is* (its essence) continues. The object of the intellect is the 'intelligible', and both 'existence' (*esse*) and 'essence' (*essentia*) are intelligible; but our grasp of the latter (essence or what it is) is gradual, a result of inferencing on the basis of the evidence or, more precisely, the activity of the thing (as a thing is, so does it act).

This growth in understanding can be seen in the light of Bayes' Rule, which seeks to determine P(H/E): *the probability of the hypothesis given the evidence.* I see the thing at a distance. What is the probability that it is a living thing? In other words, what is P(H)? It is in the air, it is moving, and it is early afternoon, so the probability that this is a remote control helicopter operated by a young boy is, I would guess, about 50%; thus, the probability that it is a living thing is also about 50%. As I make my way towards the moving "thing" or "artifact", I see that it is far too quick and agile to be a machine, and there is no open field in sight where a kid might operate a remote control helicopter, so I infer that it is more probably a living thing, a large bird of some kind. It could be a mechanical bird, but the probability is, I infer, rather low. And so my original probability P(H) has changed on the basis of this new evidence. The probability that it is a machine has been lowered to almost zero, and the probability that it is a bird has correspondingly increased; the P(H/E) is now 0.01 (that it is a machine).

This is what takes place all the time with almost everything in our day to day knowing. I recall the days, as a young teacher, when I would act on the basis of very different judgments of probability. At a track meet, for example, I would move within the javelin field with a certain degree of attention, because I judged the probability of injury to be relatively low. After an incident in which one of my students, who was inattentive, was almost killed—he was observing the events around him—, my inference bearing upon the probability of an injury increased significantly. Now, years after the fact, I ignore the rest of the track meet when in this area and keep a look out for inattentive students. Once I took a discus and decided to throw, believing that my years of experience rendered the probability of a wayward throw rather low. I released the discus too early and it soared well off course. Had someone been close by watching an event or reading a book, he or she might have been killed. That new piece of evidence changed the degree of probability of my original inference, i.e., the probability of a wayward throw.

We see people, we hear people, we watch people, etc., and we interpret them in light of what we know and what we are familiar with, and we make inferences of which we're barely conscious, and because we are not explicitly aware of the process in which new evidence alters our original inferences (their degree of probability), *we are not always explicitly aware of the space of uncertainty* (degrees of probability) that belongs to the entire collection of inferences that make up the framework or model through which we see and interpret the world and the people in it. We learn from experience, but that does not seem to change our rhetoric. We still speak with a rhetoric of certainty, and we still make assertions with a high level of confidence, and we continue to dismiss those whom we do not understand (i.e., who see things differently) or with whom we are unfamiliar. Some of us even think we have "arrived", as though we had been climbing a mountain toward the summit of understanding.

And so we can become closed to change and growth in understanding. In other words, we can become *epistemically arrogant* and overconfident. In fact, some people are so closed to the self-expansion involved in learning, especially in the moral realm, that they have clothed themselves within a facade of openness and tolerance, so as to feel and appear open. But they are not open because they refuse grow in knowledge, for they ignore evidence that challenges the probability of their judgments, especially judgments that have a bearing on their moral lives; and so they have adopted an absolute relativism. Accordingly, the individual becomes the measure of what is true and good, and all knowledge becomes a construct. Thus, whatever changes are made (individually or socially) are seen as good, because they automatically conform to the standard, which is the man (or culture) that made those changes. This is a rather ingenious form of self-deception.

52 *A Thought on Criteria*

I have often argued that there is a difference between a pretty face (or handsome face) and a "good face". A person can have a pretty face, but a "bad face", or a not so pretty/handsome face and yet have a "great face". This insight is not original, and it is the insight that is behind the old expression: "The eyes are the windows of the soul". Character is manifest in the countenance. A person of good moral character will have a good face, a beautiful face, because there is a unity between spirit and matter. The human person is a psychosomatic unity, and so the overall moral nobility that qualifies a person's character will influence his/her matter, specifically the countenance. That is why some people, who may never make the cover of Cosmopolitan or GQ, nevertheless have what I would refer to as "a good face", such as Catherine de Hueck Doherty, Father Ted Colleton, Dorothy Day, Mahatma Gandhi, St. Maximillian Kolbe, Caryll Houselander, and Elizabeth Anscombe, to name a few.

A student of mine asked one day: "What is the criteria you use to determine who has a great face?" This was a great question; for it opens up an avenue in which to explore an important knowledge issue; for the question about "criteria" is rooted in a particular epistemic framework. The answer to her question is that I have no criteria, absolutely none, and I couldn't formulate any if I tried. And yet I believe I know what I am talking about, that is, I believe I can identify a good face. It is indeed a matter of inferencing. Can I be wrong? Yes, there is no doubt about it. Can I be certain of my inference? No, I cannot, and so I ought always to be careful not to inference with a high level of confidence.

Nonetheless, the question about criteria is interesting. For I would argue that judging a face is much like judging a work of art, or a sport; it is a matter of *connatural knowledge*, not scientific knowledge. Connatural knowledge is a difficult mode of knowing to explain. Consider that the best person in the class to judge a group of performers at a piano recital is that student among us who is an accomplished pianist, and the best person to judge a figure skating competition is the figure skater among us, etc. As one becomes a better artist, his or her ability to "see", that is, to judge artistic quality is sharpened. Initially, when we were just learning how to paint, we might have thought that our work was quite good. A few years later, however, we look back and shake our heads. Our judgment has improved, for we see things now that we did not quite notice before, because we have become better artists.

In these cases, we know through a kind of inclination. St. Thomas Aquinas speaks of connaturality within a moral context: "Now rectitude of judgment is twofold: first, on account of perfect use of reason, secondly, on account of a kind of connaturality with the matter about which one has to judge. Thus, about matters of chastity, a man who has learnt the science of morals judges rightly through inquiry by reason, while he who has the habit of chastity judges rightly of such matters by a kind of connaturality."[53]

In other words, the virtuous person tends to judge rightly through a kind of inclination; he is a man of justice, or chastity, or patience, etc., for he is inclined to choose the virtuous course of action with ease; the right alternative appears to him by virtue of that very inclination.

Now this, of course, raises a number of knowledge issues, which I would rather leave for another chapter. The point I make here is that connatural knowledge is **not** criteria based. However, judges often generate a list of criteria, and for various good reasons. In the Olympics, for example, there is the possibility of biased judging, or bribery, etc. A list of objective criteria is an attempt to make more objective what in fact depends in large part on the qualities of the subject doing the judging—and it is this fact that suggests that connatural knowledge, although it is subjective, is not entirely so. It is a combination of sorts. The beauty of a work of art or a performance is in the work, or in the performance, but to appreciate it, to see it, requires that the subject doing the observing possess certain qualities.

---

[53] *Summa*, II-II, q. 45, a2.

That is why Olympic figure skating judges typically are former skaters and gymnastics judges are former gymnasts, etc.

Interviewing for positions is a phenomenon that illustrates this particular tension that exists between connatural knowledge and the more objective or scientific "criteria based" knowledge. Today, when a person is interviewed for a teaching or administrative position, there are objective criteria that interviewers are now required to follow. There are predetermined questions to ask, and someone takes notes. This way, if the hiring decision is challenged, there are objective criteria to fall back on: i.e., this person answered this question properly; the other failed to do so, etc.

I distinctly recall a principal who simply bypassed the criterion-based approach to interviewing, literally moved the papers to one side and began a conversation with the prospective candidate. He knew what he was looking for and did not need a set of artificial questions to ask. The point is reality is always much larger than the model is able to comprehend, and the problem with a strict criteria based model, at least with respect to interviews, is that some candidates interview very well, have the gift of a smooth tongue, can say all the right things, yet turn out to be the last person you would want in front of your children every day in the classroom. With an inordinate amount of attention paid to the criteria, one pays less attention to important clues that are intuitively grasped.

53 *Thoughts on Focusing and the Limitations of Human Knowledge*

Daniel Kahneman writes: "Intense focusing on a task can make people effectively blind, even to stimuli that normally attract attention." This is not only true for sense perception; it is true for intellection as well, because "nothing is in the intellect that is not first in the senses". In other words, intelligence participates in the limitations of sense perception. When we focus on a task or problem, we do become effectively blind to other aspects of a problem. For example, when I read a text in light of a question that preoccupies me, those aspects that would be highlighted or would stand out had I a different question on my mind are left in the penumbra. My attention is focused on an answer to a particular question, and so those aspects of the text that are relevant to my question stand out and are noticed. As a result, I may feel that I've never read this text before, despite the fact that I know I have read it many times before. The difference is that I now read it with a different set of questions in mind, or different interests, thus within a different framework.

Our study and knowledge of history is like that. We approach it within an already established frame of mind, that is, we approach history with specific prior interests. If I am interested in economics and the economic causes of the Great Depression, I will pay attention to historical decisions to which a historian of philosophy, for example, would not pay attention because they are not entirely relevant to his interests. I am also able to correctly see certain things as significant, to make "sense" out of them, precisely because I have within me something other than history, namely, the science of economics, which enables me to correctly interpret certain historical decisions, to grasp their historical significance and implications for the future, which would not be possible had I come at history from a different angle, that is, with a different set of interests, say questions bearing upon the philosophical ideas at the time, or with nothing more than a general interest in history.

In short, there is so much we don't see because our attention is not turned towards it. Specific ways of seeing and thus certain kinds of questions cause us to focus on very specific things, but they cause us not to notice other things that from our current angle are simply not significant, but are profoundly significant from another vantage point; that "not-noticing" is normal, and we should not be surprised to discover that there are things we never before thought of.

54 *Is All Our Knowledge a Construct?*

In the context of IB Theory of Knowledge, we often come upon the expression "the production of knowledge" employed in various contexts. The impression we might be left with is that knowledge is some kind of construct, an active producing, like a work of art. Also employed by IB is a metaphor that compares knowledge to a map.

A question we might wish to ask is whether knowledge is a construction, a production, either in part or in whole. I will argue that knowledge cannot be entirely a construct or production, only partially so. I will argue that it is more fitting to speak of the "genesis" of knowledge than the "production" of knowledge.

Firstly, it seems to me that knowledge cannot be, in its entirety, a matter of production. Knowing is indeed an activity, not a pure passivity, and clearly knowledge "comes to be". So there is a sense in which knowledge is produced. But to produce or manufacture something is to make something come to be "out of" a subject, or some kind of matter. The process of production depends in part upon the raw materials "out of which" the product is made. Art is a matter of production, and art imposes form on a pre-existing matter (i.e., paint, iron, soapstone, wood, letters of the alphabet, etc.). "What" the product ends up being is determined by the form in the mind of the artist that he imposes upon the matter.

Thus, if knowledge were entirely a matter of production, like the production of a work of art, the knower would be the measure of what is true, which means that whatever he knows is always true precisely because he knows it—for he has produced it.

If this were the case, however, the metaphor of the map would be unfitting. The reason is that a map, although it is produced, is intended to be a map "of the city" or a map "of the country", etc. That which the map is intended to represent (to make present to the mind of the one reading the map) is something other than the map, namely the city or country, and it is this (the real) that is the standard that measures the quality of the map. It is not the mind of the map maker that is the measure of the map's accuracy; the map is that through which I come to know something other than the map.

In other words, there is an "object" of knowledge, and the object is "the real", that is, real being that is outside the mind. Knowledge is a union between the knower and the known. What the knower knows, namely "real" being, exists in his mind in a new way, as "logical" being. But it is not "logical" being that I know. In other words, 'ideas' are not the object of my knowledge; rather, the ideas of 'dog' or "tree" or "a type of cancer treatment" are that "through which" I know that dog, or that tree, or what this treatment is that this person is undergoing, etc.

Knowledge is not an entirely passive affair, however. The knower contributes something of his own in the knowing process. For one, he contributes his own limited standpoint. Much of what he will come to know depends upon a host of epistemic conditions that need to be in place if he is to come to apprehend something or other, conditions such as specific experiences of certain people, places, cultures, historical situations, which in turn give rise to problems that need to be solved, which in turn give rise to specific questions, which in turn bring his mind into focus on one matter to the exclusion of another or other matters, etc. The knower is also subject to a host of biases or slants (inclinations) that he is often unaware of, but which actively contribute something to the genesis of knowledge. Many of these biases distort our grasp of the real. The ability to recognize that, however, logically implies that knowledge is not entirely a matter of production or construction. In other words, I know I can be subject to anchoring, or to an availability heuristic, or the narrative fallacy, etc., because I am able—or someone else is able—to stand outside of that, **to transcend it in some way**. I am able to see how an anchor has influenced my decision, or how my judgment relied too heavily on information that was readily available, or how a narrative, which was my own construct, has added to the content of the facts before me, introducing something that is not part of the real state of affairs I claim to understand. If we are able to become aware of these things, it follows that our knowledge is not entirely a matter of production, but partially so; for if it were entirely a matter of production, I would never know it, for I could never transcend it (i.e., I would never know the world is larger than my mind if I could never come to see what was larger than my mind in the first place, just as I would never know the world is larger than Markham if I was unable to travel beyond Markham).

There is such a thing as *a view from nowhere*.[54] Indeed, it is often the case that I will not understand something until I am in the right position, under the right conditions, or after having "walked a mile in someone else's shoes". That expression says a great deal, for after having "walked in someone else's shoes", I have discovered something that I would have otherwise missed, but once I understand it (whatever it is), what I now understand is a real objective state of affairs. For example, after living with this man or after having to work with him for a while, I now know what you meant before when you said he is neurotic, has serious control issues, is rude and obnoxious, etc.,. I see now that from a distance, I was unable to appreciate what you were talking about. I had to walk in your shoes, be his employee as you were, or his associate, etc., before I could understand it. I now "stand under" it, that is, I am now in the right "position" to grasp what I was missing before being put in that position.

What I see now, however, is true regardless of the perspective. It is a real state of affairs independent of anyone's perspective and independent of anyone knowing it, i.e., he really is neurotic, controlling, and rude, etc. It is now a view from nowhere.

Knowledge can be compared to a map in the sense that the totality of what we know is that through which we interpret or "make sense" out of the realm of the real, which is larger than the mind. When we construct an actual map, we do so on the basis of what is really so, i.e., Yonge Street really does run north and south, and it really does intersect with Bloor Street, etc., and the more time we put into the construction of the map, the better the map is likely to be. But that which the map is intended to chart, namely the actual city or country, is **the measure of** the map's quality, accuracy, or completeness. In

---

[54] Thomas Nagel, *The View from Nowhere*. Oxford: Oxford University Press, 1986.

knowledge, what we know primarily is real being, and it is the real that is the measure of the accuracy of our own intellectual map or model of reality. The map is the product of the knowing process, the model that is left over, and it is a highly influential model, and it is always incomplete and in need of development.

If all knowledge were a pure construct or production, without anything against which to measure the accuracy of what we know, then knowledge is no longer about "something", it is no longer the "knowledge of" some aspect of the real. In fact, objectivity would itself be a pure construct. But if objectivity were to become a pure product of the subject, then how is it that one would ever know what a "subject" is in the first place? Subjectivity would be lost on us, for "subject" is a correlative term; it can only be understood against the background of what is not "subject", but "object".

55 Knowledge of the Ordinary

All knowledge begins on the level of the ordinary, and every other area of more specialized knowledge, such as science, mathematics, statistics, philosophy, history, etc., takes place within the framework of this ordinary pre-scientific knowledge. Science begins on the level of ordinary experience and proceeds downward, so to speak, to uncover what is beyond ordinary sense experience, such as mitosis, or the properties of light, etc. Philosophy begins on the level of ordinary experience and proceeds upward, so to speak, reasoning to causes or reasons that cannot be investigated empirically (i.e., What is a cause? What are the rules of valid reasoning?). Mathematics abstracts from the sensible matter of ordinary experience and reasons towards an understanding of quantities (i.e., factor $z^2 - 9z + 18$).

We are, however, creatures of habit. Wisdom, science, and understanding (of first principles) are intellectual virtues, and virtues are habits, and habits are dispositions towards a specific activity, enabling us to perform that activity with ease. What often happens, however, is that we become so immersed in a particular activity, such as mathematics, or deductive logic, or a science that is heavily inductive, etc., that the particular mode of thinking to which we have become heavily disposed begins to overshadow our appreciation for the role of ordinary pre-scientific knowledge, that is, its role as the condition for the possibility of all specialized knowledge.

And so those who have been exposed only to the logic of deduction, for example, are inclined to treat all their conclusions as necessary and certain, thus failing to appreciate the degrees of uncertainty involved in most of our day to day inferences; and those exposed only to the logic of induction, or sciences that are heavily inductive, are inclined to treat all conclusions as probable, as if certainty is impossible to acquire.

A good scientist employs a method that is not only inductive, but predominantly reductionistic—to understand man in order to be able to operate on him, we have to cut him open and study his anatomy, thereby reducing him to his parts. However, his method can become so habitual that he begins to believe that everything is merely the sum of its parts. Thus, his reductionism overshadows his ordinary and pre-scientific knowledge, which is the starting point of all specialized knowledge.

The idealist, like Plato, or Descartes, or Hegel, is so disposed to focus primarily on his ideas—and not the world outside the mind—that he begins to treat those ideas as though they were the very blueprint of reality, and so he believes that his grasp on reality is far more comprehensive than it actually is. What happens is that what is in his mind, i.e., his ideas, has become the measure of the real, rather than the real being the measure of what is in his mind.

According to my ordinary and pre-scientific knowing, I live in a world of "things", or "entities", that is, beings or substances. Substance is the primary way beings exist. What is a chemist? One does not need to be a chemist to know the answer to that; he is one who studies the properties and structures of substances, such as iron, or gold, or chlorine, etc. What is a biologist? He is one who studies living substances or living things. What is a psychologist? He is one who studies the behaviour of human beings, etc. Ordinary knowledge is about the general knowledge of things or beings.

According to my ordinary and pre-scientific knowledge, water is not the same thing as oxygen. I do not need a chemistry course to know this. Five minutes under water and I am a dead man, and I cannot live 5 minutes without oxygen. A chemist's knowledge of their differences is simply more precise, but not more real.

What I know first and foremost about whatever I am coming to know is that "it is". But what is it? Initially, I can say it is something, an entity of some kind. As I observe its activity, I begin to infer with more precision "what it is" (i.e., a plant, an animal, etc.). Initially I know it is a being, a substance, and after a while I begin to discern that it is a living substance—or I may discover that it is not a single substance at all, but an artifact composed of many substances. Again, I may not know much about living substances, at least not with any scientific precision, but I know that "it is", it is "one"; it is actual and mutable. I know through ordinary experience that it has many parts, but I also know that nothing can both be and not be at the same time and in the same respect. In other words, nothing can be both many and not many at the same time and in the same respect, only in different respects. So, the substances that I know to be one have a certain relationship to their parts; the parts are not the single substance; rather, they are "parts of the one substance" or "parts of the whole". I cannot understand parts except as "parts of a whole", because to be a part is to be a part of a larger whole.

The habit of reductionism, acquired after years of good science, becomes a fallacy when it overshadows ordinary and pre-scientific knowledge. Consider the following explanation: this green piece of paper is green because it is made up of little green balls; and these little green balls are green because they are made up of smaller little green balls; and these in turn are green because they are made up of even smaller little green balls, etc. Am I explaining anything? No, I am not. In order to explain anything, one must use terms *other than* the terms one is trying to explain.

Consider that before you know anything specific about something, you know first and foremost that "it is". Being is first, and prior to being is nothing. And so the first principle, the starting point of all knowledge, is your understanding that *each being is what it is* (i.e., a carrot is a carrot, not a watermelon). One might not be explicitly aware of this, but it is real knowledge nonetheless, and observing any child at play verifies this. But the habit of reductionism can cause a person to forget this. Many scientists have said things like "solidity is an illusion...the table in front of you is not really solid, for it is made up of atoms, and atoms are mostly empty space; hence, the table in front of you is mostly empty space..."

Such thinking is very much like Plato, but the complete reverse. Plato, recall, argued that this world is not fully real; rather, the World of Forms or Ideas alone is the realm of the real; the reductionist also believes that the world of ordinary experience is not fully real,; rather, it is another world, the subatomic world that is the realm of the real, and knowing this realm alone gives us a genuine knowledge of reality, just as Plato believed that knowledge of one's ideas gives us a knowledge of reality.

But consider how reductionism contravenes the principle of identity, which you and I know immediately and without which all science becomes impossible. The reductionist says that a thing is nothing other than the sum of its parts. But those parts, in turn, are nothing other than the sum of their parts, which in turn are nothing other than the sum of their parts, etc. In other words, everything in our ordinary experience is "nothing other than", that is, everything is "other than" what it is. Nothing is what it is, but is other than what it is. Such a conclusion comes into complete conflict with ordinary experience and pre-scientific knowledge.

One could say that the reductionist is searching for "being", that is, searching for that which *is what it is*, and when he finds it, he will reduce all reality to it. But ordinary human beings need not search for being; they have found it already. Being is given in knowledge. That's what it means to know; for knowledge is a joining, a union between the knower and the known, that is, between the knower and real being. When there is a joining, there is a conception, a concept, an idea, but it is not the idea that we know; rather, the concept or idea is that through which we know the being outside the mind. You and I know beings first and foremost, ordinarily, and pre-scientifically, that is, before we engage in the more precise work of scientific investigation, or philosophy, or mathematics, etc.

Finally, statistical reasoning, inductive inference, probabilities, etc., all presuppose a more fundamental and ordinary way of knowing. Before I can calculate the space of uncertainty of a given event, or the probability of a hypothesis given the evidence [$P(H/E)$], or the probability of the evidence given a hypothesis [$P(E/H)$], I have to know "what" I am talking about. If we are talking about the probability of schizophrenia given the evidence, then clearly I know what schizophrenia is, at a rudimentary level at least. To calculate the probability of high inflation or low unemployment [p(E) + p(F) − p(EF)] presupposes that I know what inflation and unemployment are. In other words, inductive reasoning presupposes a different act of the intellect, namely, abstractive induction (simple apprehension) that is, the ability to apprehend the natures of things.

It is for this reason that knowledge cannot be reduced to any one of the specialized areas of knowledge. To do so undercuts the basic intellectual activity that renders that specialized area of knowledge possible in the first place.

56 *Denying Causality on the Basis of Quantum Mechanics*

A long-time atheist friend of mine continues to deny that the principle of causality is universal, claiming that on the subatomic level (the quantum level), occurrences take place without cause. The following is an attempt to show how such a claim simply cannot be true.

We need to keep in mind that science in general is about knowing "reasoned facts", that is, it is about knowing the 'reason for' this or that phenomenon. And so "cause" and "reason for" mean the same thing. A cause is *a principle upon which something proceeds with dependence*. If a sun burn does not depend on the outcome of the baseball game, then the outcome of the baseball game is not the cause of (reason for) my sun burn; rather, the hot sun is the cause of my burn. There is no relationship of dependence between my sun burn and the outcome of the baseball game, and science in the most general sense is about conclusions that carry the force of necessity—if one is uncertain of the truth of a conclusion, one does not yet possess science, in the true sense of that word. Granted, much of the empiriological sciences is probabilistic, because the scientific method is inductive and thus proceeds by means of slow and careful inferencing; but probability can only be understood against the background of what is certain, and empiriological science always strives for a maximum degree of certitude. To strive for science is to strive for certitude.

Nevertheless, what does it mean for an event to have absolutely no cause? It is one thing for a phenomenon to lack causal relevance and to possess only statistical relevance, such as unusual weeks in a rural hospital where more than the average proportion of girls are born, or more than the average proportion of boys are born (i.e., more than 55%)—a phenomenon that is explained not by an appeal to water quality or clean air, etc., but rather by an appeal to the law of small numbers; it is quite another, however, to claim that an event has absolutely no cause. For an event to have absolutely no cause means there is absolutely no 'reason' for the effect or phenomenon in question, and if there is absolutely no reason for the occurrence of something, then its occurrence is absolutely unintelligible. It cannot be understood; it cannot be explained at all, ever. In principle it remains forever beyond the pale of scientific scrutiny, not merely within this or that paradigm, but absolutely and without qualification. There is simply **nothing for reason to know** that would account for the phenomenon.

My friend gets to the crux of his argument thus: *"...if things happen in an entirely random manner, that would defy any ability to predict outcomes based on prior conditions, which has to be the very definition of uncausality."*

The first part of this claim is true, namely, that we cannot predict the outcomes, based on prior conditions, of things which happen in an entirely random manner. It is the final claim, however, which I believe is mistaken: "...which has to be the very definition of uncausality."

This claim is not quite right. Genuinely self-determined acts (acts of free-choice) are unpredictable, strictly speaking. I cannot predict what you as an individual are going to do tomorrow, but whatever you do, you determine yourself to do it (you are **the cause** of your actions). Indeed, radioactive decay is not self-determined activity—an atom does not freely choose to decay—, but the fact that we cannot predict which atom will decay does not necessarily entail that it decays without a cause or reason. Indeed, we may never be able to predict which atom will decay, and we may never know the reason this particular atom decayed at this particular instant rather than that atom. But there is no justification for claiming there simply is no reason for its decay, or that its decay is without a cause that explains it. Such a conclusion possesses a distribution that is lacking in the premises that precede it.

Moreover, inability to predict outcomes based on prior conditions is not the definition that expresses the very meaning of an "uncaused" event (or "uncausality", if there is such a word). The definition of "uncausality" would have to be the opposite of "causality", and so if causality entails that nothing moves itself from potentiality to actuality except by something already in actuality, "uncausality" would mean, it seems, that something can move itself from potentiality to actuality **without depending on** something already in actuality. In other words, a thing **can** give what it does not have (contradictories can be true at one and the same time). But it is impossible for the mind to make any rational sense out of such a contention; for it would open up the possibility that denying the universal scope to causality means at the same time affirming it, or to be wrong is to be right, and to do science is to not do science, and to move is to be still, etc.

My friend continues: *"If the universe observed strict causality, every word you ever spoke, every thought you ever had, would have been predetermined by prior conditions".*

Again, this is a *non-sequitur.* Moreover, this is *an if...then...argument,* (a conditional syllogism). He is reasoning—albeit validly—on the basis of a major and minor premise. The major premise consists of an antecedent clause, and a consequent clause. Now, there are strict rules for drawing a valid conclusion in a conditional syllogism, and they are all derived from the principle of causality. Affirming the consequent and denying the antecedent are invalid, because they draw conclusions that lack the force of necessity. In other words, the conclusion is "uncaused" or insufficiently accounted for. In other words, the conclusion is not "determined", but underdetermined.

But the principal problem with his argument is that he begins with an unwarranted assumption. What is the origin of the assumption that if the principle of causality is universally true, then every thought we ever had would have been predetermined by prior conditions? Why aren't I the prior condition of my thoughts and decisions and you the prior condition of your own thoughts and decisions?

At the origin of his assumption (the assumption behind his assumption), I would argue, is the intellectual habit of "reductionism"; for only reductionists hold that our thoughts are nothing but the effects of neural-biochemistry. To save free will, however, it is not necessary to deny causality on the quantum level; rather, just give up reductionism altogether. My acts are mine, they are the acts of a single agent that has the power to think and choose alternatives freely. In short, the primary mode of being is not the ultimate particles that constitute a substance. Rather, it is the substance itself.

To end his argument, he writes: *"In a strict causality universe, you would be nothing but an automaton, a biological tape recorder spouting a script "written" by a massive explosion of incoherent energy. I think we all know from introspection that in fact we do have the ability to think and make decisions."*

Indeed, we know from introspection (self-knowledge) that we have the ability to think and make choices, and I also know from introspection (self-knowledge) that the words being typed onto this page are caused by me, that I am the cause of my own acts (the prior condition that is intelligent and free), and it is this self-knowledge that enables me to understand causality in the world around me. Just as I know that a dog's yelp is an indication of pain, by virtue of my own self-knowledge, I know as well that a biological entity with many parts is really one whole, precisely because I know through that same self-knowledge that I am a single, unified whole with parts. Self-knowledge is a very real condition for the possibility of empirical science, but it is not itself scientific knowledge; and it is through that very same self-knowledge that I am able to know that this event **depends upon** that event as an effect depends upon its cause.

My friend concludes: *"Of course I don't deny **apparent causality** on a macroscopic level. The ability to predict how things will behave under specified conditions is my stock in trade as an engineer. But quantum mechanical uncertainty does not mean that we cannot know enough to predict, say, radioactive decay of an isotope. It means **there is nothing to be known**. It happens in an entirely random manner, albeit in a statistically consistent manner."*

Indeed, certain occurrences have statistical relevance only, and the tendency to explain certain phenomena in terms of certain kinds of causes is misguided. Consider a group of 100 students who are asked to flip a coin. Everyone who flips tails is eliminated from the game, while those who flipped heads continue. After six flips, only one student is left; he flipped 6 heads in a row. Now, we could all speculate on the possible causes of such an unusual phenomenon, anything from what he had for lunch, what side of the bed he got out of this morning to the color of the shirt he is wearing—or perhaps something about the coin he used. But flipping a fair coin 6 heads in a row is, although unusual, not causally relevant, only statistically so. *The sufficient reason is not found on the same level that we typically locate causes* (the food we consumed, atmospheric pressure, etc.), so in this sense, there is nothing outside of statistical relevance to know as the cause of his flipping 6 heads in a row.

But to conclude that the phenomenon in question has absolutely no cause for the intellect to investigate is simply unwarranted. It has already been investigated, and when we understand statistical phenomena, the intellect is satisfied—although not to the degree that it ends all further inquiry. This, however, does not amount to an unqualified denial of causality, only a qualified denial. To behave in a statistically consistent manner is to behave in an intelligible manner, in a way that is open to the understanding. How does one explain the laws of probability? Why is there an order that exceeds the complete grasp of an individual mind, but an order that allows itself to be understood on a different level, with mathematical certainty, leaving at the same time a large space of uncertainty? These are questions that can be asked and cannot be dismissed by the claim that there is absolutely nothing to be known.

Furthermore, it seems to me that my friend's claim is simply an instance of the round-trip fallacy: 'no evidence for a cause' is not the same as 'evidence for no cause', just as 'no evidence for a cancer' is not the same as 'evidence of no cancer'. How does a person's knowledge extend so far? Moreover, how does one prove a universal negative (i.e., No S is P)? In our experience, "No dogs fly", but how does one declare with certainty a contingent fact that "No S is P", or "No dogs fly"? Contingencies are not necessities, and certainty is founded upon necessities. "No triangle is four sided" is a universal negative proposition of which we can be certain, because "three sided" is part of the very meaning of a triangle, expressed in its definition, and so we see the necessity of the conclusion when we know what constitutes the essence of a triangle. But "there is no reason that accounts for the radioactive decay of this particular isotope" is not a proposition that contains such necessity—the claim is not evident the instant we know what radioactive decay is.

To know with certainty the truth of a universal negative that is contingent would require that we know every corner of the universe (omniscience) to be certain that "no dogs fly", or that "No Maple trees bear fruit", etc. Moreover, if something is happening in a statistically consistent manner, then it is happening lawfully, that is, according to a law. What occurs according to a law does not occur without a reason, for law *is a dictate of reason*; to behave lawfully is to behave in a way that is intelligible to reason, and to see the "reason for" something or other is to see the cause.

Moreover, randomness is not chance: a genuine chance occurrence is entirely unpredictable, for it is a disorder, an aberration. Randomness is not a disorder or an aberration; rather, to study the nature of random occurrences is to come upon an order that possesses an intelligibility that is mathematically coherent and beautiful. A chance occurrence, however, is the result of an intersection of two lines of action that are purposeful, that is, having a *final* cause (an order to an end). To behave lawfully is to behave with purpose, that is, for a reason, and to behave for a reason is to act for an end (a final cause). The agent acting need not be aware of that end (i.e., apple trees are not aware that they act for an end), nor is it necessary for us to understand the causes of an act in order to know that its behavior is lawful and thus caused in some way or other. In other words, the condition for the possibility of understanding a chance occurrence is the principle of causality.

57 What is Wrong with Reductionism?

Many young people who have good minds for science and math tend to think with a reductionist habit of mind. Such a habit of mind will tend to see the whole (i.e., the world of nature, trees, animals, flowers, human beings, etc.) as nothing more than the sum of the parts that make it up. Reductionism goes hand in hand with Scientism, the view that the only valid knowledge is scientific knowledge of the empiriometric kind (i.e., physics, chemistry, etc.).

Although the reductionist habit of mind makes for good science, it is a flawed method of explaining things in terms of first principles; in other words, it makes for bad philosophy.

Let me begin by making a point about number. Number is multitude, organized and identified and measured by unity. Multitude is plurality, pure and simple, and as such it is unorganized. Think of a continuous extension, like an unspecified quantity of milk. To number it requires a unit, such as a litre. Now, in itself a plurality is unknowable; it is known only when measured by unity. To reduce a plurality to unity is to number it, and our material world can accordingly be organized into unity. I will return to this.

Consider as well: man has two interiors. The one is physical (i.e., we can look inside his body). But no matter how much we search the physical interior of a man, we will never know what is contained in the other interior (the interior he refers to when he speaks of his "mind" or "heart"). The human person has to manifest it by acting—in this case, speaking.

There are also two interiors of any substance, like a carbon atom. The only way to grasp the interior of a carbon atom is to observe how it acts. Its activity reveals its nature. It does not have a conscious interior, as man does, but it has a determinate nature. The interior of the atom is not the parts that constitute it. Rather, the interior is the nature of the atom.

But that is just what reductionism denies. Reductionism maintains that this "thing" is nothing more or other than the parts that make it up. So, there really is no "it". "It" is a word, but "it" is nothing other than parts.

But if I understand "parts", does that not presuppose that I understand "whole"? If I know of the "parts of a thing", does that not presuppose I know "thing"? If I didn't understand "thing", I would not understand "parts of the thing"; thus, if there is no "thing" or "it", there are no "parts of it". We could not speak of "real parts" if there is no "real whole" or "real thing".

But the reductionist claims that you, as well as anything else, are nothing other than the constituent parts. But what are the parts? The reductionist would have to be consistent and maintain that each part is nothing other than its smaller constituent parts, and of course that's just what he does. What is an organ but the cells that make it up? And a cell is nothing other than the parts that make it up, that is, the parts that constitute it.

Of course, we have the same problem. How is it that I am able to grasp the notion of "cell" if the cell is nothing other than those constituent parts that make it up? What is the "it" that is constituted? The answer: the cell. But is the cell a determinate part? Does it terminate into a definite intelligible part of a larger whole? And is the whole thing (i.e., the cat) something determinate, that is, terminated as a definite intelligible whole, a thing in itself? One's answer is either yes, or no.

If the answer is yes, then the cell, or the organ, or the cat or man, is more than the multiplicity of parts that constitute it. The parts are reduced to a unity. That unity is called the cell, or the organ, or the man. That unity renders the multiplicity of parts intelligible. A raw multiplicity is unintelligible unless it is reduced to a unity; that is why we number things. An extension, for example, is measured by a unit called a yard. But a yard is numbered by the unit called a foot, which in turn is numbered or reduced to a unit called an inch. Hence, a foot is 12 inches. A number is a measure of quantity; without a number, the quantity remains unorganized.

A multiplicity does not give itself unity; the unity comes to it from the outside, from outside the multiplicity. A multiplicity considered *in itself* is not a unit, and a unit is not a multiplicity. A unit is one. An inch terminates or determines an extension, giving it determination (definition, intelligibility). A litre measures or terminates a quantity of liquid; a pound terminates a quantity of weight, allowing us to determine the weight, to know its weight (i.e., this person is 200 pounds, that milk carton is 2 litres, that table is 5 feet, 6 inches, etc.). At this point the plurality is organized into an intelligible quantity.

One may object and claim that it is not true that "a unit is not a multiplicity. A centimetre is made up of millimetres; hence, a centimetre is a unit, but it is a multiplicity at the same time."

A centimetre, however, is a unit (one one hundredth of a metre) that measures a meter, but because the centimetre is an extension, it too can be measured. To do so, we have to divide it further. A millimetre is one one thousandth of a meter. And so the unit of measure, like the centimetre, is not outside of the multiplicity spatially. Rather, it is outside of "multiplicity", that is, it is not itself a multiplicity, but a measure of multiplicity. As extended, it is a multiplicity that is open to being measured or numbered. To do so, we need a smaller unit of measure, i.e., the millimetre. The unit allows us to number multiplicity (quantity, or the multiplicity of parts outside of parts); "one" itself, however, is not a multiplicity. Multiplicity does not number or measure multiplicity, a unit does.

A single cell, similarly, is an intelligible thing. A scientist sees it as a biological unit, certainly a part of a larger whole (the organ), or a whole unto itself, if it is a single celled bacteria. He begins to analyze it and study its constituent parts.

Now, if the answer to the above question ("Is the cell a determinate part?" "Does it terminate into a definite intelligible part of a larger whole?") is no, then the cell is nothing other than "its" constituent parts, i.e., proteins, amino acids, etc. These in turn are ultimately nothing other than atoms of elements, which in turn are nothing other than subatomic particles, which in turn are nothing but smaller subatomic particles, etc.

The result is that "thing" is not anything *in itself*. It is always *other than "itself"*. A man is not a thing in itself, a dog is not a thing in itself, a flower is not a thing in itself, a single celled organism, like a bacteria, is not a thing in itself, an atom is not a thing in itself, etc.

Everything is *other than* "itself". There is no "itself". Nothing has any "interior". Nothing is what it is, but is "other than" what it is. Nothing has any determinacy. Nothing, therefore, is knowable, and everything is unknowable; for we cannot know what is indeterminate.

Once again, science becomes a fiction, a construct. This will mean that science does not uncover the intelligibility of nature, because nature is not intelligible, it is absurd and unknowable—if reductionism is true, that is. There is *nothing in itself to know*. And that is why genuine reductionists who take their conclusions to the very end are post-modernists who deny the existence of meaning and truth. Man is the measure of what is true and good, even though there is no "man" (no "thing" *in itself*).

But then one has to ask: "How is it possible to understand change?" Take the concept of evolution. When we speak of evolution, we speak of something evolving. But if there are no "things" in themselves, then "nothing" evolves. I can only understand change when I understand that something enduring has changed in some way, i.e., you sat in the sun and became tanned. Your color changes, but you are the subject of the change that endured. "Tanned" is the predicate (John is tanned). But there is no 'you', no cell, no organism of a determinate species, so what, therefore, evolves? In other words, change can only be understood against the backdrop of that which endures, that which is unchanging. Reductionism is thus incompatible with evolution.

Reductionism leads to the conclusion that categorical propositions are impossible. They are not real. For example: "John is a man" or "the cell divides" are nothing more than linguistic constructs that create the illusion of "thing". The principle of identity as well is a construct, and logic, in the end, can be nothing more than a construct.

The reductionist, however, "reasons" to conclusions from given premises. He says things like: The mind is nothing but the brain, and thinking is nothing but firing neurons, and therefore man is not essentially different than brute animals, etc. Some reductionists, not all, proceed further and will conclude from all this that we should stop treating ourselves as privileged creatures, etc. Notice the reasoning from premises to conclusions, even though logical reasoning, which depends on categorical propositions, is impossible—if reductionism is true.

Note also the reductionist's insistence that everyone admit to the fundamental truth that "man is nothing more than…" the truth *which does not exist in the first place* (since all science is a fiction). The truth is that there is no truth, just constructs. And if that is the case, it would seem that all constructs are equally valid and invalid at the same time (in other words, the principle of non-contradiction is also a construct). Which construct, therefore, is going to prevail? It is the one with the most power behind it.

If we wish, however, to hold on to our common sense and avoid this entirely irrational state of affairs, then let us return to the "yes" alternative above. If the single celled organism, for example, is a thing in itself, what is it that reduces the multiplicity to a unity, a determinate thing or entity that can be studied? It is something outside the multiplicity. One cannot appeal to the parts that make it up. The parts are organized into an intelligible whole (unity). The principle of unity is a principle that is outside the parts, a principle that embraces the whole and determines the parts to be what they are. In other words, we must proceed in the complete opposite direction of reductionism. It is the whole that explains the part or parts. Some principle belongs to the whole organism (or atom or bacterium) that determines it (and all its parts) to be what it is. That principle, I would argue, is the formal cause, or the substantial form of the thing.

58 Some Thoughts on Mathematical Knowing

Mathematical reasoning takes place on the second level of abstraction. What this means is that the mind considers quantity abstracted from sensible matter. The triangles we study in Geometry have no matter, they are not made of wood or steel, they are not soft, red or malleable, etc. Mathematical entities have no motion, they possess no disposition to act in any particular way (as does gasoline, for example), numbers are not flammable, nor do they have a boiling point. And so there is no final causality with mathematical entities, that is, they don't move towards an end, nor are they agent causes (they don't move or alter other things). The only causes mathematical entities like numbers, or lines, etc., possess are the material cause and the formal cause. The matter of number is 1, and the form is the quantity itself (i.e., 3, or 4, or 100). In other words, "what" is 100? It is 100 units, or 1 having the form (quantity) of 100. In geometry, the matter is the subject that possesses the form (i.e., the form triangle, or circle, or square or line, etc.), but this matter is purely intelligible (intelligible matter, or an intelligible subject, not sensible matter or a sensible subject).

Now, the more abstract the level, the more certain is the knowledge obtained at that level, which is why mathematics is a far more certain science than physics or biology. The more we descend to the realm of concrete sensible particulars (sensible matter), our knowledge becomes less certain. This is not to say that certainty is not possible in biology or physics (the first level of abstraction); rather, it means that it is simply more difficult to achieve certainty in our conclusions (what is the cause of this uncontrolled cell replication is harder to determine with certainty than the answer to this or that math problem).

Mathematical knowledge is very limited in terms of what it tells us about real being. A mathematical entity is not real, but logical (in the mind). For example, a point is not a real thing that exists outside the mind, neither is a triangle in its mathematical purity. I can't show you the number 5, only 5 apples or 5 people, etc. Mathematical knowing does not give us a knowledge of the "what" of things (their nature), but only a knowledge of the "how much" of a thing or an aspect of a thing, namely, a thing's measurable aspects (quantifiable aspects). When we quantify something that is not a quantity (such as a quality), what we come to understand is that thing not in terms of itself, but in terms of something other than itself, that is, in terms of quantity. That is why although there is tremendous usefulness in knowing things in terms of their measurable aspects, there is something unsatisfying about mathematical knowing. The human person desires to know the natures of things (what they are), not merely their quantities (how much they are).

Consider that from a purely mathematical point of view, 25 pennies, two dimes and a nickel, and a quarter, are all the same, for they are quantitatively equal, and mathematics is about quantities; for number is a species of quantity. Now, mathematical knowing, as we said, abstracts from the physical and considers quantity alone, leaving out quality (i.e., color, texture, sensible matter, etc) and motion (how matter reacts with other elements, boiling point, etc.). On a less abstract level, that is, on the physical level (the first level of abstraction), a penny, a dime, and a nickel and quarter are really different. A penny is made mostly of zinc, and it contains a much smaller percentage of copper. The Canadian dime is very different, so too the American dime; the dime is made up of steel, copper, nickel and silver, 92% of it being made of steel. A nickel is an alloy of copper and nickel; a Canadian quarter is made of cupronickel plated steel (60/40).

Sir Arthur Eddington's well known illustration of an elephant that slides down a grassy hillside illustrates the same point. What he says here is very revealing in terms of the mathematization of our ordinary knowledge, which is something that happens for the most part in the science of mathematical physics. He writes (emphasis mine):

Let us then examine the kind of knowledge which is handled by exact science. If we search the examination papers in physics and natural philosophy for the more intelligible questions we may come across one beginning something like this: 'An elephant slides down a grassy hillside . . .' The experienced candidate knows that he need not pay much attention to this; it is only put in to give an impression of realism. He reads on: 'The mass of the elephant is two tons.' Now we are getting down to business; the elephant **fades out** of the problem and a mass of two tons takes its place. What exactly is this two tons, the real subject-matter of the problem? It refers to some property or condition which we vaguely describe as 'ponderosity' occurring in a particular region of the external world. But we shall not get much further that way; the nature of the external world is inscrutable, and we shall only plunge into a quagmire of indescribables. Never mind what two tons refers to; what is it? How has it actually entered in so definite a way into our experience? Two tons is **the reading of the pointer** when the elephant was placed on a weighing-machine. Let us pass on. 'The slope of the hill is 60°.' Now the hillside fades out of the problem and an angle of 60° takes its place. What is 60°? There is no need to struggle with mystical conceptions of direction; **60° is the reading of a plumb-line against the divisions of a protractor**. Similarly for the other data of the problem. The softly yielding turf on which the elephant slid is replaced by **a coefficient of friction**, which though perhaps not directly a pointer reading is of kindred nature. No doubt there are more roundabout ways used in practice for determining the weights of elephants and the slopes of hills, but these are justified because it is known that they give the same results as direct pointer readings.

And so we see that **the poetry fades out of the problem**, and by the time the serious application of exact science begins we are left with **only pointer readings**. If then only pointer readings or their equivalents are put into the machine of scientific calculation, how can we grind out anything but pointer readings? But that is just what we do grind out. The question presumably was to find the time of descent of the elephant, and the answer is a pointer reading on the seconds' dial of our watch.

The triumph of exact science in the foregoing problem consisted in establishing **a numerical connection** between the pointer reading of the weighing-machine in one experiment on the elephant and the pointer reading of the watch in another experiment. And when we examine critically other problems of physics we find that this is typical. The whole subject-matter of exact science consists of pointer readings and similar indications. We cannot enter here into the definition of what are to be classed as similar indications. ...The essential point is that, although we seem to have very definite conceptions of objects in the external world, those conceptions **do not enter into exact science** and are not in any way confirmed by it. Before exact science can begin to handle the problem **they must be replaced by quantities representing the results of physical measurement.**

Perhaps you will object that although only the pointer readings enter into the actual calculation it would make nonsense of the problem to leave out all reference to anything else. The problem necessarily involves some kind of connecting background. It was not the pointer reading of the weighing-machine that slid down the hill! And yet from the point of view of exact science the thing that really did descend the hill can only be described as a bundle of pointer readings. (It should be remembered that the hill also has been replaced by pointer readings, and the sliding down is no longer **an active adventure** but a functional relation of space and time measures.) The word elephant calls up a certain association of mental impressions, but it is clear that mental impressions as such cannot be the subject handled in the physical problem. We have, for example, an impression of bulkiness. To this there is presumably some direct counterpart in the external world, but that counterpart must be of a nature beyond our apprehension, and science can make nothing of it. Bulkiness enters into exact science by yet another substitution; we replace it by a series of readings of a pair of calipers. Similarly the greyish black appearance in our mental impression is replaced in exact science by the readings of a photometer for various wave-lengths of light. And so on until all the characteristics of the elephant are exhausted and it has become **reduced to a schedule of measures**. There is always the triple correspondence—

  (a) a mental image, which is in our minds and not in the external world;

  (b) some kind of counterpart in the external world, which is of inscrutable nature;

  (c) a set of pointer readings, which exact science can study and connect with other pointer readings.

And so we have our schedule of pointer readings ready to make the descent. And if you still think that this substitution has taken away all reality from the problem, I am not sorry that you should have a foretaste of **the difficulty in store for those who hold that exact science is all-sufficient for the description of the universe and that there is nothing in our experience which cannot be brought within its scope.**"[55]

This is an important insight into the problem of all reductionism. But the point I wish to underscore here is that although number can tell us a great deal about a thing, a "measure" does not tell us "what" something is. The reason is that mathematical knowing abstracts from real motion, and since we come to know the nature of a thing (what it is essentially) through its activity (its real motions), mathematical knowing does not provide us with a knowledge of the natures of things; it can only reduce motions to "pointer readings". Consider a very simple example of two animals that are both 6 feet in length and

---

[55] Sir Arthur Eddington, *The Nature of the Physical World*. Cambridge: Cambridge University Press, 1928. 251-4. Retrieved from http://www.archive.org/details/natureofphysical00eddi

200 pounds. Numerically, quantitatively, they are equal, but one is a fish; the other is a human being. The two are qualitatively different, that is, specifically or essentially different.

This essential difference in physical and mathematical knowing can be further explicated by considering the difference between randomness and chance. Randomness is not the same as chance. As an example, consider a statistical whole, a barrel full of variously coloured jelly beans that have been well shaken up so that the units of different colors are arranged in a uniform pattern throughout the container. This uniform distribution of units in a whole is called a **random distribution**. Now, the jelly beans of different colors are evenly scattered throughout this aggregate. We will also assume that from the dimensions of the barrel and the size of the jelly beans, the number of beans in the whole aggregate can be calculated to be 100,000. And let us say that after drawing a sample of 1000 jelly beans, we find that there are 600 white and 400 black ones. From this sample, it **can then be predicted** that in the whole barrel there are 60,000 white beans and 40,000 black ones. However, such a prediction only holds for the total aggregate. If one were about to pick an individual bean out of the barrel, can it be determined with certainty which color will be picked? No, the color of any one pick can be predicted **only with probability**. Even when the actual ratio of white and black beans in the whole aggregate are known, only probable predictions can be made of individual picks. And so, the probability of picking a white jelly bean is .6, and the probability of picking a black bean on any one occasion is .4.

Randomness, however, is not the same as chance, for a homogeneous distribution, like that of the jelly beans in the barrel, is truly **an ordered collection**. There is an order of a different kind from the order that experience usually reveals and that we normally study in the sciences, like the order in the human body, or the order in nature, but there is order and pattern nevertheless (pattern, *regula*, regularity, law, lawfulness), which is why randomness can be an object of study (the mathematics of probability). What is disordered and chaotic, however, **cannot be an object of study**. For it is possible to make a mathematical analysis of a random collection; the order found to exist in the whole proves that there is an order among the individual parts even when we are unable to trace out the order itself. Statistics can be applied only to the extent that the material studied has an order.

Randomness involves the mathematical; but chance is physical, not mathematical. Chance is a real disorder; but randomness is a disorder **only for our logic**, accustomed as it is to the non-statistical methods of solving problems. As proof of its difference from randomness, consider that **chance can interfere with a random collection and thus introduce a real, physical disorder**; for example, when the sampling process is interrupted and the one counting the beans leaves the room temporarily, birds or other animals could invade the bean barrel and eat a significant quantity of the beans, thus producing a **chance disturbance** of the random aggregate.

When a problem becomes too complicated to handle through non-statistical techniques, statistics becomes a useful substitute for the more common kinds of induction. Frequently, factors in a problem concerning, for instance, the structure of matter or the transmission of biological characteristics are too numerous in themselves or in their possible combinations to admit a more direct mathematical treatment. But this kind of disorder that exists when a problem must be handled by statistical means is truly **a matter of human ignorance**, such as the failure to understand except in terms of probability the behaviour of individual beans in the above example. This "disorder" is really only an apparent disorder; it is **really an order**, as the pattern found throughout the whole aggregate in our above example indicates. It is an order whose parts we do not understand.

In radioactivity, for instance, our laws are unable to predict which individual atoms will decay or when any one atom will decay. But the behaviour of the whole aggregate, which enables us to determine a half-life period for every radioactive element, shows that we are dealing with an order, although it is **an order we do not fully understand**. In regard to quantum physics, the fact that our macroscopic world is ordered proves that there is order among atoms and their parts, even if it is an order we do not comprehend.

Order does not spring from chance; rather chance is something **secondary and relative to** an already existing order. Only in relation to order can chance exist and be understood. Take the example of meeting someone at a restaurant by chance. Your action of going out for supper at a Chinese restaurant was purposeful, intentional, and everything you did to get there (drive the car, put on your shoes, lock the door, etc.) was ordered to that end. It was not a chance event that you ended up at the Chinese restaurant, it was planned and ordered (intended). But Jimmy, whom you haven't seen in 20 years, decided to take his new wife to a movie while on vacation in Markham. The theatre is next to the Chinese restaurant. As he is walking into the theatre with his new wife, you are walking towards the restaurant; your paths cross. The meeting was a chance event. Now the meeting was not ordered. Your arrival at the restaurant was ordered, Jimmy's arrival at the theatre was ordered, but your crossing one another's lines of purpose was not ordered to one another, that is, it was not determined. It was really "undetermined" (thus unknowable); the intersection of the two orders is not itself an ordered event, i.e., flowing from a determinate and necessary cause. Rather, it is an accidental adjunct to the two lines of causality, in which each follows out its proper order and in neither of which is the meeting essentially included.

It is possible to inquire of the probability of that chance meeting, and it is possible to inquire of the probability of getting to the Chinese restaurant, but it does not follow that the two events are in reality (that is, outside of the mathematics of probability) essentially the same kind of events, i.e., probable events. They are treated by the statistician as probable events; but they are in reality different kinds of events, in the same way that 100 pennies, 10 dimes, 20 nickels, and 4 quarters are all equal or are the same from a purely mathematical point of view (numerical point of view), but are in reality something that number alone cannot determine.

Consider how physics students are taught to graph motion using a standard x-y graph.[56] On the vertical axis let's chart the distance from the zero point (perhaps the school). On the horizontal axis, one charts the time. The figure below shows someone staying at the same point, 2.7 kilometers away from the zero point (i.e., the school) for a length of time (2.5 hours).

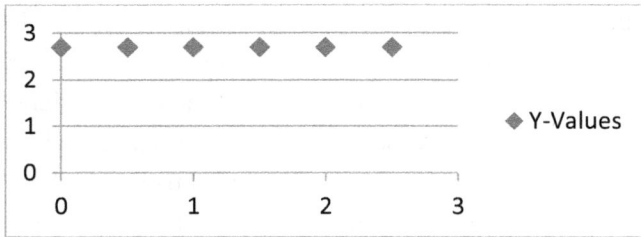

The diagram below shows a person starting from a distance 2.5 kilometers away and moving at a uniform speed of 0.5 kilometers per half hour toward the school (zero point).

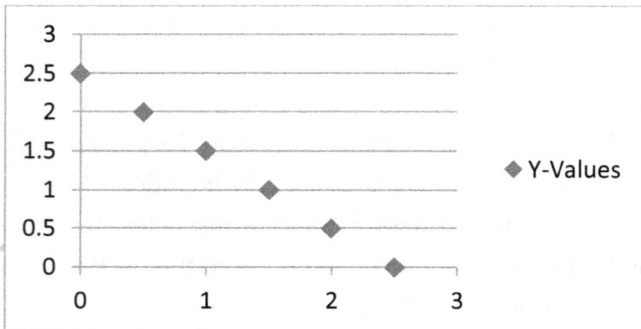

This is a typical use of mathematics to describe motion. Note that there is no introduction of actual motion into the mathematics—there is no motion in the figures above. The mathematical construct is unchanging. Now the question to ask is: "How can changeless mathematics describe change?" The answer is by leaving the change

[56] Anthony Rizzi, *The Science Before Science: A Guide to Thinking in the 21st Century*. Baton Rouge, IAP Press, 2004. 175-176.

behind. What has happened here is that time has been turned into a spatial variable, which does not change as time changes. In other words, *time is treated as if all moments existed at once*, the way space does. It is as if the one moving towards home is a one-dimensional thing that exists both at point A, B, C, etc., and at school (zero) at the same time (1.5 hours away, 2 hours away, and 2.5 hours away, etc., at the same time).

That is why it is philosophically erroneous to identify what exists in the mind (i.e., numbers, or concepts) with real entities, as many people are wont to do today, in particular those mathematical physicists who think for the most part in mathematical terms. Logical being has being "in the mind" only. For example, a point exists in the mind only, as does the number 3, or 10, or ½, etc. The point and the number 3 have no "real" existence outside the mind. The mind, on the contrary, abstracted them from the realm of real being.

Number, as an abstracted quantity, measures the real, but it is not identical to the real. To identify the logical with the real (logical being with real being) is to confuse the measure with the measured. Now some people confuse the two, and when they do, they end up saying things that sound new and sophisticated, but are in fact absurd. For example, because our knowledge of what occurs on subatomic level is had in terms of mathematics, some people with a reductionist habit of mind will say things like "This table is nothing but a probability factor…Man is simply a probability factor, etc." To speak this way is to confuse the method employed to study reality with reality itself.

Taking this to another level, a man might have originated as a result of a gamble, for example, his mother was on the pill, and she knew that the pill has a 32% probability of allowing ovulation to occur after a two-year period; she takes a gamble, and conceives. Johnny, it is said, was the result of a "probability". But that does not tell us what Johnny is. **A probability is not a thing**, but Johnny is a thing, a specific kind of thing, namely a human kind of being. The beans in the barrel form a random distribution, and there is a probability that when I pick 10 beans, 4 will be black. But the question remains: "What is a black bean? To answer: "A 40% probability" fails to answer the question, although the answer says something that is true. The same random distribution could have existed with 100,000 coins, 60% made up of gold coins, and 40% made up of pennies. A gold coin is very different than a white bean, although both can be said to be a 60% probability.

To say that a man is a probability does not say a great deal; for man is a great deal more than that, he is a being of a determinate nature capable of introspection, capable of knowing mathematical laws, i.e., the mathematics of probability, the laws of physics, etc., and he is a free being who can determine himself to this or that option. He is a being capable of knowing that he knows, knowing that he senses, and he knows the natures of things, so he can operate on animals, which is something that animals cannot do. Moreover, a man can operate on himself. A man is one who refers to himself as "I", who says things like "I" have a brain, a heart, a liver, etc., which seems to imply that the "I" is not the brain, the heart, the liver, etc., but the subject which possesses a brain, a heart, a liver, etc. And so, a man can wonder what this "I" really is. The "I" is not a "we", but can become a "we" in a certain respect. The "I" is one, for a man will say "Hey, I am the "one" who did the experiment", or "I am the one who operated on you and saved your life". In other words, man experiences himself, through introspection, as a unity, as one, not two, not three, etc. He says "I have many parts, many organs, many cells, but they are "my" parts, parts of the "one" me. He can wonder what it is that renders this multiplicity "one being". And, he can also wonder why introspection is different than a gastroscopy: I look into myself through introspection to answer the question whether or not I possess free-will, for example, but this thoughtful introspection is not the same thing as a doctor looking at the inside of my stomach through a gastroscope. What is this "second interior" to which the doctor has no access, but which only the man does (which is precisely what is meant by a private experience—his introspection can never be opened up to another person to share, it can never be public, but will always be a private experience)?

59 Thoughts on the Learning Curve

A learning curve refers to a mathematical representation of the learning process. It consists of a graph with a vertical axis, which represents learning proficiency, and a horizontal axis, which represents experience over time.

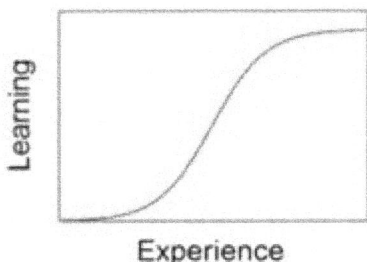

At first, learning is slow, and the experience we have of our own limitations is acute. This is visible on the graph as a slope that gradually ascends. But as time goes on, we become more proficient and we learn much more quickly. Thus, the slope of the line on the graph becomes rather steep; we feel that we are "getting it", and our learning is much more rapid. Then our learning begins to level off.

Now imagine a person saying something to the effect that learning has sigmoid properties, or learning is a sigmoidal phenomenon, or learning is a functionally derivative phenomenon, etc. We would naturally wonder what it is that person is talking about. All is he is doing, however, is employing a model and using it to represent something real, namely learning, and in the process, he confuses his listeners, at least those not familiar with calculus.

The learning curve is a mathematical model of the learning process. It is a useful model, but it leaves out a great deal of what is involved in learning. For example, learning is an activity, not a quantity. As an activity, learning is a motion. The mathematical model, which is made up of logical entities (numbers, points, lines, vertical and horizontal axes, etc.,), does not move, but is static—it statically represents a movement. The model is abstract, but learning is concrete.

The mathematical model reduces learning to a quantity, but learning is qualitative, for we learn "what" things are (i.e., human beings, substances, etc.,), or how to do certain kinds of things, i.e., manage a restaurant, look after a bunch of children, use a computer, etc.

To mathematize an activity is to abstract aspects of the activity, which leaves other aspects behind. This can be useful in coming to understand aspects of the learning process, but it also impoverishes the learning process, similar to mathematizing a human person. If the human person is always more than what can be known about him scientifically or essentially, how much more is this true with respect to the mathematization of the human person? All the more so is he more than what can be known about him when he is reduced to quantities. The same is true for the learning process. Mathematics apprehends only the quantitative aspects of reality. It's an impoverished kind of knowledge that is highly useful, clean and certain.

60 On Dialogue

One of the most important articles for a young student of philosophy to work through is Thomas Nagel's 1974 classic paper entitled: "What is it like to be a bat?"[57] Nagel argues well that we simply cannot form anything more than a "schematic conception" of what it is like to be a bat; the subjective character specific to these creatures is simply beyond our ability to conceive. He writes: "… even to form a conception of what it is like to be a bat…one must take up the bat's point of view. If one can take it up roughly, or partially, then one's conception will also be rough or partial."

He argues that our range of understanding is limited because our own experience is all that our imagination has to work with; thus, the more the other's experience (i.e., that of a bat, a mosquito, etc.) is different from my own, the less am I able to understand the "objective ascription" of the experience in both the first person and the third person. And so it follows that "there are facts that do not consist in the truth of propositions expressible in a human language".

Nagel, however, is careful to point out that this problem is not limited to "exotic cases", such as the subjective character of a bat or snake, etc., but exists also between human persons: "The subjective character of the experience of a person deaf and blind from birth is not accessible to me, for example, nor presumably is mine to him."

A mental health patient who suffers from clinical depression told me once how upset he became at a young cleric who patronizingly assured him: "I know what you are going through". The fact of the matter is he has no idea what this patient is going through. Most of us simply do not know what it is like to have suffered sexual abuse at a young age and to be suffering from clinical depression and to be subject to severe temptations to suicide.

---

[57] Thomas Nagel, "What is it like to be a bat?" The Philosophical Review LXXXIII, 4 (October 1974). 435-50. Retrieved from http://organizations.utep.edu/portals/1475/nagel_bat.pdf

The fundamental point here is true even with respect to less extreme and more ordinary instances; I only know what it is like to be you to a very limited degree. What is it like to possess your unique epistemic conditions and thus interpret the world through that epistemic model of yours? My understanding can only be partial; for I understand some people better than others, because they think very much like me, have had very similar experiences, are making the same mistakes I made in the past, etc. Such people are not a problem for me to understand well, but such people are relatively few and far between. Most people I know are very much unlike me. Not only do they have a different personality and are different in moral identity or character, they've had experiences that I will likely never have. Only on a very general level am I able to understand such people. But the more conditions for knowing that I acquire through life, the wider becomes my range of ability to understand others. All this is the result of the fact that human intelligence is limited by matter, by its close association with sense perception, space, time, memory, etc.

I will argue that we are able to gradually acquire certain conditions for knowing through authentic dialogue; for it is authentic dialogue that moves me ever closer to an understanding of the other, without ever being able to understand him completely. For dialogue to be authentic, both require a rare ability to listen, an ability to achieve an exit-of-self, and both have to be at that point in their lives where they have begun to adopt an attitude of healthy skepticism towards their current way of seeing things, that is, a practical openness to the fact that reality is always much larger than what my own limited epistemic model would suggest. This is difficult for some people, because they tend to confuse universal ideas and deductive reasoning with the overall model through which the real is interpreted.

There is a significant difference between ideas that are universal and thus encompass every particular instance of the universal, and an epistemic model that is limited and far from all encompassing. Included in an epistemic model are, among other things, deductively reasoned conclusions that require universal propositions in order to be valid;

however, although I possess the universal idea of 'equine', for example, or 'humanity', or 'radiation', etc., the idea is often poor in content, for I know very little about horses, relatively little about human nature, and certainly less about the nature of radiation. It is through induction, a process of inferencing on the basis of observed activity that I come to know the natures of things more completely, but the activity I choose to pay attention to depends upon the kinds of questions I ask, which in turn depends upon the problems I wish to solve and the aspects of these things that currently interest me. Thus, I always end up asking questions that belong to a limited and determinate area of knowledge; I may end up asking questions proper to the science of psychology, or biology, or philosophy, etc. And so included in that model through which I interpret the real are a multitude of inferences, each one of which has a power that I am often unaware of, a power independent of its degree of probability.

The epistemic model through which I interpret the real is always limited and in development, for there are so many epistemic conditions that I am currently missing that alone will permit me to understand what I am simply unable to understand without them—I believe conditions are currently missing only because I have been steadily acquiring "conditions for knowing" every year it seems, from as far back as I can remember, and I have no reason to believe the process is at an end or even whether there is such an end. But when I allow my own limited model to enter into contact with one entirely different, that is, when I enter into dialogue with another who asks different questions because he is interested in different problems, a "clash of cultures" (Popper) takes place. Depending on how I understand the nature of knowledge, I will see this clash either as something positive or as something negative.

During this "clash of cultures", many of my inferences are challenged, especially those that have crystallized into apparent certainties as a result of being left unchallenged for so long. My reasoned conclusions too are critically challenged, in particular those that are invalid, but also those that are incomplete—and my reasoning is always incomplete, whether it is deductive or inductive. The other with whom I choose to dialogue might compel me to take my reasoning further; he might challenge me to notice the limitations of the premises upon which my reasoning begins and challenge me to take another look, this time perhaps from a different angle. And how much of my inferencing is contaminated by bias?

Indeed, some biases blind, and some shed light; the other with whom I am in dialogue might be subject to biases that permit him to see what I hitherto have been unable to see, thus he may shed light on the deficiencies of my own model. Moreover, my own moral paradigm might also be insufficient. Finally, everything I have said about him can be said about me, that is, I may challenge him to expand his intellectual frame of mind.

To understand someone to the point where he actually enlarges my purview and enables me to see what I otherwise would not see, usually takes a great deal of time and effort. That is why it is normal to need to read a great book a number of times; it takes more than one reading to begin to appreciate a person's *magnum opus*; for if a person has spent a lifetime thinking about certain problems within a very specific frame of mind, how can I be expected to benefit from the model through which he interprets the real after just one reading? I have to read it, and read it again, and perhaps a third time in order to begin to re-examine all that I know, or most of what I know, in light of the new horizon with which I am beginning to become familiar. He has asked different questions, and those questions open up for me a new avenue that very often comes across as strange, at least initially. It is not enough for me to try to understand him while remaining within my own intellectual horizon; I cannot enter his world without a certain *ecstasis*, an active exit of self; for there is no enlarging of the self without such an exit of self.

It seems to me that it is fear that keeps a person from "taking leave of himself" and his comfortable surroundings, and so he remains within a small circle of authors with whom he is familiar, who do not threaten the stability of his little world. Such people demand to see everything from a very limited vantage point; the result is uniformity, a feeling of security, and a measure of control, as well as a stifling, unexciting, and exclusive point of view. The default position of such a narrow mind becomes "I am right", and so dialogue is no longer regarded as an avenue for growth in learning but is interpreted as a kind of battle, an opportunity to take on a defence of a relatively small worldview.

Reality is always so much larger than an epistemic model, just as mathematical models of some aspect of reality seem to fall short after a certain point. Similarly, the realm of the real always exceeds the scope of our own epistemic model that is made up of deductively reasoned conclusions, probable inferences, true and false beliefs, unknown biases, as well as the limited language we speak, disordered passions that affect our perception, and a profoundly limited experience of the world of people and places.

That is why dialogue can be a very exciting prospect. Great treasures can be discovered in the most unexpected places—more than once has it happened that I have discovered insights and valuable ways of looking at certain problems, very useful to a religious paradigm, from some of the most anti or simply non-religious sources.

61 Uncertainty in Science and Metaphysics

If it is true that the higher the level of abstraction, the greater the certainty, then it would follow that metaphysics is the most certain of sciences, and if it is the most certain, we would expect to see universal agreement, as we do in mathematics. Clearly this is not the case. Thus, it seems this is an instance of a hypothesis and an observational prediction, followed by overwhelming evidence that contradicts the prediction.

I cannot argue with such a conclusion; there is no universal agreement in metaphysics as there is in mathematics, thus reasoning on the highest level of abstraction does not seem to yield certainty. I am going to argue, however, that the uncertainty or tentative nature of metaphysical conclusions is very different than the uncertainty that belongs to conclusions in the natural sciences. To illustrate the difference, I would like to employ an analogy. When discussing contraception, we often speak of two kinds of failure rates: a user failure rate and a method failure rate. In the case of the former, the method works, but the person taking the pill misuses it (user failure), and thus it fails; in the latter, the person taking the pill uses it correctly, but it fails (method failure). It is said that Natural Family Planning has a user failure rate only, while the pill has both a user and a method failure rate.

The uncertainty that belongs to the physical sciences is akin to a method failure rate. The object of scientific investigation, namely a hypothesis that best explains the evidence, is for the most part uncertain, because to get there is a matter of inferencing, and there might be other possible antecedents that explain the evidence, thus testing is required to determine as far as possible whether our hypothesis is the one that best explains the evidence.

The uncertainty that belongs to the philosophy of being, however, is akin to the user failure rate. The philosophy of being takes place on the highest level of abstraction, for it considers being *insofar as* it is being. Although I may be uncertain of the exact nature of the thing before me, at the very least I am certain that "it is", whatever it turns out to be. It is not possible to empirically investigate a hypothesis belonging to the philosophy of being; what would it mean to empirically test whether or not essence and existence are really distinct? We have to reason to our conclusions; in other words, we test it rationally or dialectically, not empirically. The uncertainty is the result of the weakness of the intellect, our inability to grasp the idea or acquire the insight. Once the insight is had, such as "the act of existing is really distinct from essence", the rest is a matter of unraveling all its implications and coming to a deeper penetration and richer insight into the idea.

Human beings have different intellectual dispositions, and some dispositions or habits of mind make the philosophy of being more difficult to grasp. Sometimes people are very uncomfortable dealing with concepts they cannot picture in their imagination, or ideas that cannot be quantified in any way, and perhaps for some people the emotions incline them in a certain direction, for example, away from anything that might lead to the possibility of God's existence.

Indeed, to many people this is a very unsatisfactory answer to the question, and I am aware that I have not proven my claim. It may also seem as if what I am saying implies that one day metaphysics will have discovered all that can be discovered on that level, that metaphysical matters will have been finally settled or completely unravelled. But that is not what I am arguing, and I would doubt very much that metaphysics will come to an end. A host of metaphysical insights might appear to me to be clear and certain, and I believe I do possess some certainty in this area. My reasoning on the basis of those principles is valid and deductive, but the insights into what it means "to be" are incomplete—they have been in the past, and there is no reason for me to think that will ever change; there is far more to the story than what I have hitherto grasped. Discovering this may not necessarily cancel—although it might—what I've apprehended thus far, but only add to it significantly.

So the uncertainty, I believe, is in the user, not in the method. Science has a user failure rate, but it also has a method failure rate. Proximate causes hide behind matter, buried underneath the evidence, so to speak, and it is up to the scientist to find the cause, test the hypothesis, attempt to falsify it, etc. Ultimate causes are right before us, we just have to adjust the eyes of the mind as one would focus a pair of binoculars—it is just that adjusting binoculars takes a few seconds, while disposing the mind to think analogically about being and existence takes years.

62 Orders of Ignorance

Consider a local newspaper of a small town, like the *Auroran* or the *Markham Economist & Sun*. Read an issue and then consider just how much is going on in this small town that was completely outside the purview of your mind (i.e., I didn't know we had a world class singer among us, nor was I aware that someone is going forth with plans to open a heritage museum, etc.). And if you happen to read a story about someone or something you know rather well, consider just how much is left out of account; for you know that there is far more to the lives of those involved than what the story can hope to cover in a few columns.

There's a sense in which we can talk about a first and second order ignorance: you know that those who read a story about something you are familiar with "first hand" are only getting a fraction of what there is to know, which means they are, relatively speaking, left in the dark, or are perhaps being misled, for the story leaves so much space in between facts that it practically invites others to fill in the blanks and thereby construct their own narrative. And yet when we read a story about someone or something we are not familiar with, we are not explicitly conscious of the fact that we are getting only a fraction of what there is to know about those involved, but we are aware that this story and that initiative, etc., were outside our limited range of experience—we are surprised and perhaps delighted to learn of it. Compared to what we do know already, we feel we are given new light, even though we forget or are simply not aware that the light is scanty, thin, and probably misleading. The latter is what I would call a first order ignorance, the former a second order ignorance, known explicitly only upon further reflection.

This two-fold layer of ignorance can be multiplied, because the same principle applies to a major city's newspaper, such as the *Toronto Star* and the *Toronto Sun*. In fact, compare these two papers and you may notice that much is left out of one that the other retains, and vice versa. And once again, when a story is covered having to do with something we know well, like the school at which we teach or the parish we attend, or a person we know, etc., we notice again that much has been left out, so much, in fact, that the public simply cannot come to a sufficient understanding of this school community, parish, or person, etc., through this one story. Many will inevitably believe, however, that they now have a thorough grasp of what this community, parish, or person is about, etc., after having read the article. And yet most of what we read is unfamiliar; thus, it is easy to walk away from a newspaper feeling informed and enlightened, for there really is a tremendous amount that was, just moments earlier, completely outside our personal range of experience.

A newspaper gives us a very tiny window onto a vast area; and on the glass of that window is a tremendous amount of dust and grime that prevents us from noticing so many important details. All we are left with—compared to the totality of what there is to know in the city—are tiny pieces of information from which we can infer very little with certainty. The temptation is always to bring closure to that state of ambiguity, to construct a narrative that brings coherence to those isolated and incomplete facts, and the resulting narrative is something we're not even aware was our own construct.

Now consider this two-fold order of ignorance with respect to a national newspaper. Our "unknowing" is multiplied once again, exponentially. There is so much that is going on in the nation that we simply do not and cannot know about—we have neither the time nor the capacity—, and what we come to know as a result of reading about it is thin and insufficient, again obvious only to those who know the facts from the inside.

This order of ignorance is further multiplied when we consider an international newspaper. Read it and consider just how much you did not know about what is going on in India, China, or Turkey, etc., and that what you now know is woefully incomplete, although it may not feel incomplete. Consider too that the window any of us are given is one framed by someone on the basis of what is more likely to capture the interest of the readership, or possibly what might further a cause, and not necessarily on the basis of what is genuinely important to know.

A student once asked me to help him write a short essay he was required to write in his application to a university program he was interested in. He was to reflect on the question: "Where is the world headed?" To answer that question is like trying to figure out where an individual person is headed while being given only tiny fragments of information on what is taking place on the cellular level of his body. Your guess is as good as mine. What is going on in my own relatively small school community of slightly over 1100 students is always more than what I currently know; so much is happening outside my awareness—something I discover with every school newsletter. What goes on in that small community school is even more than what those in "governing" positions know as a group; if it can be said that they have a more comprehensive grasp of what takes place among them, that wider apprehension is had at the expense of depth and detail—the wider one stretches an elastic, the thinner it becomes.

So much of what has happened and is currently going on in my own life is outside the awareness of my colleagues, and if there are 100 other such adults in the school, then the same principle applies to me 100 times over—leaving aside the students. In other words, in this small community, there is a veritable universe of which all of us, including myself, are virtually ignorant.

Consider, as well, those people that we only later on in life have come to understand, all because we had changed in some way (i.e., came into certain experiences, grew in maturity, etc.). We did not understand them before, but we have a better understanding of them now, albeit an incomplete one. Part of the reason we came to understand them better is that we have become more like them, in some ways at least. There are, however, a myriad of people we do not understand and will likely never understand adequately, because they will remain very much unlike us—perhaps better than us, or not necessarily better or worse.

Despite all that happens outside our knowledge and control, there is an order that unfolds. The large and small societies we live in are not a chaos, but each one is a cosmos within a larger cosmos (*kosmein:* "to arrange, to adorn," from *kosmos*: "order"). And I know from within that I am not the cause of that order, nor is it under my control; I am in it, carried along in its current. No one individual or group of individuals (i.e., a bureaucracy) is the cause of that order, nor does anyone or any group have dominion over it; to have complete control of it implies it is understood in all its details, which is simply not possible. In fact, the more one tries to control this larger order, the more frustrated one becomes; to comprehend it is impossible because it is always exceedingly larger than the human intellect. Not even a teacher has complete control over a small society such as a classroom of students who have been entrusted to him; certainly he establishes the conditions necessary for an atmosphere conducive to learning, and in that sense he brings order, but he does not control his students, he has no dominion over their minds and wills, nor the circumstances of their individual lives (whether or not they get sick, their individual intellectual dispositions, the circumstances of their family, etc.). In creating optimal conditions, the teacher hopes for something to happen on its own that he is helpless to determine, as a farmer who does everything right, hopes for the best but does not determine the outcome, that is, whether there will be a good crop this year, which depends on many factors outside his control, like the weather, insects, his own health, etc.

Human knowing is profoundly limited and, most importantly, it is widely dispersed. The fact of the matter is that there is only a very tiny sphere in which what is made available to an individual is sufficient to make valid inferences. That fact, however, does not seem to stop many of us from talking as if that tiny sphere is not so tiny after all, as if there isn't a larger order beyond our ability to comprehend. We have a tendency to believe that our understanding of the community, or the city, the nation, and the world, is sufficiently complete to offer a commentary and some detailed advice with a high confidence level.

One of the most important conditions most conducive to mutual understanding and human progress is the awareness of the profound limitations that matter and sense perception impose on human knowing. It is an epistemic condition that will allow people to think and speak more slowly and listen more readily.

63 *The Relativity of Visual Statistics*

There is a clever Ted Talk given by a talented artist, Chris Jordan, entitled "Turning powerful stats into art". In it he provides artistic visuals of statistics that exceed our ability to imagine. For example, he produced a very interesting visual image, seen at a distance, of 1 million plastic cups, which is the number of plastic cups used and discarded on airline flights in the United States every six hours. He also presents an artistic visual of the number of paper cups we use per day in the United States, which is about 40 million. A day's quota of paper cup consumption in the United States stacks up on a canvas that comfortably frames the Statue of Liberty.

He goes on to point out that there are 2.3 million prisoners in the United States, which is followed by a visual of 2.3 million orange prison uniforms folded and stacked in columns, side by side. We see this after he points out that 25% of all adult prisoners in the world are Americans in prison in the United States.

Furthermore, 1100 Americans die of cigarette smoking every day, and yet the response to the 3000 people murdered on 9/11 continues to reverberate around the world and will do so for years to come; no one, however, talks about the 1100 who will die today as a result of cigarette smoking, and the 1100 who will die tomorrow, and the next day, etc.

He goes on to highlight a "tragic phenomenon", namely, the most popular high school graduation gift, which is breast augmentation surgery. To impress upon us the seriousness of the problem, he provides an image of a woman's breasts made out of a myriad of unclothed Barbie dolls.

His stated goal in this presentation is to have us "feel these issues more deeply"; only then will they begin to matter for us. The big question, he says, is "how do we change?"

That question, however, presupposes that we have come to "know" that changes are needed. The most this visual presentation can achieve is just what he purports to do, which is to make us "feel" that change is required; for although one might feel, after seeing his art, that changes are needed, no one actually "knows" that anything is amiss, at least not on the basis of his presentation. An image on canvas of female breasts made up of a myriad of used Barbie dolls, which provides a strong visual impression of the number of women in the United States that elect for breast augmentation surgery, sheds no light whatsoever on the moral nature of the issue. An image of 40 million paper cups on a canvas larger than the Statue of Liberty tells us nothing about whether or not we are overconsuming. How much smaller should the canvas have been, for a country of over 300 million people?

Allow me to create a visual of my own. The average person passes around 2000 milliliters of urine per day, which is roughly 2 quarts; we'll say that's 600 to 730 quarts per year. A pool holds 80,000 quarts of water, and a typical water tower holds 50 times that, which is about 4 million quarts. In a town of 53,000 people (i.e., Aurora), that's 32 million quarts of urine passed every year, which amounts to 8 water towers in one year. That's quite an impression we are left with. Can we make the case that the people of Aurora are peeing too much? That perhaps we need to be drinking less? After all, imagine if one of those towers were to suddenly break apart; an entire neighborhood would be wiped out in a flood of urine.

As an argument, the visual is a non-sequitur. In fact, the entire presentation is a series of non-sequiturs, albeit a very clever and enjoyable one.

Jordan insists that he is not finger pointing or blaming; rather, he is just "showing what we are". But that is precisely what he does not do; he shows us the "size" of things, what the daily number of paper cups would look like stacked up in columns and perched next to the Statue of Liberty, or the number of prison uniforms similarly stacked. These tell us nothing about what the issues are. Quantity does not tell us what we are or what anything is. 5,000 kilograms, for example, does not tell anyone whether we are talking about trucks, elephants, whales, or a pile of steel. The question about "what something is" as well as the moral nature of a current state of affairs is qualitative, but quantity is a "how much", not a "what". Visually depicting 2.3 million prison uniforms sheds no light on whether or not the justice system in the United States is fair or deficient, just as it does not follow that a school that has no suspensions or expulsions is necessarily a good school— zero suspensions might very well indicate negligence on the part of the administration. The fact that 1 in 4 prisoners around the world is an American in an American prison does not necessarily imply that other countries are doing better; it could just as well mean that America is the only country that has a legal system that actually works.

Size is relative, and what is relative can only be understood against the background of what is not relative. The height of the Statue of Liberty is not and simply cannot be a standard that measures excess consumption. Replace the 1 million plastic cups on flights with 1 million glass or ceramic cups that need to be washed with soap and hot water every 6 hours and the question of overconsumption is left unanswered; now it is simply a question of an overconsumption of soap, water, and the energy needed to heat that water. A visual statistic creates an impression, nothing more, but an impression is not an argument, much less is a feeling a reasoned conclusion. One might be passionate about a lot of things, but one might also be crazy.

64 *There is More to Knowledge than Knowledge Issues*

There is no denying that one of the most important things we need to come to appreciate more fully in the context of Theory of Knowledge is the nature of uncertainty, its roots in induction, and its scope, that is, how much of our day to day judgments are really inferences that have a probability factor that we are for the most part unaware. It is important, because we tend to make conjectures with a degree of certainty and confidence that is unwarranted. If I am not aware that there is much that I don't know and that what I think I "know" might not, in the end, be "knowledge" at all, then I am unable to learn anything new and dialogue is pointless—a point that Socrates understood well.

Now some people have made a great deal of progress in this area of epistemology, but I will argue that we should bear in mind that it remains a particular and limited area. Like any other area or mode of knowing, we can get so caught up with knowledge questions that the more important questions of philosophy, such as what constitutes good human action? Or what is the purpose of human life? etc., are simply left in the penumbra, because we are so entangled in knowledge questions—such as whether or not we can be certain of anything—that we don't feel justified in moving on to other non-epistemological questions until the epistemological ones have been settled.

I would argue, however, that already, in light of these important insights on the limitations of human knowing, induction biases, probability, etc., a fair bit of certitude is involved, including moral certitude. Thus, a number of these insights are a matter of deduction as well.

For example, we are certain that truth is the adequation between what is in the mind and "what is", because we know that "what is" (reality) is much larger than what our frail models are able to capture and articulate. We know with certainty that induction begins with the evidence, the particular facts, and proceeds towards possible hypotheses, and that confirmation of a hypothesis is not proof that it is true, and that disconfirmation is indeed proof that it is false, etc. These are just the logical implications of the rules of inference (i.e., denying the consequent). And we do know with certitude that we are subject to a host of biases that incline us towards making invalid inferences. In other words, our grasp of the real is always incomplete, and yet this is a genuine grasp of a real epistemological state of affairs—our limitations.

Furthermore, there is an important moral insight in this area as well, for we know that we ought to speak with greater hesitation, and that we ought to appreciate the limitations of our own perspective and avoid epistemic overconfidence. But these are not the product of induction or statistics; they are moral deductions. They are insights into the importance of the virtue of humility, which is a part of temperance, which in turn is rooted in an insight into the nature of justice; for it is justice that is the measure of the virtues of moderation. The moral insight is that I ought to come to a realistic assessment of myself, my limitations, and open myself to the insights of others, who often see things that I do not, by virtue of those very limitations imposed by matter (i.e., time, space, circumstance, etc.).

But why is that a moral requirement? Because I see that knowledge is a basic intelligible human good (a basic end) and that others know things that I don't. The ability to know real beings and their natures is the specific way that human beings exist as living things. Our desire to know is a desire to live, and so we see our own human life as good. And since I know beings and their natures outside of me, I know through a combination of self-knowledge and simple apprehension (the formation of concepts) that you too are of the same nature as I. Therefore, I know that 'the good' is much wider than my own private good, and so a "good man" is one who wills "the good" *as such*, not merely his own individual well-being. Willing my own good to the exclusion of others is analogous to limiting my own knowledge to what I see, thus refusing to see what another sees.

Insights such as these are easily discernable behind the claims and concerns of those who have made great progress in the area of heuristics and biases, induction, probability and the knowledge issues that arise out of them. In other words, there is far more to our knowledge than "knowledge" issues and questions. Epistemology is important, but to remain there, to focus exclusively on its issues, is to 'get stuck', and when one is stuck, one does not move, and if one does not move, one does not progress, for progression is a movement.

Sense Perception/Faith/Emotion/Language/Memory

65 Thoughts on Perception

One of the most important principles for the Theory of Knowledge is the Peripatetic axiom: "Nothing is in the intellect that is not first in the senses".[58] All knowledge begins in sensation, but it does not end in sensation; rather, it ends in intellection (supra sensible knowledge: the knowledge of existence and the natures of things). Our intellectual knowledge, however, shares in the limitations of sense perception. In other words, we come to know what things are gradually, as we perceive the world around us. Moreover, we only perceive things from a limited angle; the more angles from which we perceive a given phenomenon, the more complete is our perception and the intellectual understanding that proceeds from it.

In philosophy, we distinguish in order to unite. If we fail to make distinctions, our knowledge remains indistinct, that is, confused. What we distinguish in the mind, however, is not necessarily separate outside the mind—in other words, distinction is not separation. For example, we distinguish between substance and accident. The two, however, are not separated outside the mind. We live in a world of "things" or substances (i.e., water, gold, oak trees, birds, oxygen, etc.), and these things have modes of being that are "accidental", that is, these modes of being "inhere in" substance and modify it, not absolutely, but relatively. In other words, a substance can change accidentally (i.e., change color, or size, or position, etc.) while remaining the same substance. For example, I have known my daughter all her life, and although she has grown, it is still my daughter who has grown; she has not changed in any absolute sense. In other words, quantity is a distinct mode of being from substance. If quantity were identical to substance, a change in quantity would amount to a change in substance. Thus, we distinguish between substance and accident (in this case, the accident of quantity).

Within the history of philosophy, however, distinction soon became separation—at least for some thinkers—, and all the logical

---

[58] St. Thomas Aquinas, *Disputed Questions on Truth,* Q. 2 a. 3 arg. 19.

implications of that separation were slowly unravelled. If all knowledge begins in sensation, and all that my senses provide are sense impressions (i.e., color, texture, flavor, odor, temperature, etc.), then what justification do we have for positing the existence of a "substance" underlying these accidental modes of being? Perhaps that's all anything really is, namely a conglomeration of sense impressions regularly associated with one another. Perhaps "substance" is a construct, something we produce, or perhaps it is an *a priori* category[59]. And if sense impressions are "in us", how do we really know that there is actually anything "outside of us"?

To overcome these difficulties, I will argue that it is best to pay close attention to what it is we perceive when in the act of perceiving. I do not see color, nor do I feel texture, or taste flavor, etc. Rather, I see an apple, or more specifically, I see a red apple, and I taste a sweet apple; I am not touching firm and cold, but a firm and cold apple, etc. In other words, I sense "something", I perceive things, that is, I perceive the substance. The reason I say this is because nothing is in the intellect that is not first in the senses; if substance is not in the senses first, then how does it end up in the mind? If it is not first in the senses, then it is something that I construct or impose upon the sense data. One would then have to explain why I do that, or feel the need to do that. And then one would have to explain what is this "I" that is doing the constructing. Perhaps "I" am nothing more than a conglomeration of sense impressions, that is, perhaps there is no such thing as a single "self" that underlies the sense impressions normally associated with the self. In other words, perhaps we really don't know if there is any such "thing" as a "self", or a world outside the self.

All these possibilities that come in conflict with common sense follow from separating what is in fact only distinct. Substance is in the senses. The idea that it is "sense data" alone that is in the senses is an

---

[59] Immanuel Kant argued that what were traditionally regarded as categories of being, namely substance, quantity, quality, when, where, relation, etc., are in fact categories of knowing. In other words, "substance" is a category in the mind of the knower; as such it is *a priori*, that is, prior to experience. Thus, it is the mind that imparts substance and quality, etc., to what it knows. The result is that we really don't know things as they are in themselves (noumena), only things as they appear to us (phenomena).

abstraction. I do not sense "sense data", I sense beings, *material beings that are sensible*, that is, material beings that are able to be sensed by virtue of sense qualities (accidental modes of being) they possess. The apple is able to be perceived *because* it is colored, *because* it is hard, *because* it is extended, etc. I do not touch and bend hardness; I touch and bend a hard and malleable thing, and so on with the other senses. To claim that we perceive our sense impressions is to turn a distinction into a separation.

Some might argue: "No, you **believe** that there is a substance underneath your perception." A possible reply to this claim is that the very act of *believing* arises because there are things we cannot see, for example, a person's intentions or motives. There are causes that we cannot always determine with certainty, and so we make inferences, and we trust those inferences; but inferences have to be tested. In other words, we require some empirical evidence for the belief so that it may cease to be a belief and become "knowledge" (science). For example, I heard a knock at the door, and I believe it is the kid next door playing games again. That hypothesis has to be tested, and so I study the footage from the outdoor camera. I see it is him after all; I no longer believe it is him, I know it is him. Granted, the process of moving from belief in a hypothesis to knowledge is rarely so simple, and most of what we believe remains belief. My point, however, is that one is not justified in claiming that we **believe** there is a substance behind the perception, that is, behind the red, the wide surface that is round, the hardness, etc., because belief is intelligible only against the background of perception.

Distinguishing substance from accident and then taking substance out of the picture entirely is arbitrary. On what basis does a person claim that "substance" is "a belief"? The answer is: "On the basis that I cannot see the substance". But that is precisely the point; you can see the substance; that is precisely what you see. We don't see red, just as we cannot show you red; we see an apple that is red, and we can show you an apple that is red, that is, a red thing. Thing or substance is in the mind because it is first in sense perception.

Moreover, if we do not perceive substances or beings, then from whence arises the distinction between perception and illusion—or hallucination. Is not "illusion" or "hallucination" intelligible only against the background of what is not an illusion or hallucination, namely an ordinary perception? Isn't it a perception that finally exposes an illusion for what it really is?

There is more to what we see, however, than the simple content of a perception. There is very often an active interpreting that takes place, one that often leads to a misperception, using "perception" in a much wider sense. After speaking with a professor about student participation and interest, I found that although I disagreed with his claim that students today are indifferent, I was nonetheless unconsciously influenced by what he said, which was an inference, a hypothesis formulated on the basis of some evidence (his extensive experience as a professor). Now it is possible that my rejection of his hypothesis was not based on as much evidence as he had to support his claim, but on fear—I don't want to believe that students are indifferent.

Nevertheless, the claim he made was there in the back of my mind, and one day the students of my class were simply not answering any questions I was asking them; all I got from them were blank stares. I noticed one student in particular sitting at the back; what I perceived was a student who was utterly bored, unmotivated, not interested, completely indifferent, and that perception caused me to feel angry: "Why is he here if he is not interested in philosophy? Does he expect me to do a song and dance for him? Does he expect me to just deposit information without any contribution or inquiry on his part?" His apathy continued, and I eventually reacted with anger and warned him, only to find out later, at the end of the period, that he was not bored at all, not at all indifferent, but feeling terribly sick and about to vomit, as a result of possible food poisoning. He was very polite, as he always has been, but he simply did not know for sure what was wrong with him that morning.

I perceived a bored and indifferent student. I misperceived. My perception was "theory-laden", for a hypothesis was there in the back of my mind ready to mould the data provided by my senses. I did not, however, perceive a bored and indifferent student, but a sick student who was coming down with something. My perception was in part a construct, for it was under the influence of an inference to a hypothesis at the back of my mind, one that had only a probability of being true, an inference that required testing or further evidence, and one that was not mine to begin with, but someone else's.

My perception was accompanied by an interpretation. Do we ever perceive anything without expounding on it, that is, without explaining it in some way, without interpreting it, unpacking what it possibly means? Do we ever perceive without constructing a narrative? Is there really such a thing as a neutral observation? For the most part at least, I don't think there is. And so although I would argue that absolute skepticism is indefensible, I believe it is very important to cultivate a healthy skepticism in the face of our own knowledge claims. Our perceptions are very often—if not always—mixed with narrative constructions and influenced by unarticulated hypotheses.

66 *Thoughts on Illusions and Stereogram Images*

It is not sound to conclude that optical illusions show that our senses are unreliable, because we only know something to be an illusion against the background of a sense perception that is not an illusion. Our sense perceptions are the standard against which we discover that a "perception" is really an illusion. But optical illusions certainly do help us to cultivate a healthy skepticism regarding what it is we believe we perceive. For example, it certainly appears that the pigeons are craning their necks as they move forward (http://www.michaelbach.de/ot/mot-pigeonNeck/index.html), not to mention the "worms" expanding and contracting as they move along. [60] But uncheck the grid and it becomes evident that they are not craning their necks at all, nor are the "worms" expanding and contracting. The grid was a "perceptual condition" that made it appear that the worms were expanding and contracting and the pigeons were craning their necks. That condition caused us to misperceive, or to perceive what was simply not there. Just as there are perceptual conditions that cause us to misperceive (i.e., to see moving parts where the parts are stationary), so too there are epistemic conditions that cause us to misunderstand certain intelligible phenomena or a certain intelligible state of affairs. Remove those conditions, and we will understand more clearly and objectively. Such epistemic conditions are often psychological or emotional, they may have more to do with the limitations of the language, or the limitations of human experience, but often they are moral conditions that prevent a person from grasping the real. In other words, certain moral vices (i.e., arrogance, impatience, envy, anger, disordered fear, etc.) will keep a person from understanding what would otherwise be understood.

Stereogram images also permit some interesting analogies. For example, do you see the skier (http://www.hidden-d.com/index.php?id=gallery&oid=&pk=281);

---

[60] See Michael Bach, *Optical Illusions & Visual Phenomena*, 2015. "Pigeons Craning Their Necks". Retrieved from http://www.michaelbach.de/ot/mot-pigeonNeck/index.html

the tennis player (http://www.hidden-d.com/index.php?id=gallery&oid=&pk=278); or the gymnast (http://www.hidden-3d.com/index.php?id=gallery&oid=&pk=276)?[61]

Many students do not. Some will even begin to doubt there is anything hidden in the image at all. But it takes time to train the eyes to see the beauty of these three-dimensional images. One has to work at it, which can be frustrating and time consuming, and so it requires patience, not to mention trust that others, who claim to see the images, are not lying to you. You may even need someone to coach you on how to see a 3D image.

Similarly, there are truths that are far more beautiful and exhilarating to contemplate than any stereogram image, because truths intelligible to the human understanding have much greater scope and far reaching implications. For example, coming to understand Aristotle's notion of "prime matter" is very much like the gradual emergence of the 3D figure in a stereogram image; so too is coming to an understanding of the implications of the real distinction between essence and existence, such as the existence and nature of God as He can be understood within the natural light of reason. But some people have a different intellectual disposition, and so they tend to look at philosophical problems within the framework of a mathematical mind, or a scientific mind, which is why they have a difficult time seeing what others see, just as a majority of students will stare at a stereogram image and see nothing more than what appears to be abstract art; the reason has to do with how they are looking at the image. They look at it as they would anything else, that is, by focusing on the surface of the image. Moreover, certain epistemic conditions will keep a person from appreciating these exhilarating truths (such as a hatred of religion, or lazy mindedness, or the need to know everything through one method only, etc.), just as certain perceptual conditions keep a person from seeing what would otherwise be obvious to anyone.

---

[61] *The World of Hidden 3D Stereograms.* "Stereogram Gallery: All Stereograms". Retrieved from http://www.hidden-3d.com/index.php?id=gallery

Religious knowledge can also be compared to the gradual rise of the hidden 3D image. Behave like the person who does see it, in other words, do as he or she is doing, and continue to do so without the reward of beholding the beauty of the 3D figure, and someday the image will begin show itself. Some students, however, couldn't be bothered. Similarly, behave as a believer does, and you might begin to see what he sees. Pascal writes: "…'You want to find faith and you do not know the road. You want to be cured of unbelief and you ask for the remedy: learn from those who were once bound like you and who now wager all they have. These are people who know the road you wish to follow, who have been cured of the affliction of which you wish to be cured: follow the way by which they began. They behaved just as if they did believe, taking holy water, having masses said, and so on. That will make you believe quite naturally, and will make you more docile.' – 'But that is what I am afraid of.' – 'But why? What have you to lose? But to show you that this is the way, the fact is that this diminishes the passions which are your great obstacles…' (L418).[62]

[62] Graeme Hunter, *Pascal the Philosopher*. Toronto: University of Toronto Press, 2013. See Chapter 1, "Against Philosophy". [Kobo version]. Retrieved from http://www.kobo.com.

67 Knowing by Faith

I would argue that faith is a way of knowing, one that is not necessarily contrary to human reason. In fact, most of what we do every day is based on faith, and it isn't difficult to show the reasonableness of such faith. The "faith" I refer to here is natural faith, which involves accepting as true something somebody tells you because you have evidence that the speaker is well informed about the subject and is honest. It would be irrational to refuse to live at all on the plane of natural faith; one could argue that it is in fact impossible. For example, a child brushes his teeth. Why? Because his mother told him that it is good for him to do so. He doesn't understand why; for he does not understand the concept of tooth decay or the effects of sugar on tooth enamel. And although brushing teeth is not pleasant to him, he trusts her nevertheless. Eventually, when he is able to finally understand, he will see that it was wise to do so.

More than once in our lives will we have to take a prescription to the pharmacist; he or she will fill the prescription and we will take those pills. Unless we understand chemistry and pharmacology, we don't know what we are taking; but we trust that the pharmacist did not make a mistake, and we trust that our doctor has our best interests in mind and that what he prescribes to us is really good for us. But we do not know that with any certainty. I once visited a man in hospital who suffered a stroke because his pharmacist made a mistake and ended up giving him pills 10 or 20 times the dosage that his doctor prescribed. He'd spent a year in a hospital bed, his mind was deteriorating, and he was dying. I'm sure he's dead by now, but there's the trust – had he known, he would not have taken the pills. But was it unreasonable for him to entrust himself to his pharmacist? Not in the least; he had little choice.

I take my car in for a brake replacement. I am told that it is done, that the car will stop when I press the brake pedal at an intersection. I trust the mechanic; I don't demand that he hoist the car up, remove the tres and show me. My students place a great deal of trust in me as their teacher. I teach them all sorts of things about the history of philosophy and religion, but they don't know whether or not what I am teaching them is actually true; I could be making it up, all or part of it. They don't know, but they choose to believe me. A responsible teacher will devote a great deal of time and effort to making sure, as far as possible, that what is being taught is accurate, but even that effort involves a great deal of faith. For example, I put my faith in certain historians of philosophy; there are others I do not entirely trust.

The world of science relies heavily on faith. Scientists trust one another that they have not lied to the scientific community; for it is not possible for a scientist to repeat every experiment that has been done in the past. They trust the reported results of the experiment, that is, they trust that the scientist has not falsified data – which happens at times. Recently, there was an article in a local paper about a British doctor who published a study in the late 90s that linked the childhood vaccine for measles-mumps-rubella to autism. The study has now been thoroughly discredited. But note how the article ends: "Most scientists are to be trusted. But our systems are not ideal. We just are implicitly trustful of those we work with."[63]

Relationships of love are, by their very nature, founded upon faith (natural faith). When another offers me his or her love (whether friendship, marital, or simply good will), I am not certain that the love being offered is genuine. I do not know with any certainty whether I am loved for my own sake, or loved merely as a means to an end. But that offer of love awaits a response, and my response is rooted in faith. If I choose to reciprocate, I open myself up to possible injury (the hurt of rejection); for I have to acknowledge the possibility that the other's love will enhance and enlarge me – hence, I have to acknowledge my perfectibility and reveal it to the other. In other words, to receive another's love requires humility, an acknowledgment and a disclosure

[63] Oakland Ross, (January 7th, 2011). Andrew Wakefield's Fraudulent Vaccine Research. *The Star.Com.* Retrieved from http://www.thestar.com/life/health_wellness/2011/01/07/andrew_wakefields_fraudulent_vaccine_research.html

of my finitude; and offering love in return involves risk, that is, faith that the other will continue to receive me with all my limits.

When a married couple has promised fidelity to one another (from the Latin *fides*: faith), they have promised to remain faithful, which means he has promised her to remain true to the faith that she has placed in him, and she to remain true to the faith that he has placed in her.

Faith is reasonable because the human person is so limited in knowledge. We have little choice but to rely on one another in a spirit of trust. Try to imagine what life would be like if you were to refrain from all choices that are based on faith. You would not trust what your teachers are teaching you until you knew for yourself whether or not what they were teaching is correct. But how would you know how to read unless you relied on your teachers? How would you know what to research unless you were taught how to research as well as the names of those worthy of further research? You couldn't take your car to the mechanic until you became a mechanic yourself, and you wouldn't trust your doctor until you became a doctor yourself, and a pharmacist yourself, and a chemist yourself, and you wouldn't ever marry another because to give and receive love involves an act of faith. Life would come to a standstill. You couldn't take a taxi, bus, or plane anywhere, because in doing so you are entrusting your life to someone else, all the while believing that they are going to do what they tell you they are going to do, i.e., take you to your destination, drive safely, land the plane, etc.

Supernatural Faith

To some, it is ironic that although we readily trust others who are not entirely trustworthy, we hesitate to trust the One Person who alone is perfectly trustworthy, who cannot lie, who cannot mislead, who has no malice whatsoever in Him, who is all powerful and supremely and perfectly good, and who thus has our best and greatest interest in mind, namely almighty God Himself. If God has chosen to reveal Himself, if

He has chosen to come looking for man in order to lead him home, then our way back home to Him will require faith.

However, perhaps it is only ironic superficially, for if God reveals to man truths that surpass human reason, truths that exceed our ability to understand naturally, then the only way to possess these truths is through faith, which is an assent to truths that transcend reason. That faith must be of a completely different kind than the natural faith we've been talking about; natural faith is inadequate, for it cannot assent to supernatural truths (truths that exceed reason's grasp). It is reasonable to believe the doctor when he prescribes a medicine – unless there is good reason to suspect that he is untrustworthy. But how can reason demonstrate that it is reasonable to believe what is completely above reason, truths shrouded in impenetrable darkness? It cannot. To suggest that reason can is to suggest that what exceeds the grasp of reason is within reason's grasp, which is contradictory. We need to be given the capacity to make that act of faith in what exceeds the grasp of human reason, and what Jesus tells us about himself in the New Testament exceeds reason's ability to demonstrate. For example, he says: "I am the Way, the Truth, and the Life. No one can come to the Father except through me"; "Anyone who has seen me has seen the Father"; "I am the resurrection. Anyone who believes in me, even though he dies, will live, will never die. Do you believe this?"; "Sky and earth will pass away, but my words will never pass away"; "Before Abraham was, I AM"; "I and the Father are one"; "I am the bread of life"; "It is my Father's will that whoever sees the Son and believes in him should have eternal life, and that I should raise that person up on the last day"; "Anyone who eats my flesh and drinks my blood has eternal life, and I shall raise that person up on the last day"; etc.

On the plane of natural reason, there is no "reason" to believe him. To be able to believe him requires a quality that is above nature (supra nature). This supernatural quality that proportions the intellect and will to these supernatural truths revealed by God, enabling one to believe them if one so chooses, is divine grace, which is a sharing in the divine life. According to the Catholic Faith, baptism imparts that grace, and baptism infuses the supernatural virtues of faith, hope, and charity into the soul of the baptised, as a sheer gift. And so, if a baptised person eventually stops believing, if he or she has lost his or her faith, it is only because he or she has freely chosen not to cooperate with divine grace that enables him or her to believe. Can an unbaptised person have faith in Jesus? Indeed, but such faith (whether it is implicit or explicit) is also rooted in grace.

What enabled the Apostles to immediately drop everything and follow Jesus? According to traditional Catholic theology, they were given this interior capacity to follow him, that is, to believe him and will to believe him. They still had to choose to cooperate with that interior grace; they could have said no. They chose, however, to cooperate with that grace, not knowing where they were going, and because of that initial decision to trust the Lord, many people share in that supernatural heritage and are heirs to his promises. It all began with Mary's faith, with her *fiat*: "Let it be done to me according to your word" (Lk 1, 38). It continued with the faith of the Apostles, and then the faith of all the great martyrs and saints and missionaries throughout the ages, such as the Canadian martyrs who brought the gospel to Canada back in the 17th century, and it continued with the countless unknown faithful since that time who brought the good news of Christ's resurrection to their families, their students, and their communities.

As was said above, it is impossible not to live on the plane of natural faith, and with just a little thought, the freedom and the tremendous benefits of living on that level are obvious. Because of that natural faith, we are given the stepping stones that free us to pursue greater goods, such as further knowledge. We know things about people that we otherwise would not have known, first and foremost, their trustworthiness. We know others intimately through genuine friendships, and we know the joys of parenting as a result of a marital relationship grounded on fidelity. In a similar way, supernatural faith opens up a supernatural world that would otherwise be closed off to us. Of course, reason cannot establish this, as it can explicate the benefits of natural faith; for the starting point of supernatural faith is the grace of supernatural faith itself, not natural reason. But an analogous experience occurs. The religiously faithful acquire a new and elevated freedom as well as a knowledge of things that would otherwise be closed off to them.

Living on that plane of supernatural faith, we eventually become aware of the supernatural light that permeates our mind and life – if we persist long enough. Our prayers are answered – perhaps not always as we expected – , and we experience an inner strength to face life's difficulties, we experience the ability to forgive those we are unable to forgive before, we have a sense God's presence in our lives, we feel much less anxiety in life, we don't feel lost as we did before, we begin to see the world from a new angle, we see the hand of God in everyday occurrences, and things begin to make sense from the point of view of faith. We don't delight in the things we used to desire, and we see the emptiness of much of what the world honours, and most of all we experience within that we are known and loved by God with a love that is manifest in Christ's passion and death, and we are aware that nothing much matters anymore except making that love known to others. We begin to think of God more, of ways to serve Him and to love Him back. Life becomes joyful, rather than heavy and anxious; and all that results from living on the plane of supernatural faith.

The Dangers of Faith

Faith, however, is risky. There is always the possibility that one's trust will be betrayed – except in the case of entrusting oneself to God, who cannot mislead, deceive, or betray anyone. But how does one minimize this danger or risk factor? The answer to that question goes back to reason. If there is a good reason not to trust another, then one ought to be wary of trusting him or her. If there is no reason not to trust this person and plenty of reasons to trust him, then in light of human limitations, it is reasonable to trust him. If trusting him requires me to act contrary to reason, it is unreasonable to trust him. So too with supernatural faith; this faith transcends reason, which means that it is above reason, not below it. If what we believe about God is contrary to reason, then there is something defective about the faith, and since God is absolutely perfect, it follows that the article of faith in question cannot be from God. For example, if one believes that God is calling him to divorce his wife to whom he is validly married in order to marry another, or that He is calling one to donate sperm so that infertile couples may become parents, or that He is calling a person to murder unbelievers, etc., we know that these articles of belief are not from God, since they are contrary to the Natural Moral Law, which is a participation in the Divine Law. Many of the Mediaeval doctors of the Church (i.e., Augustine, Anselm, Aquinas, Bonaventure, etc.) devoted their lives to becoming masters of human reason in order to demonstrate that what Catholics choose to believe on faith is not contrary to reason.

C. S. Lewis' "Lord, Liar, Lunatic" argument does not prove that Jesus is who he says he is, but it does demonstrate that it is not irrational to believe his claims any more than it is irrational to believe your doctor when he tells you that you ought to take this or that medication. If Jesus is not who he claims to be (the eternal Son of God) and knows that he is not, then he is a liar, and Christianity is the greatest and most influential lie perpetuated in history. If Jesus is not who he claims to be and does not realize it – thinks he is –, then he is insane. And since the degree of insanity is measured by the distance that exists between what a person claims to be and what he actually is, Jesus is more insane than the most psychotic of mental health patients. The third option is that he is who he claims to be, the eternal Son of God ("Before Abraham was, I AM").

Of course, this does not prove that Jesus is who he says he is. Some atheists would agree that he is a liar, and some might even see him as a lunatic. But even if one does not see him as a liar or a lunatic, one still requires a supernatural quality (divine grace) to make that act of faith in him and his promises, which exceed the grasp of reason. But the proper safeguard with respect to all matters of faith is that they not fall below the threshold of human reason. For God is the author of truth; for God is Truth Itself, and the first law of being of which truth is a property is that contradictories cannot be true at one and the same time.

68 *Thoughts on Faith as Our Default Position*

When we consider just how much uncertainty, obscurity, and ambiguity characterizes much of what we refer to as "knowledge", it seems to me that faith—natural faith in the sense of trusting what someone tells you because you have evidence that lends credibility to the speaker—is in fact the "default position" of the scientist, let alone everyone else; for there is relatively little certitude and necessity in the entire body of our knowledge; the rest seems to made up of inferences that have settled into beliefs which have hardened over time; the hardening or crystallization of those beliefs lends the appearance of genuine knowledge.

Science is a search for the proper causes of—or reasons for—the things we have made the object of our search. The sciences that take place on the first level of abstraction (biology, chemistry, etc.) progress by means of inferencing to the best explanation; and anyone who has studied inductive logic knows, induction and inference to the best explanation leaves us, at best, conclusions that have high probability, and a conclusion that enjoys a relatively high degree of probability, however, can turn out to be false.

Consider, for example, the many different types of cancers there are among a myriad of other diseases, many of which we do not know the cause or cure, despite the relatively tremendous progress we've made in this area—a progress, nonetheless, that has been relatively slow. Matter renders things so much more complex and varied, and our difficulty in coming to fully understand them has everything to do with this complexity and variety; for how many centuries has it taken us to arrive at our current understanding of mental illness, for example? And yet even now much of what a psychiatrist does, he does in relative darkness; ten people with the same mental illness will not necessarily respond in the same way to the same medication, and there are more than ten to choose from. Richard Feynman couldn't be more right: "Science is an ever expanding frontier of ignorance."

Consider history; there is so much to know about what is going on in the world this instant. Hundreds of years from now, some will be looking back on this period as the object of their historical investigations. Much of their knowledge will be derived from inferencing on the basis of evidence, but it will begin with a particular interest that will establish a frame of reference in which to make very specific inferences that answer very specific and limited questions. We study history from a particular vantage point: i.e., philosophy, economics, science, or politics, etc. The best historians only know a few thin fibers of the vast fabric of human history. And just how much of that knowledge is really all that certain? How much of their narratives, coherent as they often are, are "knowledge" in the truest sense of that word?

There is an intellectual light in which we live and move, but that intellectual sphere is not as clear as we tend to think; it is thick with clouds, but the light of those certainties that we do enjoy brighten those clouds, lending the false impression that we live and move within a sphere of radiant clarity and luminosity. Moreover, we tend not to be aware of the limits of that intellectual sphere of ours; for outside of that intellectual atmosphere is a vast darkness of space, a vast realm of the unknown. That is why science is indeed an ever expanding frontier of ignorance: the more we discover, the more we come to the realization that we do not know nearly as much as we thought we did. If we were to put this to numbers, we might say that we thought that we knew .8 of all there is to know, but with the discovery of some new law, for example, we now realize that it is .4. Later on, however, we discover that this number is far too generous; we are more in the area of .2, then .1, then a 0.09, then a .04, etc. Finally, we admit that we simply don't know; for there is an ever increasing awareness of an ever shrinking bank of knowledge with every gain, an ever expanding frontier of ignorance.

Much of our day to day "knowledge" is nothing more than high statistical probabilities; for example, I really don't know that this pilot is not going to take the plane into a nose dive into the ocean, or that this doctor has my daughter's best interest at heart and is not a sociopath with a degree in medicine. I don't know what tomorrow will bring; I really don't know that I am not going to end up in the psychiatric ward as a result of a stressor that triggers a psychotic episode or sends me spiralling into a deep clinical depression. I hope that all goes well, but there is so much that is outside of my control. I was reminded of that one cold morning as I proceeded through a green light listening to my favorite music, when suddenly the melody was interrupted by the sound of the loud horn of a large truck attempting to stop for the red light; it was sliding very slowly on black ice. Fortunate that I was not as deep in thought as I usually am in the morning, because had I not stopped, I would have been slammed by a massive dump truck that would have sent me to intensive care, if not the morgue.

The past steadily recedes into the cloudy realm of the forgotten. There is so little I remember of my life as a child, as a teenager, and as a young adult. A great deal of important knowledge can be unravelled on the basis of first principles and their implications, but what we deduce, for example, from principles of metaphysics (essence and existence) is so abstract and far removed from my own direct experience that all I have succeeded in doing is demonstrating that I know more about **what God is not** than I do about **what He is**, for my knowledge of what He is depends on my knowledge of what He is not. There is a lot of knowing in that unknowing, but more unknowing in that knowing.

Our day to day life is permeated and sustained by natural faith, more than we seem to be aware of. It is our default position. Partial ignorance, uncertainty, probability, a lack of awareness of the degree of these probabilities, etc., are not the exception, but the rule; genuine knowledge that carries the force of necessity is the exception—and there is no denying that we can and do possess genuine knowledge—for at the very least, we know that there is much that we do not know, and that is indeed certain.

If faith is our default position, then humility is the most fitting posture we can take towards this epistemic state of affairs. Philosophy strives to know with certitude what can be known on the basis of first principles (both speculative and practical) which are themselves undeniable and self-evident, because they are first. It takes a great deal of work to achieve a level of certainty with respect to more proximate issues and problems, but as we apply these moral principles, for example, to particular situations, issues become increasingly more complex, requiring many distinctions and qualifications. This does not mean that moral knowledge is not possible; it only means that to achieve it requires a great deal of labour and time, that is, thinking, experience, memory, circumspection, foresight, docility, emotional well-being, caution, etc.

Now, if God is to reveal Himself, the content of that revelation can only be adhered to by faith, because what is divine transcends what is natural. Our natural mode of knowing bears upon material natures, not the divine nature. And so we require a quality that will allow us to assent to the very content of what is revealed—we require this quality because the content of revelation will be disproportionate to our natural mode of knowing. This quality is divine grace. But the very act of faith considered in itself is not disproportionate to our natural mode of knowing; for we live by natural faith—although we fail to fully appreciate the extent to which this is true. And so the scientist who prides himself on being a man of "science", that is, a man of "knowledge", of reason, certitude and proof, etc., as opposed one of faith, simply does not understand the fundamentals of epistemology. He may understand his science, but he does not understand what it means to understand and the method by which we arrive at scientific understanding. To oppose science and faith is to fail to appreciate the scientific method and the ambiguity and uncertainty that permeate it. It is to fail to appreciate the nature of inferencing and the cloud of uncertainty in which it continues to leave us, if not indefinitely, at least for relatively long periods of time. The scientist has no choice but to trust: trust his colleagues, that they have not falsified data, trust his basic assumptions about knowledge upon which science is founded; for no science establishes its own first principles, for whatever a science demonstrates, it does so on the basis of those principles. The scientist for the most part lives suspended in a space of relative uncertainty; for example, the psychiatrist will try this medication and hope, and if it does not do what he intends for it to do, he will prescribe another, all within a cloud of uncertainty but in the light of hope. An oncologist will recommend a treatment, but he has few definitive answers; all he can do is offer the little statistical evidence he has, that this treatment, for example, will increase the chances that this cancer will not return, from .76 to an .84; it may work, it may not, it may turn out to be needless, but we plod forward.

69 The Heart Has Its Reasons

The best and most beautiful things in the world cannot be seen or even touched - they must be felt with the heart. Helen Keller

One of the most famous of Pascal's *Thoughts* is the first line of #423 (Lafuma edition): "The heart has its reasons of which reason knows nothing". It is a line that does not impress unbelievers; to them, it is entirely non-falsifiable, a cowardly shield erected against all possible criticism. Believers, on the other hand, appreciate it almost immediately.

Is there any way to render an account of such a principle? I believe there is; what follows is an attempt to do so.

The first point I would like to lay down is that it is the human person who understands, not the intellect (I know *by means of* the intellect). Moreover, the human person has not just a mind, but a mind, a heart, and a network of emotions. Thus, it is not my mind that knows and my heart that loves, rather, it is the person who knows and loves by means of the two powers of the intellect and the will (heart). This is what I really mean when, for the sake of convenience, I employ expressions such as "the mind knows" or "the heart loves", etc.

Reasoning is **the third** act of the intellect. It presupposes judgments (i.e., John is a man, or that cat exists, etc.), and judgments presuppose the simple apprehension of universal ideas (i.e., man, rational, risibility, being, identity, otherness, etc.). Reasoning is both deductive and inductive; it draws out necessary conclusions from given premises (i.e., All men are rational; John is a man; therefore, it follows necessarily that John is rational), and it infers probable conclusions that are larger than what is contained in the premises (i.e., 25% of the fruit I have purchased in the last few months from this grocery store was rotten; therefore, 25% of all the fruit in this grocery store is rotten).

There is more to reasoning than this, of course; but it should be evident at this point that reasoning is not the only way the mind comes to know. For example, first principles, such as the principle of identity or non-contradiction, are not the result of reasoning, because reasoning requires these principles in order to draw conclusions. I know immediately, intuitively, that "each being is what it is" (the principle of identity), and unless it is true that "each being is what it is", I cannot reason to any conclusion. Thus, reason does not prove the first principles; it requires them in order to prove anything at all.

Hence, there is a mode of knowing that is "other than" reasoning *per se*. Pascal seems to refer to this mode of knowing as "heart knowledge". He writes: "It is just as pointless and absurd for reason to demand proof of first principles from the heart before agreeing to accept them as it would be absurd for the heart to demand an intuition of all the propositions demonstrated by reason before agreeing to accept them" (#110, Lafuma).

But I would like to move in another direction, and so what follows is not an interpretation of Pascal, but an exploration of the claim using Pascal as a springboard. It seems to me that there are certain natural behaviors that are beyond the capacity of "the reasoning intellect" considered in itself, behaviors that almost everyone understands because they understand with more than their "reason" considered in itself. For example, consider the person who, upon seeing his baby niece or nephew, gets down on all fours and begins babbling in front of him/her like a baby, making funny faces, or playing peek a boo, etc. From a purely rational point of view, he's acting like an "idiot". However, love does such things; love moves a person to act like a bumbling "idiot", and this behavior is a region that reason on its own, without the heart's lead, would not venture into; for there is nothing by which it could be led to do such things.

Now if "love does those things", it must mean that it sees something that the "reasoning intellect" by itself does not quite see. It is this "seeing" that I would like to explore more fully. There are other human behaviours, however, that I believe fall into this category of acts that seem to exceed the reach of "reasoning" considered in itself. I believe forgiveness, in particular forgiveness of a brutal crime that has left a wound that cannot be healed, is a behavior that the reasoning intellect by itself will not and cannot venture into. Try to persuade someone of the "reasonableness" of forgiveness, someone who, for example, is convinced that forgiveness dishonors those who were murdered (or unforgiveness honors them). Why should that person forgive the one who murdered his loved one? What he did cannot be undone, and many others are made to live with the painful wounds left by his brutality, for these are wounds that time does not heal.

When I talk with students about forgiveness, I find myself trying to persuade them of the "reasonableness" of doing so by pointing to the health benefits of the act of forgiveness, that harboring unforgiveness inevitably leads to intestinal disease of one kind or another, etc. Essentially, I am arguing that you ought to forgive "for your sake" (for the sake of your own health).

But how do I argue for the "reasonableness" of forgiveness not for your sake, but for the sake of the perpetrator? The latter kind of forgiveness, purely gratuitous forgiveness, is sheer gift. There is nothing he has done or can do to deserve it. The more I am forced to think of it, the more I tend to believe that this gratuitous forgiveness—for his sake and his sake alone—is a region that is outside the scope of the reasoning intellect considered in itself. Reason by itself, without the heart in lead position, cannot find a "reason" for doing so, and so forgiveness appears reckless to the rationalist who puts "the reasoning intellect" in lead position. There are many reasons that one can put forth in favor of forgiveness that refer back to the self, possibly the common good of the community, but purely gratuitous mercy offered for his sake and his alone is a region into which only the heart can take a person. In other words, love does such things.

When the heart takes a person there, his reasoning mind is taken there too—led into the fog, so to speak. The mind of such a man comes to "know" what exceeds the capacity of his reasoning, but only when he is brought into this region by the heart. Prior to this point, the heart sees (has its reasons) what reason considered in itself cannot see, and only after this point is the intellect exposed to a new realm in which are found "the best and most beautiful things in the world", one of which is gratuitous mercy and forgiveness.

Another behavior that I believe falls into this category is trust. Indeed, the reasoning mind can provide "reasons" to trust others like the doctor or the pharmacist, the mechanic, or the teacher, but the reasons refer back to the self: i.e., I need to trust my doctor, pharmacist, mechanic and teacher, etc., because my knowledge is limited and I couldn't live without such trust, i.e., I wouldn't drive, I wouldn't learn anything, and I'd be perpetually sick, etc. But trusting that another has received my love, which I offer to that person for that person's sake, and who says she loves me in return for my sake, is something else entirely. My intellect is limited, it is in the dark in the face of the mystery of love, and it is the heart that leads it into this dark region. Reasoning cannot take the lead here, unless we are talking about self-love, which is "loving another for what that person does for me"; for such love is calculating and thus rational. But think of marital love, a genuinely selfless love that chooses to entrust one's entire self to the other for the rest of one's life. Such love is risky, and it can only rest on trusting the other, that he or she will continue to receive my love, and vice versa. The reasoning intellect by itself cannot take a person into that territory; it is love that does such things

It is a very interesting experience teaching the fundamentals of the doctrine of the Trinity and the Incarnation to a group of students that includes many non-Catholics, such as Hindus and Muslims. Indeed, the doctrine itself is an article of faith and thus transcends the entire range of human knowing (i.e., purely natural intuition as well as reasoning), but a Christian is able to make some sense out of it, and what enables him or her to do so is "the heart", because God is love, and love does such things, like the adult who babbles like a baby and makes funny faces for a baby who has not reached the age of reason and does not understand. Trying to explain the Trinity and the Incarnation on a purely rational level, to those who have not chosen to believe it, often leaves them unmoved, for it inevitably comes across to them as bizarre.

So how does it work that the heart sees what the reasoning mind does not see? Perhaps it works like this: initially, the mind knows the other as another self. I know the other is basically good and naturally wills his own good, as I naturally will my own good. It is now up to me whether or not I choose to will his good as I will my own, and if I do so, it is now up to me to decide how intense will be that love for him. The reasoning intellect has no place here; rather, it is the intuitive mind that is at work here. I am alone with myself, and I see preconsciously but intuitively what kind of person I can be, and so I choose what kind of person I am going to be. I see, again preconsciously and intuitively, that "the good" is larger than this individual instance of the good that is me—you are basically good and will your own good, and so does he, and she, etc. I can be the kind of person who utters a silent 'yes' to that fact, or the kind of person who utters a silent 'no' to it. In other words, I can make myself the exclusive center of my own existence. When I do so, the reasoning or calculating intellect is free to take the lead in all matters. But when I refuse to do so—because I have uttered a silent 'yes' to the good as such (not merely my own private good), thus willing to see myself as one good among many—, I dispose myself to enter realms that are risky, realms where only the heart can take a person.

That silent 'yes' uttered preconsciously is a 'yes' to God, who is Goodness Itself, and that silent 'yes' will be the groundwork from which all subsequent acts of mine will spring and receive their life. Those acts that "the heart does" are easily recognized as extensions of that initial 'yes'.[64]

An intellect that demands an account from the heart before it follows the heart into these new and strange territories will never get it from the heart, because the heart has its reasons of which reason knows nothing. Indeed, it is the mind that knows, not the heart (will), but it is the heart that moves the person into a territory that is dark to the reasoning intellect. In the beginning, it is the mind, aware of the movement of the heart that loves gratuitously, that sees something,

---

[64] Jacques Maritain. *The Range of Reason*. New York: Charles Scribner's Sons, 1952. 66-71.

sees the other as another self and the heart freely chooses to will the best for the other as it naturally wills the best for itself.

The reasoning intellect ought to take the lead insofar as it exhorts the heart against violating reason—for love is not below reason—, but when "reasoning" is in lead position in all matters, it limits the heart to what is knowable via the reasoning mind alone. But it is the heart that decides otherwise, that is, decides to break away from the narrow strictures of reasoning and to venture into a region that is risky and rather dark to the mind at first, for it is a heart that knows its size, its littleness, a heart that refuses to make the self "all there is", for it is a heart that says 'yes' to the ever expanding grandeur of the reality.

70 *The Emotions and the Virtues that Perfect Them*

The emotions have an innate need to guided and governed by reason.[65] The result of this guidance by reason is that the human person becomes more passionate, not less. When the emotions (passions) are not disposed by virtue to readily and easily obey reason, that is, when the passions are in a governing position, the result is an emotionally disordered human being. Basically, such a person is emotionally unstable, that is, emotionally unhealthy, or emotionally immature. That is why happiness is a matter of virtue (the emotionally unstable are not happy).

Let's keep in mind that for Aristotle, it is not true that if one knows the good, one will do the good, and thus if one does evil, it is nothing but a matter of ignorance (Socrates and Plato). For Aristotle, it is more true to say that if one does the good, one will know the good. In other words, it is by possessing the virtues that one comes to know from within, through a connatural knowledge, what is the right, most noble or morally beautiful (*kalon*) course of action. That is why Aquinas pointed out that there are two ways of knowing what the right thing to do is: scientifically (the science of ethics) and connaturally. Both are important. But it is with regard to this connatural knowledge **only** that one may speak about emotions as a way of knowing. Emotions in themselves are not ways of knowing, rather, they are sensitive appetitive reactions that follow upon knowledge (sense and or intellectual knowledge). But when disposed by virtue, they provide a kind of connatural knowledge. Without virtue, the emotions actually blind the intellect.

Let us focus our attention at this point on which virtues perfect which emotions. To speak of virtue perfecting an emotion means that an emotion is disposed by a quality (good habit) to readily obey reason. For example, a person who cannot help "flying off the handle" every time something does not go his way is a person whose emotion of

---

[65] See Conrad W. Baars, *Feeling & Healing Your Emotions*. New Jersey: Logos International, 1979. 63f.

anger is not disposed to readily obey reason. Moreover, the emotions help us to execute reason's demand, that is, they "move us" in the right direction (e-motion); but emotion indisposed to obey reason is like unchanneled water that floods and destroys whole villages.

Temperance and the Emotions of the Concupiscible Appetite (love, desire satisfaction or complacency; hate, aversion, sadness)

The virtue that perfects the concupiscible appetite and its emotions is **temperance and its parts.** The object of the concupiscible appetite is the sensible and/or intelligible good (the pleasant), or the sensible and/or intelligible evil (the unpleasant).

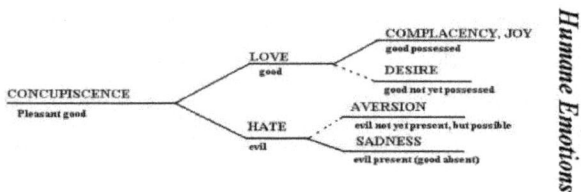

The first emotion is **love**, which is fundamentally the love of self. If I say I love pancakes, I really mean that I love what the pancakes do for me, i.e., they please me. The passion of love is not love in the highest and most human sense of the word (benevolence, which is an act of the will); for we don't destroy what we love, but we destroy pancakes when we eat them.

Now food and drink exist for our own individual preservation, so it is good to eat, and it is fitting that food tastes good. But if we love the pleasure it brings too much, we will eat and drink excessively, and that will begin to destroy us, i.e., overweight, diabetes, clogged arteries, etc. And even if our excessive love of food and drink does not harm us physically, it harms us morally, for our life becomes centered around the pleasures of food and drink, and eventually we are no longer concerned with the higher goods, i.e., spiritual goods, i.e., truth, beauty (in art, poetry, literature, etc.), the good of others, the common good of the civil community, etc.

Temperance moderates the love we have for the pleasures of touch, in particular those associated with food and drink, and sexual activity. Temperance disposes the emotion of love to obey the demands of reason, but temperance also affects the emotion of hate. If a person loves himself too much, that is, loves his own pleasure and satisfaction excessively, he will hate immoderately whatever causes him displeasure. For example, we all hate needles, but to hate that sensation so much that we refuse a reasonable vaccination is unreasonable and disordered; so too, we might have an aversion to hospitals, but we should work hard to rise above it so that we can visit the sick, especially our relatives. The emotion of sadness or sorrow can be excessive if we lack temperance. To be so overwhelmed with sorrow because you had to go without a meal is disordered. A man who has a disordered satisfaction that food brings will experience excessive sorrow when his food is delayed, or when it is not prepared to his liking—those in the food industry are very familiar with these kinds of people. That is why fasting, to some degree at least, is reasonable and morally required.

Food and drink is not the only thing that brings emotional satisfaction. Human beings have a sexual appetite, ordered towards the preservation of the species. This desire is especially vehement, which is why it needs to be disposed to obey reason. That part of temperance that moderates the sexual appetite is **chastity**. The unchaste person has a disordered love of sexual gratification. He or she is ruled by the appetite for sex, and this leads to excessive sorrow when that appetite is not fulfilled, and it leads to incalculable harm to self and others (moral and physical harm) when it is fulfilled outside is proper context, which is marriage (for example, fornication, sexually transmitted diseases, out of wedlock pregnancy, infidelity, divorce, pornography and female exploitation, sexual addiction, etc.).

We also have a natural love of ourselves and our own excellences. That love too needs to be moderated in accordance with reason.

Humility is the virtue that achieves this. A humble person knows his talents as well as his limits. Many gifted people, however, suffer from an excessive love of themselves or their own excellence. This vice is pride. The prideful person is riddled with disordered passions; he will have a disordered desire (which is an emotion) for recognition, or he will have a disordered satisfaction (which is an emotion) in his achievements, whether that is a career, or winning an argument, or winning a game, or publishing a book, etc. He will have a disordered delight (satisfaction) in being "better" than others, and that disordered passion will blind him to the excellences of others—he will not want to notice them. He will love "the spotlight", "the limelight", and he may love excessively his own looks (vanity). He or she will begin to dress immodestly, because she wants to be the object of others' attention; for she loves herself excessively and wants others to notice her and adore her as well, so she dresses so as to turn the gaze of men towards her. But those who do not love themselves excessively will dress modestly, and they will have the awareness of the need for modesty, an awareness that is lacking in the immodest (vice or disordered passion blinds the intellect).

The person who lacks humility will have an aversion for humbling situations and lowly tasks (scrubbing floors, etc.), and will experience excessive sorrow when humiliated in some way. That sorrow will also lead to anger. For example, a true saint will not be terribly disturbed at someone who calls her a "good for nothing lowlife", for she will readily agree. A proud person will be incensed at such a remark. A proud person will experience a tremendous aversion at being corrected by someone else, but a humble person will experience gratitude at being enlightened by another.

Although anger is an emotion of the irascible appetite, it does require moderation or restraint, and it belongs to temperance to restrain. An intemperate or indulgent person often exhibits uncontrolled or disordered anger when his passions are not satisfied. **Meekness** is that virtue that moderates the passion of anger to readily obey reason. Note carefully that it is reasonable and praiseworthy to experience anger at an injustice, either against the self but especially against another person; not to experience anger is "vicious" (a vice), it is a sign that one is indifferent to justice. The vice of anger refers to anger that is contrary to reason. There is no "reason" to be angry that the local Tim Horton's has run out of your favorite donuts, for example, but it is reasonable to be angry that you are being ignored by the waitress because you are black, or brown, or Muslim, etc. The former is contrary to one's appetites, the latter is contrary to justice.

Fortitude and the Emotions of the Irascible Appetite (hope, despair, fear, daring, anger)

The virtue that perfects the irascible appetite and its emotions is **fortitude and its parts**. The object of the irascible appetite is the difficult sensible and/or intelligible good (the difficult pleasant), or the difficult sensible and/or intelligible evil (the difficult unpleasant).

Let us begin with the emotion of fear. **Fortitude** disposes the emotion of fear to readily obey reason. Fear arises when we encounter a difficult evil that we judge is insurmountable. In battle, a soldier will experience fear, for there is no way to avoid the enemy's aggression, and it might very well lead to his death, but he stands his ground and defends his country and the goods that his country has spent decades achieving (freedom, education, democracy, a sound Constitution or Charter of rights and duties, etc.). At times, the difficult evil is avoidable or surmountable, so he experiences the emotion of daring (I will attempt a daring rescue that may cost me my life). But the brave soldier (fortitude) will moderate his daring so that his behavior is not reckless or foolhardy.

Now sorrow is an emotion of the concupiscible appetite, but difficult evils can generate sorrow. This sorrow will often move a person to give up on that difficulty when reason demands that one stay the course. **Patience** is that part of fortitude that disposes the emotion of sorrow to readily obey the dictates of reason; i.e., it is reasonable to be patient with a child, he's immature, doesn't know any better, etc.

The passion of hope bears upon the difficult good that is judged to be obtainable. It is noble for us to stretch forth in hope towards achieving great and honorable ends.

The virtue of **magnanimity** disposes the passion of hope to obey reason in this movement towards the honorable. The excess of magnanimity is threefold: 1) presumption, which is the mistaken and audacious assumption that "I can do anything I put my mind to"; 2) inordinate ambition, which involves aiming for something that is well beyond my capacity (I am determined to be an engineer, even though I've never passed a math course in my life); 3) vainglory (the desire to be famous, to be the object of public attention). The defect of magnanimity is pusillanimity. The pusillanimous person does not hope enough, his passion of hope is flat, so to speak; he settles for a very unheroic life that aims at nothing noble and honorable (i.e., I just work, watch TV, eat, drink, vote for the one everyone else is voting for, don't get involved, don't bother speaking out, so just leave me be, etc.). But consider a father who works long hours building houses, for example, so that his children can have what he did not have. That is often a heroic albeit uncelebrated life.

Not everyone has the means to do great things at great expense. But those who do will find it rather challenging. **Magnificence** is that virtue by which one disposes the emotion of hope to do great things at great expense; the defect of this virtue is stinginess. In this case, one's passion of hope to do great things is flattened and one becomes stingy. The excess of magnificence is extravagance. Here one spends money on oneself, and so one's hope is in oneself (which is easy), not directed out towards difficult and honorable goals at great expense.

There are a number of things we need to do every day, and some of these things are difficult and demand **perseverance**. For example, cultivating the virtues is a difficult and lifelong task that requires perseverance. It is easy to give up when things become difficult. Some people, however, do not give up when it is reasonable to do so; for example, working on a Rubik's Cube well into the night when one should get some sleep is unreasonable and thus pertinacious (pertinacity is the excess). One could say that such a person has too much love for the feeling of satisfaction of achieving a difficult task, and so from this angle one is intemperate. It could also involve the vice of pride, or excessive love of one's excellence (one cannot accept defeat).

These virtues perfect oneself *from within oneself*. They bring order and stability to one's emotional life. The two specific powers of the human person are intellect and will. The moral virtue that perfects the intellect is prudence and all its parts, and the virtue that perfects the will in its relation to others is justice and all its parts. One can only achieve temperance and fortitude through prudence, which is the mother of all the virtues, and it is the virtue of prudence that *humanizes* the emotions by cultivating the virtues of temperance and fortitude. The science of morality is prudence unpacked, and that requires special attention.

71 Thoughts on How Emotions Affect Judgment

I recall days when, as a teacher, I experienced moments of frustration and stress. Perhaps frustration is a complex emotion, a combination of hope and sorrow: I desperately want something and hope for a result, but obstacles are put before me, and I experience sorrow and anger. Early on in my teaching I began to notice how that emotional state would affect my perception of things, in particular, my judgment of how the school environment should be organized. I would see the entire administration from that limited vantage point. In other words, the passion of "frustration" had narrowed my vision, and I became aware of that. I would view their decisions "colored by" my own emotional state. Consequently, I began to relate to them negatively, with irritation. It became much more difficult to see things from their perspective, in the light of the problems and issues they had to contend with, which were much larger and wider than my own, since I was a classroom teacher and had only a limited number of students to deal with, whereas they had a much larger number to contend with (i.e., the worst students, teachers, parents, and senior administration). In any case, my relationship with administration would become rather contentious. We would argue, and the arguments were rooted in a conflict of vision.

After a while, however, I learned not to trust myself when in this state; for my perspective was too narrowed down as a result of this emotional state, so I'd resolved to wait until the frustration had passed before opening my mouth. Then, I was able take a more objective look at the situation as a whole, with my own experience in the background as one limited experience among others. The result was a much boarder perspective, more true to the complexities of concrete situations, as opposed to the simplicity of one very limited perspective.

Passion arises out of a judgment, but passion in turn narrows one's perspective, at least momentarily. That might be a good thing in certain circumstances. At a certain moment, I might be required to act decisively and with reason, and the emotions that arise out of an objective assessment of the situation have the effect of focusing my attention on the problem at hand. But when it comes to matters requiring a much larger vision or to discussing a more general problem that requires a much wider grasp of things, we need to be less "caught up" in our emotions; we need to be more stable emotionally. If a person is, in general, emotionally unstable (emotionally disordered, i.e., lacking the virtues), that habitual disorder is going to affect his or her ability to evaluate situations. His perspective will be habitually narrowed and twisted, and almost everything will be referred to himself or herself. He or she will see everything in the light of how it affects the self.

Consider a person who is lazy, unmotivated, immature, who would like to live as he did growing up, when his parents took care of him. He is uncomfortable going out into the world to take on his responsibilities. He is afraid, and he stubbornly wants to remain in the comfort of a childlike existence. How will he perceive the world? He will perceive it as a fearful place. How will that affect his perspective with regard to other things, such as the political environment? It is conceivable that he will be attracted, for example, to the political candidate who promises to raise taxes, to increase the size of the welfare state, to increase the size of government, and who talks about taking money from the wealthy and re-distributing it to the poor, etc. That will have great emotional appeal to him. If his self-love is excessive, he may not care how his lifestyle choice and his desire for a future that includes higher taxes will impact others.

Consider the person who has initiative, who is courageous enough to face the world, enter into relationships with others, make sacrifices, who is determined to contribute to the common good, to take his place in the world, etc. As he begins to experience success, he will experience the greater and more enduring joy of moral integration. He has a degree of good moral character, for he is a person of responsibility, and he experiences the rewards of his hard work, economically, psychologically, morally, physically, etc. That is going to affect the way he perceives the political landscape. He is a more just person, one who is committed to the good of the social whole and who is just in his dealings with the individuals he meets. And so his emotions (those of the concupiscible and irascible appetites) are properly ordered, for they are in line with the will for a good moral order that includes himself but is much larger than himself, that is, the will for the common good of the civil community. He will know "well-being" from within, from the inside, to a much greater extent than lazy lout, who knows little more than the fleeting pleasures of food and drink and anything else he can get his hands on. And so he (the morally noble person with initiative) will not necessarily be attracted to the political candidate who promises a stronger welfare state. He will know from within that the bar is too low, so to speak. He will be drawn to the candidate that has a plan to make it much easier to be a responsible and independent citizen.

Now, with more experience with human frailty and illness, we would hope he realizes that not everyone is able to achieve what he has achieved. Some people are visited with tragic circumstances that are beyond their control. His perspective will, if he is not too cocky, be balanced by that consideration. But if he loves his success too much, he becomes self-complacent and will fail to appreciate his limits and the role of good fortune in all of this; thus, he might become indifferent to the sick and suffering and too quick to judge their predicament. So too, his emotional complacency might be so excessive that his vision is far too narrowed and he sees everything in reference to himself.

Disordered passions blind the intellect, which in turn leads to imprudent decisions, very often to unjust decisions, and these in turn have very costly social repercussions. As an example, one morning I was driving to work, trying to think of ways to illustrate this to students; I was stopped at an intersection with a red light. I was going to proceed right, but the oncoming cars had an advanced green, and one is not permitted to turn right on a red light with an advanced green. As I am waiting for the light to turn green, a man in an SUV behind me starts to lean on his horn. I simply point to the oncoming cars and shrug my shoulders. But he continues to honk. I decide to ignore it; he obviously does not know the law. When the light turns green, I then proceed to the right, but he steps on the pedal, speeds past me, cuts me off and puts on his breaks, waving his fist.

I am somewhat taken aback at this point. He then drives off, but at the next red light, I take down his license number. What I found interesting is that this man had no idea who I was. I could have been a sociopath, a person with a long criminal record. I could have been a person with serious mental health issues, possibly armed and looking for an excuse to make someone's life miserable. He did not consider these possibilities; vehement passion blinded his mind.

One evening while sitting in a Mr. Greek Express waiting for my order, I noticed a family on the other side of the restaurant, so I watched them for a while. The father was rather large (well over 300lbs), and he looked like he was enjoying his meal, to say the least. He had his wife and two kids there with him, so I simply observed how they interact, and if the father looked over in my direction, I'd just turn my head, and then go back to watching them. At one point, the father calls the waitress over and begins talking to her as if she'd committed some heinous crime. He demanded to speak to the manager of the restaurant. The manager comes to the table and he begins talking to her in a tone that was quite distressing to anyone in earshot, for it was rather threatening (waving his knife), as if she'd backed a truck into his new car. What happened is that his wife's order got mixed up. She'd ordered chicken, not pork, or something to that effect. What struck me was the vehemence of his anger, his eyes, and the degrading way he treated that poor young waitress. His anger was completely disproportionate to the mistake that was made.

That is an example of how the disordered love of food and a corresponding inability to tolerate any kind of sorrow brought on by delay, blinds the intellect: what is not an injustice at all, is judged to be a serious violation of justice, which in turn gives rise to vehement anger. Compare that reaction to the person with an ordered appetite for food, who simply calls the waitress over and politely points out the mistake and waits. Nobody's day is ruined.

Disordered passion blinds us above all to the limits of our own perspective. The result is that we are not aware of just how limited our point of view is—we think our view is much larger and all-encompassing than it actually is, and thus *we feel so right*. At that point, it is more difficult to listen to others, we may be tempted to dismiss them, even demonize them (we continually witness this in politics). But as we get older, we should begin to see that reality is much more complex than we once thought. If that happens, we become much less self-righteous. At least that is what should happen. Very often it does not, because of the passion of pride, which is the disordered love of one's own excellence. One cannot tolerate the feeling of being wrong, for it conflicts with one's rather inflated image of oneself. And so if one insists on enjoying the passion of satisfaction in being right, then one is unwilling to listen and have one's viewpoint enlarged. The other's perspective does not "feel" the same as my own, for it is uncomfortable, it conflicts with my own, and it implies that my own is limited and that I am limited, and because my passion of self-love is excessive, I find it hard to entertain the possibility that it is true to reality.

This eclipse of a healthy sense of the limits of our own individual perspective and that narrowing in turn increases the passion to defend a particular point of view. But most importantly, "as a person is, so does he see", said Aristotle. He gave the example of a coward (one who has disordered fear) who sees the brave man as "rash" or "foolhardy". The coward does not see and evaluate correctly, for his judgment is distorted by his own self-knowledge, for he sees himself as the measure of what is reasonably brave, he does not see himself as a coward. But he fails to maintain the course of reason because of his fear. He has allowed himself to be governed by fear, not reason, and so he flees when he should stay the course and defend the defenseless, so to speak. Or, consider the foolhardy man who needlessly performs daring and risky actions when it is reasonable for him not to—since he has a wife and three children at home who need him. He sees the brave man, who acts according to the demands of reason and thus moderates the emotions of fear and daring, as a coward; and so the foolhardy man also does not see clearly nor evaluate correctly. It is the man of fortitude who evaluates correctly, for his emotions are in line with reason, and so he is emotionally inclined towards the most reasonable and noble course of action.

72 *A Note on Connatural Knowledge*

Connatural knowledge is knowledge through inclination. The word connatural comes from two Latin words: *con* or 'with' and *natus* or "birth". When a mother gives birth, the child comes forth out of her interior. We speak of things having a nature, an interior, an essential quality (essence). The French word 'savoir' means to *know how to do*, but 'connaitre' is to *know a person*. One can know a great deal **about** a person (psychology) without really knowing the person (connaitre). To know a person is to know him "from within", so to speak—in contradistinction to a knowledge "from without". This knowledge "from within" is a result of the mutual indwelling that love brings about: the lover exists in the beloved, and the beloved exists in the lover.

A morally good man who does not know **the science of ethics** can know by a kind of connaturality (or knowledge through inclination) what the right course of action is in a given circumstance. He knows **from within**, for he is inclined to choose the morally noble course of action because he possesses the virtues. This is what Aquinas is referring to in the following (emphasis mine): "Now rectitude of judgment is twofold: first, on account of perfect use of reason, secondly, on account of a kind of connaturality with the matter about which one has to judge. Thus, about matters of chastity, a man who has learnt the science of morals judges rightly through inquiry by reason, while he who has the habit of chastity **judges rightly of such matters by a kind of connaturality.**"[66]

A person can know about religion without being religious, and a person can know the faith from within, from having lived it, without being learned in the science of theology. The latter knowledge is connatural knowledge, whereas the former—theological knowledge—is not necessarily connatural. Hence, Aquinas writes: "Accordingly it belongs to the wisdom that is an intellectual virtue to form a right judgment about divine things through inquiry **by reason**, but it belongs

---

[66] *Summa Theologiae* II-II, q. 45, a2.

to wisdom as a gift of the Holy Spirit to form a right judgment about them on account of a kind of connaturality with them...Now this sympathy or connaturality for divine things is the result of charity, which unites us to God,..."[67]

How this works is difficult to understand, but the following is an attempt to explain this way of knowing. Aquinas points out: "Whatever is received into something is received according to the mode of the receiver" (Quidquid recipitur ad modum recipientis recipitur). As this pertains to knowledge, it is true that "a thing known exists in a knower according to the mode of a knower." An apple known exists in the cognitive powers of a dog according to the mode of a brute animal, and the mode of knowing of a brute animal is limited to sensation, which bears upon material singulars. But the apple known exists in the mind of man according to the mode of a man, which is why it exists in him universally and immaterially—for the mind is immaterial. In order for us to know the nature of a thing, the intellect must abstract the intelligible content (essence) of the thing from its individuating conditions and impress that intelligible content upon the passive mind. And so, my passive mind becomes the essence of the being outside me, without changing that being. My mind becomes *conformed to* the thing it knows (the mind becomes what it knows, in an immaterial way).

But how does a person who is not learned in the science of ethics judge rightly about moral matters, such as matters pertaining to chastity, or fortitude, or justice, etc.? Chastity, for example, is not an individual substance whose form or nature needs to be abstracted from its individuating conditions. Rather, it is an idea that needs to be incarnated in individual instances—note that the direction here is the opposite of what usually takes place in our knowledge of things. And so it is the human person who needs to be changed, that is, conformed to the virtue in question, and the result of being so conformed to that virtue is the ability to judge rightly concerning matters pertaining to that virtue, through a kind of connaturality. The reason for this is that a thing is inclined to act according to its nature or form. For example, a

---

[67] *Ibid.*

substance having the form of a plant is inclined to grow, reproduce, etc. A substance having the form of a dog is inclined to see things and desire them, etc. Things act according to their natures. Similarly, a person conformed to chastity, justice, fortitude, etc., will be inclined to act chastely, justly, and courageously, etc. And because we possess self-knowledge, the virtuous person knows from within, by knowing his own inclinations, what the right thing to do is.

To understand this better, consider an Olympic figure skating or gymnastics competition. To the rest of us who are not skaters, the competitors all look equally skilled, for the most part at least. But to the judge, who was a former skater or gymnast, there are obvious grades of perfection within the ranks of the competitors. The judge is able to correctly judge of the quality of each skater by a kind of connaturality; he or she knows "from within", for he or she has become athletic, has acquired the skill or quality of being a skater or gymnast, and possessing that quality from within enables him or her to judge rightly concerning matters pertaining to that specific sport. So too, a person who has become musical will be able to judge the performance of a piece much better than one who is not at all musical, and a person who is a skilled artist will be able to judge a work of art much better than one who is not at all artistic. Even a critic who has no artistic talent will be able to judge a work of art properly as long as he has a great love of art, for love brings about a mutual indwelling. Some people say they "live and breathe" art, or music, or sports, etc. In other words, it is *within them.* Their knowledge of what constitutes great art, or music, or literature, etc., stems from their very depths.

Similarly, it is the virtuous man who knows from within what is genuinely virtuous. Now, it is in this way that **emotion** can become a source of knowledge; for it is virtue that disposes an emotion or passion to readily obey reason. To possess the virtues is to have brought about order to one's passions, and this order or conformity to truth renders a person able to judge rightly concerning moral matters. So it is not emotion pure and simple that enables a person to judge rightly, but emotions disposed by good habits (virtues) that render one able to judge by a kind of connaturality. Finally, connatural knowledge is for the most part pre-conscious; in other words, one knows, but one does not always know why one knows what is right and noble.

73 *A Thought on Positive Emotion and the Bonum Universale*

Consider the emotions of excitement and exhilaration that accompany us when we venture into something new, such as a new job, or a new university, or a new program, etc. Sometimes the exhilaration is disproportionate—but we don't know it at the time. That's when, later on, we speak of being "disillusioned". We thought this would turn out to be wonderful and perpetually exciting, but after a while, "it got old".

At the root of that experience is a misjudgment. We judged something to be a greater good than it actually is. Often, we judge things to be "good without qualification", such as in the experience of falling in love with someone. To possess a good without qualification is to possess a joy that is without qualification, that is, without limits. And so we feel "oceanic", that is, we have this experience of a joy and exhilaration that sees no end, like the ocean that stretches out to infinity.

If a person is reflective and has a good memory, he or she ought to eventually figure out that the goods of this world are "finite", that is, qualified goods, and so they cannot bring perfect rest to the human heart, which is always seeking for something that will bring it rest. Indeed, our hearts desire the *bonum universale* (the good without qualification), for we desire perfect happiness. But this world is divided into those who believe that they can possess the "good without qualification" here, in this world (which is why they continue to purchase lottery tickets), and those who believe that everything in our immediate experience is finite and thus promises only limited joy.

But if the human heart (the will) desires the *bonum universale* (the good without qualification), then it must "know" it in some way. In other words, it must exist, otherwise there is in nature a motion that is absurd. For example, a plant grows, which means it is moving towards its own completion. That completion or perfection (maturity) exists as a real possibility—we speak of a mature plant, one that is fully grown. Consider hunger in an animal. That hunger is a movement towards something, namely food. Consider how absurd that hunger would be in a world where there is no such thing as food. Why then would an animal hunger? That movement (hunger) would have no correlation, and thus it would be absurd and unexplainable. The human heart moves toward a good that is without qualification. What is it that will bring rest to the human heart? What is this good without qualification? It is a good that is without limits, a good that is infinite.

Beings, however, are limited by a nature (essence) that is distinct from the act of existing (esse). But there is only one being whose nature is identical to its act of existing, and that is God (Ipsum Esse Subsistens). God is Being Itself, and since His essence is not distinct from His act of existing, nothing limits that act of existing. God is unlimited Being, Pure Actuality. And since good is a property of being, God is Pure Goodness without limits.

The human heart naturally desires God, and so it follows logically that in some way, it naturally knows God. This may be either a conscious or an unconscious knowledge—thus even a "conscious" atheist possesses a natural knowledge of the "good without qualification", he is simply unaware that this is God.

And so it belongs to "youth" to often confuse new and exciting experiences with the *bonum universale* (good without qualification), which is why the emotion of hope is often deceived into believing that "this is it, this is going to bring me the enduring happiness that I've been looking for". At the root of that hope is a judgment that this good is without qualification (unlimited). And so we can experience a tremendous high as a result of a certain experience (receiving the good news that I've been accepted into this or that program, or winning a gold medal, breaking a world record, meeting a cute and charming guy, etc.), but if that is not the good without qualification, then eventually we will come down from that emotional high and we will find ourselves no happier than when we began—the rich and famous are really no happier than you are, they simply have more convenient lives, and perhaps more pleasures.

The real secret to human life is to know how to begin possessing that *bonum universale*, that good without qualification. How does one begin to experience true and enduring joy, as opposed to perpetually fluctuating emotions (highs and lows)? One thing we can be certain of is that my own private good is not the universal good, so if I am committed to living for my own well-being primarily, then I will never come to possess genuine happiness.

74 Feeling Stupid: A Thought on Mathematics and Metaphysics

I vividly recall the few occasions while studying probability when I was convinced that "the book" was mistaken. I knew I did the math carefully and flawlessly, but the answer I came up with did not coincide with the answer given at the back of the book. I felt stupid, I was angry, and I'd concluded the book simply made a mistake. What are the chances that a 300 page book will not contain at least one or two errors? Highly unlikely, I concluded.

I recall thinking about the problem while driving home one day, and suddenly it occurred to me: I'd forgotten to factor in an important condition, so when I redid the problem, everything worked out fine. The book was not wrong; I was.

Stubbornness is not an option for me or anyone when it comes to math. We have no choice but to face the music and admit we were mistaken; to do otherwise is simply irrational, and everyone would know it; there is no hiding it.

What I found interesting in all of this was my reaction, which was one of anger, which in turn was rooted in a feeling of humiliation that I am slower and more flawed than I was willing to entertain at that moment. It was the clarity, simplicity and precision of mathematics that kept me from deluding myself further.

But what would keep me from self-delusion if the concepts were not as clear and simple as are mathematical relationships? What if the "answers at the back of the book" would take years for me to adequately grasp? What if there are no answers at the back of the book? I am referring not to mathematical but metaphysical ideas, that is, concepts within the sphere of the philosophy of being, which is a discipline that takes place at a higher level of abstraction. Our pursuit here is not quantities and their relationships, but the meaning and properties of being. Children can do mathematics, but they cannot do metaphysics.

If a person were to attempt to follow a metaphysical line of reasoning, he might struggle to grasp it, and he might begin to feel anger, which of course is rooted in a feeling of humiliation. How easy it would be to dismiss the work as mistaken, as I was able to dismiss the math, convinced as I was that the book was mistaken. There simply are no answers at the back of a treatise on the philosophy of being, and the implications of certain metaphysical truths upon my personal life and the choices that I make are far more weighty than are the truths of mathematics, and so there is greater incentive to dismiss them. A day or two is about all it usually takes to figure out where we went wrong with the math, unless a good teacher is nearby; it takes a great deal more time to begin to adequately grasp the fundamental concepts of the philosophy of being, and there are much fewer teachers in this area than there are math teachers.

Most people are already short on patience and are wont to think fast. The answers at the back of a math book keep us from believing what we would like to believe—mathematics does not permit confirmation bias—, but metaphysics does not have that luxury. If I don't want God to exist, because I have decided that autonomy is the greatest good, or that I am the measure of what is true and good, then I can and probably will dismiss these ideas that I am not disposed to grasp so readily, and there is practically no one nearby who can reveal to me my own irrationality. If they try, how easy it would be for me to accuse him of obfuscation.

It is easy to turn our back on the most lofty and most satisfying subject within reason's grasp and to spend the rest of our lives under the delusion that was spawned by our own lack of humility. I think that might be why so few in the world have allowed themselves to benefit from the insights of the greatest philosophers of being within the past twenty five hundred years.

75 Thoughts on Bigotry

Publisher Frank Sheed once wrote: "Bigotry does not mean believing that people who differ from you are wrong, it means assuming that they are either knaves or fools." This is an interesting point, because it calls attention to another way that emotion affects the intellect. He continues: "To think them so (i.e., as knaves or fools) is an immediate convenience, since it saves us the trouble of analyzing either their views or our own."[68]

There is a surprising amount of bigotry left in this country—a country that seems to pride itself on the progress it's made in this area. I am no expert in macro-economics and wish I'd studied it in university when I had the chance—I ended up studying micro-economics instead—, but when I think back over my last 26 years in teaching, I do recall that the most economically difficult decisions that had a significant impact on teachers were made by left leaning governments (the NDP and Liberals). That's not a criticism by any means; difficult financial decisions at times have to be made, and to fail to do so is irresponsible, and even the most left leaning recognize that. But I don't recall being called up to a public protest at Queen's Park, and so far we haven't been called upon to protest the latest measures. The only time we were rallied to march on Queen's Park was at the time the Conservatives were in power.

I once overheard a discussion between a couple of teachers on the latest political measures that affect us, and the discourse was rather negative. But soon the discussion turned into an attack on the conservative party, who are not in power and haven't been for a while now, and who are very low in the polls. The conservatives are not responsible for these difficult measures, but if they were in power, they'd be much worse, or so the two were claiming.

I do know that conservatives usually acknowledge beforehand the difficult measures they are going to implement so that no one is surprised—which is likely why they rarely win—, whereas the left-

---

[68] Frank Sheed, *The Church and I*. New York: Doubleday, 1974. 57.

leaning parties do no such thing, but will often lead us to believe the opposite. The latter then find themselves in an impossible place and are forced to implement the tough measures the conservatives had been all along arguing were required. And so the left-leaning parties behave like conservatives, but are treated like the socially conscious parties they have always made themselves out to be; the conservatives behave like conservatives, and are regarded as the cut-throat, cold-hearted and avaricious knaves that they have always been perceived to be.

Politics is complicated and I hope I haven't oversimplified matters, but I can't help but suspect a degree of bigotry in all of this. It seems not much different than the white man who is given a warning for driving 40 kilometers an hour over the speed limit, while the black man is padded down and fined for driving 20 kilometers over. Sheed relates the following amusing story that illustrates bigotry in all its dishonest colors:

> ...I was suddenly shown its very essence by a story told at a Catholic Truth Conference. I remember the place of this Damascus vision, it was Birmingham. I remember the year, it was 1922. And I remember who told the story, it was a new convert from Ireland, Shane Leslie. He told of two old Catholic ladies in Dublin, passing by a lawn on which an elderly cleric was throwing a ball to a dog.
> Said one lady, "That's the Archbishop of Dublin."
> Said the other—"Ah, the dear 'old gentle man, simple and innocent as a child, playing with his little dog."
> Said the first lady, "It's the Protestant Archbishop, you know."
> Said the second, "Ah, the silly old fool, wasting his time with a pup."[69]

Bigotry is rooted in disordered passion, which blinds the intellect, especially to its limitations. If I have an inordinate hope in my own excellence (pride), I am inclined to despise the person who holds a

---

[69] *Ibid.*

position different than my own; for if there is any possibility that he is right, then there is a very real possibility that I am not the superior intellect I inordinately hope to be. If that possibility is repugnant to me, then the other's viewpoint gives rise to fear; now all I need to do is look upon the other with contempt, and the threat is kept safely at a distance. Or, perhaps the problem is not arrogance at all; perhaps I enjoy an inordinate complacency (satisfaction) in the lifestyle I have created for myself—perhaps my job is easy and I am comfortable with minimal effort. Anyone who holds political views, or a vision of the country, or the company, or the institution, etc., that will demand more of me will give rise to fear. If I love my complacency more than the good that will accrue to others as a result of those greater demands on me, I will despise the person who holds the views that gave rise to those new demands.

The results of despising persons for their opposing views is that we close ourselves off from every opportunity to enlarge ourselves and transcend the limitations of our own perspective. It is best to keep in mind that human intelligence participates in the limitations of sense perception, which does not mean that intellection is sensation, but that nothing is in the intellect that is not first in the senses. The intellect abstracts from a phantasm produced by an internal sense, and an image in the imagination is a remembered phantasm. Concepts, however, are immaterial and universal—there are no images that depict them in their universality, for an image is always particular. However, reality at the concrete level is very complex, and we only know things from particular angles, even when we know things truly. Our perspective is almost always limited in some way, even when what we judge to be true really is so. Our knowledge can almost always be expanded and qualified in some way, but that qualification and expansion can only take place through a perspective, an angle, other than our own. Truth is communal. Hence, dialogue is very important. But fear and the inordinate love of self are enemies of dialogue; these are passions, and passion can blind us to the limitations of the particular angle from which we see the world.

76 *Some Thoughts on Naming*

"That's a sumac", I overheard an old woman say one Saturday morning as I was leaving a local Art Gallery. Perhaps one can argue that, no, it is not a sumac, rather, it is a tree; "sumac" is an identity that we gave to that tree, and as such it is our own construction; it is merely a tree.

One could point out, however, that no, that's not a tree; "tree" is a name we gave to that thing. So what is it? It is a being. And of course, one could reply, no, it is not a 'being' for the same reason, namely that 'being' is a designation given to this...whatever it is, so it is "outside of being".

It (the tree) has gone from being a sumac, to a tree indistinguishable from any other tree, to an 'is' that is indistinguishable from anything else, to being nothing at all. I am going to suggest that to name a thing is to co-create it, that is, to share in its "coming-to-be". It was not given its act of existence by us or by any other contingent being; there is, however, a space that belongs to every material being, a space that is ours to fill in, so to speak. It is true, that thing we call a tree is more specifically a sumac, and of course it is "called" a sumac. To name it is to bring it into focus; in a sense, it is to bring it into being 'for us" more completely. 'What it is', namely a sumac, is in part determined by a community of persons who speak. To name it is to add something to the thing; it is to impart upon it an identity that it needs. To name something is to complete it, for an unnamed thing is not yet fully what it is, for it is not distinctly known, and yet it is intended to be. In short, we help to make it be more fully, and so beings await completion by human persons for whom they exist. A thing is not fully what it is until it is named by a person, and thus it is not fully what it is until a human person enters the picture, so to speak.

God speaks things into being (Gn 1, 1ff; Jn 1, 1ff), but He creates beings for us to know, and a thing is not known until it is named. The concept is an interior word, an interior and immaterial naming. But man is a psychosomatic unity, and so the interior words of the mind tend towards a visible and audible name. God speaks things into being, but we have a share in this, for we are called to speak the things that God has spoken so that they may fully become the things God has intended them to be. And so it follows that since being and truth are convertible terms, a thing is not completely true until it is named. Truth is therefore communal; for language is communal. There is no truth, at least not completely so, outside a community of persons whose task it is to name.

The notion that truth is a "construction" is not to deny truth or to advocate for a complete relativism. Ultimately, it cannot be entirely a construct—for no contingent being has complete dominion over being—, but only partially so. If it were entirely a construct, from beginning to end, then man would be the measure of what is. Rather, truth is discovered by persons, and the truth of things unfolds before a community of knowing "subjects" (persons) for whom things exist and through whom things become "objects" of knowledge—beings are only 'objects' in a world of "subjects". What we discover in the world are beings that exist for us to discover, to know, and to delight in. Without persons, a being is not fully what it is meant to be, because without human persons who speak, a being remains nameless.

77 Thoughts on Translation

When I tell students the "swear words" typically employed by
Quebecers, they react with laughter and disbelief. Imagine someone
stubbing his toe and uttering 'cup' under his breath, or 'host', or
'tabernacle', etc. We can't make sense out of this in the English world,
at least not immediately, because the meaning of a word is, for the
most part, relative to the context or the world in which the word is
typically spoken.

The word 'meaning' in French (sens) means 'direction' or
intention, and an intention 'tends towards' something. To understand a
motion, one needs to know the context in which the motion occurs. In
the English world, a cup is typically found in a kitchen, it is used for
coffee or tea, etc. In Quebec, "calice" is the cup or chalice, which is the
sacred vessel that contains the "blood of Christ" in the context of the
Mass, and 'hostie' is the word for 'host' or the Blessed Sacrament,
which is, according to Catholics, the Real Presence of Christ under the
appearance of ordinary bread; "tabarnac" is the tabernacle that houses
the Blessed Sacrament in the Church. French swear words are
profanations of the most sacred objects of the Catholic faith. One has
to live in both worlds (both Catholic and French Canadian) to
appreciate the gravity of the utterances, which is why Muslim, Sikh, and
Hindu Canadians living in Ontario are puzzled by the words.

Consider the following, which is part of the gospel reading for the
5th Sunday in Ordinary Time: "You have heard that it was said to those
of ancient times: 'You shall not murder'; and 'whoever murders shall be
liable to judgment.' But I say to you that the one who is angry with
their brother or sister, will be liable to judgment; and whoever insults
their brother or sister, will be liable to the council; and whoever says,
'You fool,' will be liable to the hell of fire."

To those in the Western world, two thousand years after the fact,
the gravity of this reading is not felt. In fact, it is difficult to take it
seriously. But if we were familiar with first century Palestine and
Ancient Greek, we would know that there are two words for anger, *orge*

and *thumos*. The latter describes the kind of anger that is quick and short lived, the former is the kind that is long lasting, kept alive by a free and deliberate refusal to forgive and move on. The reading above, in the original Greek, employs the word *orge*, not *thumos*. Who doesn't get angry (*thumos*) now and then? And is that really the equivalent of murder? Jesus raises *orge* to the level that murder previously occupied, for the consequences are the same: answerable in court.

But there is something more serious than nursing anger against another, and that involves calling another *Raca*. The English translation makes little sense: "Whoever insults their brother or sister, will be liable to the council (Sanhedrin)". The Sanhedrin is the Supreme Court of the Jews, thus calling another *Raca* is more serious than nursing anger against another. But is calling someone *Raca* and insulting a person—as we typically do in this country—amount to the same thing? *Raca* is an untranslatable word; it describes an attitude of looking upon another human being with arrogant contempt. To do so is to murder another in one's own eyes; he becomes a worthless and brainless moron.

And finally, anyone who calls his brother *moros* will answer for it in Gehenna, which is the Greek synonym for Hell. Hence, calling someone *moros* is far worse than calling someone *Raca*. The English translation has it: "...whoever says, 'You fool'. But this too fails to capture the weight of what is being said. To call someone *moros* was to cast aspersion on his moral character. Essentially, it involves murdering a person's reputation. In first century Palestine, it would be like calling someone a traitor; to do so would cast suspicion on a person for the rest of his life. Today, it would be the equivalent of falsely accusing someone of sexual assault. That such a thing is punishable by hell fire clearly indicates that it is much worse to murder a person's reputation without physically killing him than it is to simply murder him.

We don't always know whether we've properly understood someone or something we've heard or read. What appears to be understanding may in fact turn out to be far from a genuine and accurate understanding of what has been said. A language opens up a world, because a world is wrapped up in a language, and communication is a meeting of two worlds. A translation is the meeting of a world through a mediator, and if the mediator is not entirely familiar with the world he translates, there is a high probability that what we walk away with does not represent real understanding. In other words, communication has not been entirely achieved.

78 Thoughts on Language

Even if philosophical problems were mere manifestations of our particular historical situation or of the accidental forms of our language, we probably wouldn't be able to free ourselves of them. If you are inside something like a language, the external view doesn't supplant the internal view or make it any less serious. (I can't read the words "is comprised of" without disgust even though I fully expect that in another hundred years the tide of misuse will have raised them to grammatical respectability and a place in the best dictionaries.) Recognition of the objective contingency of a language does nothing to diminish its normative reality for those who live in it. But philosophy is not like a particular language. Its sources are preverbal and often precultural, and one of its most difficult tasks is to express unformed but intuitively felt problems in language without losing them. Thomas Nagel, *The View from Nowhere,* "Introduction".

Our ideas, which are universal, are expressed in language, that is, through sounds that are perceived. Learning a language obviously involves sense perception, and so language shares in the limitations that sense perception imposes upon human knowing. Language reveals, but it also limits. It is through language that we communicate. To communicate is to create a space in which communion between persons is achieved. Moreover, language reveals a great deal about how a particular people apprehend the world in which they live, and to learn that language is to learn to see the world through the eyes of that particular people. For example, there are two words for knowledge in French: *savoir* and *connaitre.* This reveals a culture's sensitivity to the differences between 'knowing how to do something' and 'knowing a person' (connatural knowledge). Knowing about a person is not the same as knowing a person. These are two entirely different modes of knowing. The human heart longs to know persons; it is not satisfied with 'knowing about' human beings scientifically, for example.

But we in the English world have only one word for the two types of knowledge. This, I would argue, might account in part for our confusion about the nature of knowledge. In Greek, there are a number of words for love: *agape, eros, philia, storge*, etc., whereas in English there is only one word that covers all of them, namely 'love'. Once again, could this be part of the reason why we are confused about love? We fail to make distinctions, and this failure is manifest in what our language is missing. Hindus distinguish between *kama, artha, dharma*, and *moksha* to describe the four levels of happiness. Unlike Hindus, those in the western world seem to identify happiness with pleasure, which for Hindus is *kama*. Language, thus, reveals a great deal about what a particular people know and don't know. To learn another language can thus enlarge our world, that is, it can enlarge our perspective on reality and make us aware of aspects of the real that we otherwise would have overlooked.

A language is not merely a collection of conventional signs that signify an interior world of universal or common ideas. That might be true on one level, but an entire worldview is embedded in a language; to understand a language is to come to see the world from a particular vantage point. When we learn a language, all we really do initially is translate, that is, before we come to understand a language, which really takes a lifetime, we settle for translation. But translation is merely a matter of thinking within the first language, and thus within the first worldview manifest in the language; I merely translate the French into English, and so I am really thinking in English. But the more I understand the language, the more I understand the worldview embedded in it. My grasp of the language depends on my grasp of that world, but my grasp of that world depends on my grasp of the language.

When we read a translated work, we are placing a great deal of trust in the translator. We trust that he knows the world that is embedded in that language and that he understands well the world and worldview that is expressed in our language. Now translating a philosophical or scientific work is not as sensitive a task as it is when it comes to translating literature or poetry. The reason is that literature is a discourse of a very unique and special type. A literary work will compel our commitment to its argument or main point by the very representation of the object under consideration.[70] Other forms of discourse are not primarily concerned with representing its object in a beautiful or ugly way.

The scientific argument, for example, must bring up evidence extrinsic to each premise to establish both of them. For example, "All men are rational; John is a man, therefore ..." Before we can argue this way, we have to establish that all men are rational, and we do that by reasoning about the nature of rationality. For example, rationality presupposes the ability to apprehend universal ideas, which are essentially different from internal sense images, etc. Human beings give evidence of possessing ideas that are universal in character. In literature, however, the evidence in support of the premises emerges in some way from being properly expressed. In that sense, the evidence is intrinsic to the premises.

In a scientific or philosophical argument, it makes no difference in the proof if a synonym were employed for a certain word. For example, "All expensive things are valued by the rich..." or "All costly things are valued by the rich..." It really does not matter one way or another whether we use 'expensive' or 'costly'. But in poetry, the very sound of words becomes a means within the argument. For example, consider the difference:

I have travelled a lot in places where there is gold,
And lots of nice states and provinces I've seen;

... (paraphrase mine)

Much have I travelled in the realms of gold,
And many goodly states and kingdoms seen;

...

---

[70] Vincent Edward Smith, *The Elements of Logic*. Milwaukee: Bruce Publishing Company. 1957. 200-205.

The beauty of the opening of Keat's poem is lost in my paraphrasing above. Moreover, Keats himself said that in his first draft of his *Endymion*, he wrote: "A thing of beauty is a constant joy". But he eventually changed the line:

A thing of beauty is a joy for ever:
Its loveliness increases; it will never
Pass into nothingness; but still will keep
A bower quiet for us, and a sleep
Full of sweet dreams, and health, and quiet breathing.

In terms of its intellectual content, both lines are the same: "A thing of beauty is a constant joy" and "A thing of beauty is a joy forever". But in terms of their "poetic charm", the difference is significant. As V. E. Smith writes: "The second line with its short trochaic ending that trails off as though there were more to come, puts the sound into a much more genial harmony with the meaning intended. The first reading is closed, but the second is open, like the meaning of "forever" itself."[71]

The fundamental point to remember regarding the literary syllogism (argument) is that the medium of language is an essential part of the entire effect of the composition. "How" what is represented cannot be separated from "what" is represented, as it can in science in general. Paraphrasing always involves a loss of something essential to the original. This is especially true with translations of poems or great literature into other languages.

Part of the delight in reading Charles Dickens is his use of the English language. Consider the following from the opening chapter of his classic, *Oliver Twist*:

Although I am not disposed to maintain that the being born in a workhouse, is in itself the most fortunate and enviable circumstance that can possibly befall a human being, I do mean to

---

[71] Smith, *Ibid.*, 201

say that in this particular instance, it was the best thing for Oliver Twist that could by possibility have occurred. The fact is, that there was considerable difficulty in inducing Oliver to take upon himself the office of respiration,--a troublesome practice, but one which custom has rendered necessary to our easy existence; and for some time he lay gasping on a little flock mattress, rather unequally poised between this world and the next: the balance being decidedly in favour of the latter. Now, if, during this brief period, Oliver had been surrounded by careful grandmothers, anxious aunts, experienced nurses, and doctors of profound wisdom, he would most inevitably and indubitably have been killed in no time. There being nobody by, however, but a pauper old woman, who was rendered rather misty by an unwonted allowance of beer; and a parish surgeon who did such matters by contract; Oliver and Nature fought out the point between them. The result was, that, after a few struggles, Oliver breathes, sneezed, and proceeded to advertise to the inmates of the workhouse the fact of a new burden having been imposed upon the parish, by setting up as loud a cry as could reasonably have been expected from a male infant who had not been possessed of that very useful appendage, a voice, for a much longer space of time than three minutes and a quarter.

It is impossible for me to imagine how a translation of the above into French or Spanish could preserve the original charm and meaning it contains; for there is far more in it than a few simple ideas, an entire world is opened up for us.

For in literature, signs are an intrinsic part of what is known and communicated; this is not the case in science or philosophy. Moreover, as you can see, Dickens has already argued a great deal in this one paragraph. His works are literary arguments.

Another critical difference between the literary argument and scientific discourse is in the level of abstraction involved. Scientific knowledge involves intellectual abstraction; the physical or empirical sciences take place on the first level of abstraction. The mind abstracts from the particular or individual material thing (i.e., this bone, these organs, this tissue, etc.), but not from common sensible matter (i.e., bone, organ, tissue in general). The scientist studies this cadaver not in order to understand this cadaver, but to understand the anatomy of all bodies. But he does not abstract from "bone, muscle, tissue, etc.," just this bone, this muscle, this tissue, etc.

The poet, however, refuses to be taken away from the particular circumstances in which things are situated. The poet wants to communicate the universal in its concrete clothing, and so he uses particular images, sounds, sights, situations, etc. Poets and writers all have something to say, but they use sound and image, meter and rhyme to help them say it; because they simply could not say it in abstract thought alone.

That is why translation is an issue in poetry and literature. To translate a poem effectively, one really has to be a poet of sorts; it is not enough to simply know the language. One must know one's own language as well as the poet knows his original language. But contained in the very sounds and usage of words is an entire world, and so the question to ask is whether the English language can adequately disclose the world of a 16th century Spanish poet, for example. It seems to me that a translation is really a different poem.

Compare the first stanza from a poem by St. John of the Cross, Spanish mystic and poet, with the English translation. Although you might not know Spanish, just pronounce the words to yourself and note the rhythm, rhyme, and sound of the words:

En una noche oscura,
Con ansias, en amores inflamada,
oh dichosa ventura!
Sali sin ser notada,
Estando ya mi casa sosegada.

Translation into English:

On a dark night, Kindled in love with yearnings -- oh, happy chance! --
I went forth without being observed, My house being now at rest.

One need not know Spanish to see that something has been lost in the translation.

Although the literary syllogism is a weaker form of discourse, it is nonetheless true that the poet enters more deeply than the scientist into the realm of the concrete. In terms of communicating the real, it is far less abstract than science, and for this reason it is far less certain and less universal. Hence, it is in one sense less compelling upon the reader. In another sense, however, it is more compelling; for literature can be a dangerous thing. A brilliant wordsmith he or she may very well be, but if there is something wrong with his or her mind, a great deal of harm can be done and a great number of readers can be seriously misled. If, however, he is truly wise and insightful, with his craft he can do tremendous good by reaching a much wider audience than the abstract philosopher.

79 *Do Not Trust Your Memory*

I heard a homily in which the priest told us all of an incident he heard about from a funeral director, who had heard about it from a family whose aunt had committed suicide. We were told, because the priest giving the homily was told, because the funeral director was told, that the Catholic priest who presided over the funeral a few years earlier told the grieving family that their aunt was in hell, because "those who commit suicide go straight to hell". Hence, the family's strong aversion to the idea of another Catholic priest presiding over their most recent loss.

I was skeptical, to say the least, and I expressed my skepticism to a lady who was retelling the story, unwavering in her certitude that all of it was true. "Not for a second do I believe that a Catholic priest actually said such a thing to a grieving family during the course of the funeral," I said. To bolster her claim that there are priests around who are so calloused, she told us that her daughter and new boyfriend went to a nearby Church and heard a priest declare, in the homily, that homosexuals and those who befriend them are going to hell. Again, I expressed my complete skepticism. I then asked her: "What Church?" She named it, and so I named the pastor: "Do you mean Father so and so?" That's him. Immediately I informed her that I know that priest, I preach for him occasionally, and he simply would not say something so ridiculous. "He's no idiot", I insisted.

His homily was her daughter's boyfriend's first experience of the Catholic Church—a negative one at that, in their minds at least. She was adamant that the facts were accurately reported, so I said I would write this priest immediately and inquire. Of course, it was just as I suspected. He would not and could not speak such utter nonsense. The two of them simply got it wrong. "If I had stated that being friends with gays is enough to get you to Hell, then I'm condemning myself", he pointed out.

Another priest friend of mine of a nearby diocese preached a homily that touched upon the issue of same-sex marriage, and in that homily he was emphatic that those with a homosexual orientation in our society must be given all the civil rights that anyone else has, and that he would march on the streets shoulder to shoulder with them if, for instance, their right to decent housing or employment was in jeopardy as a result of their orientation; but the moral law governing sexual acts is another matter altogether, he insisted. Shortly thereafter, it came to his attention that apparently he preached that homosexuals have no right to decent housing. He confronted the man who was the originator of the rumor, and he too was emphatic that this is what my friend said. So, my friend called over another parishioner at random and asked her to repeat what she heard him preach on that topic. After hearing what was really said, the man assured my priest friend that he only told a few people, to which my friend replied: "And how many people did they tell?"

Our memories, generally speaking, are profoundly unreliable, mine included. We conflate pieces of information and the result is a new narrative that is very different from the original. A good example of this for me is a recent trip to Italy. I have positive memories of the trip and am eager to return. But the reason for this is called "duration neglect".[72] We remember peak moments that are either painful or meaningful. There were peak moments when I broke away from the group and walked the narrow streets by myself, explored some old Churches, ordered an espresso, etc. But the trip, for the most part, was a rather negative experience: it was hot, we were being walked into the ground by a woman who planned our every step, I felt I was being "ripped off" by every merchant in every town, I was fearful of our belongings back at the hotel after 150 euros went missing, etc. It was not a pleasant experience when I make the effort to recall the emails I sent a friend back in Canada. It was exhausting. And yet, I have forgotten all that, as a new mother forgets her labor pains, and now only specific moments stand out in my memory. It is the totality of those meaningful moments all conflated into one coherent narrative that I now recall. It's nice, I admit, but it is completely inaccurate.

---

[72] Kahneman, *op. cit.*, Chapter 35, "Two Selves".

We do the same thing with negative peak experiences as well. Some students of mine remember very little of what was taught in philosophy, except the 2 or 3 days we spent on sexual morality, as well as the few times sex was mentioned at the start of the course. The reason is that it was an unpleasant experience for them, because they were sexually active. That's all that stood out for them, and those moments were conflated in such a way that the entire course came to be regarded as a negative series of sexual "do nots".

One of the biggest obstacles to growth in learning and mutual understanding is the inability to recognize the uncertain and underdeterminate nature of the inferences we make on a daily basis. We are unaware of how much of what we hear we actually miss, and how much of what we miss is a constituent part of the context that renders the meaning of what is being said clear. And although feeling uncertain feels very different than feeling certain, unfortunately feeling wrong feels the very same way as feeling right, because when we make a wrongful inference as a result of insufficient evidence, we simply don't know it.

80 Thoughts on Prediction and Memory

Daniel Kahneman shows that even professional statisticians are poor intuitive statisticians.[73] Our predicting abilities are deficient, and much of that has to do with deficient memory and a tendency to neglect of base rates. Recently I had just finished marking 60 logic tests, a test for which I was anticipating a high class average, on the basis of what I had been feeling in the classroom. As I was marking the test, however, I began to change my mind. Some students were making mistakes that revealed lazy mindedness, among other things. I was feeling frustrated and rather disappointed that I would not achieve, this year, a class average of around 90% for this test, which I was sure would be the case.

When I finally inputted all my marks, I decided to check the class average, which I had come to predict would be in the high 70s, possibly low 80s. The class average for the entire test was a 90% (a 93% on the first section having to do with basic terms, a 96% on the conditional syllogism and induction, and an 81% on the categorical syllogism). Why did I eventually conclude that things were much worse than they actually were?

The reason is that I am a poor intuitive statistician. What stood out for me as significant was the disappointment I was feeling when marking certain papers; those tests that were well done met my expectations and so they did not have as significant an impact on me as those tests that fell short of my expectations. The latter were what I came to remember. I drew the false conclusion that what had greater emotional impact occurred more frequently. In other words, 6 poorly done tests on a specific section were more significant to me than 23 that were well done, and greater significance was somehow translated into greater frequency. That error led to a poor or inaccurate prediction. When I stood in front of the class and gave them my prediction—which I had no idea was completely off—, I only succeeded in raising their anxiety level.

---

[73] Kahneman, *op. cit.*, Chapter 21, "Intuitions vs. Formulas".

Peak experiences and duration neglect continue to skew memory, and in so doing, they skew our ability to make accurate predictions. Learning to cultivate a healthy mistrust of the way we might be interpreting the state of the world in which we live is prudent, especially if that interpretation is little more than an intuition, an impression that arises out of what we behold from our limited vantage point.

History/Ethics/Art/God

81 Some Thoughts on the Knowledge of History

Our memories are profoundly unreliable, and there is a great deal of subjectivity in our apprehension of the real (i.e., induction biases). Although this insight is itself an objective apprehension of a real epistemic state of affairs, it is undeniable that our apprehension of the present is fragmented, incomplete, and often mixed with error. How often do we need others to correct our apprehension and interpretation of what is happening currently? After reading a few accounts of the recent story involving the Timothy Schmaltz sculpture of "Jesus the Homeless"—that it was rejected by the Archdiocese of Toronto and New York, but blessed by Pope Francis—, I am still not clear about important details (i.e., why his offer was twice rejected, where it will finally end up, whether or not it was a gift that was rejected, whether the price was too high, etc.), and yet many of these accounts would like me to make a very specific inference that is not flattering to the two Archdioceses in question—which is likely why so many important details have been left out.

If one were to ask two people to write an account of a person's leadership, say a school principal, it is highly unlikely that the two accounts would agree. They often conflict on important points. This is not to suggest that conflict cannot be resolved or that there is no right or wrong answer; I only point out that we don't always interpret what we see correctly or accurately. I only see my own colleagues from a very limited angle, and my understanding of them is incomplete and fragmented. If I am not careful—and we rarely are—, I will make inferences on the basis of scanty evidence, and those inferences that I make are very often the alternatives (or antecedents) that have some sort of emotional appeal to me. Another colleague might see that leader differently. In fact, he or she may be in circumstances that permit a more complete and accurate grasp of a colleague's leadership qualities, for example. There are also heuristic biases that can keep me from accurately assessing the other; for example, how carefully do I pay attention to the size of my sample? Most people are woefully unaware of the inadequacy of the size of the sample on the basis of which they make modified inductions by enumeration.[74] Indeed, some biases may actually permit me to apprehend clearly and objectively certain aspects of my colleagues or a colleague; but some may turn out to be an obstacle to a more accurate assessment. Knowing which ones are a possible help as opposed to a hindrance is not always easy, but it is necessary, especially for the historian.

In this light, how much more difficult is it to come to an understanding of history—the various documents of which suffer from the same problems noted above—with any kind of accuracy? We inevitably come to an understanding of a president, for example, through the eyes of someone else. But the range of another's sight is limited, and what he sees might not be all that accurate, for whatever reason. If it is accurate, who can deny that it is open to further completion?

A good historian must inference to the best explanation; interpreting documents is a matter of hermeneutics, and the "proper" interpretation of a text depends on my own framework and the questions that I pose in the face of the evidence. An economist, for example, will have a definite interest in the causes of certain past events, and he or she will be in a better position to interpret the economic data than someone who has no background in economics. A good contrastive question bearing upon the period of the Great Depression, for example, is not "Why did the Depression occur and why did it end"; rather, we can ask the question: "Why did the Depression last so long?" An economist would ask that question because he or she knows that recessions need not last long; someone with no economic background may not think to ask such a question, and so he or she merely assumes that the end of the Great Depression

---

[74] Induction by enumeration begins with a sample and proceeds to draw a conclusion about the whole. For example, 87% of the apples on this tree are top quality. Therefore, 87% of all the apples in this orchard are top quality. To be valid, the sample must be large enough and it must be representative. Sampling from one tree is not representative, for all his best apples might very well be found in the first two or three rows. A modified induction by enumeration includes induction by enumeration, but, like the statistical syllogism, draws a conclusion about a single instance (see Chapter 17).

was brought about by decisions that preceded the end—which may turn out to be the fallacy of *post hoc ergo propter hoc*.[75]

There is a great deal we can be certain of, or nearly certain of, when it comes to the study of history. The claim that there is no such thing as a historical fact is, in my mind at least, difficult to accept. Every present occurrence recedes into the past and becomes a historical fact; so what does it mean that there is no such thing as a historical fact? Isn't my marriage a historical fact? Does it mean that nothing about the study of history is certain? Are we not certain that there was a housing boom and bust in the United States? Are we not certain that there was a Great Depression? Are we, or at least some of us, not certain that there was a ship called the Titanic that sank?

We come to the knowledge of these events through the testimony of others, and we accept that testimony on the basis of natural faith. So perhaps it can be argued that there is no such thing as a historical fact in the sense of a conclusion that carries the force of necessity, as do the conclusions of a valid demonstrative syllogism. Perhaps we can only speak of probabilities; and indeed, inference to the best explanation is a form of induction, and induction is characterized by underdetermination. Inductive conclusions lack the force of necessity; at best they have a high probably of being true. So, what is the probability that the story of the sinking of the Titanic was a complete fraud? A fabrication? What is the probability that there was no Great Depression, that the 30s was a time of great prosperity for everyone? What is the probability that there was in fact no World War I and II? That President Kennedy was not assassinated?

If certainty cannot be had, what reason is there for doubting any of the above? I am not aware of anyone who doubts that there was a Great Depression or that the Titanic sank. The probability that these are all clever constructs, fabrications that are part of a grand conspiracy of some kind, is so low that the claims are not worth serious consideration.

---

[75] *Post hoc ergo propter hoc* is a fallacy in which one concludes that because some effect (i.e., acne breakout) occurred after another event (i.e., eating chocolate), the subsequent event occurred by virtue of the preceding event.

But other historical claims are worth questioning, because their degree of probability is not so high, or not so low. The claim that Roosevelt's New Deal brought an end to the Great Depression is not so certain; in fact, it is so far from certain that it is unreasonable not to debate the issue.

It is a fact that newspapers reported on the Depression as well as on the sinking of the Titanic, that is, there were articles written at the time. It is not always clear whether the facts presented in these articles are true to reality. If today's newspaper accounts of current events can be so filled with error and misinformation, written with the intention of disposing the public to make specific inferences that agree with the ideological slant of the newspaper, isn't it reasonable to expect the same of newspapers from the 30s?

That is why the historian has to proceed like a detective. The historian is an investigator. To get as close to the truth as is reasonably possible, he will engage in an inductive method, namely, inference to the best explanation. In order to present his findings in a way that keeps a reader's attention, he will arrange those facts in the form of a coherent narrative; that narrative will, for the sake of style, leave out specific facts and include others. More importantly, that narrative will participate in the limitations that sense perception imposes upon human intelligence in general. This is not to suggest that his history is unreliable—it might be tremendously well researched and reliable; but it is always limited. There is no escaping human limitations; for there is only one way to be opened up onto the world, whether it is the world of the present or the world of the past, and that is through the purview of an individual human being who begins to know whatever he knows through sense perception, and human intelligence participates in the limitations of sense perception (we only see the world from a particular angle at any one time).

Now, finding the right contrastive question or series of questions is the way that will lead to the hypothesis from which we can infer the best explanation. Just as this often permits a detective to solve a crime, it is this stumbling upon the right question that enables a historian to solve a historical problem. Why did the Great Depression last as long as it did, when recessions throughout the 20th century have recovered on their own relatively quickly? That calls for a re-examination of the historical evidence. Perhaps we have overlooked something all these years and we never realized it, because the question was never asked, and the question was never asked because only someone with a special interest asks certain questions.

82 On the Importance of Law

When you begin to drive—if you do not drive already—, you will experience moments of tension between your private will (i.e., your will to drive uninterrupted and at a steady rate) and the rule of law (i.e., traffic lights and stop signs). It is frustrating to hit every red light on a long stretch of road, especially when you are hungry and want to get home quickly. Now imagine what it would be like if everyone on the road chose to ignore the rule of law for the sake of their own private desires. For example, instead of stopping for the red light or stop sign, or yielding at a roundabout, and patiently waiting for it to turn green, or the oncoming traffic to pass, people simply drove through without any regard for the legal system in place. We know the result would be chaos. Many would arrive late to work, many would not make it to work at all because they'd have been involved in a collision, many would be hospitalized, there would be an increase in road rage incidents, etc. Everyone would simply be looking out for himself. The purpose of traffic lights, stop signs, yield signs, speed limits, etc., is to bring about order, a just order, so that the overall end of that particular society can be achieved, and that end is the common good of the whole. The good of the whole cannot be achieved if few are able to get to work, school, or their holiday destination safely and within a reasonable length of time.

If I refuse to look beyond myself to the overall order of the whole, then I will get very frustrated when required to stop for a red light, for example. I will be tempted to run it, thus putting others' lives at risk. I can be so enslaved by passion that I am not explicitly aware that those who now have a green light have been waiting for a few minutes while I was driving and that now it is my turn to wait, for the sake of a larger order, a social order. Without that social order, my own private good cannot be achieved, because my good depends on the common good of the whole. Thus, without the ability to put aside our private desires for the sake of a larger order, that is, to make minor sacrifices for the sake of the social order, the result is inevitably social disorder.

What is it that drives people to make their own private will the rule of law, that is, to place their own will or desires over the will of the whole that is expressed in a society's laws? Since law is a dictate of reason, it isn't a reasoned decision that is at the root of the tendency to give priority to one's private will over the rule of law, but the passions. This is obvious to anyone who drives. Certain people do not control their passions; they will pass on a solid line, even while driving up a hill, putting the lives of those in the oncoming lane at risk, as well as their own lives and the lives of their passengers at risk. Such people are impatient, and since patience moderates the emotion of sorrow, which is the opposite of sensible satisfaction, these people ignore the demands of reason because they cannot tolerate the passion of sorrow which arises out of difficult situations, like traffic jams or long distances, etc.

Some people see law as their enemy and will do whatever they can to circumvent it; others have great reverence for law. It is true that different cultures or societies generally speaking exhibit different cultural attitudes towards the rule of law. At the root of social disorder are individual decisions to subordinate the good of the whole (the common good of the civil community) to one's individual will.

There are different kinds of law: civil law, which is manmade law (i.e., drinking age, voting age, income tax laws, traffic laws, etc.), and natural law that is the foundation of civil law; for there is no natural law that can tell us the proper speed limit for a highway; that has to be determined on the basis of a number of factors, i.e., statistics regarding road safety, area, weather conditions, etc. Making law is, in some ways, a matter of determining the right trade-offs. A safe speed for highway driving might be 50 kilometers an hour, but it may turn out that there is no evidence of any significant difference in safety between 50 and 100 kilometers an hour on a highway, for example. And driving 50 kilometers an hour on the highway could be very costly for others, for it would take twice as long to get from one place to another, and there are costs attached to that difference, i.e., transportation costs based on hourly wages, and only half as much can be accomplished, etc. A speed limit of 100 kilometers an hour may turn out to be safe and more cost effective, while 120 kilometers an hour may begin to show an increase in costs, at least in the long run, because a safety threshold has been crossed, resulting in more fatalities on the road, more collisions, and no significant increase in profits for businesses, etc. So a legislature decides, on the basis of evidence derived from a variety of sources, that 100 kilometers an hour on the highways in Ontario is the best alternative; perhaps a higher speed limit is called for in the prairies, for example.

The tension that often exists between one's private desires and the rule of law (civil law) is also present, very often, with respect to natural law. I have a moral obligation to pay my debts, to tell the truth, to eat and drink moderately, etc., but the passions often incline us to spend the money on ourselves instead of paying it back, or lie in order to avoid a penalty, or drink to excess, etc. Consider theft and the right to property. All of us have fundamental moral obligations to contribute to the common good of the civil community, thus to develop skills in order to create wealth, in order to purchase the property we need as a means to fulfilling those duties, for example, the duty to take care of the children we brought into this world, to feed them, protect them, educate them, etc. And so we have a right to property, because we cannot fulfill those duties without it, for example, some sort of housing, transportation, etc. But that property has to be purchased; it is not up to someone else to simply hand it to you and me; for that would imply that he has a duty to work for us without any kind of remuneration, and it could be argued that this would amount to slavery. He has just as much right to property as I have, so we all have an obligation to purchase the property we need. The duty of the state is to create the conditions that make such free exchanges possible (i.e., laws, roads, public utility services, etc.).

Money is nothing but an artificial means of exchange. So you have agreed, for example, to produce a table (since you possess those skills) for someone who has agreed to pay the cost of the materials and labor. Now, to steal is to take property that rightfully belongs to another;

thus, if I steal from you, what I am doing in effect is changing the terms of your agreements with others. For example, you earned $100 as a result of a mutually agreed upon transaction involving your skills (i.e., carpentry, accounting, or teaching skills, etc.), but I take that money when you are not looking. Essentially, what I have done is I have decided, without your permission or knowledge, that you are going to produce that table for him, but he is going to pay me for it. What I am doing is re-organizing social relationships—your relationships—in a way that serves my private desires or my individual will. In other words, the common good of the civil community is subordinated to my own private will. There is a sense in which I refuse to regard other human beings as my equals; rather, I see them as various means to my own private ends. My will becomes the highest good and everything else is subordinated to it.

83 *Self-Knowledge and the Fundamentals of Ethics*

A very important point to keep in mind is that the basic principles of the natural moral law are naturally known. We possess self-knowledge, that is, we know ourselves from within. I become aware of myself as *subject* when I am knowing an *object* outside of myself; there is no knowledge of beings outside of me unless I am also aware of myself as a subject, and vice versa. That knowledge of myself is *in the background*, so to speak. It is a *self*-consciousness; but that self-consciousness is not an objective consciousness, but a *subjective* consciousness. Indeed, I can make myself the *object* of my knowledge by focusing on myself in order to learn something about myself, such as myself as a knower, or perhaps my emotional reactions, my own psychology, etc., but that objective knowledge of myself is also accompanied by a subjective consciousness that is also in the background, so to speak. The effort to make this subjective consciousness objective consciousness is much like a cat chasing its tail.

Now, I know that I see as "good" or "desirable" a great deal of what I know. For example, I know that I am living, and I also know that I desire to live—that's why I am inclined to protect my life. I also know that I am inclined to pursue more knowledge (truth), which is why I ask a lot of questions and read a lot of books. I am also aware that I am inclined to pursue aesthetic experiences (I like to contemplate beauty, i.e., in art, music, nature, etc.). I know that I am inclined to play and to engage in making, often just for the sake of playing and making (i.e., a game of chess, cards, and producing music or painting something, or building a cabinet for the love of building, etc.). I know that I am inclined to seek relationships with people who have similar interests or qualities (friends). I am aware that I have a natural desire to marry, that is, to enter into an exclusive relationship (marriage), not merely a friendship (I may not quite understand the nature of this relationship, but there is some kind of inclination to a more than "friendship" relationship). I also am inclined to enter into a harmonious relationship with the civil community as a whole (man is a political animal who has a natural inclination to live in a *polis*, a civil community). I am also aware that I am inclined to establish some kind of harmony between the various elements of the self, for example, I often feel a conflict within me between my reason and my passions (my reason says 'no', but my emotions say 'yes'). I have also, at times, felt a conflict between my character and an action that I performed (I felt that this was "not like me"). These are times when I have experienced guilt or shame, and the desire to eliminate that is really a desire to harmonize those elements of the self. Finally, I experience a certain restlessness within me, an inclination to "transcend" myself, to seek harmony between myself and a "totally other" source of meaning (we see this religious need expressed in all cultures throughout history).

Now, since the good is that which all things desire, these natural inclinations common to all human persons are called human goods. Because they are not sensible, but intelligible, they are *intelligible human goods*. The basic intelligible human goods are human life, knowledge of truth, leisure (contemplation of the beautiful as well as play and art), friendship (various degrees), marriage, the common good of the civil community, integrity, and religion.[76]

These natural inclinations that we all have are *motivating principles (final causes) of human action*. They are the ultimate *reasons why* we do anything at all. Think of any human act and ask yourself: "Why am I doing this?" Keep asking "why" until you cannot get another answer. You'll come to the "end of the road", and that end will be one of the above inclinations. For example, why are you getting in the car? To go to Staples. Why are you going to Staples? To buy a new binder, a laptop, and some white-out. Why are you going to buy these things? I need them for school; I'm a history major (or an English major, or philosophy major). Why bother with school? Because I want my degree. Why? Because I want to teach history. Why history? Because I love history, I love learning about the past; it is intriguing, and my special area is ancient Roman civilization. Why? I just do; I've always

---

[76] See John Finnis, *Natural Law and Natural Rights*. Oxford: Clarendon Press, 1980. See also Germain Grisez and Joseph M. Boyle Jr. *Life and Death with Liberty and Justice: A Contribution to the Euthanasia Debate*. Notre Dame: University of Notre Dame Press, 1979. 359-380.

loved learning about this, for its own sake (the intelligible human good of knowledge for its own sake). Okay, why do you want to teach it? Because a nation ignorant of history is one that is doomed to repeat it, in other words, I want to help improve the world (the intelligible human good of the civil community, or the common good). Okay, but why do you want to teach it at a university and make money at it? Why not study it in private? Because I want to make my living at teaching. Why do you want to live? Because I want to live, for the sake of living (I see human life as basically good).

Just as speculative reason has a starting point, a first principle, which is "nothing can both be and not be at the same time and in the same respect" (unless that is true, knowledge is impossible), practical reason has a starting point or first principle, which is "good is to be done, evil is to be avoided". Everyone agrees with that principle, even if they are at odds with one another about what is truly good. Even the criminal starts with the principle that good is to be done, it's just that the rest of us have a problem with what he thinks constitutes the good. He certainly desires to preserve his life, seeks knowledge, leisure, friends, and harmony in himself, etc., but his acts are deficient in some way, as we'll see later. For example, instead of working to bring order to his passions and line them up with reason, he simply dismisses his conscience and follows his passions. Although he sees his own life as intrinsically good, he doesn't see yours as intrinsically good, but merely good to the degree that it is useful to him in some way.

Secondary Precepts and Self-Knowledge

The intelligible human goods are many, but they are all aspects of a single human person. Life is in you, and truth is in you, etc. Knowledge of truth does not exist in itself, but in a human being who knows. Friendship is a relationship between persons, and so friendship is not extrinsic to human persons, but intrinsic. So you and I are intelligible human goods, and all the intelligible human goods exist in you and me, either potentially or actually (i.e., you may not have any friends actually, but only potentially, etc.).

I am aware of these inclinations (human goods) through my own self-knowledge or subjectivity, but I am also aware that you are a being of the same nature as me (through simple apprehension). You too are an instance of a basic intelligible human good, and you are essentially equal in dignity to me. I naturally see my life as good, and so I know that you too see your life as good. I do not want to be harmed, because I see my life as good, so I know that you too do not want to be harmed, because you see your life as good. Now, I know that your life is truly good, because I know that my human life is truly good (it is a genuine intelligible human good), so I know that if good is to be done and evil is to be avoided, then I ought not to harm you. I also know that I ought not to do to you what I would not want done to me (the golden rule). If I see someone doing something to you that I know he would not want done to him, I am witnessing an injustice.

I also naturally know that since I ought to treat others fairly (as I would want to be treated), I ought to keep my promises. And since I know naturally that I ought to revere what is intelligibly and humanly good and that marriage is an intelligible human good, I ought to revere marriage, my own or another's, and I ought not to violate my vow of fidelity, or encourage others to violate theirs.

Everybody has, to some degree, a natural knowledge of the basic precepts of natural law. We see this in all cultures throughout history. The problem is that most people have **only a rudimentary knowledge** of the precepts of natural law. I would argue that disordered passion blinds the intellect; some people simply don't want to know the specific requirements of natural law, for fear that their lives would have to be reformed in some significant way, and people generally don't like change; they're comfortable the way they are, and they resent anyone telling them or making them feel as if they might be doing something wrong. But the difficult work of **the science of ethics** lies in rationally drawing out the moral implications of these principles as they relate to particular human acts, such as abortion, contraception, euthanasia, sexual acts, war, stewardship of riches, the use of language, self-defence, etc.

So the starting point of natural law is in connatural knowledge, which is self-knowledge of one's natural inclinations (the intelligible human goods) as well as a rudimentary understanding of the secondary precepts. The science of ethics involves reasoning and demonstration on the basis of this knowledge, which will lead to a more thorough understanding of natural law. This requires a great deal of labor—thinking, dialogue, studying the great moral thinkers of the past, etc. But the person who has cultivated the virtues possesses an acquired connatural knowledge (the connatural knowledge of the saint who knows what the just, brave, prudent, chaste, or patient course of action is, without necessarily having studied the science of ethics).

Some Basic Secondary Precepts

God is to be loved above all things [If God is Goodness Itself, the Supreme Good, then "relationship" with God is the greatest human good]

One ought to render due honour to one's parents [the family is the society through which we enter this world. We owe a debt to our parents that cannot be fully repaid. Relationship with this first society is humanly good and of the highest importance]

One ought to reverence the marriage bond [because marriage is an intelligible human good and the basis of the family]

Do not harm others, that is, one ought not to do anything that harms the common good of the civil community, that is, one must direct one's life towards the common good. [I experience my life as good, because I'm inclined to protect it. I also know that the other is of the same nature as myself and thus sees his own life as equally good. I ought not to inflict harm on others, because they are basically good]

If others are intrinsically and humanly good, then one ought not to willingly destroy an instance of an intrinsic human good for the sake of some other intrinsic good. [In other words, one must not do evil to achieve good]

Since human goods are intrinsically good, that is, ends in themselves, then one ought not to treat another human person as a means to an end. [Persons must be loved, not used; things must be used, not loved]

Since others are equally good, since they are essentially equal, it follows that one ought not to treat certain others with a preference based purely on feelings, unless a preference is required by human goods. [In other words, one ought always to treat others in a way that respects their status as equal in dignity to oneself].

The common good can only be achieved in communion with others, so if we ought to revere the common good, **one ought not to act individualistically for intelligible human goods, but in community with others**.

And since man is a rational animal who desires his own fullness of being (good), he ought to act rationally. Hence, **one ought not to act purely on the basis of emotion, either on the basis of fear, aversion, hostility, or desire for sensible goods, but ought to act on the basis of reason, in pursuit of intelligible goods and in accordance with all the precepts of natural law.** [To act purely on the basis of emotion is to act as a brute, without the guidance of reason. A specifically human act is motivated by intelligible human goods and is guided by reason]

And since each person is intrinsically good and one (integral), and since one desires to be integrated, one ought not to violate that integrity. Hence, **one ought not to lie** (an immediate violation of integrity), and **one ought to choose in accordance with one's best judgment on what to do here and now** (conscience), and **one ought to relentlessly pursue that truth of what is right and wrong, to make sure one's acts conform to the demands of the natural law.**

One ought not to take what rightfully belongs to another (property).

84 *The Elements of the Human Action*

The fundamental tendency of the intellect is towards knowing "what" things are; intelligence is the ability to apprehend the essence as well as the existence of a being. The most fundamental or primary mode of being is substance. Material beings are existing material substances of a determinate nature or essence. But human acts also have a determinate nature or species, which is why we also seek to know "what" is being done. How often have we been asked—or how often have we asked the question—: "What are you doing?"

Now imagine you are in a workshop and you are watching someone make something. He is so immersed in his work that he cannot tell you "what" he is making. You see the matter he is using out of which he will produce something (i.e., wood), but you still do not know "what" he is making. You will know, however, when he stops working. The reason is that the formal cause and the final cause coincide. The formal cause is "that for the sake of which there is coming to be", and the final cause is "that for the sake of which there is coming to be". The final cause is twofold, it is divided into a) the end of the generation (or proximate end), and b) the end of the generated (or ultimate end). The proximate end is the formal cause (i.e., cabinet), while the end of the generated is the ultimate purpose for which he is making the thing (i.e., to store plates, or clothing, or books, etc.). The end of the generation or proximate end reveals "what" it is he is making (the form); it reveals the proximate intention of his action. The proximate intention is to impose a form on matter, and it is "formal cause" that determines "whatness".

So too, a human action is "what it is" through the proximate end intended. This is the **moral object**, the first element of the human action. Shooting a gun at a human being does not tell me "what" is being done. One could very well be testing a bullet proof vest, or one could be attempting to stop an aggressor, or one could be attempting to murder someone. One has to ask: "What are you doing?" or "What are you intending?" The answer might be: "I'm testing out the bullet

404

proof vest my friend here is wearing", or "I am trying to stop this man from raping me", or "I'm trying to kill this man". These are three different species of action, that is, three essentially different kinds of acts, although from the point of view of the act as nothing more than external behavior, they are virtually the same.

The **motive** of the act, the second element, answers the question: "Why are you doing that?" This corresponds to the ultimate end (i.e., the end of the generated). Why are you killing this person? Why are you testing the vest? Why are you trying to stop that rapist? Why are you helping this old lady across the street? Why are you lying?

Finally, the **circumstances** constitute the third element of the human act. Perhaps we can describe this element as that which, taken as a whole, responds to questions beginning with "who, where, when, how, under what conditions, etc." You are practicing your short game (golf) with a wedge (moral object) in order to improve your game (motive); the only problem is that you have decided to practice in the mausoleum at the cemetery during your grandmother's burial (circumstances).

The circumstances, in some cases, will modify the act; they may add to the seriousness of the act or lessen its seriousness (lying to save another's life and lying for the fun of it). In some cases, the circumstances actually change the nature of the act, that is, they might change the moral object so that it becomes an essentially different kind of act. For example, keeping one's promises is a morally good thing to do, for it is a matter of justice; breaking one's promise is, generally speaking, an injustice. But there are circumstances in which breaking one's promise is not a violation of justice (i.e., I promised to go out for supper and to a movie with a friend of mine this Friday, but I came down with the flu, so I have decided to break that promise).

Some of us would argue, however, that there are certain acts (moral object) that are intrinsically wrong, acts whose moral species cannot be altered under any circumstances. For example, giving someone a lethal injection so that they will die (moral object), so that they will not have to suffer anymore (motive) is, we would argue, intrinsically wrong, for it is murder; the act involves the intentional attack on a basic intelligible human good, namely human life, and one may not do evil that good may come of it.

This is the fundamental difference between Natural Law and Consequentialism; according to the consequentialist, the motive and/or circumstances determine the morality of the human act, not the moral object. It is as if actions have no determinate nature in themselves, but receive their meaning entirely from the motive or circumstances. An act becomes good if the consequences are good; and bad if the consequences are bad. Thus, acts that have been traditionally regarded as intrinsically evil (abortion, euthanasia, contraception, adultery, fornication, lying, etc.) are not necessarily regarded so by the consequentialist. If adultery promises good results, then it can be justified.

According to Natural Law, however, this is not the case. Every element of the human act must be good if the act is to be morally good; if any element is evil, the entire act is evil, and there are certain acts that are intrinsically evil; for evil is a deficiency, a privation of being, a lack of something that should be there. So, if the act is morally deficient in some way, it is not a morally good act.

Moreover, morality is about character, first and foremost. We would argue that it is not about creating social conditions that are most conducive to a pleasurable or easy life. So if I willingly choose a morally evil course of action (an act that involves an evil moral object, such as adultery or lying), I become morally evil (I am an adulterer, I am a liar); for you are what you choose (will). The adverse consequences of shaping morally deficient character simply cannot be measured, contrary to what Consequentialists seem to hold.

85 *The Science of Ethics and Connatural Knowledge*

There is no science of particulars, for science is the result of demonstration (syllogism), for it is essentially certain knowledge attained by seeing things in relation to their causes.[77] Now it is the middle term that represents the cause in a demonstration, for the middle term is the cause of the conclusion. For example,

All men are rational
John is a man
Therefore, John is rational.

There is no conclusion "John is rational" without the middle term "man". "Man" is the cause, the principle upon which the conclusion depends; it is the *reason* why we can conclude with necessity, that John is rational—*because* all men are rational and John is a man.

Note also that no necessary conclusion can be drawn from two particular premises (i.e., two I statements). Hence, there is no science of particulars. At least one premise must be universal. What does all this mean for ethics? Ethics is a science, and so the science of ethics aims at universal conclusions: i.e., Injustice is a vice, lying is unjust, man ought to be temperate, intentionally killing another is always wrong, etc.

Now the virtue of prudence involves applying universal moral principles to particular situations. But particular situations are unique and unrepeatable. Indeed, situations can be similar to one another, which is why we often hear the following prelude: "…if you ever find yourself in a similar situation, this is what you ought to do…" However, although situations might be similar in many respects, they are never identical. That is why Aquinas speaks of the "quasi-integral parts" of prudence, which are: memory, understanding, docility,

---

[77] I refer here to science in the general sense as certain knowledge in terms of causes, principles or reasons; indeed, the empiriological sciences are inductive, but the aim of any science is to achieve certainty as far as that is possible.

shrewdness, reasoning, foresight, circumspection, and caution. Understanding first principles and an ability to reason are necessary if one is to apply universal principles to particular situations, but memory, docility, shrewdness, foresight, circumspection and caution are also necessary precisely because prudence concerns itself with particular situations, and particular situations are unique. Thus, one requires experience (memory), the ability to learn from the experienced (docility), and the foresight that comes from many years of experience, as well as circumspection and caution, which are missing in the inexperienced.

In other words, although it is of the utmost importance to study the science of ethics, a textbook is not going to be much help when you find yourself in the midst of particular situations that demand a response—running to the library will not work. It is going to be up to you to "incarnate" the moral truth within the heart of the situation you find yourself in. To do that is no easy task. It requires these parts of prudence, and it requires the cardinal virtues of justice (which is in the will), temperance (which is in the concupiscible appetite) and fortitude (which is in the irascible appetite).

In other words, one needs more than an abstract science. Unless all we want to do is discuss abstract moral problems and are indifferent to living and incarnating the truth in our own life, we need *connatural knowledge*.

In order to make some sense out of this, let me begin by defining prudence: it is the intellectual/moral virtue which rightly directs particular human acts, through rightly ordered appetite, toward a good end. The key phrase here is "rightly ordered appetite". A prudent man is one who has *a rightly ordered appetite*. In other words, a person who is disordered, who is unjust and lacking temperance, for example, cannot be said to be prudent, although he might be a great physicist or a good speculative philosopher. A prudent man is a virtuous man (one who makes moral truth a lived phenomenon). If a person makes imprudent decisions—and immoral choices are imprudent choices—, he is not prudent.

Now, prudence is the mother of all the virtues. But how can I be rightly ordered unless I have prudence? And yet how can I possess prudence unless I possess right appetite? These are very good questions and they are not easy to answer without appearing to be caught in a vicious circle.

First, let us review connatural knowledge. Connatural knowledge is the opposite of abstract knowledge. For example, all knowledge begins with sense experience. I see a particular thing, i.e., an animal, and I observe its behavior, and through its activity I gradually come to know "what it is" (its essence or nature). My mind conceives an idea of it through a process of abstraction. And so the word "dog", "cow" or "man", for example, are words that point in two directions; they point outwards to a particular dog, cow, or man (i.e., that is my dog), and they point back to a universal idea in the mind (canine, bovine, human, etc.). So the movement here is from the particular (this dog outside the mind) to the universal idea ('canine' within the mind).

For the sake of clarity and simplicity, let's just say that connatural knowledge begins with the idea within and moves to the particular (the concrete action). A connatural knowledge of justice, for example, is a lived knowledge of justice. The idea of justice has been incarnated into my very person. I know justice from within, because I am naturally inclined to justice, because I possess the habit or virtue of justice. A connatural knowledge of chastity, for example, is a lived knowledge of chastity. I know chastity from within, I know that this alternative before me is contrary to chastity, because I am disinclined to go there, but I am inclined to that other alternative, because the virtue in me inclines me to that option (for example, I am not inclined to go to a Swingers club or watch pornography, and I am inclined to wear modest clothing, etc.).

Again, who are the best judges of a gymnastics competition? The answer is former gymnasts. They know a good routine from within. Those who have never mastered the sport don't have it within them, and so to them, each competitor looks almost as good as the next guy. If you are not a musician, you might judge this person to be a good guitar player, but after becoming an accomplished guitarist yourself, your judgment will change. You will know what a good guitarist is from within, and you will notice things that you did not notice previously. This is true with the arts and any other sport. The knowledge of how to dribble a basketball and throw baskets is in your muscles as a result of years of practice. You may not understand the physics of throwing a ball, but you know how to throw one nonetheless.

A particular tree grows and reproduces itself because it possesses the form of tree (the substantial form). Your idea of "tree" however does not reproduce, nor does it weigh anything. A thing, by virtue of its form, is inclined to act a certain way, that is, according to its nature (gasoline is flammable, iron resists pressure, trees grow, dogs run and bark, birds fly, humans reason, etc.). Similarly, when a person possesses a virtue—not merely the idea of justice, or chastity, but the actual disposition or habit—, he possesses the "form" within himself (the accidental form or quality). The idea "justice" for example, or "chastity", or "fortitude" are now within him, as habits that dispose the will (in the case of justice) to obey reason, that dispose the pleasures of touch or the passions of the concupiscible appetite (in the case of temperance) to readily obey reason, or that dispose the emotions of fear and daring to readily obey reason, etc. Since this person possesses these virtues or habits, he is inclined towards just, temperate, and courageous acts (for a thing always acts according to its form or nature).

To possess the art of sculpting is to be inclined to sculpt well; to possess the art of music (i.e., the violin) is to be inclined to produce beautiful music easily, etc. Similarly, a virtuous person knows the virtuous course of action from within, so to speak; for he or she is inclined to it.

Now, keep in mind that the emotions affect the intellect. Disordered passion blinds the mind. "As a person is, so does he see", said Aristotle. An unjust person who puts his own desires before the rights of others is not going to be inclined to the just course of action in a particular situation (an unjust person always thinks his rights have been violated, regardless of what the judge tries to explain to him). He is going to be inclined to that option that will bring him the most pleasure. The coward is not going to be inclined to the truly courageous course of action; he is going to be inclined to that course of action that is safest for him alone—the rest can lie down and die, for all he cares. Moreover, he sees the truly brave man as reckless. But the reckless and foolhardy man who loves to run headlong into danger unnecessarily—because it raises his adrenaline level—sees the truly brave man as a coward. So too, the sexually immoral will judge the chaste woman as a prude, and the liar judges the honest man as a "goody goody".

Recall the example of the lazy lout who is attracted to the political party who promises to take care of him, or the example of the criminal who sees his lawyer as a bad man, because the jury found him guilty of rape and murder (of which he is truly guilty). Consider the lazy student who judges as "good" a truly bad teacher who gives away marks like they are candy and teaches nothing.

In order to make prudent decisions in the concrete situations of daily life, one needs rightly ordered appetite, for only the virtuous see correctly (via connatural knowledge).

But one also needs to know universal moral principles, an understanding of how morality works, what actions are absolutely impermissible, which precepts are relative, etc. This is the science of ethics, and like any science, it has developed over time as a result of reflection and reasoning. But the science of ethics can only begin to take root in a person who has made an initial decision to love the moral good (the *bonum honestum*) over the delectable good (his pleasure). That is a free decision that each one of us has made (usually at a very young age) at some point in our lives (either for the good or for the self). A person who has made a decision that translates into a love of the moral good (the common good, the good of all human persons, the moral order) over his own private good, is one who will want to know more fully what is truly good, as opposed to what is only apparently good (what appears as good, but is truly evil), and so as time goes on, he will be motivated to *draw out universal moral principles*, such as the human goods and how we ought to relate to them, what is truly right and ordered (just), what is truly honest, temperate, brave, etc., in order to continue to grow in virtue. He will be open to the moral duty to order his passions to follow (or to line up with) what he ultimately wills, which is the moral good, and so he will have the beginnings of virtue. In other words, as a young man or even a child, he will have a degree of right appetite; he will be open to a proper upbringing, which involves parental correction, and he will be open to the correction of those who represent them (teachers, persons of authority, etc.).

An immoral person will be indifferent to moral principles, truth and virtue, and often this indifference is made manifest very early on in a person's life, despite having good parents. If as a young adult such a person shows interest in the science of morality at all, it might ultimately be for the sake of justifying his own lifestyle choices.

The person who loves the moral good will grow in a scientific knowledge of the good—assuming he has the time to study or reflect upon these principles—, his will (the rational appetite) moves him to pursue the truth more completely, and his increasing knowledge affects his actions—he becomes more virtuous because he conforms his actions to what he discovers to be truly good, and his corresponding growth in virtue deepens his knowledge from within (connatural knowledge), which continues to drive him towards a deeper insight into the truth of what is morally right and good, and a more complete articulation of that truth.

In the midst of the particular situations of day to day life, the virtuous man is able to see (conscience) what ought to be done in the here and now, and if he cannot, experience will gradually help him to arrive at understanding because he is open to correction (he possesses docility). The immoral are not so open, which is why they tend not to learn from experience.

86 *As A Man Is, So Does The End Appear To Him*

This Aristotelian dictum has to do with character and its implications for knowledge. A few analogies from outside the realm of morality might help in trying to grasp this more fully. For example, assume that you've been sitting in a sauna for 30 minutes or so. Immediately afterwards you jump into the pool nearby. The water feels cold to you. Your friend, however, has just walked to the swimming pool on a cold January day, and after getting changed, he jumps into the pool. To him, the pool feels warm. The pool, however, is the same temperature for both of you. You both perceive it differently because **you are different**, that is, the two of you are differently disposed. You came from a hot sauna; he came from the cold outdoors.

A spoiled child used to eating at the finest Italian restaurants finds East Side Mario's a bland and unexciting option. A child from a family struggling financially is delighted to be taken out to East Side Mario's; for him, this is a real treat. Their judgments are different because they are differently disposed.

If a person has the virtue of fortitude, it means that he does not allow his fears to prevent him from doing what reason demands; he is able to rise above his fears in order to pursue the good. So he decides to stand up to some unjust aggressor, for example, or speak out, etc. But the coward, who lacks the virtue or habit of fortitude, is overcome by his fear (which is a passion) and thus fails to achieve the good. What is interesting is that the coward sees (judges, evaluates) the brave man as reckless or foolhardy; also, the foolhardy who are truly reckless and inordinately daring see (judge, evaluate) the man of fortitude as a coward. Thus, as a person is (character, appetite), so does he see (judge).

A person who has the virtue of chastity will see a certain course of action as intemperate and morally depraved, i.e., viewing pornography, or a one night sexual fling, etc. He or she cannot tolerate the thought of being a certain "kind of person" (unchaste). The unchaste person, on the other hand, will see the chaste person as a prude. The liar sees the honest man as strange; the honest man is distressed by the liar's lack of inhibition.

Essentially, everyone tends to see themselves as normal, that is, they regard themselves as the "norm" (from the Latin *norma*, "carpenter's square, rule, pattern,"), the ideal or measure, and so they judge others in light of the norm, which is themselves. So, the depraved man thinks he's okay, and he judges the morally noble person as rigid, uptight, etc. Thus, character shapes your vision; it affects your ability to perceive and judge soundly and accurately. This is a matter of connatural knowledge. A good musician can judge a good performance; a poor musician judges a poor musician as good. An artist thinks his works are good until years later; he looks back to his initial paintings and realizes now what he didn't realize then, namely his flaws, which his teacher clearly saw. As he acquires the quality of an artist, his judgment changes, becomes sharper and more comprehensive.

That is why arguing with someone who is closed to moral reform, one who is not open to growing in virtue, is often pointless and can be a frustrating experience. They have chosen to be a certain kind of person, and that identity does not include openness to truth, and so they will not allow themselves to see those who are morally better as morally better or more noble. They will often make remarks that are denigrating in some way, allowing their "self-normative" standard to remain undisturbed. Those who have chosen a moral identity that includes openness to truth, in other words, those who love truth more than they love themselves, will allow themselves to be inspired by those who are morally nobler than they.

Thus, accepting our moral and intellectual limitations is the condition for the possibility of progress, and on a more communal scale it is the condition for the possibility of the advancement of civilization.

87 Character Determines One's Ability To Understand

In the previous chapter, we took a cursory look at the Aristotelian dictum: As a person is, so does the end appear to him. I would like to explore this more deeply. The first point I would like to make is that "you are not what you think", nor is it the case that "you are what you feel"; rather, "you are what you will". One's moral identity (character) is determined by the free moral choices that we make. Aristotle writes: **"For our character is determined by our choosing good or evil, not by the opinions we hold**. We choose to take or avoid a good or an evil, but we hold opinions as to **what a thing is**, whom it will benefit, or how: but (the decision) to take or avoid is by no means an opinion. Also, a choice is praised for being **directed to the proper object** or for being correctly made, but opinions are praised for being true."[78]

The end, as you know, refers to the final cause, which is the purpose. Now recall Socrates who divided humanity into three on the basis of what each group regarded as the greatest good or ultimate purpose in life, that is, as man's chief end in life: 1) pleasure, 2) honors, and 3) virtue. I can make pleasure my ultimate end in life, or my own glory and honor. In both cases, I choose myself as the greatest good. Or, I can make the common good of the civil community my ultimate end, or God, etc., that is, something outside myself. The end that I choose will determine what I see as fitting, that is, a fitting means to the end that I have chosen. All this depends on my will (the rational appetite), which is ordered to a single end. The principal appetite in us, in fact, is the will, and it is the orientation of the will that defines our character, our moral identity, the *kind of person that we determine ourselves to be.*

Recall too that the final cause and formal cause coincide.[79] Both are defined as "that for the sake of which there is coming-to-be". The

---

[78] Aristotle, *Nicomachean Ethics*. Trans. M. Ostwald. New York: Bobbs-Merrill, 1962. Bk 3, ch. 2.

[79] Aristotle demonstrates the four causes that are involved in any change with examples from the realm of art. A sculptor begins working on a figure. He is the agent cause of the

agent acts for an end, for example, the carpenter sets out to build a table, but he can do so because the "form" is in his mind. And so "form" (what it is) and "end" (final cause) are really the same. What comes to be "in the end" is the form that was in his mind throughout. So too, "what" a person is (his character) and that which he makes to be his end through an act of the will (final cause) are really the same. What comes to be "in the end" is what I make of myself (character).

Now, a person's sensitive appetites (and the emotions that proceed from them) are ordered by the will, that is, they receive their direction from the will. If my end or purpose is always to feel good, regardless of how that might affect others, then I will assign my sensitive appetites the position of government; they become my advisors, so to speak. If my end is the common good of the civil community, and not myself, then my emotions will not be given a governing position, but a subservient one. If I have to do something that is a fitting means to that end, which is the common good of the civil community, I will carry it out, despite the fact that I have to go without rich foods for a while, make sacrifices, or that I might have to experience a degree of fear, etc. Thus, the entire network of the emotions is ordered according to the direction of the will, which is centered either around the self, or around the will of God, or around the demands of justice, etc.

Thus, character affects a person's ability to judge, that is, to see what is a fitting means to an end. It also affects our ability to evaluate other human beings. The reason is that we see others **in relation to ourselves**, and if we have made ourselves our own norm (from the Latin *norma*, "carpenter's square, rule"), then those who are different are regarded as falling short of the rule in some way (i.e., too small or

---

change (that by which there is coming to be); the marble he is working on is the material cause (that out of which there is coming to be); the form he is imposing upon the matter is the formal cause (that for the sake of which there is coming to be), and the purpose of his work of art is the final cause (that for the sake of which there is coming to be). Notice that the formal and final causes coincide; both are "that for the sake of which there is coming to be". The reason for this is that the final cause is two-fold: the end of the generation and the end of the generated. The artist is chipping away at the marble "for the sake of" the form. When the form is finally in the marble, his work is effectively at an end (final cause). However, there is a more ultimate end, the ultimate purpose, i.e., he wishes to honor a great poet and have this sculpture erected in the piazza. The proximate end, the end of the generation, is the formal cause.

too large). Aristotle writes: "…a brave man **seems** reckless in relation to a coward, but in relation to a reckless man he seems cowardly. Similarly, a self-controlled man seems self-indulgent in relation to an insensitive man and insensitive in relation to a self-indulgent man, and a generous man extravagant in relation to a stingy man and a stingy in relation to an extravagant man. This is the reason why people at the extremes each push the man in the middle over to the other extreme: a coward calls a brave man reckless and a reckless man calls a brave man a coward, and similarly with the other qualities".[80]

The virtues dispose the emotions, and so what the above implies is that improperly disposed emotions will affect one's ability to judge properly. The emotions affect our ability to "know". That is why Aristotle says that it is the virtuous man who judges correctly. To be virtuous is to be emotionally well ordered. He writes: "…what seems good to a man of high moral standards is truly the object of wish, whereas a worthless man wishes anything that strikes his fancy. It is the same with the human body: people whose constitution is good find those things wholesome which really are so, while other things are wholesome for invalids, and **similarly their opinions will vary as to what is bitter, sweet, hot, heavy, and so forth**. Just as a healthy man judges these matters correctly, so in moral questions a man whose standards are high judges correctly, and in each case what is truly good will **appear to him to be so**. Thus, what is good and pleasant differs with different characteristics or conditions, and perhaps the chief distinction of a man of high moral standards is his ability to **see the truth in each particular moral question**, since he is, as it were, **the standard and measure for such questions**. The common run of people, however, are misled by pleasure. For though it is not the good, it seems to be, so that they choose the pleasant in the belief that it is good and avoid pain thinking that it is evil."[81]

Now, one can have a good will, but struggle with the sensitive appetites (i.e., inordinate desire for food, sex, or inordinate fear of

---

[80] *NE, op.cit.*, Bk 2, ch. 8.
[81] *Ibid.*, Bk 3, ch. 4.

danger, etc.). It is a good will, however, that causes things to appear rightly, and so a person of good will knows that his sensitive appetites rebel against the will, which is not centered on satisfying them. He freely admits when he's made a choice to simply satisfy his appetites contrary to the demands of reason, and he regrets his decision.

In book 3, chapter 5 of his *Nicomachean Ethics*, Aristotle considers a possible objection: "But someone might argue as follows: 'All men seek what appears good to them, but they have no control over how things appear to them; the end appears different to different men.'" He replies thus: "If…the individual is somehow responsible for his own characteristics (i.e., character, character traits or virtues), he is similarly responsible for what appears to him (to be good)."[82]

And so it is true that not everyone can study the "science" of ethics, but the science of ethics is not the only way to "know" what is morally good. Connatural knowledge is acquired on the basis of how one freely chooses to shape one's own character. Character is determined by oneself, by one's own free choices, and that is why personality is not the same as character. We have all inherited certain personality traits and there isn't a great deal we can do about them—if one is a high introvert, there's no changing that, one will always feel tired after having to interact with a group of people. But character is something intimately and entirely ours and it is established as a result of the freely chosen relationship we take towards the end that we have made final (ultimate) and the freely chosen relationship we take towards basic human goods. My relationship to the latter will be disordered if I have chosen to make myself and my own delectable good the ultimate end of everything I do. For example, if I have made myself the center around which my life will revolve, then the alternative to treat another as a means to an end is regarded by me as fitting; in treating others as a means to an end, however, I become unjust in character (a user).

---

[82] *Ibid.*, Bk 3, ch. 5.

From the Universal to the Particular

But how does it come about that I choose for myself what will be my ultimate end? The following is an attempt to account for this. Before I know the precise nature of any material being in my environment, I first apprehend that what I know is *a being*. In this way, our knowledge proceeds from the general to the particular. Similarly, the first free choices that we make are the more general choices, and it is in the context of these more general choices that we make choices that are less general, as a novelist conceives the whole novel very generally, and only later begins to fill in the particular parts, chapters, paragraphs, and sentences, that give expression to the original idea. He knows where he is going from the start. In other words, the whole is prior to its parts. Now the more universal the decision, the less motivated it is by sensible goods (pleasures), and the more free and self-determined it is. But particular decisions motivated by strong passion can lessen a person's responsibility. For example, if we were to place a Hershey bar and a carrot in front of an overweight and immature boy and ask him to make a choice, we can reasonably expect that he will choose the Hershey bar, because he is immature and has little control over his sense appetites (his will is weak and his sense appetites are strong). But the more universal an idea is, the more abstracted it is from matter. So too, the more universal the choice, the more it exceeds the influence of the sense appetites.

Now, at a certain point in our lives, we make a very general choice about ourselves (by no means an irreversible choice). We choose to be *a certain kind of person*. This choice does not take place in a vacuum, but within an environment containing many different kinds of people. Very early on we choose to be "like him", or "like her", or "not like this person" and "not like that person", etc. Now, just as certain activities reveal the kind of substance that it is, for example, observing a thing flying allows us to infer that the thing is a living animal, so too, specific acts reveal a specific character. Just as things act according to their nature, human persons choose to perform activities that are in accordance with a specific character. Certain activities are consistent with a certain character, inconsistent with an opposite character.

In freely choosing certain acts, we choose to be a certain way. The actions that we choose constitute that particular way of being. For example, a child might want to be like his mother who is a kind and loving nurse, and he might want to be a person who cares for people, tends to their needs, etc. Or, a child might want to be part of this crowd and want the identity of belonging to it: "I want to be one of these, not one of them."

It is on the basis of this more general decision that other alternatives **become more appealing**, for they are more in accordance with the kind of character that the person originally chose for himself. Conversely, certain alternatives drop out of consideration—lose their appeal—because they are inconsistent with the kind of character he has chosen for himself. For example, he does not choose, like other kids he knows, to spit at seniors as he rides his bike past the nursing home every day because he does not want to be that kind of person. He loves those people. Why? Because he has chosen to, not for any ulterior motive (although that is a real possibility), but ultimately because that is the kind of person he has determined himself to be, the kind of person who relates to people in a way that loves them for their own sake.

It is possible for a person to choose to always look out for himself first, to make himself the very center around which his life will revolve. For example, a person can decide that feeling comfortable is more important to him than the wishes of others, or even the well-being and rights of others. He might *accept* that this is the kind of person he has become, that is, one with a less noble identity than that of a person who has made a better, less self-centered, choice. He experiences himself as rather unsightly as a result of that general decision and the choices that ensue, but he accepts that identity (in other words, he couldn't care less), and he will probably do his best to hide from the subtle awareness of his relatively rotten character. He does not intend that unsightly character, but he does intend to make himself the center of his life; it just so happens that this renders him unsightly to others and to himself, so he will attempt to disguise his true character and attempt to appear better, perhaps as a paragon of virtue, in order to procure the affirmation of others. This is where "personality" comes in to the picture. Sometimes people with depraved character will fabricate specific personality traits that are very attractive to others, precisely in order to hide one's true character and to win favor and adulation, etc.

There are always certain choices that are consistent with the general decision that we make about ourselves, and there are choices that are inconsistent with it. As was said, these latter tend to lose their appeal. For example, if I decide that I always want to be "top dog", and I want others to either love me or barring that, fear me, then things like doing volunteer work or giving generously to charitable causes, tend to lose their appeal, unless they can be a means of maintaining a facade. Watching certain kinds of shows or applying for certain courses of study, etc., will also lose their appeal, while other alternatives will have greater appeal. Consider, for example, how appealing education becomes to a person who has made a commitment that requires some years of schooling.

It is not necessarily possible for us to determine exactly when this very general choice was made by a particular person, but some of us remember moments in our own childhood when we became conscious of having made a simple and general decision to be "like this person" or to strive to be "like that person", or to be "a good person", or "a notorious person", etc. There is no need to search for the cause of this decision; the choice is self-determined, or self-caused. The power to choose freely is really the power to "make oneself", and what is made, the character that is established, is more intimately ours than anything else that we might possess. We are the kind of person that we are because we willed that identity into existence.

The person who has made a general decision to put his own delectable good (private good) second, so to speak, and to give first place to the good as such (i.e., the moral good, the common good, the good that is larger than the self), will begin to judge rightly concerning the means to the end he has decided upon. If he errs, he will make adjustments to line himself up more perfectly with his ultimate end. Now, recall that Aristotle said that "the chief distinction of a man of high moral standards is his ability to **see the truth in each particular moral question**, since he is, as it were, **the standard and measure for such questions**." Unfortunately, those of low moral standard typically make themselves the standard and measure for moral questions, which is why the coward regards the brave man as rash, and the foolhardy judge the brave as cowards, etc. We have made ourselves our own standard, our own *norma* or rule.

To the degree that our will and the sensitive appetites are disordered, that is, to the degree that our love of self is disordered, our judgment will suffer defect. To the degree that our appetites (will and emotions) are rightly ordered, to that degree will our judgment be right.

But isn't it possible for two people, who have the same ultimate end, to have opposing judgments or an opposing vision of what is the best means to a given end? Indeed it is possible. As an example, consider two devoutly religious people. The religious person claims he does not make himself the measure, but God is the measure. That may be true, but as a person is, so does he see. How does a Christian see Christ? And how often is his vision of Christ determined by his own moral identity? Wouldn't you say it is possible to misrepresent Christ without being fully aware of it? That is why the acronym WWJD (What Would Jesus Do) that in recent years has begun to appear on ankle bracelets is really quite pointless. What I judge he would do is going to be very different from what you judge he would do, if and only if *we are different*. People of like character tend to see "eye to eye". But even bishops are often in conflict in their judgments on the best course of action—not to mention more serious matters of morality. So it seems the religious person still makes himself the norm; and that norm is a true measure to the degree that his appropriation of Christ is complete. In other words, the holier the man or woman is, the closer will his vision conform to Christ's.[83] The problem, however, is that we are

---

[83] If Catholics are right about the charism of infallibility, they need not worry about matters of faith and morals; only matters of less importance—but important nonetheless—are impacted by the holiness of Church leaders.

never fully aware of just how short we fall from the 'norm' that is Christ. The holiest people among us have the highest level of skepticism regarding themselves and thus the least amount of confidence.

Intrapersonal Asymmetry

Another problem to consider is that all of us suffer from some degree of inordinate love of self. The moral life should be a continual effort to bring order to that love of self, but it is this disordered self-love that is the principal contributor to a certain asymmetric phenomenon in which we judge others differently than we judge ourselves. We have a view of ourselves, often not true to reality, and we favor evidence that confirms that "hypothesis" about ourselves—a highly favorable one—, and we tend to allow our mistakes—which disconfirm our "hypothesis"—to drift from memory. This is confirmation bias applied, pre-consciously, to ourselves. We favor pieces of evidence that confirm our own self-estimation, and we leave those disconfirming pieces of evidence in the penumbra.

However, we welcome the disconfirming evidence when it has to do with our evaluations of others. We avoid or pay little attention to disconfirming evidence that challenges our self-estimation, relegating it to a region in which it becomes easily forgettable, but this is not what occurs when it comes to the mistakes of others.

This may explain why we often become angry at the mistakes of others. Our perception of others' errors is similar to what occurs in hindsight bias. At the beginning of a judgment, there is tremendous opacity as a result of the various possible alternatives that can explain a given situation, or the various possible ways of choosing to respond to a situation. In hindsight, the opacity seems to have disappeared; we've simply forgotten about it. If we predicted correctly, we take credit for it; if we err, we find it easy to forgive ourselves, after all, "we knew it all along". When others err, we conveniently forget that they too were and are subject to the same initial opacity that characterizes the present; it is as if in their case we substitute the opacity that overshadows the starting point of a judgment or decision with the clarity that appears at the end: "You should have known".

This forgetfulness makes possible our anger or impatience towards the mistakes of others, but this forgetfulness is in turn rooted in disordered love of self, something we are not entirely aware of—at least not explicitly.

Concluding Thoughts

And so we are more in the dark than we think. Thus, we really ought to learn to approach moral questions with a healthy skepticism towards our own way of seeing things; for although we can reason our way to conclusions that show that we have made wrong choices, we are usually not honest and open enough to welcome that correction. Both laziness and pride keep us from making the effort to think hard about our moral convictions and admitting that we are not as "good" as we might have thought. We are not aware of the deficiency in the norm or standard we hold ourselves up to, that is, ourselves as the norm, and so we judge in light of a measure that is probably deficient—insofar as it is a lifetime's work to grow in prudence, humility, temperance, fortitude, etc. This is true even for those who are devoutly religious. Moreover, we are profoundly limited by sense perception, by time and circumstance, lack of experience, poor memory and duration neglect, an intrapersonal asymmetric bias that keeps us from appreciating the unique perspective of ordinary persons, a proven incapacity to predict, the limits and constraints that result from inductive inferencing which characterize most of our day to day reasoning, the resulting lack of familiarity with the rich history of every ordinary human being we encounter—not to mention the resulting lack of understanding of the rich history of the world, much of which is lost to even the best historians—, and despite understanding the tools of probability (statistics), the accuracy of our numbers depend on our knowledge base which is far more constrained than statistics would lead us to believe.

Add to this our tendency to disordered appetite (the wounds of Original Sin) which in turn clouds our moral judgment, it seems quite miraculous that human beings have not managed to completely destroy themselves and the world in which we live.

88 *Some Thoughts on Modesty*

If the good of a thing consists in its proper operation or function, its final cause,[84] then all we have to ask in order to begin to understand what constitutes modesty is: "What is the purpose of clothing?" What is its function? The obvious answer is to protect us from the elements. But once that is accomplished, can we adjust or modify our apparel in some way in order to serve a secondary purpose? Some of us said that clothing is for the sake of self-expression. That is true; who can deny it? So, what is it that a person tries to express in his choice of apparel? If we can answer that question, we are closer to solving this difficulty.

The school uniform expresses the fact that you are a student of this school. That identity, however, is temporary. The choice of clothing you would wear to a funeral would express something in you, i.e., your sorrow. People often wear black, because black was at one time an unfashionable color. At a funeral, one does not want to appear to be concerned about looking good; we want to express that we are not interested in ourselves at this time, but that our hearts "go out to" the one who has lost a loved one and who is grieving. Wearing bright and joyful colors to a funeral calls attention to you, they do not express the feeling of grief, and so they do not express a sense of solidarity with those who have lost a loved one. So we can argue convincingly that the "wrong" apparel manifests a lack of empathy. It fails to accurately express one's interior, or what one's interior ought to be (i.e., solidarity with the grieving).

Similarly, we dress for a party accordingly; we wouldn't wear a black suit and a serious demeanour. Moreover, the reason clergy wear black is that at one time, as was said above, black was unfashionable, and clergy and religious (nuns, monks, etc.) saw dress as an expression of one's interior disposition (one's character). They chose to dress unfashionably in order to express that they are unconcerned about the

---

[84] For example, a good computer is one that functions well, a good knife cuts well, a good dog runs and fetches sticks and rolls over when commanded, and a good man reasons well and chooses well.

goods of this world and that their lives are directed towards eternal goods (i.e., the kingdom of God). To be joyful and at the same time to dress unfashionably is to give genuine witness that one's joy does not come from the goods of this world, that is, from looking good.

But what about those who are not priests, monks, sisters, etc. The moral requirement is to dress modestly. But what does that mean? What is modest for one culture or time period is immodest for another. So how do we know? The same way we know the good of anything; we look to its final cause. **The purpose of clothing is to express one's character, that is, who you are**. Now, our fundamental moral obligation is to cultivate morally beautiful character (the *kalon*). Thus, one should dress "beautifully", that is, in a way that expresses "beautiful character". That does not necessarily mean always dressing "to the hilt". Dressing simply may be an expression of one's character; dressing professionally may be an expression of one's character, etc.

Now, we are drawn to people of like character, and we are drawn to clothing or apparel that expresses who we are, or who we want to become. So, "Is this or that person dressing modestly?" Does this person dress himself or herself with reasonable restraint? The following questions may help to answer this question: When we look at this person, what do we see? Do we see a morally beautiful person? Or do we see too much? Does the clothing draw us towards this person *as a person*, that is, *as a person of intelligence and moral beauty?* Or does the apparel draw us to this person *as someone who can possibly satisfy a sexual appetite (lust) within us?* If you are a woman, you can ask yourself: "Does this apparel accurately express who I am?" If you are a person who wants to arouse another or others sexually, then you will dress accordingly. The problem in this case, however, is your character; you are the kind of person who would like to be reduced to an object of sexual consumption, or the kind of person who has little regard for the moral integrity of others insofar as you intend to focus their gaze on you in a way that compromises their character. It may also be indicative of a lack of due self-respect. Why? Because you are more than that; but some women are so desperate to be loved that they will go to great lengths in order to be loved and desired.

Now some women are just not aware that what they are wearing is inappropriate (unbefitting a person of morally beautiful character), because they are unaware of how their apparel is affecting others, in particular those of the opposite sex. Women are not visually stimulated, but men are. Some women are unaware of this, so they are oblivious to the effects of their revealing clothing. They might also assume that "if everyone dresses this way, it must be okay."

Moreover, some men are not attracted to women of good character, that is, women who are intelligent, prudent, shrewd, and morally beautiful, because they know that they cannot sustain their facade for long, that these women will eventually see through them and thus reject them. They are drawn to women who are not so smart, not so emotionally healthy, but needier and of lesser moral character. Such women are willing to do what it takes to be accepted; they are more open to being used. The woman who dresses in a way that appeals to that kind of man (character) is opening up a path to trouble; she is attracting to herself the wrong kind of person.

The more we think about this, the more we should see that these questions are not easy to resolve. We should avoid the two easy alternatives to difficult moral questions: the extremes of absolutism and relativism. There is an objective standard, namely reason, but its application is not fixed and unchanging like a steel ruler. It is more like the measuring tape tailors use: it bends to various situations, but the standard remains universal (15 inches is 15 inches, even though every neck is somewhat different). Some instances of women's apparel are easily identifiable as immodest, others are barely immodest and barely modest, thus very difficult to determine; other instances are safely in the modest range, and others still are without much doubt excessively modest (they hide a woman's character by making her look either ugly or funny, or strange, slightly off, when in fact she isn't strange or off).

In the end, I cannot say for certain whether or not a bikini is immodest. It says a lot that at one time, no one but strippers would model it. Cultural arrogance allows us to easily dismiss those of another period as sexually repressed; it is quite possible, however, that there is something wrong with us. I do lean heavily towards the old style swimwear, only because when looking at such women, they remain beautiful and personal. Many women on the typical beach these days appear desirable; very few strike me as beautiful and personal. This is not to deny that they are morally beautiful and personal; rather, their chosen apparel simply fails to reveal it.

89 Inclination to God and the Moral Sense: Some Thoughts on Knowledge and the Natural Moral Law

There are a number of ways of knowing involved in a person's sense of moral duty, that is, his sense of the natural law. Involved are intuition, connatural knowledge, self-knowledge, and reasoning. Moreover, a large portion of that knowledge, in most people at least, is not explicit and conscious, but remains implicit and pre-conscious.

Aquinas argued that every human being, whether he realizes it or not, possesses a natural knowledge of God; it is a confused and general knowledge—this is true even for the "atheist". It is this knowledge that is the source of the moral sense, a natural awareness of a moral order that includes a host of natural obligations. This moral sense can be dulled or enhanced, depending upon how we choose to respond to its command in the deepest recesses of our conscience, that is, whether we choose to obey it out of reverence for a good we know is larger than ourselves because it embraces everyone, or whether we choose to disregard it for the sake of the delectable. The evidence for this natural knowledge is in man's behavior, in his search for 1) the sufficient reason that explains the existence of things, and 2) in his desire for happiness. The following is an attempt to explain this.

God and the Intuition of First Principles

I would like to begin with *the principle of sufficient reason*, which runs thus: "Everything which is, to the extent to which it is, possesses a sufficient reason for its being so that it is capable of explaining itself to the intellect. In other words, whatever is, has *that whereby* it is."[85]

Consider the example of a broken window. You come home one evening and find that your living room window has been smashed. You immediately wonder how that happened. In other words, you seem to know that there is a sufficient reason for this window being broken. Now, "whatever is, has that whereby it is"; and so this broken window

---

[85] Jacques Maritain. *A Preface to Metaphysics*, London, Sheed and Ward, 1948. 97-105.

has that whereby it is broken (i.e., the reason), either in itself or in another. If it has "that whereby it is" in itself, then it contains within itself, within the very notion of "broken window", the reason for its being broken. If that were the case, then just knowing that this window is broken is enough to know the sufficient reason for its being so, and thus you would not ask the question: "Why is this window broken?" The reason would be contained in itself, and so it would explain itself. But that is clearly not the case, since you wonder how the window got broken.

Notice, however, that you do not wonder how you are able to carry on an intelligent conversation with a friend; there is nothing about that which you find puzzling. The reason is that the "sufficient reason" for the conversation is contained within your friend's very nature, for he or she is a human person, that is, a rational animal, and an individual with a rational nature is capable of communicating concepts through language—that's what it means to be rational. But a flower is not capable of such communication, and so if a flower were to pose a question to us, we'd be wonder struck.

If *that which is* has that whereby it is through another, then it depends upon that 'other'. Thus the broken window has its sufficient reason for being broken in something outside of it.

Now when we see something existing, or an inanimate thing moving, we naturally inquire of the reason until we possess the sufficient reason, at which point we are sufficiently satisfied. The reason for the moving ball is the pitcher's act of throwing (the efficient cause). Knowing the efficient cause, however, is not always sufficient. If a neighbor tells us that the boy down the street threw the ball through the window, we continue to search for the reason more deeply, until we find the sufficient reason—a "throwing arm" is insufficient. It is not enough that his arm was moving and caused the ball to move through the air, thus breaking the window. We know that arms don't throw things; it is the agent as a whole that throws things, and so we naturally want to know "why" he threw the ball in the first place. In other words, we're looking for the final cause of the action (the end, purpose, or motive). If it is determined that he threw the ball to his friend during play and the pitch was wild and thus he accidentally broke the window, we now possess the sufficient reason. But if that is not the case, we continue to search for the reason. If we learn that he threw the ball at the window because he was angry with you and wanted revenge for an injustice he believes you committed, then we are coming closer to the sufficient reason that explains the broken window.

Now, consider the principle of identity: *each being is what it is* (a carrot is a carrot, an oxygen atom is an oxygen atom, etc.); there is quite a bit packed into that first self-evident principle. In knowing anything at all, I know first and foremost that *it is* (it exists). Being is first in my knowledge of anything. I may not understand who or what is approaching, but I know generally and confusedly that something is approaching; after a while, I come to realize that it is an animal. After a bit more time, I realize that it is something possessing a canine nature. Finally, I realize it is my pet dog that was lost. That realization is accompanied by a sense of relief.

In this apprehension of my approaching dog, I know "what" it is (a canine creature), and I know "that it is" (my dog *has* existence). The formulation of the principle of identity—"each being is what it is"— contains two apprehensions: the simple apprehension of a being's nature or essence (what it is) and the judgment of its existence (that it is). But my dog's existence is not contained in her nature (canine)— otherwise I would not have been worried that she might have been killed; for whatever belongs to a thing's nature belongs to it necessarily. Thus, the ability to think belongs necessarily to a rational nature, and "3 sides" belongs necessarily to a triangle, etc., and so if behind this door there is a human being, it is necessarily the case that he or she has a rational nature and thus cannot not be rational, and if there is a triangle behind this wall, it may not be made of wood and painted yellow, but it necessarily has 3 sides (it cannot not have 3 sides).

Existence, however, does not belong necessarily to my pet dog's nature; otherwise my dog would necessarily exist, and could not **not** exist (just as a triangle cannot not have 3 sides, etc.). In other words, the sufficient reason for my dog's existence is not contained in its nature, but is outside of it. More to the point, the existence of anything that I apprehend, whether it is a human, a cat, a plant, or a mineral of some kind, etc., is not contained in the nature that I grasp through simple apprehension. I apprehend existence through a distinct act of the intellect, namely existential judgment.

And that is precisely why we wonder why there is anything rather than nothing at all. We want to know the ultimate meaning of things, the purpose of life, the origin of existence, etc. We do so because the sufficient reason for the existence of things is outside the things themselves that we know, and so we are constantly seeking to discover the causes of things. Sure, we now know why your eyes are blue, and why your cells multiply, and why you should moderate the amount of sodium in your diet, etc., but we continue to seek for more answers to our questions, for we want to know why you and everything else exists in the first place. We have a desire to know the ultimate causes of things, the first causes, and being (existence) is absolutely first. To know the cause of the origin of the whole is to understand the whole.

Of course, most people do not have all this worked out in explicitly formulated concepts and first self-evident principles, but they do, nevertheless, have a real knowledge of the "insufficiency of being", even if it is only a preconscious one. But there is more to this. If I possess—even confusedly and pre-consciously—a knowledge of the insufficiency of things to explain their own existence, then I know that things *depend* on something outside of them in order to exist (to be and continue to be). In other words, if the sufficient reason for their being is not within them, it is outside of them, in another. And since the most obvious agents of a living thing's generation are its parents who are themselves beings whose sufficient reason for their own existence is outside of them, whose parents in turn are beings whose sufficient reason for being is outside of them, and so on, etc., I am aware (even confusedly and perhaps pre-consciously) that all things depend for their existence on a being who contains within himself the sufficient reason for his own existence, that is, a being whose existence and essence are one and the same, and who is thus independent.

If I were to provide an analogy, think of a beautiful chandelier hanging above your head in a ballroom, but you are positioned in the room such that you cannot see the ceiling, only the chandelier and the links of the chain by which it is suspended. Now in your mind, it matters not how many links in the chain there are; the ceiling could be so high as to require hundreds of thousands of links. Nevertheless, each link is dependent upon another (i.e., the one is holding up the link below it because it is being held up by the one above it, which in turn is being held up by the one above it, etc.). The very fact that there are hundreds of dependent links makes no difference to your knowledge of the insufficiency of the links as an explanation for the chandelier being suspended above. Multiplying them into the millions, even trillions, does not in the long run satisfy you by offering you the sufficient reason for its suspension. You know that there must be a ceiling from which the links are attached—millions of dependents do not amount to an independent.

And so, one does not even need to see the ceiling, but one knows nonetheless that there is a sufficient reason for the chandelier being continually suspended above our heads, which is why if we want an explanation for its suspension, we look to see the ceiling, or whatever it is that is radically different from the dependent links in between. Whatever it is, we know it is a stable origin that enjoys an independence not belonging to the links.

Now, it is not necessary to think of this in terms of a long series of causes stretching back into the past; that would be to misunderstand the point being made. If the sufficient reason for a thing's very act of existence is not contained within it, then there is no need to search for it in another being in the same predicament (i.e., a parent). Every being in such a predicament is immediately dependent upon *this efficient cause who is the sufficient reason for the existence of all things.*

Human beings have a more or less confused knowledge of this, and they've always had this knowledge. This is what most people have always referred to as God. But those who refuse to do so, i.e., atheists, are nonetheless still in search for "the origin" that they expect will explain and thus provide the sufficient reason for the very existence of the universe. In other words, their search for this sufficient reason shows that they understand, even if only pre-consciously, that there really exists a sufficient reason, *otherwise there would be no "reason" to search*.

The Desire for the *Bonum Universale*

There is also another angle from which we can look at all this. You and I are moved to act, to pursue, to search, to work, to accomplish, etc. Whatever we choose to do, we do so for the sake of an end (final cause).

Consider any activity whatsoever—your neighbor fixing his car, for example. Why is he doing that? He's acting for an end, namely, that the car will continue to function. And why would he want the car to function? So that he can get from one place to another. And why would he want to drive from his home to, let's say, his workplace? Well, he wants to work. Why does he choose to work? In order to support himself, etc.

As we can see, it is the end that gives meaning (direction) to one's activity, and it is an end that is the reason (the cause) for the previous movements or actions. The end is the final cause, or *that for the sake of which* there is activity. The final cause (end) is the mover that moves the agent to action. The ultimate end is the ultimate reason, that is, the ultimate mover of one's actions.

So let us ask the question: "What is the ultimate reason why we do anything at all"? The answer is happiness. We seek happiness, and the happiness we seek has certain characteristics. We seek a happiness that is **enduring**; for example, were we to achieve that happiness, we would not say to ourselves: "I want this to come to an end". We want a happiness that endures. We want a happiness that is not precarious, in other words a happiness that does not depend upon contingent factors like the weather, thus, we seek a happiness that is sufficient unto itself (i.e., free of the risk of loss). We seek a happiness that is complete, that is desired entirely for its own sake and not for the sake of something else. That is why we continue to seek, regardless of how much we already possess, for our current state of happiness is always incomplete, temporary, and not entirely self-sufficient.

The human heart (will) is restless. It is always searching for more, no matter how much it already possesses. Now if we seek this unqualified good (end), it must mean that *we know it in some way*; for we do not desire what we do not know—the will can only tend towards what the intellect presents to it. So what is it that we know, which is behind the will's tendency to a happiness that is unqualified, complete, enduring, and self-sufficient? What we know is that there is an unqualified good that is complete, enduring, and sufficient unto itself—otherwise we would not desire it. We may not know clearly and explicitly what that is, but we know it confusedly and generally at least, which is why we continually tend to it.

This is the good that we love before and above all things, and this ultimate end is the reason why we recognize the goodness in all other human goods in our life, i.e., our friendships, our work, our leisure, our insights, etc., just as our neighbor sees all those things that contribute to the achievement of his end, which is the functioning of his car, as good; for example, he sees his tools as good, his garage as good, his tires as good, oil as good, etc. They are all good in view of the good of a functioning automobile, but a functioning automobile is good in view of his work, which is good in view of his very life that his work helps to sustain.

My life and all other human goods are good because they are related to the ultimate end, which I naturally love more than I love myself—for I am not the *bonum universale*, for if I were, I would no longer seek anything outside myself. Indeed, my life is good *for its own sake*, but it is also relatively good, that is, *in relation to* higher goods that are specific to my nature. For example, it is good to be alive, and so I know that food and shelter are good for the sake of that life. But I seek more than just living. Indeed, it is good to be alive for its own sake, but

I also want to live in order to continue to possess truth, to love, to raise my children, pursue justice, and friendships, etc. I pursue a life rich in human goods, but behind all this is a pursuit of something supremely good, a self-sufficient happiness that I do not find within myself or as yet in the world. I certainly desire my own perfection, my own fullness of being, but that desire is for something other than me, namely the *bonum universale* (universal or unqualified good). If I were to possess it, I seem to be aware that I will possess perfection and thus happiness—otherwise I would not pursue it. I desire a universal good, an unqualified good that will bring me an unqualified happiness.

I do not know how we can avoid the conclusion that this self-sufficient happiness, which is the ultimate end of everything we do, coincides with the sufficient reason for the being of all beings. My search for the sufficient reason for being and my search for happiness converge towards the same point. Being Itself (that being whose nature is to be) and the universal good (the possession of which constitutes my perfect happiness) are one and the same.

This one end is God, whether we are explicitly aware of it or not. In fact, Aquinas' demonstrations of God's existence are simply ways of showing that what we already know confusedly and generally is in fact what we mean by God. To repeat, although an atheist rejects the idea of God's existence, he pursues nonetheless the origin that he expects will explain and provide the sufficient reason for existence. Perhaps he thinks that sufficient reason is going to be located in a particle, or in an equation for a theory of everything, etc., but it is the difficult work of philosophy that involves attempting to determine whether these or other such things constitute the sufficient reason for the existence of things. Similarly, a person might believe that his greatest happiness, the ultimate end, is the possession of power or unlimited wealth or fame, etc. So too, it belongs to philosophy to test that supposition through reasoning. Regardless of all this, what is clear is that these people and everyone else are aware of a sufficient reason for being and a *bonum universale* (universal good), for their actions reveal such an awareness.

The Moral Sense

There is much more to this pre-conscious and confused knowledge of the universal good than what we've unpacked up to this point. We experience reality as intelligible, good, and beautiful, even though its goodness, intelligibility and beauty are limited. Now, all these properties (intelligibility, goodness, and beauty) have to do with order. This is especially obvious in the case of beauty; a beautiful symphony is ordered, harmonious, and radiant with meaning. We speak of beautiful days, beautiful sunsets, beautiful skies, etc. If there is beauty to reality, there is an order to reality.

That is why we have a sense that the origin, the sufficient reason for existence, is intelligent, good and beautiful; for we all know intuitively the principle of causality, that for every effect, there is a cause, and the effect cannot possess what the cause is lacking, for that would suggest that something comes from nothing (or that nothing and something are identical, which is absurd). And that is why human beings, from as far back as we know, have an awareness of a God (or gods) that is in some sense personal (intelligent and volitional) and who is deserving of acts of gratitude and thanksgiving. He is the origin of the order found in things, considered in themselves and taken as a whole.

Now the world we live in is characterized by movement (change). Things are in motion; there is change in the universe, and every agent moves for the sake of an end, a final cause. A thing's final cause tells us the good of the thing, that is, it tells us what completes it. A plant moves, but its motion is towards its own completion, i.e., a rose develops in order to be a rose most fully and completely. That is why we understand what constitutes a good and healthy rose, a good and healthy dog, etc. Without that knowledge, we couldn't treat diseases in plants and animals, for we can only know what is pathological in light of the good of the thing (i.e., we only know that cancer is bad because we know what constitutes human health).

Now I know from within that I am inclined to an ultimate end, namely happiness. I also know from within that I am inclined towards a number of ends (intelligible human goods, such as life, the possession of truth, the knowledge and appreciation of what is beautiful, personal friendships, marriage and family, a just social order, etc.). I also know that this and that person over there are of the same nature as myself (human), and I know through observing their behavior that they too are inclined to these goods, and ultimately to the universal good, because everything they do is also for the sake of happiness. We all experience our own lives and the lives of one another as fundamentally good.

And so I know that the good is *much more than* my own private good; I know that it is much more than your private good. I know, therefore, that there is a common good that is larger than my own private good, just as each player on a soccer team is aware of a common good, which is the team's victory. Each player will share in the victory and will be glorified by it. This common good, however, is larger than the individual player's private good, for example, the player's individual scoring record. Note that the team's strategy is ordered for the sake of victory (the common good). Every action on the part of the individual players is ordered towards the common good, and a player's acts are judged to be good to the degree that they are ordered to the common good, which is victory. To score is good because it contributes to the end to which all their actions aim, but if a player were to get carried away and begin performing dazzling tricks with the soccer ball, which then leads to the other team scoring a goal, his actions would be judged by his teammates as bad—albeit skilled. Were he to continue in that vein, he would eventually be benched, because his behavior is harmful to the team (and thus every player on the team, including himself). His actions lack order towards the good of the whole, perhaps as a result of having an inflated ego, a passion for praise, etc. He has the potential to be a great player, but does not achieve excellence because his actions on the field lack due order towards the good of the whole, that is, the common good.

Each one of us has **a sense of a moral order** which includes us (our own good), but which is also larger than us considered individually (it embraces the good of everyone). I know from within that I am a moral agent, and that I have a natural inclination towards the universal good that I can't do anything about (I necessarily will my own happiness), but I am aware that I have the freedom to make choices that establish me in a certain relationship with my ultimate end, this personal God, who is the origin of the order of creation. If I sense that He is personal, even confusedly and pre-consciously, then I sense He has a will and that the order of creation manifests His will, just as the order I behold in a work of art is an expression of the will of the artist.

Plants and animals are not moral agents. The movement of a plant is such that as long as it is watered and planted in the proper environment, it will mature and become what it is inclined to become by nature; so too is this the case with brute animals. Both plants and animals achieve their own good naturally. But human beings, on the other hand, have the ability to freely determine themselves towards their own fullness of being or in a way that arrests that maturation. A moral agent can choose to fulfill his nature or destroy it.

As a moral agent, I have the ability to think and make free choices, thus determining myself to be a certain kind of person, that is, shaping a moral identity for myself. This is what we mean by moral character. By my free choices, I determine myself to be a person of good character, or a person of deficient (evil) character. This means that I am either the kind of person who freely chooses to love the moral good before my own private good (the delectable good)—which involves freely choosing to love your good and everyone else's (the common good), or I am the kind of person that loves my own private good (the delectable good, the pleasant good) over the moral good (which is larger than me).

The human person detects within himself a law, which is a command or rational dictate, to which he feels called to obey, and it is a command to respect the order of creation in all things, in himself and in the social order. He knows from within that he respects that moral order by freely choosing to do what he understands to be *good as such*, as opposed to what is simply pleasurable for him. For example, I know that you are of the same nature as myself (through simple apprehension), and I know from within that it is good for me to be alive (I desire to live). Now I desire to possess certain property *for the sake of* preserving my life, for example, I own a pair of shoes, a jacket, my own lunch box, etc. I know that you too possess property for the same reason, and that it is good for you to do so—in other words, it is "right" (Latin: *jus*) and ordered for you to do so, not disordered— property is ordered towards the preservation of life, which in turn is ordered towards knowledge, personal relationships, and other human goods, and finally the ultimate end (the *bonum universale*). The social order, which includes the economy and the order of justice, exists for our shared good (common good), and I know that I would not want you to take my shoes and lunch box just because you happen to like them (I need them), and so *I know from within* that I ought not to take yours (because I know that you are of the same nature as myself), even though possessing them would bring me some kind of emotional satisfaction.

If it is right and ordered for you to own them, it is wrong and disordered for me to take them simply because I like them. When my emotions incline me to take your property when you are not looking, simply because I desire them, I now have a choice before me: to resist that inclination for the sake of an order larger than me, or give into it, thus choosing my own emotional satisfaction (pleasure) over the order of justice (over your good). In choosing the latter, I am choosing to treat myself preferentially. Although I know you to be equal in dignity to me, I am treating you in a way that fails to respect that equality, and thus that larger moral order. I am twisting that order, elevating my desire for emotional complacency above your right to own and share in the good. I am aware that I am violating a natural law, that is, a natural command or dictate of reason to respect an order that is larger than me.

Think of how a criminal behaves when he is caught and confronted—he often reacts with violent indignation. And how does a criminal behave when he discovers he's the victim of a theft? Also with violent indignation; thus he is aware that theft is a violation of a right, but he is indifferent to the rights of others and incensed when confronted with the truth of his disordered character.

Just as a bad but skilled soccer player behaves without order towards the good of the whole, so too a morally bad person chooses without due regard for the good of the whole, that is, the entire moral order. In doing so, he goes against his deepest awareness of that order, that is, he violates his conscience. He is disordered within himself, for his emotions are not disposed to submit to the demands of reason, thus he is intemperate, and he lacks the fortitude to sacrifice his own love of the delectable good for the sake of the good of the whole. Moreover, he is an unjust person, for by his own will he is a disordered part of the social whole.

Now the human person naturally loves God more than he loves himself. I know, for example, that I am not the "universal good", which I naturally pursue. I also naturally love the good of the whole more than the good of the part. For example, if someone comes towards me swinging a baseball bat, I naturally raise my arms to defend myself; I am placing a part of myself in harm's way in order to protect the whole, thus I naturally love the whole more than the part, for the whole is a greater good than the part, which is good on account of the whole. Similarly, I see that I am part of a larger social whole (not a mere part, to be sure), and I naturally love the social whole more than myself. All this is natural and inevitable; there is no moral nobility in this. But as a moral agent, I must now freely choose in accordance with that natural inclination. For me to choose my own private satisfaction over the good of the social whole (which reflects back on me for my well-being, as a team's victory is also the good of the individual player), is for me to choose in a way that is contrary to my own natural inclination (my own good). In other words, immoral choices put me on a path to self-destruction. Furthermore, I never do experience the "pleasurable good" that I choose above the moral good, at least not in any lasting and significant way, because the delectable good and the moral good are not necessarily opposed; rather, the former (*bonum delectabile*) is the fruit of the latter (*bonum honestum*). Immoral choices only succeed in bringing fragments of the delectable good, temporary pieces that lack breadth and depth, which is why immoral choices lead to greater restlessness, not greater peace. An immoral person is his own worst enemy, not to mention an enemy of the civil community as a whole.

Consider that by virtue of the close relationship between the moral sense and the sense of God's existence, it is no coincidence that moral reasons tend to be at the root of atheism. To violate that moral order of which my conscience makes me aware is to dampen that voice, to suppress that sense of a natural and personal command or dictate (natural law). To eradicate that sense completely is, I suspect, difficult to do, and even more difficult to dampen that sense consistently, which is why those of depraved character will expend a tremendous amount of energy trying to show that God does not exist and that to believe so is delusional and infantile. It is also no coincidence that atheists and agnostics who choose to obey the directives of that moral sense as it is made known to them in the deepest recesses of their conscience, very often come to a more explicit awareness of God's existence and become great converts.

I would argue that all that we've unpacked and made explicit up to this point is known, more or less confusedly, vaguely, and pre-consciously, by every human person who has reached a certain level of reason. What is particularly disturbing, however, is the increasing number of people who choose every day to place their own pleasure (*bonum delectabile*) above the moral good (*bonum honestum*), in little acts of theft, lying, deception, cutting corners, insurance fraud, etc. In doing so, they not only place themselves on a path of self-destruction (personal dis-integration or dis-integrity), they also create disorder in the world, for their disordered actions have wide and costly social repercussions to which they are frankly indifferent. But they know this fundamental conflict within themselves, they are aware of it and are ashamed of it, they don't love it, which is why they spend a great deal of energy trying to hide it, for they know that others, persons of virtue in particular, would find them unsightly, as they find themselves unsightly.

90 *Moral Relativism and the Beautiful*

The meaning of life may never have been a more pressing issue than it is today, when the world's evil and senselessness stand exposed for all to see. I am reminded of visiting a cinema in Berlin, some four years ago, and seeing a film on the life of a predaceous water beetle in an aquarium. It was a vivid illustration of the ruthless struggle for survival that goes on in nature. Creatures were shown devouring one another, and the beetle invariably got the better of fishes, mollusks, salamanders, and so on, thanks to the technical perfection of two weapons: the powerful mandible with which it crushed its victims, and the toxic substance with which it poisoned them. Such has been the way of nature for eons, and such it will be for an indefinite time to come. If the spectacle repels us, if we experience a sense of moral nausea at the sight of such scenes as were filmed in the aquarium, this proves that in man there exist the seeds of another world, a different plane of being. It would not be possible for us to feel so revolted if this animal life were the only kind of existence we could imagine, if we did not feel an inner call to bring about a different way of life. Prince Evgenii Nikolaevich Trubteskoi. *A World View in Painting.*

"Relativism" is derived from the word 'relative', which describes a 'relation'. Moral relativism is that school of thought which maintains that there are no actions that are absolutely wrong, that good and evil in human action are relative to something else, i.e., the culture in which we currently live, or social consensus, or my individual situation, that is, what I see fit, etc. Moral relativism goes back to the ancient Sophists, for example Gorgias, not to mention the ancient hedonist Epicurus. We see it in more sophisticated garb in the thought of Nietzsche and Sartre in the 20th century. Currently, moral relativism is the default position; but it wasn't always so.

The classical non-relativist position (natural law) on the contrary, holds, among other things, that there are certain actions that are absolutely wrong and which no circumstances can justify, such as adultery, abortion, active euthanasia, and that social consensus can be wrong. This position goes back to Socrates, Aristotle, Augustine, Aquinas, etc. Cicero speaks of the natural law, and more recently

Martin Luther King Jr in his Letter from the Birmingham Jail says some very eloquent things about this law. John Finnis, Germain Grisez, and Joseph Boyle are three contemporary analytic moral philosophers who have articulated rather extensively the principles and implications of natural law.[86]

To appreciate the radical difference between relativism and the non-relativist position in morality, I'd like to call your attention to the essential difference between man and brute animal. The greatest delight an animal experiences is sense pleasure, that is, the satisfaction of its passions. The human person, on the other hand, is capable of a higher delight, a cognitive delight, namely, the experience of beauty. Man is the only animal who leisures, and leisure is about the contemplation of the beautiful. When we experience the beautiful, the intellect delights in the intelligibility, integrity and harmony of the real world outside the self. This experience of the beautiful includes the possession of truth— because truth is complex and harmonious—, the contemplation of works of art, or the delight in watching a well-executed strategy of a game, etc.

Recently while on retreat in a Monastery in New York State, I visited a local art gallery with a friend. I was very much impressed by the beauty of the art; the artists captured well the beauty of the landscape that we beheld driving there. The delight was not the same as the experience of pleasure. Pleasure is entirely in the self, but the delight of the beautiful is of an ecstatic kind (from the Greek *ecstasis*, or exit of self). A truly beautiful work takes you out of yourself and brings you in touch with the radiance, unity and harmony of the real world outside the self.

Relativism comes out of a very different conception of the human person, one that sees the human person as essentially no different than a brute animal. For animals, pleasure is the highest delight. Jeremy Bentham, 19th century British philosopher, formulated the utilitarian principle: "the greatest-happiness for the greatest number of people".

---

[86] See John Finnis, *Natural Law and Natural Rights*. Oxford: Clarendon Press, 1980. See also Germain Grisez and Joseph M. Boyle Jr. *Life and Death with Liberty and Justice: A Contribution to the Euthanasia Debate*. Notre Dame: University of Notre Dame Press, 1979.

But the word happiness here does not have the same meaning as happiness (*eudaemonia*) in Aristotle or Socrates. For Bentham, happiness is pleasure.

Now pleasure is relative. A particular pleasure is not universal, nor is it stable; for it constantly changes. To impose stability or permanency on pleasure would in fact be cruel. Imagine a mother who responds to her child's delight in his favorite meal by promising that she will serve him the same meal every day, with the same dessert, followed by the same television show every night, night after night, etc. This would soon become a maddening existence. I am reminded of the Twilight Zone episode entitled *A Nice Place to Visit*, in which criminal Rocky Valentine thinks he's died and gone to heaven, because he's given all the money he wants and is allowed to spend it in whatever way he wants. His desires are satisfied in everything he does. He soon finds this kind of existence meaningless and in the end intolerable. He then asks permission to go to hell, or what he refers to as "the other place". He is then told that he is in the 'other place'. His hell is to spend eternity delighting in the satisfaction of his every pleasure.

Relativists cannot understand the non-relativist position, and the reason is that pleasure always gets old; what pleases can even become revolting. The relativist sees the non-relativist as wanting to impose stability and permanency where none should be imposed, because life is about the greatest pleasure for the greatest number. Why should I settle for the same woman year in and year out? Why should I raise this child whose birth will disrupt my plans? When pleasure is made to be the highest good, permanency makes no sense whatsoever. Picasso is a great illustrator of this. He had many mistresses, and at the beginning of his relationships, he would often draw them a sketch in traditional art form, as a kind of love note. But in time his mistress would become revolting, as does anything that has become an object of consumption. And so he came to experience their ugliness, and that would appear in his paintings. He would distort them, thus expressing the ugliness he came to behold in them. These works are caricatures.[87]

---

[87] What I am arguing here is conjectural and tentative.

Our current culture is relativistic; as I said, that is the default position today. That was not the case when I was growing up—relativism was the position of a few rebels. Now, as pleasure dulls, people crave more and at higher intensities. Notice that today there is a hunger for extreme pleasures, thus more demand for extreme sports and extreme forms of entertainment. We are easily bored, because pleasure is at the center of our existence, and relativism is the only moral position that makes sense for a culture in which pleasure is at the center.

As I was looking at these beautiful works of art in a gallery in Upstate New York, I suddenly wanted to paint again. Then I remembered something that I'd briefly forgotten, namely, how tedious painting is. It is work, taxing, not a constant state of artistic exhilaration that lasts all the while you are painting. The work is slow and monotonous. But if you are a good artist, the result is a work of beauty, and for others, it is an experience that is ecstatic, an experience of being lifted out of oneself and into something larger than oneself. Experiencing beauty is not about consuming, but about being lifted up into something larger, a reality that overflows with radiance and meaning.

Now, not all of us can be fine artists; we don't have the time, inclination, or talent. But all of us are called to be artists of the highest kind. We are called to be sculptors of beautiful character. Morality is about 'character'. The word 'morality' is from the Latin *mores*, and 'ethics' is from the Greek word *ethos*, both of which mean 'character'. Character is not the same as personality. One can have a great personality, but depraved character—criminals usually have charming personalities; and one can have a dull personality, but great and noble character. Our highest achievement is the sculpting of noble character. The Greek word *kalon*, which appears in the *Nicomachean Ethics* of Aristotle, is best translated as the morally beautiful (from the Greek *kaleo*, 'attractive'; for what is beautiful 'attracts'). Character describes the kind of person we make ourselves to be by the choices that we make. There are certain kinds of actions (i.e., murder is a different kind of action than self-defence, etc.), and only certain kinds of people choose certain kinds of acts. The moral life is about becoming a certain kind of person, a morally beautiful person.

Like all artistic production, the work is slow, hard, tedious, and monotonous. It involves sacrifice and self-discipline, but the end is the production of a beautiful work, namely morally beautiful character.

None of this makes any sense to the moral relativist. For him, it is pleasure that is the highest delight; and so for the relativist, morality is about making those choices that create the conditions most conducive to a life of pleasure (the greatest pleasure for the greatest number). Happiness is a matter of having (having enjoyable experiences), but for the non-relativist position, happiness is a matter of being (a matter of character).

A moral choice establishes a relationship between the will and intelligible human goods, which are aspects of human flourishing. A noble character relates well to human goods; a good will is one that wills the good wherever there is an instance of it. Deficient character establishes a deficient relationship to the good; a partial or qualified love of the good; there is, rather, a disordered love of self. In other words, the self is loved as the ultimate end, and everyone else is loved insofar as he or she serves that end. That is why it is okay to abort a child if it is inconvenient, for example.

The happiness of the relativist is pleasure; but the happiness of the non-relativist is an ecstasy, an exit of self, akin to the experience of the beautiful. Man differs from brute animal in that he possesses **intellect** and **will**. It is through these two powers that the human person can *become something other than himself*. Aristotle pointed out long ago that when we know the nature of a thing, the essence of that thing exists in the mind of the knower. The mind becomes what it knows in an immaterial way. Through knowledge, I become *more than what I am*, without ceasing to be what I am. I am *what I know*. This is an intellectual self-expansion. However, through the will, I can also become someone other than myself. I naturally will the best for myself, but I do not naturally will the best for you. I have to freely choose to do so. I naturally love myself and want the best for myself, and I know that you too desire the best for yourself. I can choose to will the best for you *as if you were another me, another self.* I have that ability to go outside myself and exist *as you*, without ceasing to be myself, so that I am no longer one, but two. And if I love a third person as another self, then I become three, and four, and five, etc.

A morally good person loves human goods whenever and wherever he finds them. A morally beautiful human being is an expanded human being, one who lives outside himself in the other. The artist paints, labors, so that you can be brought out of yourself and experience the beautiful, that is, in order that you experience ecstasy. So too, the morally noble man or woman disciplines the passions and cultivates the virtues so as to be able to love ecstatically, selflessly, to exist outside himself or herself in the other, for the good of the other.

The difference between the happiness that follows upon moral integrity and the life of pleasure is hard to convey, especially if one has not experienced it. The highest kind of happiness is much greater than the ecstatic delight in the beautiful; it is like that insofar as delighting in beauty is an experience of being taken out of oneself. But think of the exit of self that is involved in loving another *as another self.* When we are so loyal to the good, to every instance of intelligible human goodness, that wherever there is a human person, that person is loved for his sake, as another self, we have expanded ourselves. The happiness of others becomes our own. That's a very difficult thing to achieve—we are far more selfish than we are aware of. But the happiness that results from such an expanded mode of existence is so deep and pervasive that its description means very little to those who have not begun to taste it. It is the happiness of existing both outside the self and more deeply within the self. Just as it is only in knowing something outside myself that I become present to myself, so too, the more I exist outside myself through an act of the will that loves the other as another self, the more fully do I become the person that I am.

The moral life is all about cultivating the virtues, which are habits, and as you all know, bad habits are hard to break, and good habits are hard to acquire. The intellect is perfected morally by the virtue of prudence, the will is perfected by justice, the concupiscible appetite and its emotions are perfected by temperance, and the irascible appetite and its emotions are perfected by fortitude. A prudent, just, temperate and brave person is a morally beautiful human being. Moreover, moral beauty imparts a kind of physical beauty. What takes place on the level of the soul spills over into the realm of matter; a morally noble human being radiates beauty in a way that Hollywood simply does not.

So how do you sculpt ugly character? Be a relativist. Picasso exhibits the ugliness that relativism begets. In a relativistic world, everyone eventually is going to find you ugly, and in due time you are going to find everyone else ugly. What is new will appear exciting, but it will soon get old, just as a new dish is exciting and tasty at first, but it gets old, and in time it may even become revolting. In that case, you search for a new restaurant or a new recipe. That's why relativism naturally leads to adultery, fornication, contraception, divorce, etc. Things get old, and so we want to experience what is new, but traditional non-relativist morality, by imposing permanency, takes the fun out of life, or so the relativist believes.

How do you sculpt morally beautiful character, and thus a morally beautiful countenance? Commit to the good; follow the eternal law; love that law, which is larger than you, me, and the civil community as a whole. Learn to love human beings for their own sake, not for the sake of what they do for you. That is the secret to looking beautiful, and that is the secret to a life that is beautiful, heroic and meaningful.

91 *A Note on Final Cause in Human Action*

The **final cause** refers to the end or purpose of a process. Every agent acts for an end, and the end of an act is two-fold: a) the end of the generation (proximate end), and b) the end of the generated (ultimate end). In a typical accidental change, for example in the realm of art, the end of the generation coincides with the formal cause. The formal cause is: *that for the sake of which there is coming to be.* For example, the sculptor is carving for the sake of realizing the form in the matter. He will stop working (end) when the form is completely realized in the matter. When that occurs, his work is perfected (*per*: through; *factum*: made). The end of the generated is the ultimate end, the ultimate purpose for which he made the sculpture, or clay pot, or painting, etc.

It is the end of the generation (the proximate end) that tells us *what* is in the mind of the sculptor. His idea is the form he intends to impose on the matter. Thus, the proximate end—at least for us observers—reveals "what" it is he is making. In other words, the essence of his act (what he is doing) is determined by the proximate end (i.e., He is making a flower pot; she is going for a leisurely jog, etc.). And since the proximate end is the formal cause, it is the proximate end that determines the action to be the "kind of act" it is. We know what someone is doing through the proximate end that is intended.

The *ultimate end* (end of the generated), however, will give us deeper insight into the nature of his act. For example, a person is making a gun, but his ultimate end will tell us whether this 'production' is part of a murderous plot, or whether it is simply artistic expression, or perhaps is carried out for some non-violent practical purpose (i.e., a starter's pistol).

To sum up, the form determines the substance to be what it is, but in the realm of action, it is the end or final cause that is the form of the action, for the end determines the action to be the kind of act it is. To get a better handle on this, consider two men firing a gun at a human being. In one case, the shooter is firing a gun at a man *in order to* stop him (he's running at the shooter with a knife). The other shooter is firing a gun at a man *in order to* kill him. The ends in both cases are entirely different, and that is why the two acts are essentially different. The former is a self-defensive act; the latter is a murderous act.

Now, there are many actions a person performs, each one defined by its end (both proximate and ultimate). But the totality of one's actions, that is, one's entire life, is also directed to an end, which is an ultimate end. The ultimate end of a person's entire life that he intends ultimately in doing all that he does will determine the kind of life he is living. In other words, the very meaning of his life is given by this ultimate end.

Consider now the thought experiment we did in class; everyone agreed that it is possible for a person to have a life inundated with pleasures and still find himself unhappy. We also agreed that a person can achieve everything he has ever set out to achieve and in the end remain unhappy. Indeed, it is possible to have achieved all that one has set out to achieve and yet be happy. But if that person is happy, it logically follows that his happiness is not the result of having achieved everything he has set out to achieve. To show this, imagine two ladies who both graduated from university with honors, married with a family, and each one has become a family physician and lives in a large house. However, one is happy, the other is unhappy. If that is a possible scenario, then it follows that the happy woman is happy not by virtue of the fact that she graduated with honors, became a doctor, is married with children, etc. If that were so, the other would necessarily be happy as well.

So, what is the reason for her unhappiness? The two lives are virtually identical from the point of view of their activities and achievements. But one says her life is without meaning, the other says her life is meaningful. It follows that their lives must be radically different from another point of view. If they are radically different in kind, and if the kind of life one is living is determined by the ultimate end (just as the kind of act one performs is determined by the proximate end), then the two lives are radically different in kind because each of them has a radically different ultimate end.

How are they different? Let's say that one lady has devoted her life to her own personal fulfillment, which is a more respectable way of saying that she is devoted to herself ultimately. If the other lady (the happy one) has also devoted her life to the fulfillment of her personal dreams, then ultimately her life is no different in kind. But if her life is radically different in meaning, it must follow that her ultimate end is not 'herself', but something outside herself. Let's say the ultimate end of her life is to serve not her own will, but the will of God. Thus, the two lives are radically different in kind. The one life is secular and ultimately self-centered; the other is religious and 'other-centered'.

Does this account for their radically different internal states? I would submit that it does. Two people can have very similar achievements, i.e., graduation from a prestigious university, a career in medicine, marriage and family, financial success, etc., and live very similar lives in appearance, and yet feel radically different about their own lives. The one may be unfulfilled, bored, and unhappy, while the other is fulfilled, motivated and full of joy. The difference, I will argue, lies in their ultimate ends, which are not identical. The one life is directed beyond the self to something larger than the self, the other is directed ultimately to the self, or to the fulfillment of his/her will.

This is an artificial scenario, to be sure, and does not constitute proof or demonstration by any means. But let us return to a point about knowledge and will. When we know something, we become what we know in an immaterial way. The object of our knowledge exists in us 'intentionally'—not physically. Knowledge is thus a way of existing. I exist as that tree, or dog, etc., without ceasing to be myself. In knowing anything, I become larger than what I am, without ceasing to be what I am. We all have a desire to know, for we all desire to intellectually self-expand. But there is another way to become enlarged that is even less self-centered, and this is through the will. I know that person as another being of the same nature as myself, and through self-knowledge I infer that he too wants the best for himself. I can freely choose to join my will to his and will the best for him as I will the best for myself. In this case, I go outside myself, so to speak, and become him, that is, another self. This is self-expansion, but different from that of knowledge. In knowing him, he becomes me (exists in me in a new way, i.e., intentionally) without ceasing to be himself, and without my ceasing to be myself. But in love (willing the best for him for his own sake, not for my sake), I exist as another self outside myself, in him, without him necessarily even knowing about it. I have become two, and if I love another person for his own sake, I have become three, four, etc. It is in man's nature to become another through knowledge and love, but to become another through love requires a free act of the will. I will argue that happiness directly corresponds to the self-enlargement that is genuine love of another. Thus, happiness is an activity, not a passivity; it requires a free act of the will that is directed outside the self towards other human persons.

No matter how rich in wealth or achievement a person's life is, if it is directed ultimately for the sake of personal fulfillment, the person in the end will be deeply and radically unsatisfied. He will only find his own fulfillment when he ignores it and concerns himself with the happiness of human persons outside himself.

Can a person have as his ultimate end the happiness of others (plural) without concerning himself with God? The problem here is that in this case, one's ultimate end is not single, but plural (others); it is singular in idea only (i.e., humanity). One's ultimate end must be an end that is a real being, not an idea. A person's greatest happiness is going to be the knowledge and love of the highest being. If I really love each human person (not just an idea, like "humanity"), then I love the Real Being that is the origin of the human person, namely God Himself, who is the origin and end of all beings. Happiness is only found in loving God and neighbor.

92 *A Thought on Paradox and Purpose*

There is a strange paradox about the human person, and it is this: God loves each one of us as if there is only one of us, as St. Catherine of Siena points out somewhere, and yet there is **not** only one of us, but many of us beyond counting. Each one of us is significant, that is, important, to a degree that we cannot fully appreciate—as if you are the only one that exists. Yet, once again, you are not the only one that exists. When we see ourselves as one among a myriad of human beings beyond counting, we often get the distinct impression that we are profoundly insignificant and unimportant, about as insignificant as a blade of grass—which isn't all that significant.

Consider that when we listen to a symphony or a choir, we don't pay attention to each note. Compared to the whole, each note is insignificant. But every note is profoundly significant; for if one person sings one or two notes off key, that stands out and something is clearly amiss. A trained choir director would hear it and it would cause him some discomfort; a conductor would hear the flute or violin or clarinet play that wrong note and he would not be indifferent to it. Thus, although from one angle an individual note is insignificant—for it lacks the depth and beauty of the whole piece—, we can see that each note is profoundly significant and contributes to the beauty of the whole.

And when we hear the piece being played, we don't pay attention to the individual notes, but each note, when played in tune and situated in its proper place, surrenders itself to a kind of "invisibility", that is, it makes its contribution and in doing so allows us to pass over it. It does what it is supposed to do, and in doing so allows us to forget it, or fail to notice it *as an individual note.*

The life of the individual person is supposed to be lived like that. We are profoundly significant, but we are called to take our place and allow ourselves to be struck so as to resound, as one among a myriad of different notes, and the whole is a symphony that glorifies God, that communicates the divine beauty, which is simple and inexhaustible, but which can only be imperfectly communicated and expressed through a diversity of notes. We are called upon to allow others to pass us over, that is, not to notice us; but we are called to take our place and play our part, so as to contribute to the symphony that glorifies God, that proclaims His beauty and greatness.

93 The Radiance of Personhood and the Splendor of Chastity

The human being is a person, but to be a person means much more than being an individual. The etymology of 'individual' underscores the fact of being 'undivided', that is, being a single and unified whole. A cat, however, is an individual, and so too an oak tree; but they are not persons. The very word 'person' is from the Latin *persona* (*per*: through; *sona*: sound). Thus, a person is a "through sound". What does this mean? Historically, the sound referred to in the etymology of this word refers to the words that pass through a mask (in the context of the theatre). In other words, a person is communicator, a speaker. He radiates sounds that have meaning, that is, he communicates ideas through words, and in so doing, he enables others to enter into a shared space. A person is one who, by communicating with another person willing to receive that communication, establishes a degree of community. Through communication, persons create and live within a larger reality, a good that exceeds the limits of the individual self.

Since the Middle Ages, "person" has been defined as an individual substance of a rational nature (Boethius). To possess a rational nature is to be capable of apprehending the "reasons for" or causes of things. It is the ability to grasp the meaning of a thing's motions (activities). Brute animals perceive motions, but they do not grasp the meaning of those motions. To grasp the meaning of a thing's motions (i.e., sickness, growth, the significance of hand signals, hand writing, etc.) is to apprehend the reasons for the motions of things, that is, the motions of things in terms of their causes. Now there are four causes, so to apprehend the motions of things in terms of their causes includes the agent cause, but it also includes the final cause (the purpose or end of the motion) and the formal cause (what that motion is: i.e., sickness is a pathology, etc.), not to mention the material cause. Now, since a cause is a principle from which something proceeds with dependence, it follows that to understand the reasons for a thing's motions is to understand the principles upon which those motions depend. And so a person is one who apprehends "necessities", for a cause is the 'reason for' such and such, and so the connection between an effect and its source or principle is a necessary one, that is, it is one of dependence (the effect depends on the cause). This motion depended on that source or principle (waving depended upon that man, and it depended upon his purpose (final cause) of offering a greeting, etc., and so this occurred as a necessary consequence of that, etc.

Let's look at this from another angel. A person possesses the ideas of things; and these ideas are universal. To be able to reason, or to pronounce on the reasons for this or that happening, requires an ability to grasp universal ideas, for there is no reasoning without universal ideas—recall that no conclusion can be drawn from two particular premises, for the middle term must be distributed at least once. A person possesses universal ideas precisely because his mind is an immaterial power. As a result, persons are capable of complete self-reflection; a person knows that he knows, and he knows that he seeks the 'reasons for' certain facts in his experience. He is aware that he is continually searching for the causes of things, and discovering one cause does not satisfy his intellect entirely, for he continues to seek more deeply into the causes of things. He will only be satisfied when he comes to possess, in knowledge, the cause of that which is absolutely first about things; and that which is first, to which nothing is prior, is being or existence. Man is a seeker, and he seeks to know the sufficient reason for being, and he will not be satisfied until he possesses it.

The 'sound' in *persona* refers to language (or words spoken), and words have a meaning, which is to say that they have a direction. The meaning of a 'sound' that is a spoken or written word is in the idea inside the mind, the interior word. The interior words or concepts point towards the thing or things outside the mind, because the idea inside the mind is intentional. This means that it signifies or intends the thing outside the mind. The idea is a *pure sign* whose sole function is to signify or intend. For example, my idea of 'canine' or 'feline' is not what I know, it is that *through which* I know the particular being outside my mind that is a cat.

To speak is first and foremost to conceive an interior word (idea), and an interior word 'intends' or tends towards some being. Now, to "intend" is to have reference to, to refer to, or to have a relation to. An idea has a relation to the being of which it is an idea. To speak audible words is to radiate something; it is to radiate a different kind of light, namely ideas. The human person is not locked within himself, he radiates his deepest self by communicating what he has become through the ideas he has conceived within himself. He is pregnant with the inner life of ideas, and he communicates those ideas through words. He must radiate, for he "exists for" something beyond himself.

To be a person is to "exist for". That is why a fundamental need of each human person is 'to be important'. The reason is that to be important is to be "important for" someone. And so a person's perfection consists in "existing for" another or others. If there is nothing to which his existence can be ordered, then his existence is felt to be pointless, that is, without a point, without a direction or end. Such an existence is felt to be meaningless; for it is without direction.

Indeed, Sartre is right in pointing out that man is a 'pour-soi' (for self), because he is conscious of himself, whereas a chair is not conscious of itself, it does not exist for itself, but purely for another. However, man's self-conscious existence is a relational existence, for he *is conscious of himself only when knowing something outside himself*, something other than himself. His sense of self emerges simultaneously with the knowledge of beings other than him. There is no 'coming to himself' in any kind of self-awareness without being opened up upon the world outside himself. He is a *pour-soi* primarily because he is a *'for another'*.

And so, a person is a being who knows, who possesses ideas. But to know the nature of a thing is to become that thing in an immaterial way. The nature of the being I know exists in me immaterially and thus universally. Thus, knowledge is a kind of self-expansion; in knowing something, I become **more than** what I am (my mind is that being immaterially), without ceasing to be what I am (I am still a human being).

That fundamental thrust to "exist for" that is at the root of the need to be important is also at the root of the need to expand through knowledge. As Aristotle said, 'all men by nature desire to know', that is, they desire to become more than what they are without ceasing to be what they are. The human person has a natural appetite or desire to 'exist for', that is, to exist in relation to a reality outside his own mind. Thus, he is not sufficient unto himself. No man is an island, as Irish poet John Donne wrote. If the human person does not exist "for somebody", he is of no importance. But a person is essentially a 'for another', and so to exist without a sense of importance is a kind of 'death'; like a sun that has ceased to radiate, or a sun that radiates without anything there to receive its illumination.

In other words, the human person has a need to be loved and to love. He has a need **to know he "exists for",** which means he knows he is important for someone or others and is thus loved, and he has a need **"exist for",** which means he has a need to love (to illuminate in some way).

Now, as was said above, in knowing anything, the human person becomes what he knows. But when he loves another, he wills the good of the other *as another self.* His self-knowledge enables him to know that this 'other' is a being, a person, a knower like me, and he too has a natural desire to exist for, that is, a natural desire to be important. And so I can choose to acknowledge his importance and to will his good (the true goods he desires) as if he were me. In loving him, I expand, for I become that other self, and I affirm his 'existence for'. I actually treat him as another me, without ceasing to be me. In love, there is a going out of the self into the other, *without actually experiencing all that he experiences.* I will his good for his sake.

To be a person is to be capable, therefore, of a two-fold expansion: one of knowledge, and the other of love. Knowledge and love are relational. Now because the human person is rational and since love is not love unless it is freely given, the human person has a freedom that other things do not possess. Every other thing below man has a natural inclination towards its own perfection, and it will realize that perfection or maturation as long as conditions are right. In other words, if we water a plant and make sure it gets enough sunlight, it will grow to become fully what it is. The same is true for brute animals, although their care might require a little more than water and sunlight.

The human person, on the other hand, is inclined towards his own perfection, but he has the ability to freely determine himself towards a course of action that will inevitably destroy him. His fundamental thrust as a 'person' is to 'exist for' others, but he may choose an existence that is entirely self-centered (he may choose to exist primarily for himself). In doing so, he freely chooses to live in a way that is contrary to his nature. The result of such a general course of action is greater unhappiness, for a person's happiness is directly proportionate to the degree of his self-expansion.

Some Fundamental Needs of the Human Person

The human person has a fundamental inclination to possess truth. But truth is a relation; it is the conformity between what is in the mind of the person and what is (being). And so the human person has a fundamental need to be measured by the real, that is, to be enlarged by the real or to conform to the real, to have it exist in him according to his specific mode of being (as a knower). But, he also has a fundamental inclination to be known. In other words, he has a need to be loved. As was said, he needs to "exist for", that is, to be "important for", another or others.

The human person, because he is essentially relational, has a fundamental need for justice, which means "rightly ordered social relations". Injustice is a disorder. Now we naturally love the whole more than we love the part. We see this, for example, when a person under attack suffers defensive wounds. He places his arms in harm's way to protect the whole. Now although the human person is not reducible to a mere part of the social whole—for he is a whole unto himself—, nonetheless, he is still a part of a larger whole, and he naturally loves the good of the whole more than he loves himself. That does not mean, however, that he is necessarily a just person. In order to be a just person, he must choose to act according to that natural love, and not contrary to it, that is, he must freely choose acts that are consistent with a love of the whole that is greater than the love of self, and that is not always easy, for he has a quasi-natural inclination to seek himself (the wounds of Original Sin).

The human person has a fundamental inclination to happiness; for he is a seeker; he seeks to know the sufficient reason for the very existence of things, and in every one of his choices he ultimately pursues a happiness that is final, eternal, and sufficient unto itself. He knows, albeit confusedly and generally, that there is an ultimate end that is the sufficient reason for being, that is eternal and sufficient unto itself, and he knows, perhaps confusedly and pre-consciously that this sufficient reason for being is intelligent, good, and beautiful, and thus personal, since he experiences the world as intelligible, desirable, and beautiful. Each human person naturally knows through a pre-conscious and rapid reasoning process that God exists (although he may not necessarily know this to be God), and he has a need to be always searching for God until He is found.

Now the human person has a moral sense, or a sense of duty. In other words, the human person is a moral agent, and he has moral needs, that is, a moral inclination. He needs to become more than what he is through the free decision to love that which is other than himself, and he cannot fulfill this need if all he chooses to pursue is the delectable good—which is a good that only he can enjoy. He knows that he is not the only person in the world, that there are others who are like him, namely human persons who have the same basic needs or inclinations. He understands through his own self-knowledge or self-consciousness that there is often a tension within himself, a tension between his own appetite for the delectable good, which is a private good, and another good that is larger than himself—the good of the other or others. He recognizes a fundamental moral "ought" and that he ought to treat another in a way that agrees with (or is true to) what the other actually is. For example, if he is a human person equal in dignity to me, then I ought to treat him as such; I ought not to reduce him to the status of an instrument for my own private good, because I know from within that such behavior is repugnant to me—for I desire to be "important for" someone in an absolute sense, not relatively and for a short time only, like the existence of a pencil or a flashlight, which has importance only when needed, and not in itself; for no instrument is loved for its own sake.

The common good or the good of the whole cannot be achieved unless each person responds faithfully to that sense of duty to freely love the whole more than the self. And so I have a need for integrity or integration. In other words, I not only desire order within the social whole—even though I choose in a way that frustrates that order—, I also desire order within myself, among the various aspects of myself, such as my passions and reason, and between my choices and my already established moral identity (character)—even though I choose in a way that is contrary to right reason. My sense of duty includes bringing order from within me because it is not possible to bring about order within the social whole unless there is order within each of the parts of the whole, especially in light of the fact that a person, who is part of the social whole, is a whole unto himself with many aspects (i.e., intellect, will, the emotions of the sensitive appetite, his established character, and his potential acts).

Now this shared or common good of the social whole includes much more than economic prosperity; the human person is a moral agent, he has a fundamental need for moral integrity. He is part of a larger moral order, for he is part of a community of moral agents, namely human persons. Nevertheless, a community of morally disordered persons will inevitably have negative economic repercussions, and that is because man is more than a consumer, he is a person—if he were a mere consumer, moral integrity wouldn't matter. And so if we reduce the human person to a consumer and regard economic prosperity alone as the ultimate perfection of the individual, we will inevitably experience the never ending frustration of economic failure, to some degree at least—for injustice and human selfishness are costly (for they generate mistrust, excessive caution, an atmosphere of alienation and over competitiveness, anxiety, despair, etc.).

And so "the good", or the moral order, is much larger than my own private good, that is, my own "delectable good". Moreover, my own personal good depends upon the good of the whole (the moral order) and how I freely choose to relate to it; and so it follows that the way I choose to relate to the moral order is the way I freely establish my relationship with God, who is the lawgiver behind the natural moral law (man's sense of duty and all its moral implications or precepts). My choices determine my moral identity (moral character), the kind of person that I am—which is not the same as my personality (I do not "make" my personality, but I do make myself to be a certain kind of person by my own free choices). Either I freely choose to love God and the moral order more than I love myself, or I freely choose to love myself above all, contrary to my deepest need. My happiness thus depends upon moral choices that incorporate me into something much larger than myself; I need to "exist in" something larger than myself, and I can only do so on condition that I freely choose to "exist for" something other than myself, and on condition that others freely and gratuitously receive the gift of my existence.

My character, in turn, affects the way I see the world: "As a person is, so does he see" (Aristotle). If I choose a self-centered existence, I begin to see you as a means to my own private ends; if I am an unjust person, I see any course of action that demands from me some kind of sacrifice as an injustice; if I am a prideful and arrogant human being, I see whoever is smarter than me as a threat; if I am a lazy lout, I regard those who are willing to spoon feed me as my friends, and those who demand I take some initiative as my enemies, etc.

And so although I have a need for justice, my choices might be made for the sake of my own "delectable good", and the result is deficient character, or vice, which are bad character traits (habits), such as cowardice, intemperance, impatience, arrogance, vanity, dishonesty, leniency, etc. So although I desire a just social order, my choices help to prevent that, because they are selfish, but I never end up seeing or acknowledging that. And so I have become my own worst enemy; for I need to love and be loved, but my choices are unloving and they give rise to resentment in others, and so I end up alienating myself from others, to one degree or another.

Personhood and Sexuality

Intense passion, such as the passion of pleasure or satisfaction, is very different from the general state of human happiness or well-being. It is very difficult to make this clear for those who do not already know this from within; for it usually takes years of life experience and a keen sense of self-awareness to grasp the distinction. But the distinction is clear and obvious to those who choose to love the moral good (the moral order) more than they love themselves.

The most a brute animal can expect in terms of happiness is the perpetual satisfaction of its sense appetites. The human person, on the other hand, also has passions, but his emotions have a much wider range; the human person can get excited about objects outside the animal's range of cognition: we get excited about the prospect of flying overseas to visit historic places and museums, we can get excited about commitments that promise a great deal of hardship, but which have as their object the good of another or others, such as the prospect of having and caring for a baby or a large family, or serving a community in some way. Human emotions are personal; the passions are humanized when taken up into the life of the intellect and will. The emotions become most fully what they are when they are disposed to obey reason and the demands of the moral order.

Consequently, it is possible to experience pleasure that is momentary and intense, but which leaves one in a lesser state, that is, unhappier in the end, because the act which produces the pleasure does not lift the person into a larger reality. Allow me to employ an analogy that compares the moral life to a soccer game. Exercising my dazzling skills as a soccer player before a large crowd of people might be pleasurable, but skillfully contributing to a play of which I am only a part and which ends with another player scoring a goal for the team, bringing about the larger good of victory for everyone, in the end brings me a greater good and thus a greater happiness—because we naturally love the good of the whole more than our own individual good. But if my emotions are so disordered that I am inclined to my own delectable good and choose on the basis of that inclination, that course of action leaves the team frustrated with me, although it flatters my ego and brings me momentary enjoyment. In the end, it deprives me and the team of victory. And so my acts ought to be taken up into something larger, namely the order of the game itself, ordered to a common good (victory).

Again, this is difficult to communicate to those who have not experienced the subtle difference between this general and underlying state of moral well-being that we can call joy, and the pleasure of intense passion and the relief it often provides; and so to continue the analogy, it is difficult to persuade the egotistical player that a greater happiness can be had by ordering his activity to the shared good of the team. And the distinction is especially difficult in the area of sexuality, not so much in extreme cases of adultery or casual sex—most people of relatively decent character understand the morally repugnant nature of these acts—, but more so in reference to sex acts performed in the context of a committed relationship that is not marital, or masturbatory acts that are mutual and between married couples. It is particularly difficult because committed friendship is a good thing that promotes the fullness of one's personal existence, and the sexual act is often regarded as a genuine part of that relationship, sharing in its goodness. The following discourse, however, aims to clarify how *such acts are really not at all genuine parts of such non marital friendships but are additions that actually erode and harm them*, and that the wisest and most prudent course of action for a young man or woman is to keep oneself for one's spouse, to practice fidelity even before marriage, and to avoid masturbatory acts within marriage (i.e., oral sex, anal intercourse, or sexual intercourse that is merely a response to an urge). I am aware, however, that the only ones who are going to appreciate the reasoning in all of this are those who genuinely love the moral good more than they love their own feelings of complacency, those whose lives are already freely ordered towards the source of all that is good, namely God, who is Goodness, Truth, and Beauty Itself; outside of that, all moral discourse defending traditional sexual morality, no matter how precise and true to reality, will appear thin and unduly scrupulous.

Having said that, let me begin by pointing out that sexual union in its full meaning is not a union of parts, but a union of persons. The sexual act has a meaning much greater and richer than the sexual acts of brute animals. The sex acts of brute animals are ordered towards the preservation of the species, they are instinctual, and the animal experiences nothing more than vehement desire and the passion of satisfaction. For many people as well, that's all sex is on the human level. But the only way to make any sense out of traditional sexual morality is to keep in the forefront of the mind that sexual union is a union of persons.

The basic orientation of a morally good life, one that responds faithfully and completely to the moral sense, is a relational one, an existence that radiates beyond the self. It involves not merely knowing, but loving the other and others as another self, to will his good and the good of the whole, not for my sake or for my own delectable good, but for the sake of the good as such. All my passions must be ordered to that end, and when they are ordered to that end, they serve reason, and when they are made to serve reason, my passions become fully humanized. I become an ordered person within a larger order, as a working starter motor or distributer contributes fully to the functioning of an engine (such analogies fall short in that man is indeed a part of the whole, but not a mere part).

Some genuinely human acts (freely willed) result in intense pleasure, and such pleasure is part and parcel of the act for a **reason**. A brute animal is not conscious of the reason in its case; only a rational creature can detect the reason—i.e., for the preservation of the individual, and the preservation of the species (i.e., eating is for the sake of the preservation of the individual, and sexual desire is for the sake of the preservation of the species). A human person's desire for food is also for the preservation of the individual; a brute animal does not know this, but a person is capable of knowing this and ordering his appetite to that end. We eat to live, and to live is good. Thus, his appetite ought to be ordered, freely and intelligently, for the sake of his own preservation, thus for the sake of his over-all health. Unhealthy eating is thus disordered; excessive eating is also disordered, for it contributes to the individual's demise (i.e., diabetes, heart condition, clogged arteries, etc.). In other words, such a person's appetite is inclining him to do something which results in the opposite of what it is intended to achieve. But there is also a moral component here. Man is a moral agent. A man with a disordered appetite lacks complete self-possession. He lacks control; he is controlled by his sense appetite, and so his behavior is somewhat less than fully human, in that it is less under the dominion of a will subject to reason. He is becoming self-indulgent, pleasure oriented, a slave to passion, to some degree at least.

Joy, however, results from a life of virtue, because a life of virtue is an ordered life, a life that is taken up, as a result of the free moral choices of the person, into something larger than the individual person, namely the common good of the civil community as a whole. A person who is ordered within himself, through the possession of fortitude and its parts as well as temperance and all its parts, is a person who can be inserted within the civil community as a whole as a healthy part of the social whole. He is one who loves the common or shared good more than the delectable good. If he loves the moral good, then he wills order from within himself (he wills to cultivate temperance and fortitude, or integrity) and wills to take his place within the civil community, for the sake of the common good of the civil community. The intemperate, generally speaking, freely choose the delectable good over the shared good, or the good of the whole; for they are somewhat indifferent to how their own emotional state affects the civil community. In fact, it can be argued that they don't even love themselves enough—their character. They care more for how they "feel" than what they might become (character). Disordered acts, such as intemperate acts, i.e., gluttonous acts, are indeed pleasurable and provide a sense of relief, but because they are not ordered to their proper end and are rooted in an excessive love of one's emotional complacency, they distort the character, rendering it disproportionate; for it becomes lopsided, comparable to a large beer belly, or another disproportioned area of the body.

It is the same for sexual acts. The goodness of these acts, like all human acts, consists in their order within a larger whole. The first point is that sexual acts are ordered towards the preservation of the species, and so in the human being, the will must be freely ordered to that end, towards the good of the whole, not merely the pleasure of orgasm. This does not mean that the sexual act must always issue in children; it means that this end is the key to understanding the complete meaning of the act.

The sexual act is pleasurable, that is, it is sensibly good, but the reason for that is the end, which is the species, the civil community as a whole, or the common good—if the sexual act were not pleasurable, would the species be preserved? The union of marriage is for the sake of the common good of the civil community, and the family is its basic unit, and so he ought to love his wife for her own sake, and that love must be part of his love for the common good of the civil community as a whole, and vice versa. He marries her to care for her, because she cannot care for herself when she is with child. She and her child need his protection, which is much more than financial. His love of her is a great service to the civil community as a whole. The two must love one another not as a means to an end, but as an end. At the same time marital love is a part of a wider love of the civil community as a whole, for marriage is ordered to the common good of the whole.

And so his sexual act, to be fully personal (*persona*), must be an expression of that marital union, that is, ordered towards it. His commitment to marriage is a good much larger than himself considered individually, a commitment which among other things promises hardship, difficulty, and sacrifice. The act is pleasurable, but the end he ought to intend in the act is not his own pleasure, but something beyond himself, namely the good of his spouse, the expression and celebration of that marital love. That marital union is much more than a friendship. It is a commitment to be a one flesh union, which is an institution, and an institution of persons is for the sake of the common good (the public welfare). A child is the fruit and testimony of that one flesh union.

Masturbatory acts simply bring pleasure, the pleasure of orgasm. They have no capacity to be ordered towards anything beyond the pleasure of orgasm; for they are neither unitive nor are they procreative. They are inevitably closed in on themselves, comparable to the act of eating for the mere taste of food. But the act of sexual intercourse between a husband and wife who have given themselves completely to one another, thus instituting a marriage ordered towards the good of the civil community, does not result in pleasure alone, but in something more. This is a sexual act of mutual self-giving in which the two receive the entire gift of self (including fertility). It is a sacrificial act, albeit a pleasurable act, and that is because marriage itself is sacrificial; it is a giving that includes a great deal of hardship, because it involves begetting and raising children—which is a difficult task—, self-denial, learning to adjust to another's ways, flexibility, etc. The act of sexual intercourse between the married couple is an act of marriage; not all sexual acts that can occur between a married couple are marital acts, that is, acts of the social institution that marriage is. Oral and anal intercourse, for example, lack an order towards the larger social reality that marriage is. They might in some way resemble the marital act, but they lack its complete meaning. The act of marital self-giving results in intense pleasure, but it is an essentially self-giving act, for it is a complete giving of one's bodily self, which includes one's fertility, and it is a giving that is completed by the free decision to receive the total and personal self-giving of one's spouse. The result is a union of persons, not merely a union of parts. Acts of self-giving, genuinely charitable acts—whether they are accompanied by pleasure or not—

cause a genuine expansion of the self and thus bring about a greater sense of integration or integrity, and thus a greater joy.

Non-marital intercourse and masturbatory acts cannot achieve that; all they achieve is pleasure. But because the will consents to the act—which is a less than fully human action, since it is not ordered to a union of persons and procreation, thus not ordered to the civil community as a whole, as is marriage and its acts—, the person is left in a diminished state, not so much the state of an expanded self, but a shrunken self, a more dis-integrated self (the passions are not integrated towards an end proposed by reason, but are indulged in for the sake of sensible satisfaction), and the result might be more pleasure, but a superficial character and a depressed or empty state of sorts, the opposite of joy, a subtle sorrow or sadness, the emotional state of having become shrunken (for the act is directed ultimately to the self, that is, to pleasure, which is in the self).

94 Burley's Principle and Moral Integration

One of the most important insights central to theories of plausible reasoning bears upon the systemic nature of our best estimates about what is true. Truth is systematic; it is a complex whole whose parts are tightly interconnected and interdependent. The limited sets of data through which we formulate our best estimates about particular matters (scientific, economic, political, moral, etc.) is highly information sensitive. These sets of data form a systemic whole in which the parts, i.e., the data or pieces of information, are so interdependent that a change in one part will require a change in another. In other words, new information that is inconsistent with much of the information in our current set of data can do a great deal to upset the neatly stacked applecart of our conceptual framework and cause us to make adjustments, that is, to dismiss information that is inconsistent with the new data. The history of science is a beautiful illustration of this process.

This fact underpins a point made by medieval logician Walter Burley (ca. 1275 to ca. 1345) who said: "When a false contingent proposition is posited, one can prove any false proposition that is compatible with it."[88] As Nicholas Rescher points out: "...Burley's Principle has far-reaching implications. Given the interconnectedness of facts, any and all fact-contradicting assumptions are pervasively destabilizing. As far as the logic of the situation is concerned, you cannot change anything in the domain of fact without endangering everything. Once you embark on a contrary-to-fact assumption, then as far as pure logic is concerned, all the usual bets are off. Changing one fact always requires changing others as well: the fabric of facts is an integral unit, a harmonious system where nothing can be altered without affecting something else."[89]

---

[88] *Treatise on Obligations*, quoted in Nicholas Rescher. *Conditionals*. London, MIT Press, 2007. 79.

[89] *Ibid.*, p. 83.

I believe there is a moral parallel here; what is true in the cognitive domain is true in the moral domain. The human person is a single entity, but a morally complex whole. The human person is a moral system, so to speak. Just as a contrary-to-fact assumption has far reaching implications, that is, as new information inconsistent with our current set of data requires us to readjust that set in order to restore consistency and establish maximal plausibility, so too something similar takes place within the fabric of a person's complex moral nature; certain actions are inconsistent with the overall demands of right reason, and making peace with such actions has far reaching implications.

There are four faculties or powers that belong to the human person that are open to being disposed to a certain course of action; other faculties are not so open. For example, there is nothing I can do about my poor eyesight or poor hearing; no moral choice I make will improve my vision, hearing, or any other sense—all I can do is rely on technology to help improve them. In the same way, there is no moral choice one can make that will increase one's height or fertility, for example. But the human person does have a number of emotions (sensitive appetitive reactions) which can be disposed in a certain way through choice and repeated action, not to mention the specifically human faculties of intellect and will. Achieving a good human life is principally about disposing these faculties so that they readily conform to the demands of right reason; this is what it means to cultivate the virtues.

There is in everyone a fundamental drive towards self-preservation: I see my life as fundamentally good—which is why I naturally defend my life when it is under attack. However, there is more to human life than mere existence. Human nature is a manifold that embraces a diversity of intelligible and incommensurable goods that are loved for their own sake, and it is the totality of these intelligible human goods that constitute human well-being. I will my own fullness of being necessarily; but I have to choose to will your good as I will my own good. The latter is not natural, but the former is natural. Without choosing to will your good as I will my own good, I cannot achieve the well-being I naturally desire for myself, because a constituent part of that manifold that embraces a diversity of intelligible human goods is benevolent friendship and genuine concern for the common good of the civil community. Hence, we naturally love ourselves, but we do not naturally love ourselves well. To love oneself well is a matter of choosing well, and that is a moral achievement that does not happen overnight.

Returning to the cognitive domain once again, for me to introduce an inconsistency into a consistent set of data is to bring about a host of cognitive repercussions whose reverberations extend out even beyond my ability to understand at the moment. Similarly, for me to choose a course of action that is contrary to virtue, a course of action that is inconsistent with the good of moral integrity (integration), is to initiate a change that will reverberate throughout the moral system that I am. That vice will not be isolated, because the intellect, the will, and the entire network of human emotions—although distinct—are not separate powers, but are interconnected, for they are the emotions of a single unified entity, a human person.

A disordered appetite is fundamentally a disordered love of self, but there are a number of different appetites: the concupiscible (spawning the emotions of love, desire, pleasure, hate, aversion, and sorrow), the irascible (spawning the emotions of hope, despair, fear, daring, and anger), and the rational appetite or will. The defect of temperance, or indulgence, which can be a disordered appetite for the pleasures of food, for example, is fundamentally a disordered love of self; so too is a disordered appetite for drink or the pleasures of sex. But so too is impatience, which amounts to a disordered love of satisfaction, and so too pusillanimity, which is a defect of magnanimity, rooted as it is in a disordered love of ease. Human beings are differently disposed, that is, they have different temperaments; someone may not have a disordered appetite for food, but a disordered appetite for "peace and quiet", or a disordered appetite for praise, etc. Whatever a person's specific difficulties, at the root of it is disordered self-love. The moral life, from this angle, is about bringing harmony, order, or consistency within a set of elements, so to speak, that is, harmony between the various elements of the self, just as the point of reasoning well is about bringing consistency or systemic coherence to the entire set of data at our disposal, in order to achieve maximal plausibility.

A disordered appetite for food is a vice of the concupiscible appetite, whose perfection is the virtue of temperance—not justice, nor fortitude, nor prudence. But this does not mean that justice, the virtue that perfects the will, is unaffected. A person might be good willed and hate injustice, but love food or sex inordinately. By virtue of the systemic unity of the human person, this vice, which belongs to a particular sensitive appetite, will nevertheless affect the rational appetite (the will), because the decision not to restrain one's love of self on the level of the sensitive appetites is itself an act of the rational appetite. The will permits this disordered love of self. It may take a while for the effects of this vice to seriously affect the will just as a tear in the fabric takes a while to enlarge, or as it often takes a while for the implications of a piece of inconsistent data to be drawn out explicitly, but if a person neglects to address that moral inconsistency, he may find himself making choices that years earlier were unthinkable to him.

Fortitude is the virtue that affects the emotions of the irascible appetite. But it takes fortitude to restrain the concupiscible appetite, specifically the emotions of love, desire, satisfaction as they bear upon the most vehement pleasures. Moreover, it takes a just will, one responsive to the debts owed to others (i.e., the debt to speak the truth, the treat another in a way that respects his/her status as equal in dignity, etc.) if one is to rise above the emotions of fear or sorrow in order to exercise proper restraint over the concupiscible appetite; so the degree of one's sense of justice is the measure of one's fortitude and temperance. Also, fortitude is more than daring—daring can be reckless; hence, true fortitude requires good judgment (prudence). But to carry out a brave action that is truly good requires a love of the good as such, not just one's private or individual good. For example, if I am risking my life to save another, I am both brave and just, but I am also temperate, because that risk to my life is a risk of a serious loss of pleasures—the danger I face might seriously compromise my ability to enjoy the rest of my life, if it does not kill me.

The moral life is a fabric; if I lie to another (a vice contrary to justice) in order to create conditions that are convenient, not only do I lack trust in divine providence, I love my own convenience more than the equal status of the other—for I have violated his right to be treated in a way that respects his status as equal in dignity to me. To lie in order to create conditions conducive to the overall good of an institution or the society at large is also to act without an adequate sense of one's cognitive limitations—likely rooted in a defect of humility, which is a disordered love of one's excellence; for it is impossible to trace all the trajectories that will result from such a lie, but one acts as if one can, or as if there are no repercussions because they are unseen at this time. The thief too is willing to subordinate another's right that others respect his property as well as his status as equal in dignity, all for the sake of the thief's satisfaction of his desire for that property, however small is the amount. All this constitutes a disordered love of self. But what exactly do I love excessively that permits me to violate justice to that extent? At the root of it may be my own piece of mind, or financial gain, or a love of praise, or a love of physical gratification of some kind, etc.

A disordered will also affects the intellect in a number of ways. Excessive passion concentrates the mind, narrowing it on the satisfaction of the passion in question. For example, excessive hunger tends to limit the mind's attention to the alleviation of that hunger so that it becomes very difficult to think of anything else. Fear does the same thing: the mind is concentrated on ways to protect the self from a perceived threat. A life centered on the satisfaction of the passions is cognitively limited in unnatural ways, nor is such a person likely to be open to a life directed to the various kinds of justice, which involves others and a consideration of their rights and my obligations to them. The excessively passionate are relatively indifferent to the common good of the civil community as a whole, but they are not indifferent to whatever has relevance to the self and the satisfaction of the passions. This of course has political implications as well; for such people are disposed to vote not necessarily for the party that promises to establish conditions that will promote the good of the entire civil community, but the party that best serves their private interests, for it is their private good that has become the narrow focus of their lives.

The intellect is affected by a disordered will in another way: if I love my private good more than the good as such, then my readiness to conform to "what is" (the real) will be compromised—for truth is a conformity of the mind to the real. What I want to be true takes priority over what actually is true. At this point we begin to erect different confidence thresholds for the truths we want or do not want to believe in. I will not allow myself to see what I do not wish to see, and so I will demand an inordinate amount of evidence before I acknowledge that I have been wrong or that a certain course of action is the best one. I also establish very low confidence thresholds for what I want to be true, and what I want to be true is that which is most congenial to what it is I want, which is inordinately directed to the self.[90] In this way, character shapes the intellect; it can darken the mind or permit the mind the freedom it needs to pursue what is true.

To sum up my main point, a failure to restrain the emotions of the pleasure appetite, whether that is sexual pleasure, or the pleasure of food and drink, or the pleasures of an easy life, etc., brings about a disorder that extends beyond the concupiscible appetites to include the irascible emotions, the will, as well as the intellect, analogous to Burley's insight that when "a false contingent proposition is posited, one can prove any false proposition that is compatible with it". To introduce vice into one's life, no matter how small, and making peace with that vice, begins a slow process of moral unraveling—other vices

---

[90] See Arie W. Kruglanski. *The Psychology of Closed Mindedness.* New York, Taylor & Francis Books, 2004. See also Alfred Mele. *Self-Deception Unmasked.* New Jersey: Princeton University Press, 2001.

consistent with it are gradually spawned. That unraveling can be contained, but it will take some energy to bring that moral unraveling to a halt. The price is an underlying conflict of conscience that one must live with for the rest of one's life—and this can be tiring. The only way out of this is not to make peace with that vice, to renounce it, that is, moral repentance.

Concluding Thoughts

Moral unravelling (dis-integration) has very real social repercussions. Disordered love of self and a limited ability to restrain one's passions will have obvious economic repercussions; it will affect a person's work ethic, his sense of responsibility, his ability to make sacrifices for the sake of the organization for whom he/she works, his or her ability to be trusted by others, not to mention the obvious social consequences, such as the stability of a person's marriage, and the emotional life of the children should that marriage fall apart, which in turn has very costly social and economic consequences impossible to trace in all their details.

That is why belittling the serious treatment of specific areas of ethics, such as sexual ethics—derisively designated as "pelvic morality" by many social justice advocates—is misleading and not true to the facts. There is no doubt that there are more serious and pressing moral matters than certain issues of sexual ethics, and sometimes it is more prudent to focus at the moment on moral battles that can be won and use the time and resources at our disposal to carefully lay down the conditions that will permit a victory in the distant future. And indeed, corruption in high places is very serious, far more serious than a 14-year-old adolescent boy tempted to masturbate or two teenagers fornicating in the backseat of a car. There is, however, no such thing as merely "pelvic" immorality. Sexual emotions involve every other faculty of the human person and affect persons as a whole. To be unconcerned with sexual morality for the sake of more important moral issues is to overlook the unified moral fabric of the human person and the systemic nature of truth, that is, the single and coherent set of cognitive moral data.

It is always difficult to provide a sufficient explanation for certain contemporary social phenomena, such as the difficulty entrepreneurs currently experience filling job openings that demand a rigorous work ethic, reliability, a sense of justice, common sense, and prudence, etc., but it is more difficult to believe that the moral permissiveness of the past 50 years has nothing to do with many of these social difficulties we are facing with today's generation of young people. The focus of political reform has typically been limited to the level of the political system, but political organizations are made up of individual persons, and evil exists on the level of the system only because evil principally exists on the level of the person, who is a moral system in himself. Genuine political reform cannot neglect this primary level if we expect to make any social progress.

95 Is a Developmentally Disabled Child Inferior to a Non-disabled Child?

In studying the hierarchy of material substances in the material universe and the various powers (faculties or potentialities that inhere in the substantial form) of living substances, the question always arises: "Are developmentally disabled children inferior to the non-disabled?" The question arises because the criterion for determining whether a substance is superior to another lies in a thing's powers; animals have more powers (potentialities to activity) than a plant, which only has the three powers of growth, reproduction, and nutrition. An animal has all these as well as the powers of sensation (external, internal, and sense appetite, and locomotion). Man is superior to animal in that he has all the powers of the levels below him, but more, namely, intellect and will.

A disabled child, however, lacks certain powers that a non-disabled child has, such as the ability to see (blindness), or the ability to walk, or reason at a normal level, etc. Can we not conclude that the non-disabled are superior to the disabled?

The answer is, no, we cannot. There are two kinds of superiority corresponding to the two modes of being, namely substantial and accidental.[91] We can distinguish between essential superiority and accidental superiority. Man is essentially superior to brute, and animals are essentially superior to plants, etc. We can even discern a hierarchy within the hierarchy of animals. For example, a horse is superior to a worm, etc. But there is no specific hierarchy within the human level, that is, there are no various species of man as there are species of animal, or species of plant life. All human persons are essentially equal, but we are not all accidentally equal. Consider the accident of quality, which is divided into affective qualities, habit/disposition, abilities, and

---

[91] I am referring to Aristotle's ten categories of being. The primary mode of being is substance; beings exist primarily as substance. But there are secondary modes of being that exist in substance, namely quantity, quality, relation, where, when, activity, passivity, posture, and environment.

figure. Each of us has certain intellectual and physical dispositions; some are disposed to be better athletes (i.e., faster runners, better swimmers, etc.); some are intellectually disposed, for example, to the mathematical, or the historical, or the political, etc. Some people achieve high marks in the sciences, but very low marks in the humanities, and vice versa. We are not all equal, at least not accidentally. But we are all essentially equal.

A disabled child is still a human person. A child born blind still has the faculty of sight, but that potentiality cannot be realized by virtue of some kind of damage to the organ of the sense of sight (i.e., eye or optic nerve). An intellectually disabled child still has an intellect that is capable of intellectual abstraction, judgment and reasoning, but these activities are seriously impaired as a result of brain damage—this is not to suggest that the mind is the brain, only that the mind depends on the brain which produces phantasms.

We do not say that a child is disabled because it does not have wings, nor do we insist that a dog is disabled because it cannot reason. It does not **belong to the nature of** a human being to have wings, nor does it **belong to the nature of** a dog to have intelligence. But it does belong to the nature of a human being to have the ability to reason, and so if a person cannot reason, he or she suffers from a genuine disability. But it is a **human person** that suffers the disability. It is not the activity itself (second act) that renders one essentially superior; rather, it is the nature of the being (first act) that renders one essentially superior, for it is first act that determines the substance to be the kind of thing it is. Its activity only follows upon that first act.

The increasingly popular viewpoint that the lives of disabled children are of less value (the quality of life mentality) than the lives of healthy children is rooted in a failure to distinguish between first and second act. **You are not your activity.** You are not living (first act) because you are breathing (second act or activity); rather, you are breathing (second act or activity) because you are alive (first act). In the same way, you are not a person because you are thinking; rather, you are thinking (second act) because you are a person (first act). A bird that cannot fly because its wings have been clipped or because it is physically deformed in some way is still a bird (first act). So too, the severely disabled child is still a human person and has more value than the healthiest and most useful and productive animal; for animals exist to serve the needs of man, but man exists for his own sake. The developmentally disabled are among us to provide us with the opportunity to learn to love human beings not for what they might do for us, but for their own sake. When we have finally learned to love others for their own sake, not for the sake of their usefulness and productivity, only then have we become the persons we are meant to be. A culture like ours that increasingly neglects or destroys its most vulnerable (abortion and infanticide) and values only the useful is one that increasingly resembles the pre-civilized and barbaric. Although we have progressed technologically, there is plenty of evidence that we have digressed morally.

96 *Some Thoughts on Knowing Others and Being Known*

After giving a retreat talk that included the story of my hitchhiking adventure to the United States back in 1979, a woman whom I have known for years said to me: "I feel I know you now". I was surprised, but it did get me thinking about a fact that is so mundane that we are no longer explicitly aware of it. We see human beings around us all the time and for the most part they are "nonentities", insignificant, just a number among a myriad of other human "nonentities". Their relative insignificance corresponds to the degree to which we lack knowledge of their personal history; they are insignificant to us because we don't know all that led up and went in to constituting the human being who stands before us in line for a coffee, or to make a withdrawal, etc. All we see is the current moment at the end of this person's long history, which is a rich narrative we know virtually nothing about.

But that doesn't stop us from constructing our own narrative on the basis of the scanty evidence before us, i.e., a piercing, a tattoo, his or her countenance, clothing, accent, tone of voice, etc. The narrative we construct may coincide with the truth of who he or she is in some respects, but our narrative is always so much thinner in comparison to the reality of this relatively unknown person before us.

Very often, after discovering something about our personal history, people will say things like "Wow, I never knew that about you; I am shocked, I never would have imagined...I see you differently now...etc." Such reactions only reveal that they had us all packaged up and figured out in their own minds. They believed the narrative which they were not even aware they weaved. In their minds, what they imagined and the inferences they made were, for all intents and purposes, "all there was to know about us". Their narrative construction was based on whatever evidence was available, and they ignored the possibility that unavailable evidence is much like the iceberg underneath the water, which is a world of evidence containing clues that would disconfirm many aspects of the narrative we constructed to explain or make sense of the person before us.

The narratives we construct are often little more than a collection of inferences rooted in our own limited experience of others. It is natural to construct them, but it is epistemically arrogant to treat them with a high level of confidence; and yet this is precisely what people do. We should, on the contrary, make every effort to cultivate a healthy skepticism in the face of those inferences and an attitude of openness to reform. The human person is always more than what we believe him to be on the basis of narrative construction, and he is forever more than "what" we can know about him scientifically (because essence and existence are really distinct). When we stand before a human being, we are before a mystery, and we must approach that mystery with great reverence.

The fundamental need of every human being is the need to be known, that is, to be understood. That's another way of saying that our most fundamental need is to be loved; for if we are not loved, we are not understood. The need to know another and be known by others is a need to love and be loved. At the root of all moral disorder and deprivation is precisely this desire to be known, a desire which is typically disordered, which is why one is led into moral disorder.

The world we live in is one that perpetuates this interpersonal alienation, because we have become indifferent to knowing others and to the mystery that is before us in the stranger; others are a collection of nonentities, and we are aware that we are nonentities to others. The rich history behind each person, if known, would render each one far more significant and alive to us than he or she typically is; they would not be a collection of nonentities any more than the face of a brother or a long lost friend in a large crowd would be just another face. Moral depravity is fundamentally an attempt to recover what has been lost—I do not mean to suggest, however, that those who do evil are fundamentally blameless.

We have a fundamental need to establish an identity, and that need, which is good, is at the root of pride; for pride is a disordered love of one's own excellence. It is fundamentally, however, a desire for uniqueness. The fact of the matter is that we are unique, we do have an identity, and that identity is discovered—as is the nature of all things—in our origin, the principle through which we came to be. In other words, our identity is discovered in the Word through whom we came into existence (Jn 1, 1ff).

The more we know the *Logos*, the Word through whom all things came to be and who became flesh (Jn 1, 14), the more we discover our unique identity. Outside of that, we will desperately seek to establish an identity by distinguishing ourselves from others, separating ourselves, rejecting what others are and what they have to say and offer, all in favor of what we are and have to say and offer. The prideful do not want to know what will ultimately reveal their limitations; for they are not yet secure in the knowledge of who they are, a security that would permit them rest in the knowledge of their own radical limitations. Envy spawns jealousy and slander, which is a longing for a kind of knowledge: the envious delight in knowing the faults of others; that is all they want to know, for they do not want to risk knowing anything that might suggest there is something in the other that is larger and more excellent than what they are able to discover in themselves.

Not only are pride and envy rooted in a longing to know one's own unique identity, that is, a longing to be known, but so too are the sins of the flesh. "I do not know man" says Mary to the angel at the Annunciation. Sexual union is an intimate mutual act of allowing oneself to be known by another. But sexual disorder (i.e., acts of oral sex) is a disordered desire to know and be known.

The problem with excessive love of self, which sins of the flesh intensify, is that they slowly nurture indifference to others, to their sufferings, etc. In other words, sins of the flesh cause charity—which involves an exit of self—to grow cold. Anger as well is rooted in the experience of not being adequately known and loved; for it is a response to an injustice, and for a human being to live in a world indifferent to knowing him and coming to recognize his own unique identity is profoundly unjust. Avarice is a disordered love of possessing, which is the disordered desire to live and remain alive, for what lives is a knower. We want to continue to know and be known.

The desire to know and be known is fundamentally a desire for God. He knows us, for His knowledge causes us 'to be'. All men by nature desire to know, says Aristotle, and that desire is a yearning for Him, who is the First Cause, which is why the pursuit of science is ongoing; it will remain so until we know Him. We also yearn for a happiness that is enduring, complete, and sufficient unto itself; it is the happiness of being known completely and forever, and knowing the one who knows us this way and who thus reveals to us our true identity.

Hell is the prideful rejection of what God knows and an unjust usurpation of what is proper to God; who I am (i.e., my character or moral identity) is determined by me, but I have a moral obligation to determine an identity that is in accordance with what God knows, that is, with what He intends me to be. I do that first, on a fundamental level, by obeying the basic precepts of natural law; for the natural moral law is a participation in the eternal law. Those in darkness demand the right to establish their own identity independently of Him, which is ultimately a desire to be *the* unutterable mystery. But only God is the unutterable mystery; for I am a mystery uttered by the Word, but the Word is uttered by the Father, and the Father is uttered by no one. Moreover, the Word is not uttered by any creature; any utterances within the Trinity are contained within the Trinity. Those who choose Hell desire to be "like that"; yet "that" is impossible.

Those in Hell want what is impossible to achieve, so their will is forever frustrated. They want to be in the position of God; they wish to remain mysterious, inaccessible, elevated above and in a class all their own. That the sun shines on them is a torment to them, that is, that God knows them through and through, is a torment, even though it is that knowledge that causes and perpetuates their existence. They desire to be known on their terms; they have rejected their creaturely status and do so perpetually.

The aim of the spiritual life, its purpose, is to know ourselves in the Word: to know how much we are loved. When we finally know that we are loved, when we know ourselves as we are known, that is, when we are given the new name that we alone will know (Rev 2, 17), then we will be at rest. As we progress in the spiritual life, the restless desire for our own identity decreases, for we discover it as we choose in accordance with his will.

Love, however, does not do away with all desire, only restless desire. The more we know that we are known, the more we desire to love others, to know them, to communicate to them their loveableness, to help them on towards their origin. That love too is the root of the suffering of the second beatitude: "Blessed are those who mourn". We want what others want for themselves, but often people do not understand who they are or what it is they truly want—that is our default position. Human beings are very complicated, and there are innumerable stages persons have to go through, and thus many delusions that have to be shattered, and that does not come to an end in this life for those well along the road of the spiritual life. They continue to climb, but they remain among us with patience, and pray and suffer with us, and are there when we need them, all the while rejoicing in the ever expanding ignorance brought about by their ever increasing intimacy with the Word that is their origin.

97 Is Beauty in the Eye of the Beholder?

Aquinas defines the beautiful as that which, being seen, pleases (*id quod visum placet*); hence, why we are not inclined to describe a work of art as beautiful if it fails to please us. So how can a work of art that fails to please be genuinely beautiful? Does Aquinas support the post-modern dictum that "Beauty is in the eye of the beholder"? It might seem so, but I don't believe this is entirely the case. Allow me to explain.

No one can deny that beauty is in the eye of the beholder, or that 'pleases when seen' is part of the very meaning of the beautiful. But we need to ask: "What causes the pleasing in the first place?" The answer is a work of art that is of a certain quality. Without that quality or set of qualities, the work would not please, and would not likely be described as beautiful.

There is no doubt that a genuinely beautiful work of art may leave a person unaffected, but that might not necessarily mean that the work lacks beauty, any more than blindness in a person implies that things have no color, or that imbecility implies that things have no intelligible structure. It is entirely possible that something in the observer is lacking, a quality or combination of qualities that enables him to discern the beauty in the object he beholds. What those qualities are is not easy to determine.

Allow me to consider some basic observations about human beings and their reaction to things in the world. Most people do not stop to behold the beauty and charm of worms on a wet road, but they will often slow down to view horses in a meadow. Moreover, flowers tend to evoke a deeper emotional reaction than say a bag of freshly mown grass, which is why people bring their loved ones flowers instead of weeds.

As we move up the scale of the hierarchy of being, things exhibit greater complexity. A flower is more complex than a stone, a rabbit is more complex than a flower, and a child is more complex than all of them. The very idea of complexity implies a plurality of some kind; so too does the idea of harmony, which is an ordered state of things or a thing's properties—for there is no vocal harmony without a number of voices.

The greater the multiplicity or complexity of parts, the greater is the potential for a much more complex and richer harmony. Two shades of red, for example, do not have the same potential for harmony as does the entire color spectrum, nor do two notes on a keyboard have the same potential as does the entire piano. Beauty has something to do with the harmony that we behold in things. As Catholic philosopher Jacques Maritain points out: "If beauty delights the mind, it is because beauty is essentially a certain excellence or perfection in the proportion of things to the mind."[92] That is why Aquinas assigns three conditions to beauty, namely, integrity, proportion, and radiance (clarity).

Integrity refers to an integration of parts. It implies completeness or fullness of being. All things desire to be most fully, to be all that they can be and for as long as they can be; thus, "goodness" means fullness of being. A good life is a complete life; a good meal is a complete meal, etc. No one of sound mind would delight in the news that one's newborn baby is missing an arm or a leg, for we know the child desires to be most fully, and we want what is best for the child, which is why good parents will do all they can to alleviate the deficiency. The mind delights in fullness of being, which is why integrity pleases.

Proportion refers to order and unity. The intellect is not pleased with disorder, but it is pleased with unity for the same reason that it is pleased with integrity; for "oneness", like "goodness", is a property of being. The more fully a thing is, the more unified and ordered it is.

Finally, the intellect is pleased with radiance or clarity. Radiance refers to intellectual light, or meaning. The object of the intellect is the intelligible. The greater the intelligibility, the greater is the delight of the mind. Stories are more pleasing than a display of fireworks, because

---

[92] Jacques Maritain, *Art and Scholasticism With Other Essays*. Trans. J. F. Scanlan. Kessinger Publishing. 20. See also *Art and Scholasticism*. Trans. Joseph W. Evans. Retrieved from http://www3.nd.edu/Departments/Maritain/etext/art5.htm. Chapter V.

stories have more meaning; for the pleasure involved in a fireworks display is short lived and merely sentient, but a good story is remembered for a long time, tweaks one's sense of wonder, warms the heart, teaches eternal truths, etc.

Returning to our earlier example, a horse has more integrity, proportion and radiance than does a worm; for it has more being. Hence we tend to find horses more beautiful than worms, a flower more beautiful than a blade of grass, etc.

Beauty in the Work

But what makes a work of art beautiful? I believe that it is a mistake—a common one—to assume that beauty in things and artistic beauty mean exactly the same thing. This misconception leads people to conclude that the better the art, the more realistically will it represent the object of the work. But a painting, for example, is not the same kind of thing as a scene or a thing outside the mind; beauty in the work is very different. In other words, the conditions of integrity, proportion and radiance exist differently in the painting than they do in things outside the mind.

A work of art is an expression of something in the artist, and so it says something of the artist himself as well as something of the world outside him. We see the world *as he sees* the world. What is most important with regard to beautiful works of art is precisely this vision of the artist.

A good artist is one who sees more than the ordinary man. For him, what he beholds overflows with meaning (radiance). The world "speaks" to him, it utters a word to him, and if he has the technical wherewithal, he is able to communicate what he sees to others through what he makes (a poem, a sculpture, a building, a painting). Often he is unsuccessful, because he is unskilled, and so he practices. Eventually, with enough practice, he can produce a work that corresponds to what he knows or sees. He can communicate the rich and superabundant radiance he apprehends in beholding the world around him and in so doing awakens others to a depth of reality of which they were, up to that time, unaware. Hence, a good artist teaches others to see the beautiful.

A beautiful work of art is complete (integrity) in what it communicates to us, but what it communicates is a vision that is penetrating, that reaches to the meaning or radiance in which things super abound. That is why we find good paintings more beautiful than ordinary photographs. A picture—I do not refer here to the art of photography—simply communicates what is there on the surface. But a painting communicates what is not always explicitly apprehended, but intuitively grasped by others and often unconsciously known (radiance). A good painting exposes a world, a history, it is vibrant with activity; it can disclose suffering, or joy, or both, and it can express something about what life means for some at its profoundest level. It does this in a way that is tight and orderly (proportion).

Appreciating the Beautiful

In order to be beautiful, therefore, it is not necessary that a work of art, for example a painting, correspond exactly and realistically to the object seen. Realistic art is not always and necessarily the most beautiful art. Rather, it is necessary that the work correspond to what the artist—who is a poet to be sure—sees when he sees the world, i.e., the shoes, or the landscape, the people, etc. It is a poor work to the degree that it falls short of that intuitive gaze.

In order for the beholder to discern the beauty in the work, that is, to find the work pleasing to his intelligence, it is necessary first that he be intelligent—brute animals do not delight in man's art. Also, he must be someone who has lived and suffered; he must be, to some degree, a contemplative. Unless he is able to see what the artist sees, he will fail to recognize anything of significance in the work. And so it is possible for a relatively inexperienced and superficial human being to take greater pleasure in a work of lesser quality (beauty) than in a genuine masterpiece.

Consider the expert who judges a figure skating or gymnastics competition. For many of us, all the competitors appear equally proficient, and we might struggle to determine who the better athletes are. But the expert skater or gymnast who is in the position of judge has no difficulty, for he readily sees defects in the performance that the untrained overlook. The more we become involved in the sport, however, the better able we are to see what we could not see earlier. The same is true for the arts. The expert guitarist knows what good guitar playing sounds like, just as the gifted composer knows the difference between a symphony that is little more than a "cheap imitation" of a Mozart and one that is brilliantly and masterfully composed.

There is, however, no simple formula by which a person might determine whether or not a particular work of art is truly beautiful; but since art aims to express the beauty that the artist apprehends in the world around him, to appreciate the genuinely beautiful requires not only a certain level of intelligence and a contemplative disposition, but as well--I would argue--a certain level of moral character, the kind of moral character that makes it possible to appreciate the moral radiance behind a face, a circumstance, or natural scenery, etc. As Aristotle knew, one sees according to one's character; when he said this, Aristotle was not referring to works of art. Nevertheless, the kind of relationship a person establishes between himself and God, who is the Supremely Beautiful, will certainly affect his or her ability to see His "fingerprints", so to speak, upon all that He has touched.

To sum up, it is not enough to say that beauty is in the eye of the beholder. Beauty is first and foremost in things. It is in the work if the artist has the poetic intuition to see the wealth of meaning in things and if he has the technical wherewithal to express what he sees. The beauty in the work of art is beheld and appreciated if the beholder is intelligent, and has lived enough, suffered enough, and is contemplative enough to see what the poet has come to see and made visible in his work.

98 *Thoughts on Artistic Beauty*

In the summer of 2014, I visited the National Gallery of Modern Art in Rome (Galleria Nazionale d'Arte Moderna), and I certainly did enjoy the 19th century Italian art. I do recall not enjoying the most contemporary art in the museum. I saw a work that was part graffiti, and I found it very uncomfortable to look at. But what does that mean? What does that say about the work itself? All I can gather from this experience at this point in time is that the work makes me feel uncomfortable. I think it would be arrogant of me to use that experience as the criterion to judge the work as deficient. Perhaps if I'd spent a few years in the Bronx working among the poor and the dispossessed, surrounded by graffiti, and having come to learn something about those who spray paint graffiti, their reasons for doing so, what it means to them, etc., my experience would be something else entirely. I have no idea whether or not this is true; I hesitate, however, to make myself the measure of what counts as beautiful art. Indeed, I do not like Baroque paintings; nor do I like neo-classical art; I do like iconography, Impressionism, Franz Marc, a great deal of abstract art, etc., but I don't exactly know why, except to say "because they are beautiful".

On a very abstract level at least, we can begin with the principle that beauty is a property of being. Whatever "is", is beautiful insofar as it is—just as whatever "is", is one, true, and good to the degree that it exists (the more fully a thing is, the more good and beautiful it is). What this means in the context of a work of art is very difficult to determine. Vivian Maier captured beautiful moments with her camera. She captured what "is", but she did so with skill. It requires skill to capture the beautiful, but prior to that, one must be able to see it, to recognize it. Just as one has to be good to recognize the good (i.e., a just man recognizes immediately the just course of action whereas an unjust man misses it), I would argue that connatural knowledge is also involved in the recognition of beautiful art (i.e., the more one excels in an art, the easier it is to distinguish between a great work and one that is not so great). But having said that, there is still much that is left unexplained. What does it mean to recognize beauty? Why is Vivian Maier's picture of a very poor and dishevelled man on the street with a slight smile so beautiful? Why do I see beauty in a particular patient of mine who suffers from clinical depression, and who stands there beside my car, unshaven, overweight, and happy to be heading off to Mass? This patient, his life, his suffering, his gentleness, his understanding of mental illness, his fragility, the scars he carries, etc., all this 'is', and there is a beauty that I can discern, but it is certainly not discernable to everyone. I would imagine that a good photographer, like Vivian Maier or Diane Arbus, would see it, and of course they would have the skill to capture it.

And so I think it is safe to say that a necessary condition of a good artist is the ability to see. Certain *epistemic conditions* are necessary in order to appreciate great art (whatever that is) and in order to actually produce great works of art, because art begins with seeing. The artist sees, and from that vision arises a desire to capture it, to communicate it, and in doing so, he teaches others to see. As Diane Arbus said: "I really believe there are things nobody would see if I didn't photograph them".[93]

But Diane Arbus also said: "A photograph is a secret about a secret. The more it tells you the less you know."[94] Can one say the same thing about any good work of art? Is a painting also a secret about a secret? And is it part of the beauty of a work that the more it tells you, the less you know? The work tells you a secret, and it continues to tell you something, and it's as if the work draws you into an ever expanding frontier of ignorance. This is what physicist Richard Feynman said about science (an ever expanding frontier of ignorance), and many scientists speak of the beauty of science, mathematics, and the cosmos. In other words, they see truth as beautiful. That science is an ever expanding frontier of ignorance is part of the reason the scientist experiences the scientific process as exhilarating and beautiful,

---

[93] Diane Arbus, *Diane Arbus: An Aperture Monograph.* New York: Aperture, 1972. 15.
[94] William Todd Schultz. *An Emergency in Slow Motion.* New York: Bloomsbury, 2011. Chapter 1: "Essential Mysteries" [Kobo version]. Retrieved from http://www.kobo.com.

for the universe is overwhelming, it possesses an intelligibility that is larger than a single individual or community of individuals.

I would not reduce art to pure subjectivity, as if to say that beauty is merely in the eye of the beholder. There are some people who find neo-classical art or art from the baroque period pleasing. Who am I to say that they are superficial? And yet I must admit that I believe that to be the case. Am I right? Or is this a kind of arrogance? Our taste changes, and it changes as we grow in knowledge and experience, that is, as certain epistemic conditions are gradually put in place. That is what leads me to believe that beauty is not merely in the eye of the beholder, that it is also in the work—it is just that certain conditions are now in place that enable me to appreciate the work. So, could it be the case that the very fact that I find certain works displeasing today is simply the result of my lacking certain epistemic conditions? Perhaps that is the case, but how is it possible to know this in advance? It seems to me that I would only know this the moment those conditions are in place, that is, the moment my eyes have been opened. Thus, can I ever be sure that my artistic judgment that a work falls short is reliable? Very often it is a mental prejudice that keeps me from enjoying a work. But when we love someone, we allow ourselves to see the world from his/her point of view; we try to understand those we love. We are willing to allow our mental prejudices to dissipate, and the result is our world is enlarged significantly. Perhaps our range of appreciation for art is so narrow because we simply don't love enough.

99 *Natural Ways of Knowing About God*

I have always agreed that the existence of God can be demonstrated by reasoning on the basis of the real distinction between essence and existence. The argument can be expressed succinctly, as Aquinas does in a number of places.[95] Once a person gets a handle on this distinction, the rest of the argument can be understood quite readily. Knowing "what a thing is" (essence) does not tell me whether or not it exists; the apprehension of the existence of a being is the result of a distinct act of the intellect (existential judgment), distinct from the apprehension of a thing's essence or nature (what it is). The essence can exist in my mind (i.e., as a concept), or outside my mind as a single existent. Knowing "what a cat is", for example, does not tell me whether cats actually exist; they might have been extinct for centuries now, and all my knowledge of "what they are" comes from books. But a real existing cat in front of me is a *habens esse*, which is

---

[95] "Whatever belongs to a thing is either caused by the principles of its nature (as the capacity for laughter in man) or comes to it from an extrinsic principle (as light in the air from the influence of the sun). Now being itself cannot be caused by the form or quiddity of a thing (by 'caused' I mean by an efficient cause), because that thing would then be its own cause and it would bring itself into being, which is impossible. It follows that everything whose being is distinct from its nature must have being from another. And because everything that exists through another is reduced to that which exists through itself as to its first cause, there must be a reality that is the cause of being for all other things, because it is pure being. If this were not so, we would go on to infinity in causes, for everything that is not pure being has a cause of its being, as has been said. It is evident, then, that an intelligence is form and being, and that it holds its being from the first being, which is being in all its purity; and this is the first cause, or God." Thomas Aquinas, *On Being and Essence*. Toronto: Pontifical Institute of Mediaeval Studies, 1968. 56-57. The most important line here is "And because everything that exists through another is reduced to that which exists through itself as to its first cause, there must be a reality that is the cause of being for all other things, because it is pure being". Recall chapter 8, "Is Everything Relative?" The point was made that if something is relative, it can only be relative against the backdrop of that which is not relative, or absolute. If everything were relative, we'd have an infinite series of relatives, and that would mean that I would never achieve a definitive understanding of anything that is relative, such as the statement "John is tall"; for I can only understand that "in relation to" something other than John. If that something other is relative, then I can only understand it in relation to something other than it, etc. Eventually I have to come to an end, to something that is understood "in itself", otherwise, the series of relatives goes on to infinity. That would mean that in order to understand that "John is tall", I would have to understand an indefinite number of factors. Indefinite means 'without end'. The same principle is in play here: "...everything that exists through another is reduced to that which exists through itself as to its first cause".

Latin for "that which **has** an act of existing". Existence does not belong to its essence or nature. In other words, the act of existing is not a predicate. [96] The act of existing does not add anything to the nature of a thing; rather, it is a being's act. Without the act of existing, there is nothing.

Let's consider this from another angle. Whatever belongs to the essence of thing belongs to it necessarily, thus if existence belongs to the essence of this cat in front of me, then this cat necessarily exists and cannot not exist. If it cannot not exist, it existed always and will always exist. But that is clearly not the case. The cat has a received act of existing, as you and I do. Thus, you and I as well as that cat are contingent beings; you are not a necessary being, neither am I, nor is this cat. In other words, existence belongs to us contingently— contingent upon receiving an act of existing.

The question at this point is: "What is the efficient cause of the received act of existing of a contingent being (a being whose essence is distinct from its own act of existing)"? There are only three logically possible options: 1) the contingent being is the cause of its own act of existing; 2) a contingent being other than itself is the cause of its act of existing; 3) or a non-contingent being (whatever that might be) is the efficient cause of its act of existing. The first option is impossible; for nothing can bring itself into being; for it would have to exist before it exists, which is simply absurd (a being cannot give what it does not have). The second alternative, we would argue, is also impossible, because a being can only act within the limited powers of its nature; for example, plants can grow, but they cannot sense; animals can sense, but

---

[96] "If we simply say *that* a certain thing *is,* the judgment in question is a judgment of existence, and it is a perfectly correct one: it is complete without any other term requiring to be understood, with only one term and a verb, that is, the subject and the verb *is*.... Existential propositions, which deal with nothing else than actual existence, are no fitting objects of consideration for the logician. They raise no formal problems, because they do not deal with forms, but with existence, which itself is the act of all forms....Existential judgments are meaningless unless they are meant to be true. If the proposition, "Peter is," means anything, it means that a certain man, Peter by name, actually is, or exists. *Is* does not predicate anything, not even existence; it posits it, and such a proposition has no business to be quoted in formal logic, except as an example of a whole class of propositions which are not the business of the logician." Etienne Gilson, *Being and Some Philosophers*. Toronto: Pontifical Institute of Mediaeval Studies, 1952, 2nd edition. 201.

they cannot do calculus, etc. The act of existing, however, is not within nor is a part of the nature of any contingent being, but is distinct from its nature (outside its nature)—otherwise it would be a non-contingent or necessary being. That is why contingent beings can only produce (bring something into being from something already existing), but they cannot impart the act of existing (bring something into being from nothing). The only alternative left is that the efficient cause of a being's act of existing is a non-contingent being, which is a being whose nature is to exist—it is within its power to impart the act of being, because it is its own Act of Being. A non-contingent being is a being that cannot not exist, because its essence is identical to its existence. It does not have existence; it is its existence (*Ipsum Esse Subsistens*, or Subsistent Being Itself). The *evidence for* the existence of Subsistent Being Itself is the continued existence of contingent beings.

Without a non-contingent being, it follows that everything that is, is contingent. In other words, the sufficient reason for each being's existence is not within it; existence does not belong to it necessarily. If everything that is, is contingent, then the entire order of reality is contingent, because the entire order of reality is nothing but the sum of the parts that constitute it, which are the beings that make it up. To be contingent is to "depend upon something other than itself", but if the entire order of reality depends *upon nothing*, then the entire order of reality is independent; thus, it is both dependent—because it is nothing other than the sum of its dependent parts—and independent at the same time and in the same respect. This, of course, is contradictory. If the entire order of reality considered as a whole is independent, then it must be something more than the sum of its parts, or something other than the sum of its parts. In other words, it is a reality that is "necessary". But an "is" that is necessary is just what atheism denies.

After getting to this point with my students—which usually takes about four days—, I would often say to myself: "This was a rather long way around the barn. Why not just start with the idea of a necessary being, a being that cannot not exist? Since it cannot not exist, then it exists". That, however, would constitute a kind of ontological argument, the first one of which was made famous by St. Anselm: "God is that greater than which nothing can be thought; hence, God exists".[97] Since I was taught that the ontological argument was unsound, I didn't bother to pursue it, that is, until I read Graeme Hunter's defense of Leibniz's very succinct version of the ontological argument.[98] The more I thought about it, the more I became convinced of its soundness, which begins with the idea of a necessary being and proceeds to conclude that it exists, as is typical of an ontological argument. I call this the shortest proof of the existence of God.

---

[97] St. Anselm writes: "Assuredly, this being exists so truly [really] that it cannot even be thought not to exist. For there can be thought to exist something whose non-existence is inconceivable; and this thing is greater than anything whose non-existence is conceivable. Therefore, if that than which a greater cannot be thought could be thought not to exist, then that than which a greater cannot be thought would not be that than which a greater cannot be thought – a contradiction. Hence, something than which a greater cannot be thought exists so truly [really] that it cannot even be thought not to exist." *Proslogion*, ch. 3, in *Anselm of Canterbury*, trans. Jasper Hopkins and Herbert W. Richardson. Vol 1. Toronto: The Edwin Mellen Press, 1974. 94.

[98] Graeme Hunter, *Pascal the Philosopher*. Toronto: University of Toronto Press, 2013. See Chapter 1, "Against Philosophy". [Kobo version]. Retrieved from http://www.kobo.com.

100 The Shortest Proof for the Existence of God

The shortest proof for the existence of God is the following: **If a necessary being is possible, then it exists** (Gottfried Wilhelm Leibniz, 1646 – 1716).

A Possible Explanation

If we were to write the logical form of this kind of statement using the symbols of modal logic (modal operators), it would look like this:

$$\Diamond\Box p \rightarrow \Box p$$

$\Diamond$ 'it is possibly the case that…'
$\Box$ 'it is necessarily the case that…'
p is an assertion, i.e., it is raining outside.
$\rightarrow$ if…, then…

This is translated as: **'If it is possibly the case that ($\Diamond$) it is necessarily the case that ($\Box$) it is raining outside (p), then it is necessarily the case that ($\Box$) it is raining outside (p).'**

And of course, that is true, provided we don't restrict the meaning of necessity and possibility. Another way of looking at this is the following: **If it is the case that it is raining outside, then it is necessarily the case that it is raining outside *as long as it is raining outside.*** Thus, denying the proposition by asserting **it is not raining outside** would necessarily be false. Hence, it is necessarily raining outside, *as long as it is raining outside.*

Moreover, given that it is raining outside, the assertion "it is possibly the case that it is raining outside"—made by someone who has spent the day inside a room without windows—, is true. In other words, *necessity implies possibility.*

The converse, however, is not true: *if it is possibly the case that it is raining outside,* it does not follow that it is necessarily the case that it is raining outside. Thus, possibility **does not** imply necessity. However, **possibility is precisely an openness to necessity, that is, has a reference to necessity**.

Now let's define our terms: **necessity and contingency, or necessary and contingent.**

> **Necessary**: *cannot not be*. I.e., a triangle **cannot not** have three sides; it is necessarily three sided. A man **cannot not** be rational; he is necessarily rational (note: he may act irrationally, but only a rational being can act irrationally).

> **Contingent:** may or may not be (possibly so), I.e., a triangle may or may not be yellow, or may or may not have 6 inch sides, etc. A man may or may not be blond, tall, blue eyed; or today may or may not involve rain; tomorrow may or may not be a snow day, etc.

The question is whether **existence is contingent or necessary**. Does existence belong to you necessarily or contingently? We can answer that by considering the following: **If existence belongs to you necessarily, then you cannot not exist. If you cannot not exist, you always existed and will forever exist. You would be a necessary being (a being that exists necessarily).**

You and I, of course, did not always exist, but began to exist, and we will cease to exist (leaving aside the question of the immortality of the soul). So, consider the following proposition:

> **If a contingent being is possible (i.e., your future baby, or a pet cat), it necessarily exists.**

Clearly, this is false; *possibility does not imply necessity.*

Consider as well the following:

If a square circle is possible, then it exists.

The problem here is in the antecedent (the 'if' clause): a square circle is not possible; the idea is contradictory (it is a logical contradiction, so it cannot be realized). In other words, square and circle cannot co-exist in one and the same plane figure; for if it is circular, it does not have right angles, and if it is square, it does not have a boundary consisting of points equidistant from a fixed point.

Now consider Leibniz's proof:

If a necessary being is possible, then it exists.

A necessary being is possible, for necessity logically implies possibility, but not vice versa (i.e., $\lozenge\square p \rightarrow \square p$): If it is possibly the case that it is necessarily the case that **this being is** (p), then it is necessarily the case that **this being is**. If a necessary being is not possible, that is, if it is logically contradictory, then it does not exist (just as a square circle is not possible). But a necessary being is not logically contradictory, for necessity implies possibility, and possibility is an openness to necessity (in other words, the two concepts are not incompatible). A necessary being is a being that cannot not exist. It is possible, therefore, it exists necessarily.

Concluding thoughts

This is not to suggest that we possess an innate and *a priori* knowledge of God (knowledge prior to experience). Our knowledge in general begins with real contingent beings: "Nothing is in the intellect that is not first in the senses". It is not the idea of Subsistent Being Itself that is first in our knowledge, but the apprehension, through existential judgment, of real contingent beings; I apprehend that things are, and I gradually apprehend "what they are" with increasing precision. What the above argument might suggest, rather, is that it is easier to prove the existence of God than it is to prove anything else, because the existence of God can be proven by a consideration of the idea alone of a necessary being.[99] The argument may not compel, but a sound argument is not the same thing as a compelling argument.

---

[99] Graeme Hunter pointed out to me that if we read Kant's famous criticism of the ontological argument with a knowledge of S4 and S5, we will see that he has an S4 concept of modality and that his critique is a consequence of it.

101 *A Thought on Leibniz's Ontological Argument (LOA)*

It seems to me that those who, from a Thomistic framework, oppose the Leibniz version of the ontological argument (LOA) are claiming that our idea of a necessary being does not prove that there is actually a necessary being, because real being is not implied by the idea of that being. In other words, an idea is a possibility with respect to real being (i.e., my idea of the Saber-tooth tiger is an apprehension, however incomplete, of its essence, and essence and existence are really distinct). And so the argument continues: this idea, i.e., the idea of a necessary being, is a possibility. The "what" of a necessary being may or may not exist.

Firstly, my idea of a Necessary Being (NB) is just that, an idea in my mind; in other words, my idea is not in fact the necessary being. Rather, the idea bears upon (is about) a being that, we are saying, "cannot not" exist (must exist, necessarily exists). We have the idea of a NB, and we don't need to do anything more than consider it to know that it necessarily exists (outside my mind). As long as it is possible, it exists. The reason is that what is possible is a being that is necessary, that is, a being that cannot not exist. Therefore it exists—unless, of course, it is impossible.

Contingent beings (CB), on the other hand, are a different matter. We must have evidence for them, because the idea of a CB (i.e., the Saber-toothed tiger) bears upon a possible being, one that may or may not exist, that does not necessarily exist. Now, does the idea of a NB bear upon a possibility? No, that would involve a contradiction. Consider the following statement: A necessary being that cannot not be may or may not be. Indeed, that is contradictory.

So, it seems to me that to deny LOA is to suggest that: *A necessary being (a being that cannot not exist) may exist or may not exist; and we need more than the idea to know whether or not it exists.*

But that, it seems to me, is a contradictory claim. A necessary being cannot be something that may or may not exist, any more than a circle may or may not be circular.

102 The Necessary Being That Just Won't Go Away

An objection to the ontological argument (OA), in particular
Leibniz's version (If a necessary being is possible, then it exists), is that
one can tag on "necessary" or "being" to the definition of anything,
i.e., an exotic fruit, a unicorn, a Hobbit, etc., and then proceed to
conclude that it necessarily exists, without the need for any empirical
evidence. In other words, theists indeed have a concept of God, but
"necessary being" (a being that cannot not exist) is made part of that
concept, and the conclusion is then drawn that God necessarily exists.
It is convenient, not to mention entirely arbitrary. Moreover, it is a
circular argument, an instance of the fallacy of begging the question
(assuming the point that needs to be proven).

This is an important objection. A possible reply is that tagging
"being" onto a concept essentially reduces it to the necessary being. In
other words, making being a part of a concept, such as an exotic or an
imaginary fruit, utterly transforms the concept into something else
entirely, namely, the necessary being, of which there can only be one.

Consider that whatever belongs to the concept of a thing belongs
to it necessarily. "Rational" belongs necessarily to the concept of man,
and "three-sided" belongs necessarily to the concept of triangle, etc.
Tagging "being" onto a concept indeed renders it necessary, but what
is left of everything else in the definition? Consider the concept of
"dinosaur"; it includes a number of parts, such as "living", "sentient",
"cold-blooded", and "vertebrate", etc. Now these parts of the concept
are not parts of one another. For example, "vertebrate" is not part of
the concept "living"; for if it were, all living things would be
vertebrates—and anything that is not a vertebrate would not be living,
which of course is false. In the same way, "sentient" is not part of the
concept "living"; for if it were, all living things would be sentient; yet
flowers are living but not sentient, etc. "Sentient" is outside the
concept "living", as are "vertebrate" and "cold-blooded".

living/sentient/vertebrate/cold-blooded

In other words, each part of the concept is "outside of" every other part; they are "parts outside of parts". But insert "being" as a part of the concept and something happens:

being/sentient/vertebrate/cold-blooded

All the other parts (sentient, cold-blooded, vertebrate, etc.) are now outside of "being", since all parts are outside of one another. Outside of being, however, is non-being:

Being/non-being/non-being/non-being

Non-being, however, is nothing, and so nothing is outside of the "part" being, which means that being is not a part, but the whole:

Being

The entire concept is reduced to "being itself", and whatever belongs to the concept belongs to it necessarily. Therefore, Being Itself is alone necessary. Tagging "being" onto a concept, such as "dinosaur" does not give us a dinosaur that necessarily exists; rather, it reduces it from "dinosaur" to the necessary being (God).

Finally, if being or existence were part of "vertebrate", "living", "sentient", "cold-blooded", "fruit", "man", etc., then these latter would necessarily exist and could not *not* exist, which is manifestly false. And so being or existence is not part of the concept of anything, but is rather the whole of the necessary being.

There can only be one necessary being for the same reason that being cannot be one part alongside other parts; for if there were two necessary beings, what would distinguish this Being Itself from that Being Itself? It would have to be something that they are not or do not have in common. What are they? They are Being Itself. And since outside of being is non-being, nothing distinguishes them, and so Being Itself is ultimately one, not many.

A contingent being whose concept does not include being or existence can only be known to exist empirically, and not logically, that is, by a consideration of the concept alone. A necessary being, on the other hand, cannot be known empirically (through sensation), but it can be known to exist by a consideration of the concept alone (logically), at least according to advocates of the ontological argument.

103 *The Necessary Being: Some Implications*

Once it has been established that a necessary being exists necessarily, one can begin to draw out some further implications.

1. Is there only one necessary being?

A necessary being (NB) is one that exists necessarily; as a circle cannot not be circular, the NB cannot not be. Consider what would be implied if we were to think of the NB as "being itself". In other words, just as a contingent being (CB) is "what it is", i.e., a man is human, a cat is feline, a dog is canine, etc., a necessary being is also what it is, and it is Being Itself Essentially. If so, could there be more than one of it/them?

The idea "animal" can be divided into "living" and "sentient"; the idea "man" can be divided into "animal" and "rational"; anything that has quantity can be divided into parts. But "being" cannot be divided. The reason is that outside of the idea of being is non-being, which is nothing. If we divide being, we are left with either: a) being and being, which are identical, or b) being and non-being. Non-being, however, is nothing, which means in b) we are left only with being. Thus, it would seem there cannot be two NBs. They would be identical; and nothing would distinguish them. Thus, it would seem that the NB is one, not many.

2. Is the necessary being absolutely first?

The NB cannot not be, thus it always is. Hence, there is nothing prior to it. And since there is only one NB, there is no distinct being that is co-eternal with it.[100] Thus, it would seem that the NB is absolutely first.

---

[100] Christians believe that God the Son is co-eternal with God the Father. To believe that does not contradict what is said here, because the Second Person of the Trinity is not a distinct being from God, but a distinct Person. The Trinity means that God is three Persons in one divine nature.

3. Is the necessary being a-temporal?

Time implies a before and an after, and so it depends on change. To change is to acquire something that was lacking (i.e., a new position, a different color, a different size, etc.), or to lose something that was had. It would seem that the NB cannot change, for outside of being non-being. Hence, it would seem that the NB is a-temporal.

4. Is the necessary being a quantity?

If the NB is one and undivided, and if a quantity is divisible into two, then it would seem that the NB is not a quantity. Thus, it has no parts, and so it is not composed of particles of matter. And if the NB has no quantity, it is not located in any place. It is literally "nowhere".

5. Is the necessary being independent?

The NB is absolutely first, thus it would seem that it is absolutely independent. To depend on something other than oneself implies that there is something outside oneself on which one depends. If we think of the NB as "being itself", and outside of being is non-being or nothing (nothing is prior to it), it would seem that the necessary being is absolutely independent.

6. Is the necessary being infinite?

If the NB is Being Itself, and if outside of being is non-being, then it would seem to follow that there is nothing outside of the NB that limits it. And if the NB is pure Being Itself, then nothing within the NB limits it, unlike a contingent being, whose act of existence is limited by a determinate nature distinct from its unique act of existing.

A Final Thought

Truth is a logical relation; it is the conformity between what is claimed and what actually is. Thus, **truth is being** insofar as it is known (i.e., it is true that the Brooklyn Bridge is real and that I once walked across it).

Good is also a logical relation, it is that which all things desire. If we desire something, we see it as good in some way. All things desire to be and to the fullest extent (i.e., plants grow, animals eat, humans defend themselves, etc.). Thus, "good" is **being as desired**.

Beauty as well seems to be a relation of the same type; for the beautiful is that which, when seen, pleases. What is beautiful is radiant with intelligibility, proportionate, and whole (integrity). **Beauty is being** in all its radiance, proportion, and integrity **as known and delighted in**.

In other words, one, true, good, and beautiful as properties of being, and so whatever is, is one, true, good, and beautiful to the degree that it is. If the necessary being is Being Itself, in the highest degree possible, then it would seem that the necessary being is Truth Itself, as well as Goodness Itself and Beauty Itself without limits.

104 Intuition and Abstraction in Statistics and Metaphysics

There are three degrees of abstraction, and although abstraction tends to impoverish what it is we know, it has the advantage of allowing us a freedom to deduce conclusions that would otherwise be impossible to deduce. The more abstract our reasoning, the more certainty we can expect to enjoy; the less abstract, the richer that knowledge is, but the less certainty we can expect to possess with regard to conclusions. Abstraction offers generality and precision without entirely eliminating areas of uncertainty.

For example, all of us have an intuitive understanding of the central limit theorem—given certain conditions, the mean of a sufficiently large number of independent random variables will be normally distributed, that is, in the form of a bell-shaped distribution or curve. For example, a number of buses filled with students from Father Michael McGivney are on their way to the Art Gallery of Ontario for a field trip. One bus took a wrong turn and is lost somewhere in the city. It is up to you to find that bus and determine, through observation alone and without anyone on the bus communicating a word, whether or not that bus is one of the number that left our school for the Art Gallery. You may very well succeed on a hunch. For example, if the bus holds 45 students and 40 are an equal distribution of Italian, Irish, and Macedonian, you'd probably conclude, immediately and intuitively, that this was not the McGivney bus. Random samples are like the population from which they are taken, and so if this is a truly random sample, it will not deviate far from the composition of the entire school population. Statistics allows us to reduce this intuitive hunch to a precision judgment. The population of McGivney is over 1000 students, and only a small minority of these students are Italian and Irish—let's assume that there are a total of 50 white students in the entire school (probably too high an estimate). What is the likelihood that a bus of 45 McGivney students, randomly assigned to a bus, would average 90% of the white population? Highly unlikely; for only 5% of the school population is white (Italian, Irish, Macedonian), and the rest are a mixture of Indian, Sri Lankan, Filipino, Chinese, Jamaican, etc. 89% of this sample is white (Italian, Irish, Macedonian), and 11% is brown. To calculate our standard error, we use the following formula: $\sqrt{p(1-p)/n}$.

Our sample from the lost bus consists of 89% white students, 11% brown students. Thus, $\sqrt{.89(1-.89)/n} = .046\pm$ or 4.6%. Our standard error is 4.6%±. We know that roughly 68% of the time, we can expect the sample proportion to be within one standard error (above or below the average) of the final result. 95% of the time, we can expect the sample proportion to be within two standard errors of the final result (9%± according to our sample). 99.7% of the time, we can expect the sample proportion to be within three standard errors of the final result (13%± according to our sample). This means that 68 times out of 100, the recovered bus (if it is from McGivney) will be within one standard error of the proportion of the entire school, 95 times out of 100 it will be within two standard errors, and 99.7% of the time it will be within three. Thus, the probability that our sample is two standard errors above or below the mean is 5%, or .05. The probability that our sample is three standard errors above or below the mean is 0.3%, or .003 (p-value < .003). So, the proportion of white students at school, if this sample is a properly representative one, should be at least 84%. A 95% confidence level requires 2 standard errors, which is 9%±. In this case, if this sample was properly drawn, McGivney should be made up of 80% white students. But of course, it is not. Our sample is well over 3 standard errors above the percentage of white students at the school. Thus, it is highly improbable that this sample of students on this bus is from McGivney.

What does this mean? It means that a science (mathematics) that occurs at a higher level of abstraction (the second level of abstraction) allows our hunch, which lacks precision and certitude, to become more precise; thus, it offers us a greater degree of certitude. In many cases, statistics actually corrects our intuition. We might look at a bus and notice 10 white students, while the rest are Indian, Chinese, Sri Lankan, Jamaican, etc., and we might be inclined to conclude that this is probably the McGivney bus. But is it likely that a bus of McGivney students randomly assigned to it would contain 10 white students? Calculating the standard error would provide us with greater precision. It actually turns out that such a sample is more than two standard errors above the proportion of McGivney students that are white. Hence, it is more likely than not that this sample would have come from a school with a higher population of white students (i.e., 20%, rather than 5%). The mathematics does not entirely remove the uncertainty, but it clarifies and determines the range of uncertainty with mathematical precision and certainty.

Metaphysics does much the same kind of thing with regard to our intuitive sense of God. Man has an intuitive and imprecise sense of the existence of God. He knows immediately that 'from nothing comes nothing', and that an indefinite series of causes is indefinitely non-explanatory, and if the effects (the universe) are experienced as intelligible, good, beautiful and unified, then he infers that the cause is intelligent, good, beautiful and one to a super-eminent degree (for the effect cannot be greater than the cause).[101] And so he is moved to discover his origin as much as that is in his power, for he knows that his understanding of himself has everything to do with understanding his origin.

Man also desires happiness, one that is complete, unending, and sufficient unto itself; but everything he finds here is insufficient unto itself, temporary, and incomplete, which is why nothing brings rest to his restlessness. The happiness we find never endures. But how can we desire what we do not know? We cannot. So, on some level (a pre-conscious level), we must know that something sufficient unto itself, eternal and complete, exists, because we desire it, and we cannot desire

---

[101] Maritain writes: "There is...a pre-philosophical, simply natural knowledge of God's existence. It can be described as starting from the primordial intuition of existence, and immediately perceiving that Being-with-nothingness, or things which could possibly not be—my own being, which is liable to death—necessarily presuppose Being-without-nothingness, that is, absolute or self-subsisting Being, which causes and activates all beings. This pre-philosophical knowledge can also be described as a spontaneous application of the principle: no artifact is possible without a maker." *On the Use of Philosophy*. New Jersey: Princeton, 1961. 60.

what we do not know. What we explicitly come to believe answers to these characteristics is often mistaken (some think happiness is found in unending wealth, or pleasure, or fame and honors, etc.). Nonetheless, the preconscious knowledge of something sufficient unto itself, complete and eternal, is still there.

The entire life of aboriginal man is religious in meaning. For him, the entire cosmos is a book that speaks of God. It is simply not true that the Aborigines adored rocks, the sun, the moon, etc., as gods, any more than Catholics adore statues of stone, bread, and wine, etc. Rather, for him these are visible signs and manifestations of the sacred.

Primitive man employs all sorts of symbolism that has natural religious significance, such as the rock, the storm, the sun, the night sky, etc. These are hierophanies (from *hieros*, "sacred" and *phainein,* "to reveal"). The sky (the "heavens") is a symbol and expression of the permanence of God. For example, when we say that we shall go to heaven when we die, it does not mean we are going to the stars; it means we are returning to our Origin, who is unchanging and vast beyond our ability to conceive, like the sky. The storm too is a symbol and manifestation of the power of God, and we see this symbol continued in the Old Testament: "In his majesty he gives the storm its power and breaks off the hailstones. The thunder of his voice makes the earth writhe; before his might the mountains quake. A word from him drives on the south wind, the angry north wind, the hurricane and the storm" (Sirach, 43: 13ff).

The rock has theophanic value, first of all, because of its permanence and power of resistance; human beings come and go, but the rock endures. Because the rock is solid, we can lean on it and it will not give way. We see this symbolism in the New Testament, for Christ is the "rock" on which we are to build our lives, and according to Psalm 18, 2: Yahweh is my "rock". As Danielou writes: "The cosmic religions are essentially the discovery of God through His manifestation in the hierophanies of the universe. This is why they are basically, in their roots, religions of nature. The rhythm of natural life constitutes their fundamental source."[102]

It seems to me that these are very much like intuitive hunches. But a higher level of abstraction enables us to hone those intuitions to greater precision, without eliminating mystery and the cloud of unknowing.

To repeat what I've already said more than once, there is real distinction between "what" something is (essence) and its very "act of existing" (esse). Knowing "what" something is does not tell me "whether or not it is". You are "what" you are, that is, you are human; but the act of existence is possessed (to have). In other words, you *have* existence. A being, as Aquinas points out, is a *habens esse*, or 'that which has an act of existing'. A being is a composite of essence and existence.

Whatever belongs to the essence of a thing belongs to it necessarily. Rationality, for example, belongs to the nature of man, and so if a being is a man, that being is necessarily rational, and if he is necessarily rational, then he cannot **not be** rational. That is why the 'act of existing' does not belong to the essence of a thing (i.e., a dog, a tree, a flower, a man, a carbon atom, etc.). If it did, then that thing would exist necessarily, and thus it could not **not** exist, and thus it would have always existed.

And so the *sufficient reason for* the act of existing of any existing thing is not found within the nature of that thing, but outside it. And since a thing only acts according to the powers of its nature, within the limits of that nature, no being whose essence is really distinct from its act of existing can impart the act of existing upon what simply does not exist. That is why we do not create, but only produce things from already existing matter.

Thus, the sufficient reason for the received act of existing (esse) of a being whose essence is distinct from its existence is a being whose essence is identical to his act of existing, that is, a being who is pure

---

[102] Jean Danielou, S.J. *Introduction to the Great Religions.* Indiana: Fides, 1964. 15-16. See also Mircea Eliade. *Myth and Reality.* Waveland Press, Illinois, 1998.

subsistent existence (Ipsum Esse Subsistens). His nature is to be; thus, He cannot not be, but necessarily is.

The properties of being are 'one', 'true', 'good', and 'beautiful'. Whatever is, is one. And since truth is the conformity between what is in the mind and what is, then being is the measure of the true. If something is, it is true, to the degree that it is. And since all things desire to be most fully, good and being are convertible terms (whatever is, is good to the degree that it is). So too, whatever is, is beautiful to the degree that it is. What exists most fully is most beautiful.

And so if God is Being Itself, then God is One, True, Good, and Beautiful. Whatever has being, has it from God, and so God is the measure of what is and thus the measure of what is true. If God is Being Itself, then God is Goodness Itself, and thus Beauty Itself. Finally, there can only be one being whose essence is to exist; if there were two, something would have to distinguish the two; one would have to possess something that the other does not possess. But both are Being Itself, and outside of being is non-being, or nothing. Hence, nothing would distinguish them, which means there is only one Being Itself, not two, or three, etc.

Furthermore, God (Being Itself) cannot be a quantity, because quantity is divisible into parts, and parts are a multiplicity. But there cannot be a multiplicity of 'Being Itself' as there can be a multiplicity of humans, or cats, or flowers, etc., as we just demonstrated. So God is immaterial, indivisible, and absolutely simple. He is also unchanging, because to change is to either acquire or lose a mode of being (I lost weight, or I acquired a new skill, or a new place), but God is the First Cause of whatever is. He cannot lack any perfection, because nothing exists outside of Him that He did not cause to be.

And so it follows that since God is the First Being, He is the First Truth, the measure of all that is true, and thus He is ultimately what everyone who pursues knowledge (science) is seeking. Science is a knowledge of things through their proper causes, but new discoveries never bring an end to our search; we continue to search, because we seek the cause that is absolutely first.

Finally, since God is Goodness Itself without limits, then He is the end that we seek in the pursuit of any and all finite goods that motivate us to action. Goods delight the will, but there are no finite goods that bring complete rest to the will, and so the will continues to pass over these goods in search of something ultimate, complete, enduring and sufficient unto itself. God alone answers to these properties.

God is Beauty Itself, without limits, and so everything that is beautiful announces its origin. We seek to delight in the beautiful, but like the good, we pass over these beautiful works, moments, sounds, etc., in search of the Supremely Beautiful, that which is Beauty without limits. Our experience of the beautiful is not so much a pleasure that is within us as it is an ecstasy, an 'exit of self', or an experience of being lifted out of oneself, which is what a beautiful work of art, for example, accomplishes, bringing us in touch with the radiance, integrity and harmony of the real that is outside of us. We long for ecstasy, one that will never end, and again, only God, who is Beauty Itself, answers to that yearning.

Primal man knew this, albeit pre-consciously, intuitively, and without precision. His rituals, which are rich with symbolism, demonstrate much of this. But metaphysics, or the philosophy of being, brings more precision to what he grasps intuitively and vaguely.

105 Some Thoughts on Atheism and Ways of Knowing

After debating atheists for well over 20 years, I am still puzzled by the atheist who demands empirical evidence for the existence of God. What strikes me, in particular, is the knowledge problem associated with it, that is, the need for evidence. From my vantage point, it is similar to a fish who demands evidence for the existence of water. The fish sees everything in the water, but not the water, because our proverbial fish "expects" water to be like the things he observes in it. The problem is he fails to see that "in which" the things exist. Water cannot be something in the water, for it would have to be water and "other than" water at the same time, which is a contradiction.

I imagine a boy raised in a household surrounded by beautiful art—his sister is a brilliant painter, his brother a brilliant pianist who plays beautiful compositions throughout the day, his father a brilliant sculptor, etc. Most of us who appreciate art know that when we are continually exposed to it in one form or another, such as classical music or painting, we slowly and eventually come to see what all the fuss is about. The music, for example, begins to "grow on us". Now imagine a new friend of the boy visits the house and is informed of the many instances of beauty that he will encounter in it; he simply does not see it, however. He demands evidence of this so called "beauty", empirical and measurable evidence. Of course, this is not something that is amenable to observation in a test tube, as it were; beauty is not something subject to measurement. And so his demand is unmet, and he remains a skeptic.

I have never met anyone who demands empirical evidence for beauty, nor have I ever met anyone who consistently demands "sufficient" evidence before believing anything or anyone. One simply cannot function without trusting others, with or without "sufficient" evidence—I am not even certain what counts as "sufficient"; but I know I don't have sufficient evidence that this man behind the wheel, at the stop sign, is not going to put his foot on the gas pedal and run me over as I cross the street, nor do I have sufficient evidence that the owner of this cafe did a thorough background check before hiring this young lady and that she is not going to poison the coffee I ordered, etc. All I have is a statistical inference based on what I have experienced up to this point, which is no guarantee that something radically new and perhaps even devastating is not about to change my life.

So why is it, I ask myself, that certain atheists demand sufficient evidence for one thing, but not for a myriad of other things? A possibility—and I do offer this only as a possibility, not a certainty—is that he does not want to believe that God exists, and this "not wanting" really does affect what it is he permits himself to know and see. Indeed, there are people who have acknowledged that they do not want to believe that there is an eternal life of unimaginable happiness for themselves and for their children. There are people who find the idea of God (the First cause of all that is, all knowing, supremely good, judge of the living and the dead, etc.) repugnant, because it implies that I am not first, that there is an authority greater than me and that I probably should be concerned about whether I have made choices in conformity with what that authority demands or requires, etc. I wish to be my own god, so I do not like the idea of the existence of a deity other than myself. A person who does not want to believe that God exists will not permit himself to see it.

Perhaps another possibility is that they really do wish to believe that God exists but experience no capacity whatsoever to assent to such an idea.[103]

---

[103] That, of course, is disputable theologically. According to Catholic teaching, God wills salvation for everyone, and everyone is given sufficient grace to come to the knowledge and love of God. Furthermore, the very existence of God is evident through his effects: "For what can be known about God is evident to them, because God made it evident to them. Ever since the creation of the world, his invisible attributes of eternal power and divinity have been able to be understood and perceived in what he has made. As a result, they have no excuse" (Rm 1, 19-20). However, perhaps there are psychological reasons that a person is explicitly an atheist; it may be possible that implicitly or preconsciously she has not rejected divine grace and so is not the atheist she believes herself to be. In light of the complexity of the human person and how much more there is to learn about human nature, the limitations of human knowing and our radical proneness to error, it is probably a wise decision to guard against drawing any conclusions bearing upon individual human persons; ultimately, we just don't know.

There are different modes of knowing. One does not arrive at an appreciation for the beauty of a piece of music through inductive reasoning, nor through a kind of deduction; nor is it even a matter of faith. One simply opens himself to the beautiful. When a person is young, however, it often happens that he refuses to open himself to the beautiful as it is "embodied" in a particular piece of music because the kind of music is incompatible with the identity he has chosen for himself. For example, he likes heavy metal, or rap, and he despises those who like classical music; they are boring, highbrow snobs, and he refuses to associate with them in any way, so he refuses to open up himself to see what they see, to take the time required to finally see the beautiful in something so old, for example.

It is possible that something similar takes place with regard to belief in the existence of God. One may not want to believe in God's existence, because it is incompatible with an identity that one has chosen for oneself, and so the atheist closes himself to this particular way of knowing or seeing, at least as it bears upon this particular object of thought, i.e., God.

Some people—I'm not speaking of atheists necessarily—have a need to be right, always. If a person has a need to always be right and always first, they will limit themselves to a mode of knowing, an intellectual frame of mind, a single model or paradigm through which to see the world, one with which they are comfortable and which allows in only what one is willing to know, and refuses entry to what is strange, different, and demanding. What happens is very slowly, gradually, the ego is built up and enlarged, and they end up deifying themselves somehow. After many years, they find it very difficult to give up this habitual way of existing; it's like having to give up an old leather jacket that one has worn for years and has grown accustomed to.

This might be the reason an atheist stubbornly persists in his atheism, but it also may be the reason the fundamentalist, whether Christian (Catholic or Protestant), Muslim, Hindu, or Jew, etc., stubbornly persists in his religious rationalism.

106 Meaning and Non-Existence

If both ends of our lives are bordered by non-existence, life is fundamentally meaningless. I believe the reason is that meaning has to do with purpose. Thus, someone who does not believe in God can find tremendous meaning in life, as long as his life has purpose. The French word for meaning is *sens (sense)*. In English, we often say: "That does not make any sense", which is to say: "That has no meaning". But the French word *sens* is also translated as 'direction'. A life with forward direction has meaning; one without direction lacks meaning. The expression "spinning my wheels" is telling. When you are spinning your wheels, your car is stuck; it is in the mud and not going anywhere. In other words, there's no direction. A motion that is without direction is meaningless, it is impossible to make sense out of it, thus it is relatively unintelligible. It is the end, the purpose or final cause that renders a motion meaningful or intelligible. So the question is: "Is there any ultimate meaning to human life?" What gives my life ultimate meaning?

I used to read tombstones when I would have to wait a few hours for my mechanic to fix my car—there was an old cemetery nearby. I often thought: this person buried here under this tombstone two hundred years ago is completely unknown to me; he lived a relatively short life, even though it was 75 or so years, but all the moments he lived are gone. Virtually no one thinks of that man now. I think of my grandfather once in a while, but what I call to mind is an image I have constructed; I never knew him; and I call that image to mind only rarely.

What gives your day meaning? Today you were busy doing this and that and other things, and it all took place for a purpose; at the end of the day you are in bed, and you remember all that took place. Your memory sees the day as a whole; you see how every action converges into that moment at the end. The present moment is full of meaning, for it is that moment that gives meaning (direction) to all that went before, because all that went before took place for the sake of that point (there was a point to it all); all that took place was ordered to a definite end—it had direction. And then you fall asleep, sort of like death. You wake up the next day, but imagine if you and I could not remember the day before? That present moment would be deprived of a very rich meaning.

If, at the moment I hit the last period, this entire text vanishes, it would have all been for naught, a complete waste of time and I would feel frustrated. Everything I'm doing now is ordered towards completing this text. Once it is done, the whole thing is before me, every moment that passed, every letter typed, will be summed up into a single whole before my gaze. In other words, it is the end that gives meaning to all that goes before, to every part that is ordered to the end, that is, to the single whole or final product. Once this text is complete and brought into being, it endures, and all those moments I spent, all those letters I typed that were ordered to a single end, all that activity that had a direction, a meaning, an intelligible structure, endures. The meaning endures; of course, it only lasts as long as the text endures somehow.

It is the present moment that gives meaning to the past. If death (or non-existence) has the final word over our life, then life really does lack ultimate meaning, and nihilists would be right. Life would have no enduring and ultimate meaning, and for some, that's perfectly okay, at least that's what they claim.

But I would argue that we naturally want life to have a final and enduring meaning, an ultimate meaning. Man keeps seeking, and life is meaningful to the degree that man seeks, and atheists can be some of the greatest seekers.

It is an eternal present that will give an eternal and ultimate meaning to every moment of a person's historical existence. A life without any enduring and ultimate meaning would be much like spending years writing a book and have no one read it. By the time you type the last period, it disappears. It was all for naught. You could argue that it was not all for naught, that you enjoyed writing it while it lasted, and you would be right, but the writer would be very frustrated nonetheless. Or, you could argue that a few people had read it, a small circle, just as only a limited number read a best seller, and then it is forgotten, and a new best seller is on the market. And that's true too, but every writer would like his work to endure, to be a classic, to be continually in print. It keeps the 'meaning' of his labor alive.

We seek meaning, and we seek a meaning that endures. We naturally seek happiness, and the happiness we achieve is never enough; for we continue to seek. What are we looking for? Even those who are happy and apparently very satisfied still seek. There remains a restlessness in the human heart; what will bring the heart rest? Many don't even know, but all we can say at this point is that they are seeking a happiness that is complete, enduring, self-sufficient; they are seeking an enduring meaning.

If that man buried under that tombstone two hundred years ago is completely and utterly forgotten, if there is nothing about him that exists anymore, if there is no record of him, no memory, or nothing more than a skinny little memory in the minds of relatives who never really knew him, who recall his name once every three years or so, then everything he did and everything he became has no ultimate meaning. Even if he influenced a number of people, who in turn influenced others, etc., his life as well as every other life will, in the end when all human beings are dead and this planet is no more, cease to have any meaning at all. It was all for naught, ultimately speaking. All human life would have no ultimate meaning, only a relative meaning.

I would argue that even the most apparently insignificant life has ultimate meaning. We may never know here what the full meaning of this person's life is, but we will in eternity. To see God as He is in Himself is to see that Being who is Eternal Truth Itself. He is the end, the final cause of all final causes, the ultimate purpose of all motion and change. We will know all things in knowing Him, and He will be infinitely knowable. And so the good and charitable deed that you do in secret, and the sacrifices you make for someone in secret, things that no one knows about, will have an enduring meaning, an eternally enduring significance, and we will see that apparently insignificant deed in light of the whole, as we would understand a sentence of a novel in light of the ending of that novel. Its significance will endure eternally. It will have a significance that even you didn't fully understand, and so you will rejoice in the significance or meaning of each one of your actions in a way that is not open to you now, because you do not yet grasp its full significance.

The purpose of the gradual loss of memory that accompanies old age is, I believe (but cannot prove, of course), to help prepare us for that eternity; for this life is about preparing for eternity. When we gradually lose our memories of this trip and that adventure, and when we lose our ability to climb that mountain or swim that lake, etc., we begin to focus less on what is passing away and more on what is eternal within the very heart of us, in the depths of the interior castle of the soul, to use St. Theresa of Avila's expression. There we are alone with God, who alone is our happiness. He alone answers to our search for a happiness that is enduring, complete, sufficient unto itself, because He alone is eternal, fullness of being, and thus sufficient unto Himself. To know Him and to know that we are known by Him is perfect happiness. Human persons are always seeking to know and to be known (they express themselves; they want to be loved, which presupposes being known). To know other human persons, however, and the mysteries of a contingent universe is delightful, but insufficient; to be known by others is also delightful, but insufficient. The human heart continues to restlessly seek; it is looking for God, who is fullness of being, truth itself, beauty itself, goodness itself, and it desires to be known by Him. But of course, you and I are already known by God, because His knowledge causes us to be. Only then, in eternity, will we know that we are known (now we only believe we are known, or we know it indirectly through philosophical reasoning), and that direct knowledge that we are known and loved will be a source of unspeakable delight.

Appendices

Appendix A   A Note on Analogy and Analogical Usage

Equivocal

We speak of terms that are equivocal, univocal, and analogical. Equivocation involves using the same term with an entirely different meaning. For example, we speak of a river bank as well as a piggy bank. "Bank" means something completely different in each usage. Consider the following syllogism:

All barking creatures are dogs
The Oak tree has bark (is a creature with bark)
Therefore, the Oak tree is a dog

This, of course, is an invalid syllogism, because it involves the fallacy of equivocation. "Bark" in the major premise (the explosive cry of a dog) has nothing in common with "bark" in the minor premise (the tough outer sheath of a tree), except the sound of the word. The two terms are *equivocal*.

Univocal

Univocal usage involves terms that are used each time with <u>exactly the same meaning</u>. For example: "All men are intelligent; John is a man; therefore, John is intelligent". The term "intelligent" is used with exactly the same meaning in the major premise as it has in the conclusion.

Consider the term "animal" when it refers to a fox, a bird, a dog, a cat, etc. The term "animal" has exactly the same meaning in every case, and that meaning is "living sentient creature"; or, $3 \times 4 = 4 \times 3$. Here, the number 3 means exactly the same thing in "3×4" as it does in "4×3", and so too the number 4.

Analogy (Analogy of Attribution and Analogy of Proper Proportionality)

Univocal usage has its limits, however. Consider the following example from a former professor of mine, Dr. F.F. Centore:

All exceptional people are in mental hospitals
All philosophy students are exceptional people
Therefore ...

Or, consider the following:

All intelligent beings apprehend universal concepts
Dobermans are intelligent dogs
Therefore, Dobermans apprehend universal concepts.

The terms "exceptional" and "intelligent" do <u>not</u> have exactly the same meaning within their respective syllogisms, which is why the reasoning is invalid. The terms "exceptional" and "intelligent" are used analogically, not univocally. When we speak of a certain kind of dog as being intelligent, we don't mean that they literally have the ability to apprehend universal ideas or the ability to reason. What we typically mean is that this kind of dog is very trainable and learns certain behaviors more easily than other kinds of dogs or other animals, like cats.

What is analogy? Analogous usage involves the use of terms having a meaning that is *partially the same* and *partially different* in different contexts. For example, we speak of a good day, a good husband, and a good meal; we speak of a true diamond, a true friend, and true love, etc. The good and the true are used here analogically, not univocally; they do **not** have exactly the same meaning in each context.

An exclusively univocal mode of thinking does not permit us to understand "goodness" and "truth"; these are only understood by analogy. A good meal, for example, *makes us feel good*. To an exclusively univocal thinker, a good person would be one who "makes us feel good".

However, when we understand that "good" is an analogical term, not a univocal one, we can then begin to see that "good person" means much more than "a person who makes us feel good".

Let's explore this further, and then return to our examples. There are two kinds of analogy: 1) **analogy of attribution**, and 2) **analogy of proper proportionality**. Let's look at analogy of attribution first.

Consider the word "healthy". It can be predicated of such things as medicine, diet, and complexion. For example: Cough syrup is healthy; Janet's diet is healthy; Sarah has a healthy complexion. Strictly speaking, however, cough syrup is not healthy, nor is a diet healthy, nor is a complexion healthy. Health exists **primarily** in a living organism. Cough syrup **helps to bring about** health in the living organism, a diet **helps to maintain** health in Janet, who is a living organism, and Sarah's complexion is **a sign or indication of** health that exists primarily in Sarah, a living organism. The three terms "medicine", "diet", and "complexion" **all have a relation to** "health", which is the **primary analogate**, and each one has a different relation to "health" (one is a sign, the other a cause, etc.), but they are all similar in that they can all be referred or attributed to health in some way.

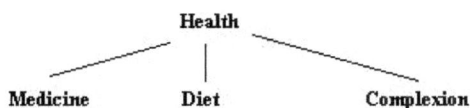

Health

Medicine   **Diet**   **Complexion**

"Medical" is another analogical term (analogy of attribution). We speak of "medical building", "medical instruments", "medical vehicle", "medical advice", "medical book" and "medical doctor". A building is not primarily medical, it is simply a building; rather, a person who possesses the "art of medicine" is primarily medical. The other terms, "medical instruments, vehicle, advice, etc." are all related to the "medical person" (i.e., instruments he uses, the ambulance that takes the patient to the doctor, the book from which he learns about the art of medicine, advice that comes from a person learned in the medical arts, etc.).

In analogy of attribution, the various analogous terms are related to the prime analogate (i.e., the doctor, or the living organism) **extrinsically**, not intrinsically. "Medical" does not exist intrinsically in the building, nor does it exist intrinsically in the scalpel.

The analogy of **proper proportionality** is analogy in the most perfect sense of the word. Consider:

2 is to 4 **as** 500 is to 1000. Or,

$$\frac{2}{4} \quad \frac{500}{1000}$$

The terms in the one are different from the terms in the other, but they have a common relation or proportion, namely, 2 is half of 4, and 500 is half of 1000.

Consider that "winter is to snow **as** fall is to leaves", or, "birds are to wings as sharks are to fins".

Let's return to our examples above: a good day, a good husband, and a good meal, and a true diamond, a true friend, and true love. The good and the true are used here analogically (according to proper proportionality), not univocally; they do not have exactly the same meaning in each context.

A good person is not the same as a good meal, nor is a good day the same as a good person. They are a similar in proportion or relation. The good is "that which all things desire" (Aristotle), and as Aquinas points out, what all things desire first and foremost is their own perfection. So "good" has to do with desire, in particular the desire for fullness of being or perfection. Now, since the good is the object of desire (that which we desire we see as good), a good meal is one that is desirable, that tastes good (of course it means more than that, at least to health conscious eaters). A good man, however, is not one that makes us feel good, but much more than that; rather, he is a person of moral integrity or perfection, and perfection is what all things desire first and foremost.

Thus, the "good" is partially the same and partially different in the two contexts of a good meal and a good person. They are the same in that they have to do with desire; they are different in that the one has to do with the desire to satisfy a sense appetite (good meal), the other with a desire for "fullness of being".

So too, a true friend, a true diamond, and true love. Truth is the conformity **between what is in the mind and what is** (reality). A true friend is one who is faithful, one whose behavior conforms to her promise; a false friend turns out to be a user, one who misleads us into believing that she is a faithful friend who loves you for your sake. A diamond is an allotrope of carbon and it has certain refractive properties; a fake diamond will have a low refractive index. And of course a love that is true is faithful and enduring, because it loves the other for his/her own sake, not for the sake of the self; and so true love conforms to what it means to love, whereas a fake love appears to be genuine, but it eventually reveals itself for what it is, namely self-love.

So in all these uses of the term "true", there is a real and common relation or proportion, and that is the relation of "conformity to". Unlike analogy of attribution, the terms of the analogy are not extrinsically related to a prime analogate (i.e., health or medicine); rather, the analogical term (true, or good) is **intrinsic**. The proposition, the stone, and this person (Robert) are really and intrinsically true, that is, they really do have a conformity to something that renders them true.

This proposition is to the real **as** this stone (diamond) is to the essence of diamond **as** this person is to the essence of friendship.

Proposition (i.e., John is 17)	this stone (diamond)	this person (Robert)
Reality	the real nature of diamond	the essence of friendship

Philosophy (in particular Metaphysics or the philosophy of being) requires the ability to think analogically. That is why strong univocal thinkers, like mathematicians and physicists, can often have a hard time with philosophy, especially metaphysics.

For example, causality is also an analogical term, not a univocal one. In other words, it is unrestricted. A cause is a principle from which anything proceeds with dependence (that on which a thing depends in being or in coming to be). As such, a cause need not involve motion, collision, and time. In other words, causality is not restricted to things colliding into one another, thus moving one another. The middle term of a syllogism, for example, is the cause of the conclusion, it is that on which the conclusion depends. For example:

All even numbers are divisible by 2
Numbers 10, 2240, and 1 million are even numbers
Therefore, numbers 10, 2240, and 1 million are divisible by 2

"Even numbers" is the middle term, and it is the cause of the conclusion. In other words, there is no understanding of the conclusion without understanding the cause; for the effect (conclusion) depends upon the cause.

Now a univocal thinker who has a good mind for physics, for example, often has difficulty with this, because he tends to restrict causality to the "mechanical", i.e., one moving thing pushing another thing so that it moves. The latter is genuine causality insofar as the resulting motion **depends upon a principle that accounts for it**, namely the initial thing that was moving. But causality is broader than that, just as being is broader than motion—causality is as broad as being. But some physicists will deny universal scope to the principle of causality because what occurs on the quantum level cannot be accounted for in terms of the **laws of classical Newtonian physics**. The *non-sequitur* here is rooted in the fact that although all mechanical causality is genuine causality, not all causality is mechanical (just as all tasty meals are good, not all that is good is tasty, i.e., a good medicine. Furthermore, without causality—I don't mean "mechanical" causality—, our ability to reason to a conclusion in order to possess "science" becomes impossible—insofar as the middle term of a syllogism is the cause of the conclusion.

Appendix B. Reductionism, Analogy, and the Priority of Being

Reductionism is the habit of mind that reduces the whole to the mathematical sum of its parts (i.e., man is nothing other than his chemistry, which in turn is nothing other than...). It is first and foremost a methodology, but for many it continues to be a way to explain the ultimate nature of things, which in turn carries with it significant moral and even political implications.

I believe the definitive way to expose the fallacy of reductionism is to focus attention on what we know naturally, but not always explicitly—with respect to the priority of being. What I mean to say is that being is first. If anything is prior to being, then it "is", and being is still first. Moreover, being cannot be second or subsequent, for that would mean "non-being" (or nothing) is prior to being, which would immediately establish being, once again, as absolutely first.

Before we know anything in detail about an object of knowledge before us, we know that "it is". Thus, being is necessarily first in our knowing. The "what" that exists (i.e., you, or a dog, or a carbon atom, etc.) follows upon being and is a "that which is". The fundamental way that beings exist in the world is, generally speaking, as a "that which is". In other words, beings exist primarily as "things" or "entities" possessing a certain "whatness", a distinct intelligible configuration, as well as a kind of independence (in other words, a thing exists 'in itself', not 'in another'). That is why we know immediately, self-evidently, without reasoning to the conclusion, that each being is what it is (the principle of identity).

The most fundamental question that arises in the face of the objects of our knowledge is: "What is it?" In other words, "what is 'that which is'?" Our question reveals that we want to know more fully the basic intelligible configuration (what it is essentially) of that single being that exists in itself (whatever that might be).

Furthermore, the "thing" (or 'that which is') is prior to quantity (parts outside of parts), which corresponds to the question: "How much of 'that which is' is there?" For example, how much does the cat we gh, or how large or extensive is it? Quantity is not a 'that which is'; rather, quantity only 'exists in' a 'that which is', which exists in itself. For example, I cannot show you fifty pounds, only a fifty pound 'thing'. The question "What is that?" is fundamentally different than "How much of it is there?" The former is "qualitative"; it bears upon the fundamental way beings exist, that is, as a certain kind of thing. The fundamental or primary mode of being is "entity" or "substance", not quantity (parts outside of parts).

To sum up, before I know anything specific about the object of my knowledge, I know at least that it 'is'. If it 'is', it is one and 'in itself'. I then move to know "what" that being is more specifically. And so although essence (what a thing is) and existence are not two separate principles, existence is prior to essence, not in the order of time, but in the order of dependence (there is no essence to know unless it first exists).

Univocal versus Analogical Thinking

The difficulty that some students encounter in trying to rise above the reductionist habit of thinking often stems from their habitual tendency to think univocally; students with good minds for science and math are disposed to think univocally, because scientific and mathematical terms are for the most part univocal. But the only way we grasp the first principles of material being—principles that cannot be perceived or imagined, but only understood—is to think by way of analogy. Allow me to explain.

We speak of terms that are equivocal, univocal, and analogical. Equivocation involves using the same term with an entirely different meaning. For example, we speak of a river bank as well as a piggy bank. "Bank" means something completely different in each usage.

Univocal usage involves terms that are used each time with exactly the same meaning. For example: "All men are intelligent; John is a man; therefore, John is intelligent". The term "intelligent" is used with exactly the same meaning in the major premise as it has in the conclusion.

Analogous usage involves the use of terms having a meaning that is partially the same and partially different in different contexts. For example, we speak of a good day, a good husband, and a good meal, or a true diamond, a true friend, and true love. The good and the true are used here analogically, not univocally; they do not have exactly the same meaning in each context.

An exclusively univocal mode of thinking does not permit us to understand "goodness" and "truth"; these are only understood by analogy. A good meal, for example, makes us feel good. To an exclusively univocal thinker, a good person would be one who "makes us feel good".

However, when we understand that "good" is an analogical term, not a univocal one, we are able to see that "good person" means much more than "a person who makes us feel good". He is, rather, a person of moral integrity or perfection, and perfection is what all things desire first and foremost. A good meal is good because it is "desirable"; for the good is the object of desire. Thus, the "good" is partially the same and partially different in the two contexts of a good meal and a good person. They are the same in that they have to do with desire; they are different in that the one has to do with the desire to satisfy a sense appetite (good meal), the other with a desire for "perfection".

Causality and Analogy

Causality is also an analogical term, not a univocal one. A cause is a principle from which anything proceeds with dependence. As such, a cause need not involve motion, time, or physical contact. The middle term of a syllogism, for example, is the cause of the conclusion, it is that on which the conclusion depends: "All men are rational; John is a man; Therefore, John is rational". The middle term "man" is the cause of the conclusion, that is, the conclusion proceeds with dependence upon the middle term. There is no understanding of the conclusion without understanding the cause; for the effect (conclusion) depends upon the cause. The cause in this case is not a moving cause, but a universal idea (man).

Now a univocal thinker who has a good mind for physics, for example, often has difficulty with this, because he tends to limit causality to the "mechanical", i.e., one moving thing pushing another thing so that it moves. The latter is genuine causality insofar as the resulting motion depends upon a principle that accounts for it, namely the initial thing that was moving. But causality is more extensive than that, just as being is more extensive than motion; causality extends as far as being, which encompasses everything.

But some physicists will deny universal scope to the principle of causality because what occurs on the quantum level cannot be accounted for in terms of the laws of classical Newtonian physics. This conclusion is a non-sequitur, and it is rooted in an error of distribution: All mechanical causality is genuine causality, but not all causality is mechanical; just as all men are animals, but not all animals are men. Furthermore, without causality—I don't mean "mechanical" causality—, our ability to reason to a conclusion in order to possess "science" becomes impossible insofar as the middle term of a syllogism is the cause of the conclusion.

It is univocal thinking that is responsible for both the fallacy of reductionism and the difficulty in coming to understand the first causes of material being. Reductionism is good scientific methodology, but as a philosophy (i.e., a way to explain the ultimate nature of things), it is simply the logical fallacy of composition (attributing to the whole what belongs only to the part, or vice versa). Reductionism as a "philosophy" consists in using scientific knowledge as first principles and drawing philosophical conclusions on the basis of those scientific principles (i.e., DNA determines the organism to be what it is; reality is ultimately indeterminate, etc.), as if science is able to uncover the first causes of mobile being. Let's pursue these causes further.

Matter, Form, and End

"Matter" is a first cause. It is a principle from which coming-to-be proceeds with dependence. But matter is an analogical term, not a univocal term (analogical as well are: "form", "being", "true", "good", "beautiful", "potency", "act", "subject", etc.). "Matter", as the term is commonly employed in the world of science (that which has mass and extension) is partially the same and partially different than the "matter" that is one of the first principles of a material nature (which is the object of the general science of nature, or the philosophy of nature).

"Matter" as the term is employed in the world of science and what we in the world of philosophy call "first matter" are partially the same insofar as they are both subjects of contraries, that is, matter always possesses a determination of some kind and is an openness to a contrary determination. For example, the sheet of iron is in the form of a square but open to being shaped into a passenger door. First matter, on the other hand, is the first or ultimate subject of a material thing's intelligible structure or form (whatness), and that very subject is a thing's openness to or potentiality for another intelligible structure or form. They are partially different in that the first matter of a material being is not extended, cannot be manipulated nor apprehended through sense perception, as the extended matter of the physical sciences can be. Whatever can be manipulated, sensed, or measured, is an already constituted thing or entity with extension and a host of sense qualities and other properties.

"Form" or intelligible structure is a first cause as well—not a mechanical cause. It is partially the same as "form" in the sense of a figure, insofar as figure determines or shapes extended matter, which is the subject determined by that shape (i.e., iron shaped into the body of a car). But the ultimate form or intelligible structure of a single material being (form possessed by first matter) is partially different than a visible figure; the latter we can perceive with the senses, the former we only know through the intellect (although I can picture a rectangular door, I cannot picture 'humanness').

One cannot come to understand the first causes that constitute an existing material nature (first matter and first form) with the help of the imagination, because these principles are not extended, they are not parts, and so they have no sense qualities. They are only known through the intellect by way of analogy.

A material being is an existing nature, it is a "what" that has existence, an actual being of a certain intelligible configuration (i.e., it is a dog, not a cat; it is oxygen, not carbon). And the most obvious fact about material beings is that they are mutable, that is, a material being can become something else entirely, a fundamentally different kind of thing (a different form). Any material being is actually something, but potentially something else. That potentiality and actuality of the whole is the first matter and first form of the single material thing that is the object of our knowledge. And just as extended matter (i.e., a piece of iron) cannot be without some 'shape' or other, first matter is never without some intelligible form or configuration.

Another cause upon which all science depends is final causality. But once again, this type of causality is not "mechanical" agent causality. Nevertheless, it is the cause of every other cause, and so it is primary. For example, without a purpose (end), a carpenter will not be motivated to build (act); but if one needs something on which to rest things (end), that end determines what he will make (table) and the matter out of which he will make it (wood).

But final causality is involved in the acts of every existing thing, rendering things intelligible; for we only know the nature of a thing through its activity, and we only understand an activity through its end.

A Latin word for law is *regula*, which means rule or standard. To act according to a law is to act according to a rule. Lawful acts are regular, or standard. In other words, an agent (whatever it is) that acts according to a law, acts for an end. This means that an agent is not indifferent to the end for the sake of which it acts. Water is not indifferent to what properties it will exhibit, nor is a fertilized oocyte indifferent to the end of its development. The boiling point of water is not 100 Celsius one minute and some other temperature the next. Iron is not malleable one instant, but brittle the next, etc. A fertilized egg does not at times become a chicken, at other times a cow, at other times a child, etc. If you are playing snooker and you aim the white ball towards the red ball at a particular angle, the red ball is not indifferent to the end to be realized; it will move in a defined direction. If not, winning at snooker would merely be a matter of luck, not skill. The resulting motion is not indeterminate, but regular and intelligible (lawful). If agents were indifferent to the ends to be realized, their acts would be irregular, unknowable, unintelligible, and utterly unpredictable.

The reason science depends on final causality is that a motion is intelligible through its end (definable; fin; end). The reason is that the final cause and the formal cause coincide. The formal cause of a change is that for the sake of which there is coming-to-be (change). What this means is that all change is a transformation of one kind or another. But the end of the process is achieved precisely when the form has been realized in the subject (matter) that is undergoing change, or when the subject is "made through" (perfected)—the form of table is possessed by the wood. The final cause (the end of the generation or change) is thus that for the sake of which there is coming-to-be. That is why we only possess an idea of a motion (what it is) through its end. For example, we know that cooling is occurring when water begins to freeze, or that heating is occurring when water begins to boil.

But final cause also includes the end of the generated, which is the ultimate purpose (end) of the change or coming-into-being. Once the organ of the eye or the kidney or the lungs has fully developed, we can ask: "What is its purpose?" It is precisely their motions (directed towards an end) that will reveal it.

Now, what is it that moves? It is a being, or part of a being, that moves, so it is the end that reveals just what that being is; i.e., the relatively full grown apple tree reveals what that seed is, namely an apple seed. A being moves towards an end repeatedly (regularly) because it is a determinate kind of thing. In other words, its acts "terminate" or come to an end (fin), and they do so regularly, disclosing just what that being is. Acts that do not terminate or come to an end would be indistinguishable from any other act, and the being that acts indeterminately would be indeterminate, indistinguishable from any other being. Such a being would not be "what it is". As such, it would have no identity; hence, it would be indefinable (without fin' or end); nothing about it could be an object of scientific inquiry.

The Priority of Being

When considering material things, we must not lose sight of the fact that being is first; for nothing acts unless it first is. Now it is not the essence of a thing that makes that thing to be, for the essence is "that which has a to be (esse)" and answers the question "what is it?" I can know what a thing is without thereby knowing whether or not it is. I am a human kind of thing, but I am not my existence. Rather, I possess existence, that is, I have an act of existing. The act of being is the act of all acts, including the act of matter (which is the substantial quality or form, imparting to matter its actual "whatness") as well as all other modes of being that exist in material things, such as quantity, when, activity, passivity, etc.

A contingent being (as opposed to a necessary being) is an existing nature; it is a "that which has an act of existing". Hence, a contingent being is capable of not existing; for if it possesses an act of being, it can also be dispossessed of its act of existing. My cat exists, but it did not always exist, nor will it always exist.

Now, our quest for understanding reveals something fundamental about things. What our questions reveal is that everything which exists, to the extent to which it exists, possesses a sufficient reason for its being so that it is capable of explaining itself to the intellect. In other words, whatever is, has that whereby it is. This is the principle of sufficient reason.

Whatever exists has "that whereby it is" either in itself or in another. If it has "that whereby it is" within itself, then it is that whereby it is. If it has "that whereby it is" through another, then it depends on that whereby it is. For example, if we chance upon a broken window, we naturally wonder what it is that caused the window to break; we look for the sufficient reason for the broken window. The sufficient reason (that whereby it is broken) is either in the broken window itself, or outside of it, in another. If the sufficient reason is in the broken window itself, we would not inquire of the reason. Since we ask: "How did this happen?" it is clear that the sufficient reason for the broken window is to be found outside of it, in another (i.e., the kids were playing baseball and Billy hit the ball out of the park and into the window).

Returning to the question of existence, a contingent being (an existing nature) possesses an act of being, and it can also be dispossessed of its act of being (my grandmother's cat no longer exists). So what is the sufficient reason for the act of existing of a contingent being? The sufficient reason, or "that whereby it is", is either in itself, or in another. No contingent being (one that may or may not be, i.e., the cat) contains within itself the sufficient reason for its act of existing; for if it did, it would be "subsistent being itself"; its "whatness" (essence) would be to exist. It would not possess existence; it would be its own act of existing.

Now whatever belongs to the nature of a thing belongs to it necessarily. For example, a human person is necessarily rational, an animal is necessarily sentient, a living thing is necessarily self-moving, etc. A being whose nature is to be would necessarily be, and could not not exist. Moreover, this being whose nature is to be (subsistent being itself) would necessarily be one, not many. To understand this, suppose there are two beings that are "subsistent being itself". The only thing that could distinguish "being itself" from "being itself" is that which is outside of "being itself". But outside of being is non-being, or nothing. Hence, nothing distinguishes them, so they are one. Hence, there is only one necessary being, not two. And it is this non-contingent being (God, or Being Itself) that is the sufficient reason for the act of being of all contingent beings.

What does God impart to beings? The answer is their unique acts of existing, really distinct from their natures. God cannot bring into existence a being whose nature is to be; for there can only be one necessary and non-contingent being, not two, and it is a contradiction to suggest that a necessary being has a received existence. It follows that a contingent being is a being of a certain "whatness" (kind or nature), a determinate kind of thing, distinct from its act of existing. Being is first, "whatness" (essence) follows—not in terms of time, but in terms of dependence; "whatness" depends on the act of being, and the act of being depends upon "subsistent being itself", or God.

Now, if what is brought into being is an existing material nature, it is a "what" that is mutable, or moveable (a hydrogen atom, or a horse, or a man, etc.). It is a particular existing mutable being with certain modes of being inhering in it, such as quantity (having parts outside of parts), sensible qualities, dispositions, where, when, relation, etc. These latter exist only in and through the being's act of existing. Quantity, for example, does not have independent existence.

Now, existential causality is not something that occurs at a first point in time, only to withdraw itself so that what exists may continue to exist on its own. That is how many people, thinking univocally, tend to conceive of creation (such as the creation of the universe). But that kind of causality is "horizontal" and is proper to secondary causes that are not "existential", but efficient causes of particular motions, like the cause of the movement of a billiard ball, or the fertilization of an oocyte. Existential causality—and God is the first and only existential cause—is "vertical", so to speak. That is to say, it is perpetual and continuous. It does not occur in time, because time is a mode of being dependent upon and inhering in material beings that move. Time exists only in and through the act of existence of mobile beings. In other words, time is not prior to being, rather, being is prior to time, for time depends on material beings in order to exist, and material existing natures exist by virtue of a received act of being, which in turn depends on the first existential cause that is subsistent being itself, or God. In other words, there is no absolute time, followed by the creation of material beings in time, followed by the actual movement of material things. On the contrary, there is the bringing into being of an existing material nature, and this existing material nature is preserved in being by its first cause so that it is able to act; it moves in certain ways (i.e., locomotion, or growth, or qualitative changes, etc.), and time follows upon that movement as its number according to a before and an after.

Nothing (no being) can bring itself into being, and for the same reason no contingent being can preserve itself in being—for I can do all sorts of things to preserve my life, such as drink water, take medicine, eat, etc., but I cannot perform these acts unless I am first made to be and my act of being is perpetuated or preserved. A being only acts according to the limited potentialities of its nature, and existence is outside my nature, for I have an act of existing; I am not my act of existing. That, of course, is true of all contingent beings whose natures are distinct from their acts of being, which is every other being besides God, whether we understand their natures or not. Hence, God is the first and perpetual (preservative) cause of the act of being of contingent beings, including material contingent beings.

Now, "one" is a property of being. Whatever is, is one. Two beings are not one, but two. It is always a single whole that exists primarily, a whole being of a certain "whatness" or intelligible configuration. A material whole has parts outside of parts. Those parts are many. But a being cannot be both one and many at the same time and in the same respect (that is contradictory); rather, a being is one and many at the same time, but in different respects.

A material being's extension is continuous either homogeneously (i.e., a gold brick) or heterogeneously (i.e., bones, nerves, muscle, etc.). The parts of a whole are ordered to the whole because they are its parts. That ordering is an intelligible ordering, because the whole is intelligible. In other words, we can make sense out of the parts of the human anatomy (or the parts of a cell, or an atom, etc.,) because the whole human being is an existing nature, a being with intelligible content. The parts of a being exist in the one being, and they exist through the act of existing of that being in which they inhere. They have no separate existence, otherwise they are not parts of that being. But it is a nature that exists (having a determinate intelligible 'whatness'), so the parts that exist in and through the one being are parts of a nature. Hence, they receive their essential configuration (their intelligibility) from that nature, for they are its parts. That is why every part of the human body is human; but not every part is every other part (this part is not that part, etc.).

If there is multiplicity in a being, as there is in material beings with quantity, that multiplicity is reduced to a unity through a single unifying principle by which the whole is intelligible. Now, there is a twofold intelligibility to an existing material nature. I know that it is (existence), and I also know what it is (essence), albeit incompletely. That unifying principle by which a multiplicity is reduced to existing parts of one being is the act of existing, and the unifying principle by which that multiplicity is configured to a single "what" (i.e., my eyes are human, my bones are human, and my nerve cells are human, etc.) is the first or substantial form of the thing that is possessed by its first matter. The principle by which a being of a certain nature is multiplied into an indefinite number of individual instances having the same nature is matter having determinate dimensions (dimensive quantity). A being's mutability is rooted in its ultimate subject, which is the potentiality of the whole being (first matter) to possess some other substantial quality or form, and thus be some other determinate thing; and that potentiality or matter is real (it is not extended, nor colored, etc.); it is the real subject of a material being's intelligible configuration (to be 'matter' is to be a subject of form).

The principle of potentiality and actuality of the whole material being are not parts, for parts exist in the category of quantity. Moreover, there are no pre-existing parts as one would find at a hardware store. Rather, parts or particles are parts of wholes. If what we will later on designate as a part now exists by itself (or in itself), then it is no longer an actual part, but a whole unto itself; it is only potentially a part of a whole.

What this means is that an existing material nature is not a result of particles behaving lawfully. Being, one and determinate, does not result from the activity of a multiplicity of contingent beings, no matter what they are; contingent beings cannot impart being, they can give only what is in their nature to give, not what is outside of it, and the act of existing is outside (not 'outside' as in the category of place) the nature of a contingent being that possesses it. That is why a multiplicity of existing natures cannot impart existential unity, for they cannot impart being. If they become incorporated into an existing material nature (whatever that might be, i.e., an atom, a salt crystal, an animal, a plant, etc.), they cease to be what they are—if they did not, we could not speak of a single thing, such as a single atom, or a single dog, or single plant. To cease to be what they are in this case means that they (wholes unto themselves, i.e., a hydrogen, carbon, and oxygen atom) have become a part of a larger whole (i.e., a living organism). A whole exists on its own, with its own act of being; a part, however, does not exist on its own; it exists through the being of which it is a part.

To deny this is merely to shift the level of discussion to another level. Whatever level that turns out to be, one will have to account for what one eventually comes to regard as the fundamental mode of real being and the "what" of those beings, their movements and principles, without begging the question. But no matter what that level is on which we choose to carry on a discussion that attempts to explain the ultimate constitution of material being, we always give evidence in our language that we understand, consciously or pre-consciously, something of the first principles of mobile being. Our language reveals what we know, that there is always a single subject with two contraries (possession and privation). Whether we speak of not knowing the position and velocity of an electron at the same time (an electron possesses position and velocity), or a particle possessing wave properties, etc., there is always a pre-scientific knowledge that exercises a kind of dominion over the entire scientific process. When a person refers to the indeterminacy principle as the uncertainty principle, for example, he reveals his understanding that formal and final cause coincide, for what is indeterminate is unknowable, for we cannot 'terminate' our understanding of a thing's momentum, thus we cannot grasp the end (term) towards which it moves.

The Novel: An Analogy

In order to better grasp the relationship between "part and whole", the following analogy may prove helpful. A book is made up of parts, the parts are made up of chapters, the chapters are made up of paragraphs, the paragraphs are made up of sentences, the sentences are made up of phrases and words, and the words are made up of letters. When a novelist writes the book, he begins by writing a letter, such as the letter "t". When we read the book, we begin with the first letter of the first word. The novel comes to be at the end of the writing process, and our understanding of it is relatively complete at the end of the reading process.

But it is the whole that comes first absolutely (the whole is prior not in terms of time, but in the order of dependence). A letter of the alphabet, i.e., "c", is more open to determination (has more potentiality, or less actual meaning) than is a word, i.e., "cool", and a word is more open to determination than a phrase, such as "cool glass of water", but a phrase is more open, has more potentiality, than the full sentence: "After a jog on a hot day, you should be sure to replenish yourself with a cool glass of water". A full sentence, however, is more open to determination than is a paragraph. We do not think one letter at a time, nor do we think one word at a time. We think of an entire idea, and then we think of the best way to express that idea, searching as we do for the proper matter (the right words).

To be less open to determination is to have more meaning. A letter is very poor in property and has far less intelligibility (meaning) than a word. The letter "e" means much less than the word "love" or "truth". When the letter "e" becomes part of the word "love", it becomes part of a larger whole, with far more meaning than the letters "e" "l" "v" "o" taken separately. We can do a lot more with the letter "e" than we can do with the word "love", precisely because "e" has greater indeterminacy, that is, less intelligibility and thus less meaning. "Love" has greater intelligibility, that is, more definition than the letter "e".

If I were to ask a group of students to write any meaningful word using the letter "e", they'd have no difficulty. Ask them to write anything using the word "love", and they would have to think a little harder. Ask them to write something that incorporates the phrase "love is blind", and they'd have to think even harder, but they could do it. But ask them to write an entire paragraph that incorporates the sentence: "A certain kind of love is blind, for it is passion that has a tendency to blind the intellect, and so the kind of love that blinds is an emotion, not an act of the will", and they'd spend much more time thinking about how to incorporate it into a larger idea. They'd need to think of a much larger meaning (idea), one that exceeds the limited intelligibility of the part; for the meaning of that sentence exceeds that meaning contained in the phrase "love is blind". "Love is blind" is open to further determination, but it does not and cannot determine itself to that larger end, an end that gives full expression to the idea contained in the full sentence above. Rather, it must be determined by something that possesses that larger meaning. The simple phrase does not possess it, just as the word "love" does not possess the idea contained in "love is blind". Considered in itself, the part does not possess the meaning of the whole; otherwise it would be the whole. The part is made to serve the whole through the whole, by existing as part of the whole.

Shakespeare conceives the whole before writing, and it is the intelligible whole that determines and shapes every part of the play, i.e., the letters, the words, the phrases, the sentences, the paragraphs, the scenes, the acts, etc. The intelligible whole that Shakespeare conceives is not in the book, but remains within him - it is part of his interior. But existing natures (beings) have their own interior; they have their own nature (only an intelligent creature, man, is intelligently conscious of that interior).

Now, as we move towards the subatomic level, we are moving towards a level that is real, but not as rich in property. The realities we discover at this level have a greater openness to determination (potentiality). For example, the electron is more open to determination (more potential) than the atom, the atom more open to further determination than the molecule, and larger more complex molecules have more potential than a flower, etc. In other words, the atom has less potentiality (more definition) than the electron (the electron is a part of it; if it is not a part of it, it is potentially a part of it, but actually a whole unto itself, but poorer in property than an atom). A protein molecule has less potentiality than a carbon atom, and a horse has less potentiality (more meaning) than a protein molecule.

Now just as the idea of the entire novel determines the configuration of each part, not vice versa, so too does the substantial form of a material being communicate its own intelligible configuration to every part of that being. The parts do not determine the whole, and the whole is not an effect of the parts, for that would suggest the parts are prior to the whole, which means they would be wholes unto themselves. But they can only be parts if they cease to be wholes. If four beings resisted the pressure to relinquish their existence to become parts of a greater whole, but combined with one another, the result would be four beings, not one.

Now, once a novel or play has been read, we finally come to understand it; for we only understand something when we know it as a whole. All the parts of the novel serve the whole, the single idea that exists in the mind of Shakespeare. But after a time, the reader forgets the details. Nevertheless, he knows the novel or play as a whole: "I know that book, I've read it before", he says. "So I'd like to read something I don't know. Let me look for another book." After a few years, he might decide to re-read the novel. His initial knowledge of the whole begins to acquire a greater precision, perhaps one he once had, but lost over time.

It is the knowledge of the whole that is always the condition for the possibility of knowing its parts. At the beginning, it is knowledge of a relative whole (i.e., the sentence in relation to the words, the paragraph in relation to the sentences, or the chapter in relation to the paragraphs) that is the condition for the possibility of understanding the parts we are reading. Unless I understand each word within the order of the whole sentence, I do not understand what I am reading. The words have meaning, that is, a direction or movement forward towards an end. Each move forward brings me closer to the whole idea (either of the sentence, or of the paragraph, or of the chapter, or of the whole novel). Each whole enables me to understand each part of it completely.

The entire meaning contained in "love is blind" allows me to grasp the particular nuance given to the word "love"; it enables me to understand something about love, in particular, something the author wishes to convey to me about it. By itself, the word "love" does not convey that larger meaning. But consider our previous example: "A certain kind of love is blind, for it is passion that has a tendency to blind the intellect, and so the kind of love that blinds is an emotion, not an act of the will". My understanding of "love is blind" is much more complete, it is far more nuanced and somewhat richer, in light of the whole for the sake of which it was phrased. If, as a result of a loss of memory, I cannot retain the words in order to discern the movement or direction in the writing, I end up knowing each part in isolation from the whole. Hence, I cannot grasp the whole.

But the whole idea determined each part, which is why each part together moves forward to convey the overall meaning. If my memory works, I remember the whole word, the whole two words, the whole three words, the whole four words, and the meaning, which always exceeds them individually, gradually comes to light. The words only exist in view of the whole, and the whole determines the sequence of the words, providing them with their moving power, that is, their ability to carry the reader along.

Now, the greater the potentiality or openness to determination a thing has, the greater is its poverty, and the greater a thing's poverty, the less causal power it enjoys. In other words, the greater the indeterminacy of a thing, such as the letter 'a' in comparison to the meaning of a complete novel, the less it has to impart. It has, rather, a greater openness to receive a richer determination.

As reality moves towards the quantum level, it moves towards a level of greater poverty or indeterminacy - which is consistent with the popular designation of Heisenberg's uncertainty principle as the 'indeterminacy' principle. To deny causality on this level is not entirely irrational, for in light of the principles we've been discussing, perhaps it is to be expected. But the quantum level is no more the cause of what takes place on the ordinary macroscopic level than the letters of the alphabet are the cause of the novel.

It is the idea of the novel (the story) that is the final and formal cause of the novel; the words and sentences are determined by it and are ordered to serve it, that they may communicate it. In other words, the story is not an emergent property; rather, it is the parts that express the entire idea that emerge as an effect of a prior cause.

This order that the analogy of the novel uncovers is an order that exists with respect to every "whole", every being and every substance on the periodic table as well as every living entity. An empiriometric understanding of the physical universe at any level is genuine and real, but it is not and cannot be an ultimate explanation, that is, an explanation in terms of first causes. The empiriometric sciences are an intelligible account of secondary causes (i.e., the heart really pumps blood, DNA really brings about certain traits in an organism, etc.) that presuppose the existence of intelligible natures in the first place.

Appendix C. Chance and Spontaneity

Many people in the world of science will often employ terms like 'indeterminacy', 'chance', 'probability', etc., and using knowledge from the world of science they will often attempt to draw philosophical conclusions about the nature of reality as a whole. Some still claim that everything that happens does so by chance, or everything is a result of probability, or that reality is fundamentally indeterminate, etc. But at the root of these claims is a vague and imprecise understanding of what these terms really mean.

Radioactivity, for example, is a statistical process. The half-life of an element is defined as the time required for half of the atoms present in a given aggregate to decay. Take radon as an example; it has the half-life of 3.825 days. What this means is that half of the radon atoms initially present will have decayed 3.825 days after one begins to observe them. We cannot determine statistically which of the atoms in the aggregate will decay; the fate of individual atoms is beyond our ability to know at this point.

But some people have a tendency to infer that since we cannot predict exactly which atoms will decay, the decay is a matter of chance. This conclusion, however, is unwarranted. It is true that if I were to say which atom was going to decay within the next 3.825 days, there is only a chance that I'd be correct. And if I turned out to be right, that would only have been by chance; for it is completely unpredictable which individual atom will decay. But one cannot conclude from this that the decay itself is 'by chance'.

The Meaning of Chance

In order to explain chance more thoroughly, I am going to offer a careful commentary on book two, chapters five and six of Aristotle's Physics, which treats the philosophical question of what it means for events to happen by chance. He writes:

First then we observe that some things always come to pass in the same way, and others for the most part.

In other words, John wakes up every morning at the same time and spends his morning in the same way, i.e., he goes for a half hour jog. Or, this tree always bears apples, and they ripen, and they fall of the tree in October and November.

Aristotle continues:

It is clearly of neither of these that chance is said to be the cause, nor can the 'effect of chance' be identified with any of the things that come to pass by necessity and always, or for the most part.

Hence, it is not by chance that John gets up every morning at the crack of dawn and goes for a jog.

Already, from these first two lines of chapter five, we can begin to deal with the relationship between radioactive half-life and chance. If it regularly comes to pass that half of the radon atoms in a given aggregate will decay after 3.825 days, we cannot say that their decay occurs by chance.

Aristotle continues:

...some events are for the sake of something, others not. Again, some of the former class are in accordance with deliberate intention, others not, but both are in the class of things which are for the sake of something. Hence it is clear that even among the things which are outside the necessary and the normal, there are some in connexion with which the phrase 'for the sake of something' is applicable. (Events that are for the sake of something include whatever may be done as a result of thought or of nature.)

John puts on his shoes 'for the sake of something', namely for the sake of jogging. He does not put on his shoes necessarily. It may not even be normal for John to put on his shoes and jog (perhaps it was a result of watching a special on TV). Even so, he acts 'for the sake of something'; thus, what happens here does not happen by chance. It is only when things 'come to pass incidentally' that we say they have come to pass 'by chance'.

Aristotle writes:

> For just as a thing is something either in virtue of itself or incidentally, so may it be a cause. For instance, the house building faculty is in virtue of itself the cause of a house, whereas the pale or the musical is the incidental cause.

The *per se* cause of my house is the skill (house building faculty) of the builder, which he acquired over many years of apprenticeship. It is not in virtue of his flute playing that my house was built. A flute player did indeed build my house, but the faculty of flute playing is not the per se cause, but an incidental cause. It is by chance that the carpenter who built my house is also a flute player. But it is not by chance that the carpenter who built my house owns a hammer, or is capable of reading blueprints. The joining of 'flute playing skill' and 'carpentry skill' is incidental, that is, by chance.

Now, we cannot conclude that since it is by chance that our carpenter is a flute player, his flute playing itself is an effect of chance. He may have wanted to be a flute player ever since he was a child, studied flute in high school and university. He became a flute player 'on purpose', so to speak. Perhaps he got interested in flute playing by chance, for instance, he was sent to the store to buy milk and decided to take a different route, upon which he stumbled upon a flute player playing his flute under a tree. But again, stumbling upon a flute player playing a flute under a tree is incidental to buying milk at the corner store. The intersection of the two events is 'by chance'.

Aristotle continues:

> That which is per se cause of the effect is determinate, but the incidental cause is indeterminable, for the possible attributes of an individual are innumerable.

In other words, the cause of purchasing the milk can be determined (being sent to the store, walking towards it, and presenting the money, etc.). So too are we able to determine the cause of the house (the builder who has the faculty of building). But we cannot determine the incidental cause. It is not possible, for instance, to determine that he is a flute player by looking at the completed house. The incidental cause is indeterminate. And so Aristotle writes:

> When a thing of this kind comes to pass among events which are for the sake of something, it is said to be spontaneous or by chance.

In other words, chance events come to pass among events which are not chance happenings, that is, events which are for the sake of something.

That is why *it is not possible for every event to be a chance event.* What is incidental can only be seen as such against the background of what is per se (through itself). If all was chance, no causes could be known or determined. If the causes of all the houses in the neighborhood were incidental causes, we could not determine the cause. For instance, consider that the cause of my house was a flute player having no building skills, my neighbor's a ballet dancer, John's house a truck driver not necessarily having any building skills, etc. The relationship between the effect and the cause would be unintelligible and indeterminate; thus, science, which is a knowledge of things through their proper causes, would be impossible.

Now, in order to say that the radon or plutonium atom decayed by chance, one would have to know the proper cause of an atom's decay. Only then would we be able to say that its decay was brought about by chance. We cannot, as was argued above, say its decay was a chance event simply because we cannot determine the cause. Our inability to determine the cause and 'chance' do have something in common, namely indeterminacy, that is, *an inability on our part to determine the incidental cause in a chance event*, and *our inability to determine which atom will decay*. The former belongs to the indeterminacy of chance events (the indeterminacy of incidental causes), the latter has nothing to do with incidental causes. These represent two different kinds of indeterminacy; to argue that the indeterminacy involved in knowing which atom will decay means that it decays 'by chance' is to confuse the two; for although I do not know which apple is going to fall off the tree next, I cannot conclude 10 minutes later that this apple that just fell, did so without a *per se* cause.

Aristotle writes:

> It is necessary, no doubt, that the causes of what comes to pass by chance be indefinite; and that is why chance is supposed to belong to the class of the indefinite and to be inscrutable to man.

This is why if all causes were reduced to incidental causes, science would be impossible. For what belongs to the class of the indefinite is inscrutable to man.

He continues:

> ...to say that chance is a thing contrary to rule is correct.

Consider that the Latin word for 'rule' is *regula*, which means a straight length, a ruler, a pattern, model, or law, and from which are derived the words 'regular' or 'regularly'. It is not regular that builders are flute players, or that kids on their way to pick up milk become interested in flute playing. Again, if everything was a result of chance, there would be no formulated laws (*regula*) of physics.

Aristotle distinguishes between 'chance' and 'spontaneity'. He limits the use of the word 'chance' to agents capable of deliberation. He writes:

> ...what is not capable of moral action cannot do anything by chance. Thus an inanimate thing or a lower animal or a child cannot do anything by chance, because it is incapable of deliberate intention; nor can 'good fortune' or 'ill fortune' be ascribed to them, except metaphorically,...The spontaneous on the other hand is found both in the lower animals and in many inanimate objects. We say, for example, that the horse came

'spontaneously', because, though his coming saved him, he did not come for the sake of safety.

Consider 'spontaneous combustion'; the cloth soaked in oil bursts into flames not by chance, but spontaneously. There was a determinate cause of the change. No one set it on fire, and we were unable to determine when it would burst into flames. But we do not say that it happened by chance. Hence, Aristotle writes:

> ...it is clear that events which (1) belong to the general class of things that may come to pass for the sake of something, (2) do not come to pass for the sake of what actually results, and (3) have an external cause, may be described by the phrase 'from spontaneity'.

Consider Aristotle's example of the horse that moves spontaneously. He moves not for the sake of avoiding the explosion that is about to take place, but because he moved and was saved as a result, we say that he was one lucky horse. He moved spontaneously. What came to pass did not come to pass for the sake of what actually resulted (the horse's life was saved). The oil soaked cloth burst into flames and burned down the shed. But the combustion did not come to pass for the sake of burning down the shed. Its combustion was spontaneous.

Aristotle uses the example of the stone that struck the man as he was walking under a bridge.

> The stone did not fall for the purpose of striking him; therefore, it fell spontaneously, because it might have fallen by the action of an agent and for the purpose of striking.

The man will run and look to see if anyone is on the bridge looking down with a handful of rocks. If so, the rock did not fall spontaneously. But if there is no one around, and the man sees other loose rocks falling as a result of the age of the bridge, he knows that the rock fell spontaneously.

We continue to use the word 'chance' in connection with such scenarios, but it was not by chance that the rock fell; rather, it was by chance that the rock hit the man. If a physics student was dropping stones in order to time their fall, and one of the stones or rocks hit the man under the bridge as he was passing under, we would say that the rock hit the man by chance. Here we have two lines of action "for the sake of some end" which intersect 'by accident', that is, incidentally. But in the situation in which no person is on the bridge experimenting with rocks, and in which the rock falls spontaneously, there is a determinate reason why that rock fell at that particular time—perhaps an engineer or a chemist would be able to figure out the reason. But it was 'by chance' that it hit the man under the bridge.

Similarly, when we say the atom decayed by chance, it is only so according to our perspective, that is, in relation to us. There are no grounds for maintaining that there is no determinate reason why the atom decayed, which is what we would be saying were we to maintain that it really did decay by chance, and not merely from our perspective. In short, we might be able to predict, using the tools of statistics, the number of deaths that are going to occur next year, but it in no way follows that my death (if I happen to be part of that number) was 'by chance'—I could have been dying of cancer for a few years.

Aristotle concludes his chapter:

> Spontaneity and chance are causes of effects which though they might result from intelligence or nature, have in fact been caused by something incidentally. Now since nothing which is incidental is prior to what is per se, it is clear that no incidental cause can be prior to a cause per se. Spontaneity and chance, therefore, are posterior to intelligence and nature. Hence, however true it may be that the heavens are due to spontaneity, it will still be true that intelligence and nature will be prior causes of this All and of many things in it besides.

In other words, it is not possible for chance and spontaneity to be the per se cause (first cause) of the universe and all that happens therein. Chance is an incidental cause and can only be known in light of the per se cause. It is only in light of the carpenter's skill and his product that I understand that his skill as a flute player, or a poet, or a iconographer, etc., are incidental (chance) with respect to the house he built.

As a further illustration of what is meant by chance, consider the following: Tom gets up every morning (regularly) and opens the door of his house to get the paper, but on this day, Friday, May 18th, he didn't come to the door to get his paper. It is not the case that on Fridays he doesn't come to the door to get his paper; rather, he picks it up every day, including Fridays. It's just by chance that on this Friday, he did not pick it up. There is nothing in the nature of being a Friday that requires Tom to not pick up the paper. The fact is he got sick and couldn't get out of bed. It is "by chance" that it happens to be on a Friday. There is no per se connection between Tom not getting the paper and Fridays, or the 18th day of May. If on every May 18th, Tom would not come to the door to get his paper, then it would not be "by chance" that he didn't get the paper. May 18th is the anniversary of his father's death, so he does not go to the door, but has some routine he regularly engages in every year on this day. It was only by chance that May 18th fell on a Friday this year. There is nothing in the nature of being May 18th that requires that day to be a Friday.

Now, what is the probability that Tom will not be getting the paper in the morning due to illness? If he typically gets sick twice a year, perhaps we can determine that there is a very low probability that Tom will not get the paper on the morning of such and such a particular day, or a rather high probability that he will not be getting the paper on two occasions this year, but which two days we do not know. It is likely to turn out that on two occasions Tom did not come to get the paper due to illness: February 3rd and July 22nd.

Now, is there a per se reason why Tom got sick? He went to a party on February 2nd, shook hands with one who had a bad cold, then Tom went to the table to the dish full of peanuts, grabbed a handful and ate them, the virus on his hand was transferred to the peanut and entered his body, and the next morning Tom was not feeling well. The mathematics, of course, cannot tell us this, but does that mean that this causal series was non-existent? No, it does not.

Why did he get sick on July 22nd? On July 21st, Tom was riding a street-car and was hanging on to the pole to keep himself from falling, but earlier that day a man with the flu was holding on to that pole. Tom picked up the virus, went home, and the next day woke up feeling sick. Why didn't his immune system destroy it? Because that night Tom had three glasses of wine, and alcohol suppresses your immune system temporarily. Hence, it was weakened.

Probability was not able to provide us with any kind of qualitative information like we have above, but that does not mean that there isn't any qualitative information to be had.

Now, we can say that it was 'by chance' that it happened to be February 3rd and July 22nd in this sense: there is nothing in this date (February 3rd) that entails illness. It has nothing to do with dates. So too, there is nothing about the date July 22nd that entails "flu"; the meeting of "illness" and "July 22nd" was purely incidental. It had to do with where Tom was on this particular day and on what he was doing on this day, and on who he was in contact with.

Now what some argue is that since probability has determined that there is a very high probability that Tom will not come to the door to get his paper in the morning due to illness on two separate occasions this year, Tom got sick on those particular days "by chance". But with regard to the actual days, Tom got sick by chance; for one does not get sick every single year on those days; one's sickness has nothing to do with those days as such. Nevertheless, he got sick for a determinate reason, and this is the case even if the reason remained forever outside our ability to determine with certainty.

Now, chance is still involved here. For example, Tom goes to the Bill's party, and Bill's party is a regular and yearly occurrence, but this year Dave came, and he has a bad cold. The intersection of "Dave having a cold" and "Bill's party" is by chance. Bill's party does not require somebody with a cold. It was by chance that someone showed up with a cold. But it was not by chance that people showed up. They were invited, and they chose to accept the invitation. Dave came because he broke up with his girlfriend and was lonely, so Dave did not come to the party by chance (but it was by chance that this party came two days after he broke up with his girlfriend).

Dave did not come to the party by chance, neither did Tom get a cold by chance. He got a cold on that day by chance (insofar as the date is concerned), but he did not get a cold by chance. Moreover, it is not true that Tom did not pick up his paper by chance; there was a definite reason: he was sick. But it was by chance that on Friday, he didn't get his paper; it just happened to fall on that day.

The mathematics of probability leaves out a veritable universe of information. Predicting that Tom will be sick 2 or 3 times this year and will not get his paper on those mornings, whatever they turn out to be, does not imply that everything that happens to bring that about was by chance or indeterminate. If all that information is closed off to us, it only means that it is closed off to us, not that there is nothing there for us to know.

Appendix D Logic Exercises I

For the following propositions, circle the subject, underline the predicate

1. All giraffes are tall
2. No clown likes ice-cream (is an ice-cream lover)
3. No president is a pervert
4. Some Italians like Irish music (are people who like Irish music)
5. Some students are not hard working

Circle the middle term for the following syllogisms

All Prime Ministers are French speaking.
Paul Martin was a Prime Minister.
Therefore, Paul Martin was French speaking.

No $ is &.
All & is X.
Therefore, No X is $.

All Cats are soft.
Some soft animals have whiskers.
Therefore, some cats have whiskers.

All chocolate bars are sweet.
Some sweet things are orange.
Therefore, some orange things are chocolate bars.

All men are animals.
John is a man.
Therefore, John is an animal.

All good Catholics attend Mass on Sunday.
I attend Mass every Sunday.
Therefore, I'm a good Catholic.

Underline the major terms in the following syllogisms, and bracket the minor terms.

All McGivney students like curry chicken.
All curry chicken is spicy (spicy food).
Therefore, all McGivney students like spicy food.

Some chicken is rubbery.
All rubbery things are unpleasant to eat.
Therefore, some chicken is unpleasant to eat.

Dogs hate cats.
All cat haters are vicious.
Therefore, Dogs are vicious.

Circle all distributed terms in the following syllogisms.

Some dogs are cute (cute things).
Some cute things are furry (furry things).
Therefore, some furry things are dogs.

Some students are not Italian.
All students wear a uniform.
Therefore, some of those who wear a uniform are not Italian.

All horses eat hay.
No human is a horse.
Therefore, no human eats hay.

All basketball players are tall.
John is a basketball player.
Therefore, John is tall.

Some cars are expensive.
Some expensive things are fast moving.
Therefore, some cars are fast moving.

Some dentists are tempted to suicide.
Some who are tempted to suicide like chocolate bars.
Therefore, some dentists like chocolate bars.

No Russians live on Yonge Street.
No McGivney student is Russian.
Therefore, no McGivney student lives on Yonge Street.

No new books are dusty.
Some books are not dusty.
Therefore, some books are not new.

Circle T if true, F if false

1. T F (O) ⊢ I
2. T F ∼(O)⊢ I
3. T F ∼ (E) ⊢ A
4. T F E ⊢ ∼(A)
5. T F E ⊢ ∼(I)
6. T F ∼ (A)⊢ I

Check your answers in Appendix H

Appendix E Logic Exercises II

The left hand column contains categorical arguments; the right hand column contains conditional arguments.

All A are W. Some W is O. Therefore, Some A are O. [ ] Valid [ ] Invalid Reason:	If you can type fast, you will be grateful later on. You can type fast. Therefore, you will be grateful later on. [ ] Valid [ ] Invalid Reason:
All Cats are soft. Some soft animals have whiskers. Therefore, some cats have whiskers. [ ] Valid [ ] Invalid Reason:	If you are exposed to mold, then you will get a cold. You have a cold. Therefore, you were exposed to mold. [ ] Valid [ ] Invalid Reason:
All horses eat hay. No human is a horse. Therefore, no human eats hay. [ ] Valid [ ] Invalid Reason:	If you pray, God will draw close to you. God did not draw close to you. Therefore, you don't pray. [ ] Valid [ ] Invalid Reason:
All sunny days are warm. Some warm days carry the risk of sunburn. Therefore, all sunny days carry the risk of sunburn. [ ] Valid [ ] Invalid Reason:	If you eat right, you will be healthy. I don't eat right. Therefore, you are not healthy. [ ] Valid [ ] Invalid Reason:
All A are B. All C are A. Therefore, C is B. [ ] Valid [ ] Invalid Reason:	If you learn to think critically, you won't be deceived as much. You fall for everything, it seems. Therefore, you didn't learn to think critically. [ ] Valid [ ] Invalid Reason:
All books by Scoffield are easy to read. "Principles of Truth" is a book by Scoffield. Therefore, "Principles of Truth" is easy to read. [ ] Valid [ ] Invalid Reason:	Eat lots of vegetables and fruit, and you reduce your risk of cancer. I eat lots of veggies and fruit. Therefore, I have reduced my risk of cancer. [ ] Valid [ ] Invalid Reason:

Check your answers in Appendix I

Appendix F Necessary and Sufficient Conditions.

1. T F   Oxygen is a necessary condition for human life.

2. T F   Food and water are together sufficient conditions for human life.

3. T F   Being 19 years of age is a necessary condition for buying alcohol in Ontario.

4. T F   A thunderstorm is a sufficient condition for the ground to be wet.

5. T F   Sunlight is a necessary condition for the roses to bloom.

6. T F   Sunlight is a sufficient condition for roses to bloom.

7. T F   Being a male is a sufficient condition for being a father.

8. T F   Being a father is a sufficient condition for being a male.

9. T F   Being a male is a necessary condition for being a father.

10. T F   Being 20 years old is a sufficient condition for being a university student.

11. T F   Being a university student is a sufficient condition for being at least 16 years old.

12. T F   Eating too much is a necessary condition for being overweight.

13. T F   If B is a necessary condition for A, then A is a sufficient condition for B

14. T F   The competent possession of an artistic skill is a necessary condition for recognizing one's own artistic incompetence.

15. T F   Being wealthy is a sufficient condition for being able to afford a good lawyer.

16. T F   Intelligence is a necessary condition for wisdom.

17. T F   Education is a sufficient condition for wisdom.

18. T F   Education is a necessary condition for being an intelligent person.

19. T F   Self-possession is a necessary condition for possessing virtue.

20. T F   Possessing the virtues is a sufficient condition for being wealthy.

21. T F   Being famous is a sufficient condition for happiness.

22. T F   Being famous is a necessary condition for happiness.

23. T F   Being happy is a necessary condition for being famous.

24. T F   Being happy is a sufficient condition for being famous.

25. T F   Being rich is a sufficient condition for happiness.

26. T F   Being rich is a necessary condition for having influence.

27. T F   Marital fidelity is a necessary condition for a good marriage.

28. T F   Marital fidelity is a sufficient condition for a good marriage.

Check your answers in Appendix J

Appendix G The Logic of Induction

Circle the correct answer

1.

85% of polled grade 9s thinks that Rohan should be elected President of the Student Council.

Therefore, 85% of the students at McGivney think that Rohan should be elected President of the Student Council.

Valid Inductive Argument.   *Invalid Inductive Argument.*

2.

80% of the citizens of this country think abortion is wrong. Since Billy is a citizen of this country, Billy thinks abortion is wrong.

There is an 80% probability that this statement is true.
There is a 20% chance that this statement is true.

3.

35% of the remarks made by Steve are insulting. The next remark made will be insulting because Steve will make the remark.

It is improbable that this statement is true.
It is highly probable that this statement is true.

4.

600 of the tickets in the drum were purchased by grade 12s, 90 of the tickets were purchased by grade 11s, 60 tickets were purchased by grade 10s, and 50 of the tickets were purchased by the grade 9s. The winning ticket will be drawn from the drum. Hence, the winning ticket was purchased by a grade 12 student.

The conclusion is probably true.
The conclusion is probably false.
No probable conclusion can be drawn.

5.

75% of polled students at McGivney think that we need to change the uniform.

Therefore, 75% of all the students at McGivney think that we need to change the uniform.

The students polled were the IB students in grade 9 (pre-IB), 10 (pre-IB), 11 and 12 IB.

Valid Inductive Argument.
Invalid Inductive Argument.

6.

75% of polled parents think that we need to change the uniform.
Therefore, 75% of all the parents think that we need to change the uniform.

The parents polled were selected from 50 grade 9 students (randomly chosen), 50 grade 10 students (randomly chosen), 50 grade 11 students (randomly chosen), and 50 grade 12 students (randomly chosen)

Valid Inductive Argument.
Invalid Inductive Argument.

7.

87% of polled Catholics from Holland are in favor of IVF.
Mr. McManaman is a Catholic.
Therefore, Mr. McManaman is in favor of IVF.

This is a good statistical syllogism.
This is an invalid modified induction by enumeration.
It is a good statistical syllogism in that it has a high probability of being true, even though it is actually false that he favors IVF.

8. "I spent my last two weeks of August last year in Rome, and although Italians drive fast, I didn't see one accident. I am now convinced that because people drive so fast in Italy, they are naturally more aware, more alert, more on the watch for pedestrians. In Canada, people drive more slowly, so they

are not as aware, hence the reason I've witnessed many accidents within the past 5 years."

What kind of argument is the above?

Deductive (categorical syllogism)
Statistical argument
Conditional argument
Induction by enumeration.

9. "I've been dating this guy for 3 months now, he's really charming, he's nice to me, and whenever we get together, we have a great time. Only two or three times did I have my doubts about his character. All the other times were great. That's why I've consented to marrying him—all future times with him will be great as well. The wedding is next week."

The conclusion in the above is a form of:

Deduction
A statistical argument
Induction by enumeration
Modified Induction by enumeration

10. "Betty, Jason, and Carole had the highest overall average, in the nation, upon graduation from high school. They all went to St. Mary's High School. Therefore, St. Mary's High School is the best high school in the nation."

This is necessarily true.
This is an invalid induction by enumeration.
Given the evidence, it is highly probable.
This is a good statistical argument.

11. Attacking your next-door neighbors, killing them and taking their property is immoral.
War involves going into a neighboring country, killing people and taking their property.
Therefore, war is immoral.

This is an analogical argument
This is a statistical argument
This is an induction by enumeration
This is a modified induction by enumeration

12. The school principal interviews a candidate for a full-time teaching
position (history). The interview is about a half hour in length. The candidate
answered the questions in accordance with what was expected, she dressed
well, she was young and energetic. It did not take long for the principal to
make the decision that this young lady will get the position. She interviewed
so much better than the previous candidate (John), who was nervous and
didn't think on his feet very well.
What kind of inductive reasoning was the principal engaging in?

Induction by enumeration.
Analogical induction.
Statistical reasoning
Deductive reasoning

Check your answers in Appendix K

Appendix H. Answers to Logic Exercises

For the following propositions, **bold** *the subject, underline the predicate*

1. All **giraffes** are <u>tall</u>
2. No **clown** <u>likes ice-cream</u> (is an ice-cream lover)
3. No **president** is <u>a pervert</u>
4. Some **Italians** <u>like Irish music</u> (are people who like Irish music)
5. Some **students** are not <u>hard working</u>

Bold the middle term for the following syllogisms

All **Prime Ministers** are French speaking.
Paul Martin was a **Prime Minister**.
Therefore, Paul Martin was French speaking.

No $ is **&**.
All **&** is X.
Therefore, No X is $.

All Cats are **soft**.
Some **soft animals** have whiskers.
Therefore, some cats have whiskers.

All chocolate bars are **sweet**.
Some **sweet things** are orange.
Therefore, some orange things are chocolate bars.

All **men** are animals.
John is a **man**.
Therefore, John is an animal.

All good Catholics **attend Mass on Sunday**.
I **attend Mass every Sunday**.
Therefore, I'm a good Catholic.

Underline the major terms in the following syllogisms and bracket the minor terms.

All McGivney students like curry chicken.
All curry chicken is spicy food.
Therefore, all [McGivney] students <u>like spicy food</u>.

Some chicken is rubbery.
All rubbery things are unpleasant to eat.
Therefore, some [chicken] is <u>unpleasant to eat</u>.

Dogs hate cats.
All cat haters are vicious.
Therefore, [Dogs] are <u>vicious.</u>

Bold all distributed terms in the following syllogisms.

Some dogs are cute (cute things).
Some cute things are furry (furry things).
Therefore, some furry things are dogs.

Some students are not **Italian**.
All **students** wear a uniform.
Therefore, some of those who wear a uniform are not **Italian**.

All **horses** eat hay.
No **human** is a **horse**.
Therefore, no **human eats hay**.

All **basketball players** are tall.
John is a basketball player.
Therefore, **John** is tall.

Some cars are expensive.
Some expensive things are fast moving.
Therefore, some cars are fast moving.

Some dentists are tempted to suicide.
Some who are tempted to suicide like chocolate bars.
Therefore, some dentists like chocolate bars.

No **Russians live on Yonge Street.**
No **McGivney student** is **Russian.**
Therefore, no **McGivney student lives on Yonge Street.**

No **new books** are **dusty.**
Some books are not **dusty.**
Therefore, some books are not **new.**

Circle T if true, F if false

1. **T** **F** (O) ⊢ I
2. **T** F ~(O) ⊢ I
3. T **F** ~ (E) ⊢ A
4. **T** F E ⊢ ~(A)
5. **T** F E ⊢ ~(I)
6. T **F** ~ (A) ⊢ I

Appendix I

The left-hand column contains categorical arguments; the right-hand column contains conditional arguments.

All A are W Some W is O Therefore, Some A are O [ ] Valid [**X**] Invalid Reason: Undistributed middle term	If you learn to type now, then you will be grateful later on. You have learned to type. Therefore, you will be grateful later on. [X] Valid [ ] Invalid Reason: Affirming the Antecedent
All Cats are soft Some soft creatures are whiskered Therefore, some cats are whiskered. [ ] Valid [**X**] Invalid Reason: Undistributed middle term	If you are exposed to mold, then you will get a cold. You have a cold. Therefore, you were exposed to mold. [ ] Valid [**X**] Invalid Reason: Affirming the Consequent
All horses eat hay No human is a horse Therefore, no human eats hay. [ ] Valid [**X**] Invalid Reason: Any term distributed in the conclusion must be distributed in the premises.	If you pray, God will draw close to you. God did not draw close to you. Therefore, you don't pray. [**X**] Valid [ ] Invalid Reason: Denying the Antecedent
All sunny days are warm. Some warm days carry the risk of sunburn. Therefore, all sunny days carry the risk of sunburn. [ ] Valid [**X**] Invalid Reason: Undistributed middle term.	If you eat right, you will be healthy. I don't eat right Therefore, you are not healthy. [ ] Valid [**X**] Invalid Reason: Denying the Antecedent
All A are B All C are A Therefore, C is B [**X**] Valid [ ] Invalid Reason: No rules are broken.	If you learn to think critically, you won't be deceived as much. You fall for everything, it seems. Therefore, you didn't learn to think critically. [**X**] Valid [ ] Invalid Reason: Denying the Consequent
All books by Scoffield are easy to read. "Principles of Truth" is a book by Scoffield. Therefore, "Principles of Truth" is easy to read. [**X**] Valid [ ] Invalid Reason: No rules are broken.	Eat lots of vegetables and fruit, and you reduce your risk of cancer. I eat lots of veggies and fruit. Therefore, I have reduced my risk of cancer. [**X**] Valid [ ] Invalid Reason: Affirming the Antecedent

Appendix J

1. **T** F Oxygen is a necessary condition for human life.
2. T **F** Food and water are together sufficient conditions for human life.
3. T **F** Being 19 years of age is a necessary condition for buying alcohol in Ontario.
4. **T** F A thunderstorm is a sufficient condition for the ground to be wet.
5. **T** F Sunlight is a necessary condition for the roses to bloom.
6. T **F** Sunlight is a sufficient condition for roses to bloom.
7. T **F** Being a male is a sufficient condition for being a father.
8. **T** F Being a father is a sufficient condition for being a male.
9. **T** F Being a male is a necessary condition for being a father.
10. T **F** Being 20 years old is a sufficient condition for being a university student.
11. T **F** Being a university student is a sufficient condition for being at least 16 years old.
12. T **F** Eating too much is a necessary condition for being overweight.
13. **T** F If B is a necessary condition for A, then A is a sufficient condition for B
14. **T** F The competent possession of an artistic skill is a necessary condition for recognizing one's own artistic incompetence.*
15. **T** F Being wealthy is a sufficient condition for being able to afford a good lawyer.
16. **T** F Intelligence is a necessary condition for wisdom.
17. **T** F Education is a sufficient condition for wisdom.
18. **T** F Education is a necessary condition for being an intelligent person.
19. **T** F Self-possession is a necessary condition for possessing virtue.
20. **T** F Possessing the virtues is a sufficient condition for being wealthy.
21. T **F** Being famous is a sufficient condition for happiness.
22. T **F** Being famous is a necessary condition for happiness.
23. T **F** Being happy is a necessary condition for being famous.
24. T **F** Being happy is a sufficient condition for being famous.
25. T **F** Being rich is a sufficient condition for happiness.
26. T **F** Being rich is a necessary condition for having influence.
27. **T** F Marital fidelity is a necessary condition for a good marriage.
28. T **F** Marital fidelity is a sufficient condition for a good marriage.

---

*There is a sense in which this is true. Very often a poor singer or painter will believe he is good and is dumfounded that others do not share his opinion. As a person becomes more competent artistically, he will begin to see how deficient his earlier performance was. There are, however, many people who have no artistic talent whatsoever and readily see it and admit it.

Appendix K

1.

85% of polled grade 9s thinks that Rohan should be elected President of the Student Council.

Therefore, 85% of the students at McGivney think that Rohan should be elected President of the Student Council.

Valid Inductive Argument.   **Invalid Inductive Argument.**

[The sample is unrepresentative]

2.

80% of the citizens of this country think abortion is wrong. Since Billy is a citizen of this country, Billy thinks abortion is wrong.

There is an 80% probability that this statement is true.

There is a 20% chance that this statement is true.

[Over 50%; this is a good statistical argument]

3.

35% of the remarks made by Steve are insulting. The next remark made will be insulting because Steve will make the remark.

It is improbable that this statement is true.

It is highly probable that this statement is true.

[Under 50%; this is an invalid statistical argument]

4.

600 of the tickets in the drum were purchased by grade 12s, 90 of the tickets were purchased by grade 11s, 60 tickets were purchased by grade 10s, and 50 of the tickets were purchased by the grade 9s. The winning ticket will be drawn from the drum. Hence, the winning ticket was purchased by a grade 12 student.

The conclusion is probably true.

The conclusion is probably false.

No probable conclusion can be drawn.

[75% of the tickets were purchased by grade 12s; this is a good statistical argument]

5.
75% of polled students at McGivney think that we need to change the uniform. Therefore, 75% of all the students at McGivney think that we need to change the uniform.

The students polled were the IB students in grade 9 (pre-IB), 10 (pre-IB), 11 and 12 IB.

Valid Inductive Argument.
Invalid Inductive Argument.

[This is a modified induction by enumeration; it is invalid because the sample is unrepresentative. IB students represent a minority of the school population]

6.
75% of polled parents think that we need to change the uniform. Therefore, 75% of all the parents think that we need to change the uniform.

The parents polled were selected from 50 grade 9 students (randomly chosen), 50 grade 10 students (randomly chosen), 50 grade 11 students (randomly chosen), and 50 grade 12 students (randomly chosen)

Valid Inductive Argument.
Invalid Inductive Argument.

[The sample is large enough and representative]

7.
87% of polled Catholics from Holland are in favor of IVF.
Mr. McManaman is a Catholic.
Therefore, Mr. McManaman is in favor of IVF.

This is a good statistical syllogism.
This is an invalid modified induction by enumeration.
It is a good statistical syllogism in that it has a high probability of being true, even though it is actually false that he favors IVF.

[The sample "Catholics from Holland" is not representative. One will have to sample from other countries]

8. "I spent my last two weeks of August last year in Rome, and although Italians drive fast, I didn't see one accident. I am now convinced that because people drive so fast in Italy, they are naturally more aware, more alert, more on the watch for pedestrians. In Canada, people drive more slowly, so they are not as aware, hence the reason I've witnessed many accidents within the past 5 years."

What kind of argument is the above?

Deductive (categorical syllogism).
Statistical argument.
Conditional argument.
Induction by enumeration.

[It is also invalid; for my experience was a sample of Italy. It was limited to one city, and it was limited by a period of only two weeks, and most Romans are on vacation in August]

9. "I've been dating this guy for 3 months now, he's really charming, he's nice to me, and whenever we get together, we have a great time. Only two or three times did I have my doubts about his character. All the other times were great. That's why I've consented to marrying him—all future times with him will be great as well. The wedding is next week."

The conclusion in the above is a form of:

Deduction
A statistical argument
Induction by enumeration
Modified Induction by enumeration

[One could make the case that it is also invalid; thus an imprudent decision. 3 months of dating is a small sample, and for that reason it may be unrepresentative. Furthermore, she ought to pay attention to those 3 red flags]

10. "Betty, Jason, and Carole had the highest overall average, in the nation, upon graduation from high school. They all went to St. Mary's High School. Therefore, St. Mary's High School is the best high school in the nation."

This is necessarily true.
This is an invalid induction by enumeration.
Given the evidence, it is highly probable.

This is a good statistical argument.

11. Attacking your next-door neighbors, killing them and taking their property is immoral.
War involves going into a neighboring country, killing people and taking their property.
Therefore, war is immoral.

This is an analogical argument
This is a statistical argument
This is an induction by enumeration
This is a modified induction by enumeration

12. The school principal interviews a candidate for a full-time teaching position (history). The interview is about a half hour in length. The candidate answered the questions in accordance with what was expected, she dressed well, she was young and energetic. It did not take long for the principal to make the decision that this young lady will get the position. She interviewed so much better than the previous candidate (John), who was nervous and didn't think on his feet very well. What kind of inductive reasoning was the principal engaging in?

Induction by enumeration *(it can be seen as an induction by enumeration)*
Analogical induction *(if the principal was inferencing on the basis of a candidate with similar properties)*
Statistical reasoning
Deductive reasoning

Suggested Reading

Adler, M. J. *How to Think About the Great Ideas. Ed. Max Weismann.* Chicago: Open Court, 2000.*

Bastiat, Frederick. *That Which is Seen, and That Which is Not Seen, 1850. Retrieved from http://bastiat.org/en/twisatwins.html.*

Chabris, Christopher., and Simons, Daniel., *The Invisible Gorrilla.* New York: Crown, 2010.

Danielou, Jean., *S.J. Introduction to the Great Religions. Indiana: Fides, 1964.* _____. *God and the Ways of Knowing. Trans. W. Roberts. San Francisco: Ignatius Press, 2003.*

Eliade, Mircea. *Myth and Reality. Waveland Press, Illinois, 1998.*

Gigerenzer, Gerd *(2004). Mindless statistics. The Journal of Socio-Economics 33. 587-606. DOI: 10.1016/j.socec.2004.09.033.*

Gilson, Etienne. *Methodical Realism: A Handbook for Beginning Realists. San Francisco: Ignatius Press, 1990.*

Hacking, Ian. *Introduction to Probability and Inductive Logic. Cambridge: Cambridge University Press, 2001.*

Hallinan, Joseph T. *Why We Make Mistakes. New York: Broadway, 2009.*

Huff, Darrell. *How To Lie With Statistics. New York: W. W. Norton & Company Ltd. 1982.*

Hunter, Graeme. *Pascal the Philosopher. Toronto: University of Toronto Press, 2013.*

Kahneman, Daniel. *Thinking Fast and Slow.* New York: Ferrar, Straus and Giroux, 2011.

Lipton, Peter. *Inference to the Best Explanation.* New York: Routledge, 1991.

Maritain, Jacques. *A Preface to Metaphysics,* London, Sheed and Ward, 1948.

McRaney, David. *You Are Not So Smart.* New York: Dutton, 2011.

Nagel, Thomas. *"What is it like to be a bat?"* The Philosophical Review LXXXIII, 4 (October 1974). 435-50. *Retrieved from http://organizations.utep.edu/portals/1475/nagel_bat.pdf*
_____. *The View from Nowhere.* Oxford: Oxford University Press, 1986.

Prichard, H. *A. Knowledge and Perception: Essays and Lectures. Oxford: Oxford University Press, 1970.*

Popper, Karl. *The Myth of the Framework, New York: Routledge, 1994*
_____. *Conjectures and Refutations.* New York: Routledge, 2002.
_____. *The Logic of Scientific Discovery.* New York: Routledge, 2005.

Rescher, Nicholas. *Plausible Reasoning.* Pittsburgh: University of Pittsburgh Press, 1976.
_____. *Induction.* Pittsburgh: University of Pittsburgh Press, 1980.
_____. *Empirical Inquiry.* London: The Athlone Press, 1982.
_____. *Epistemology.* New York: State University of New York, 2003.
_____. *Presumption and the Practices of Tentative Cognition.* Cambridge: Cambridge University Press, 2006.
_____. *Error.* Pittsburgh: University of Pittsburgh Press, 2007.
_____. *Conditionals.* London: MIT Press, 2007.
_____. *Epistemic Principles.* New York: Peter Lang, 2017.

Schultz, Kathryn. *Being Wrong: Adventures in the Margin of Error.* New York: Harper Collins. 2010.

Scruton, Roger. *Beauty. Oxford: Oxford University Press, 2009.*
_____. *The Uses of Pessimism. Oxford: Oxford University Press, 2010.*

Sowell, Thomas. *The Vision of the Anointed New York: Basic Books, 1995*
_____. *Applied Economics. New York: Basic Books, 2004.*
_____. *A Conflict of Visions. New York: Basic Books, 2007.*
_____. *Intellectuals and Society. New York: Basic Books, 2010.*
_____. *Economic Facts and Fallacies. New York: Basic Books, 2011.*

Taleb, Nassim, N. *Fooled by Randomness. New York: Random House, 2004.*
_____. *The Black Swan: The Impact of the Highly Improbable. New York: Random House Trade Paperbacks, 2010*

Tversky, Amos; Kahneman, Daniel *(1974). Judgment under Uncertainty: Heuristics and Biases. Science, New Series, Vol. 185, No. 4157. (Sep. 27, 1974), pp. 1124-1131. Retrieved from http://links.jstor.org/sici?sici=0036-8075%2819740927%293%3A185%3A4157%3C1124%3AJUUHAB%3E2.0.CO%3B2-M*

Trueman, Carl R. *Histories and Fallacies: Problems Faces in the Writing of History. Illinois, Crossway. 2010.*

Walton, Douglas. *Informal Logic: A Pragmatic Approach. 2d. ed. Cambridge: Cambridge University Press, 2008*